The One Year® Book of Amish Peace

The One Year® Book of

AMISH PEACE

Hearing God's Voice in the Simple Things

TRICIA GOYER

Tyndale House Publishers, Inc.
Carol Stream, Illinois

Visit Tyndale online at www.tyndale.com.

Visit Tricia's website at www.triciagoyer.com.

TYNDALE, Tyndale's quill logo, *The One Year*, and *One Year* are registered trademarks of Tyndale House Publishers, Inc. The One Year logo is a trademark of Tyndale House Publishers, Inc.

The One Year Book of Amish Peace: Hearing God's Voice in the Simple Things

Designed by Ron Kaufmann

Published in association with Books & Such Literary Agency, 52 Mission Circle, Suite 122, PMB 170, Santa Rosa, CA 95409.

Citations for portions of text taken from other sources appear at the end of the book and are noted by devotional date and the last words of the quoted masterial.

ISBN 978-1-4143-7980-7

Printed in the United States of America

19   18   17   16   15   14   13
7   6   5   4   3   2   1

Introduction

I never planned on writing about the Amish or learning about their customs and being inspired by their faith. It all started with a simple question from a friend: "Have you ever thought about writing an Amish novel?" I hadn't. Most of the novels I had written were set during World War II or other times in history. I pushed the thought out of my mind, but it resurrected later that day.

Out of the blue I remembered I knew a couple who'd grown up Amish and who'd lost two daughters in a buggy and semi truck accident. I hadn't seen them in months. . . . How would I ever contact them?

It "just so happened" that I ran into their daughter the next day! I knew this wasn't a coincidence. God was up to something.

Meeting Ora Jay and Irene Eash led me to write numerous Amish novels. As I did research for these books, I visited with Amish families, toured Amish country, and read a pile of books about the Plain people and their faith.

As I read, I found myself being challenged . . . and changed. No, I had no intention of leaving my "modern" life, but I did seek to incorporate their peace into my own ordinary days. I've been more intentional in caring for my family. I've reached out to friends and neighbors. I've dug into God's Word to discover the peace He has to offer us, Amish or not. I discovered that day-to-day Amish life revolves around seasonal rhythms, and I started looking at my own life to see how I could simplify things and bring more calm to our busy home.

My hope is that this devotional will guide you to that same peace. Not simply peace in your surroundings (although we can take steps toward that, too), but Peace—Jesus, our Prince of Peace.

I'm eager to take this journey with you. May the end of this book—and the end of the year—find us with more joy and contentment in our hearts than ever before.

Tricia Goyer
SEPTEMBER 2013

WINTER

Recipe for Amish Breakfast Casserole

1 pound sliced bacon, diced
½ pound breakfast sausage
1 medium sweet onion, chopped
8 eggs lightly beaten
4 cups frozen shredded hash brown potatoes, thawed
2 cups (8 ounces) shredded cheddar cheese
1½ cups (12 ounces) 4% cottage cheese
1¼ cups shredded Swiss cheese

———————————— ■ ————————————

In a large skillet, cook bacon and onion until bacon is crisp; drain. Sauté the sausage until it is cooked through. In a large bowl, combine the remaining ingredients; stir in bacon mixture and the sausage. Transfer to a greased 13-in. x 9-in. baking dish. Bake uncovered at 350° for 35-40 minutes or until a knife inserted near the center comes out clean. Let stand for 10 minutes before cutting. Makes 12 servings.

JANUARY 1

Looking Forward

Anyone who belongs to Christ has become a new person.
The old life is gone; a new life has begun!

2 CORINTHIANS 5:17

An Amish family gathers around the kitchen table to celebrate God's goodness in bringing a new year. Grandparents, parents, and children join together with the glow of the lantern casting rings of light upon their heads. A pot of pork and sauerkraut sits in the center of the table. True to the Swiss-German heritage, pork—more specifically, fattened pigs—symbolizes wealth and looking to the future. Interestingly, unlike most animals, which can easily turn their heads, pigs can't look backward. We should all be so forward thinking!

When the Amish immigrated to America, they brought with them many cooking traditions. Sauerkraut, potatoes, and spaetzle are still popular on Amish tables and come from their Swiss-German roots.

After dinner the Amish family joins in a traditional New Year song: *Die Zeit ist angekommen, das freudige Jahr. Gott wolle euch geben ein gutes Neujahr.* "'Tis time now to welcome the happy New Year. God grant you to live and enjoy the new year."

Amish families sing of fortune and blessings, but even as they look forward to the coming year, their gazes also lift to unseen eternity. The song continues, "In heaven before the great heavenly throne, God grant you reward in that heavenly home."

What are you looking forward to? Perhaps you smile as you anticipate family togetherness, a graduation, or a new life to come. Or perhaps, as one year rolls into the next, you're in the midst of a season of sadness or loss. Whether you look ahead with hope or anxiety, remember Who sits on the great heavenly throne. Because we belong to Jesus, we can say, "The old life is gone; a new life has begun!" He is our reason to celebrate the new year, the days and seasons of our lives, and an endless eternity of rejoicing.

■ ■ ■

Heavenly Father, the newness of the year pales in comparison with the new life You give through a relationship with Jesus Christ. Help me to look ahead to eternity with a grateful heart, no matter what this year brings. Amen.

The Rhythms of Nature

Even the stork that flies across the sky knows the time of her migration,
as do the turtledove, the swallow, and the crane. They all return at the proper
time each year. But not my people! They do not know the LORD's laws.

JEREMIAH 8:7

Snow covers the silent ground, and an Amish couple sits by lantern light looking through a seed catalog. Outside, a cold wind rattles bare branches, but in their mind's eye the husband and wife are considering the seasons to come: the earth's thaw and a hint of warmth on the breeze, followed by spring planting. Green shoots sprout, and fields are cultivated to protect young plants from the threat of weeds. Then, later, comes the harvest. Cutting, raking, bundling, drying. The loving Creator designed an arc of life and growth. Even when winter's cold grasp holds the world outside our windows, we know that it only lasts so long.

Sometimes in our world of to-do lists and electronic devices we miss the rhythm of nature. We trade our fall sweaters for winter parkas but forget that seasons are about more than simply adjusting our clothing choices. God's creatures know the journey of the seasons, and the Amish understand too. They live and work in the rhythms of nature. Just as spring is a time of hard work, winter is a change of pace. Do you live by this too?

> **The first requirement for prayer is silence. People of prayer are people of silence.**
>
> **PROVERB**

Have you lost touch with the rhythms of nature? Do you forget to pause and consider the natural world? Take a moment and look outside your window. What we see outside is a reminder to us to still our lives and our hearts. There is a time to plow, a time for growth, a time of harvest, and a time to be still.

Is there a way to add stillness to your day? Do you have ten minutes to sit before God? Look at your calendar. Can you carve out some extra time for rest or quietness, knowing that another season of work is right around the corner?

■ ■ ■

Dear heavenly Father, treating each season of life as the same is so easy—with a similar to-do list and the same urgency about my work. Help me to rest today. Open my eyes to the rhythm of nature and still my heart—not for the sake of stillness, but so You can speak. Amen.

Deep Roots

Blessed are those who trust in the LORD and have made the LORD their hope and confidence. They are like trees planted along a riverbank, with roots that reach deep into the water. . . . Their leaves stay green, and they never stop producing fruit.
JEREMIAH 17:7-8

Where do the roots of your faith come from? I didn't meet my biological father until I was twenty-eight years old. After we met—and forged a relationship—I discovered the roots of my own faith. They were deep roots. My grandfather had been a church planter. My great-great grandfather had been a missionary in Canada. My great-great-great grandfather had been a missionary and circuit preacher to early settlers of Indiana. There are even Christian books written about some of my ancestors. Amazing!

No one can claim the Amish never worry, but a popular saying among the Amish is "Why worry if you can pray?"

Likewise, the roots of Amish faith go deep. Amish roots stretch back to sixteenth-century Europe. During the time of the Protestant Reformation, the religious ancestors of the Amish were called Anabaptists (rebaptizers) because they baptized adults who had previously been baptized as infants in a Protestant or Catholic church.

These Anabaptist groups spread rapidly, and religious authorities rose up against them. In a span of just a few decades, more than twenty-five hundred men and women died in prison, were burned at the stake, were drowned in rivers, or lost their heads to executioners' swords. Yet instead of withering or dying away, the persecuted Anabaptists scattered into rural hideaways, where the groups continued to grow and bear fruit despite the hardship. As these people gradually fled to other parts of the world, they carried their faith with them.

The type of faith these men and women had comes only when we sink our roots deeper into the living water and discover God is always enough. Think about your personal history. Do you have a heritage of faith? If so, thank God. If not, ask God to make *you* the one who will spread the Good News to anyone along your path.

■ ■ ■

Lord, thank You for the Christian believers who went before me, for their faith and their example of staying strong and letting their roots grow deep into You during hardship. Help me, Lord, to trust in You with that same hope and confidence.

Knots of Faith

*I thank my God through Jesus Christ for all of you, because your
faith in him is being talked about all over the world.*

ROMANS 1:8

Every other week the Amish hold worship services. Instead of meeting in a church building, they take turns hosting worship in their homes. They gather to hear God's Word and to worship, and they sing songs without instruments—twenty, fifty, or even a hundred voices praising God together, just as their forebears have done for hundreds of years. The songs are sung slowly, with each syllable stressed, the joined voices swirling around the women's prayer kapps and the men's bare heads.

Amish hymns are drawn from a collection called the *Ausbund,* first published in 1583 and the oldest Christian songbook in continuous use. At the core of the *Ausbund* are fifty-one songs written by Anabaptists imprisoned in the Passau (Germany) castle dungeon between 1535 and 1540 for their beliefs. These hymns embody the prayers of those prisoners. What peace the Amish must draw from these hymns, knowing their ancestors faced harsh challenges yet found a way to set their prayers to song.

"The *Ausbund* . . . does not contain any musical notes and the melodies are passed down from one generation to the next."

*The one who is not faithful in the smallest thing,
and who still seeks his own good which his heart desires—
how can he be trusted with a charge over heavenly things?
Let us keep our eyes on love!*
Ausbund 119:14

Like the Amish, we, too, can draw strength from worshiping with other Christians and from realizing that the God who cares for us is the same God who has strengthened and uplifted believers through all the moments in history. Each of us has a place in passing on the praise. May we be faithful to do our part.

■ ■ ■

Heavenly Father, how thankful I am for the men and women who've gone before me, who've faced hardships and still lifted their prayers to You through songs of worship. May my life become a knot on a thread of faith that stretches before my life and beyond it. Amen.

Cold Winds of Trouble

God's breath sends the ice, freezing wide expanses of water.
JOB 37:10

The news hit me like pellets of hail from the gray sky outside. Bad news about the health of a family member numbed me. Even though the sun still shone outside the window, the world around me felt faded, chilled. *Lord, why did You let this happen?*

Like everyone else, the Amish face hardship. Accidents happen, children stray, a life is cut short. Yet as trials hit, the Amish, in spite of their pain, find the strength to offer a difficult but simple prayer: "Thy will be done." They wouldn't think of questioning God—how prideful that would be!

Accepting the pain this world brings is hard at times. Our souls are made for eternity and long for the "no more tears" that heaven promises. Yet having faith in God means trusting Him in the hard moments of life—through the pain that numbs us and the hardships that make us lose sight of the good gifts God gives us. The truth is, we need God's light most during those dark days.

> Sometimes God calms the storm, but sometimes God lets the storm rage and calms His child.
>
> PROVERB

Second Corinthians 4:6 says, "God, who said, 'Let there be light in the darkness,' has made this light shine in our hearts so we could know the glory of God that is seen in the face of Jesus Christ."

What season is it in your heart today? If cold winds of trouble blow around you, can you still feel a hint of warmth as you worship God and read His Word? Consider God's light shining in the darkness. Picture the "glory of God that is seen in the face of Jesus Christ." The truth is, we may always love Jesus—even on the bright days—but we see Him in a new way when He shines brightly in the darkness of difficulty.

The sun will emerge again in God's proper time. Until then, draw near to God, and continue to seek Him no matter what season of life you're in.

■ ■ ■

Heavenly Father, it's winter not only outside my window but also, in some ways, deep in my heart. I desire to draw near to You. Give me the willingness to do so. Help me to see Your glory in the face of Jesus, and warm my heart with Your presence. Amen.

Old Christmas

Arise, Jerusalem! Let your light shine for all to see.
For the glory of the Lord rises to shine on you.

ISAIAH 60:1

In a dark time in history a light shone. God's glory encased itself in the small form of a babe. When the Lord shines in our lives, we have reason to celebrate . . . and you may be surprised that for many Amish, January 6 is the day chosen to do just that.

People all over the world celebrate Christmas on December 25, but many Amish communities celebrate on January 6, or Old Christmas. Tradition states that twelve days after the birth of the Messiah, the wise men arrived in Bethlehem and, upon finding the baby Jesus, offered precious gifts.

The song "The Twelve Days of Christmas" was inspired by twelve days of feasting that culminated in "Old" Christmas. Like the December 25 celebration, Old Christmas is celebrated with family gatherings and simple decorations and gifts. Considered a more holy day, many Amish families fast until noon and then celebrate together with a large meal. On our calendars you'll see the date marked as Epiphany.

Whether you choose to celebrate Christmas on December 25 or January 6, remember that every day is one worthy of celebrating the Light of God, Jesus Christ. Take a moment and consider how His light has transformed your life. Remember that the light of Jesus coming to earth is just a glimpse of what we'll experience some day in eternity: "No longer will you need the sun to shine by day, nor the moon to give its light by night, for the LORD your God will be your everlasting light, and your God will be your glory," we read in Isaiah 60:19.

In response to Christ's gift to you, offer a simple gift to a friend today, whether it be a kind word, a hug, or a warm smile and prayer.

> Don't plan on doing any after-Christmas shopping at Amish businesses on January 6. Those (and those staffed by Amish) are closed that day.

■ ■ ■

Dear heavenly Father, we spend the days leading up to our Christmas celebrations attempting to make Jesus "the reason for the season." Instead, Jesus is the reason for life, hope, and eternity! As many Amish families celebrate the birth of Christ today, I desire to join them in my heart. I rejoice in the indescribable gift of Your Son!

Winter to a Mother's Soul

Your wife will be like a fruitful grapevine, flourishing within your home. Your children will be like vigorous young olive trees as they sit around your table.
PSALM 128:3

Scripture refers to mothers as fruitful vines and to children as olive trees. Most Amish homes are very good at producing "trees," with six to seven children (and some have more)! Can you picture the smiling faces, from toddlers to teens, surrounding the table? Can you picture all the bare feet that need to be scrubbed at bedtime, and all the dirty laundry?

For an Amish mother, raising children is best compared to gardening. There are seasons of planting, sowing, work, *dirt*. Then, like the coming of winter, the harvest arrives, and the empty plot remains. Winter arrives in a mother's soul when her children are sent out—to work in another area or into their own homes to "grow" their own families.

You'd think mothers of large families would get used to their children moving away as they venture into adulthood. For most Amish this means marriage, but it could also mean an older son leaving for work or an older daughter taking a job in another district as a *maud* (maid) or teacher.

Letting go of a child is never easy—not even for Amish mothers. Children are held close for many years and then are released with tears. Yet just as a garden nourishes a family, the time and attention a mother offers are not for her own enjoyment. Sometimes the work of mothers is most fruitful when it benefits others, as children have a positive impact on the community, begin new families, and send "shoots" of their own.

Consider the young people in your life. Offer prayers for them today. If you are rolling up your sleeves and doing laundry or dishes for little ones, use this time to lift up prayers for them. If the children in your family or extended family have already left home, consider spending a day helping and encouraging a young mom as she cares for her own family. In either act of service, God will be glorified.

■ ■ ■

Dear Lord, sadness comes when I see my children, nieces, and nephews growing older. Sometimes I want to freeze time and enjoy the young ones for just a moment longer. Instead, help me to do my part in sending out shoots that will benefit Your Kingdom. Amen.

Afresh Each Morning

Great is his faithfulness; his mercies begin afresh each morning.

LAMENTATIONS 3:23

Working outside in the crisp air. Cutting firewood and piling it. Husband and wife work side by side and see the satisfaction of their labor. There's a smile between them. A thank-you at the end of the day. The woodpile will last yet a while. This is just one of the ways Amish families gather their provisions to carry them through the cold winter months.

Jars filled with the produce from autumn's harvest line the shelves of the pantry—not as many jars as before, but enough, the husband and wife hope, to last until fresh fruit and vegetables are again in season. The barns have caches of grain to feed the livestock through the winter, and pens are filled with clean straw to keep the floors tidy. Yet even as the Amish family depends on their stored resources through winter, their souls need daily maintenance, daily gathering in the Word, and renewal through daily prayer.

We read in Isaiah 33:2, "Lord, be merciful to us, for we have waited for you. Be our strong arm each day and our salvation in times of trouble." To claim God's mercies, God's followers don't rely only on stored-up resources but also on time spent daily with God. Many Amish families have a time of Bible reading and devotions in the morning and a time of prayer together at night.

Canning food has long been the tradition of the Amish. Most Amish women can hundreds of quarts of food every year. Not everything comes from their gardens—sometimes they trade produce with friends or buy it from local farmers.

Do you have a similar practice? You may calculate much in your own life: your shopping list, your budget, your calendar. You may "store up" for a rainy day, but don't treat your moments with God in the same way. Open yourself to God's goodness in the morning. Take time to feel His smile at the end of the day.

■ ■ ■

Dear heavenly Father, sometimes I act as if a good Sunday sermon will carry me all the way through Friday, or as if worship songs from the radio will give me a boost for the day. These things are certainly good starts, but they aren't enough. Give me the desire to spend more and more time with You each day so that I can recognize and experience Your new mercies to me.

Gently Patience Comes

If we look forward to something we don't yet have,
we must wait patiently and confidently.

ROMANS 8:25

Patience is a virtue worked into the fabric of everyday Amish life. The pace of a horse on a country road affords time for contemplation. When Amish farmers plant seeds, they don't expect to get a crop to harvest overnight. Ralph Waldo Emerson once wrote, "Adopt the pace of Nature. Her secret is patience." The Amish embrace and live the truth of this statement.

Are you impatient about something today? Are you waiting for an answer, good news, relief? If you're like me, you might wish that God would work faster in your circumstances. You want a harvest of joy or peace, but all you see outside is frozen ground. You can't picture anything different, and the waiting begins to wear on your soul. God anticipated that you'd feel this way, and He provided exactly what you need in order to wait patiently—Himself.

North American Amish have more than ninety varieties of buggies. Tradition and the bishop of each community set the standard for what kind of buggies the group will use.

Our hope grows as we turn our attention away from our own desires and toward the One who gives all life and goodness. When we understand who God is, we will better understand who we are. When we allow Him to love us, we love others better in numerous ways—including being patient: "Love is patient and kind. Love is not jealous or boastful or proud" (1 Corinthians 13:4).

Today if you are struggling with being patient, find a moment to reconnect with the world God has made—the world of slow-growing trees and of clouds that move lazily across the sky. The world of icicles and frosty windowpanes. As you look at creation, ask God to plant a seed of patience in your heart and to show you how to nurture that seed with prayer and faith, just as an Amish farmer does with the seeds he plants.

■ ■ ■

Lord, I often want quick answers and fast solutions, but when I rush ahead, I not only miss the beauty found along the journey, I also miss walking in step with You. Slow my heart and my steps to match Your perfect pace.

Soul Stitching

[Boaz said,] "Come over here and sit down, friend."

RUTH 4:1

The Amish sewing circle is a gathering of women working together with a common purpose. The quilt is the object of their work, but when women nestle side by side, sharing recipes, good news, and worries, their hearts and souls are stitched together too. Amish live, work, and worship with those who reside next door, down the road, and around the corner. They not only know the names of their neighbors but they also bake with them and their daughters.

Spending time with friends is often one of the first things we cut from our busy schedules. We may have neither the skills nor the interest to belong to a sewing circle, but each of us can make time for friends. The colorful moments of shared lives brighten the dreariest days. The pieced-together scraps of memories create the story of who we are.

The Bible shares numerous stories of friendship. David and Jonathan's friendship bonded them closer than brothers. Ruth found friendship in her mother-in-law, Naomi. Jesus crossed the countryside sharing the Good News of God's plan with twelve close friends. More than that, Jesus calls *us* friends too: "I no longer call you slaves, because a master doesn't confide in his slaves. Now you are my friends, since I have told you everything the Father told me" (John 15:15).

If you have even one good friend, hold her tight and be blessed. If you have a circle of friends, consider yourself rich indeed. The shared laughter and tears keep us close and stitch our hearts together. Most of all, remember that Jesus is your best friend—no matter what.

> "Most people assume that Amish quilts were done completely by hand but this was not the case. Many Amish quilts were pieced using a treadle sewing machine but the beautiful quilting was always done by hand."

■ ■ ■

Father in heaven, my heart overflows with gratitude for my friends. I know these relationships weren't formed by chance; they were tailor-made by You. Show me today, Lord, one person to reach out to in friendship. Stitch my life together with others' through the power of Your love.

Passing On the Element of Faith

After that generation died, another generation grew up who did not
acknowledge the LORD or remember the mighty things he had done for Israel.
JUDGES 2:10

You might be tempted to believe that little about the Amish way of life has changed over the years. But as the generations come and go, there are small changes to be seen. Some younger mothers use disposable diapers and buy items from a thrift store rather than make all their household items themselves. The older generation may watch such things and wonder, *Is this a sign that the younger generation will become lazy about the foundations of their faith, too?* Sometimes there is evidence of this—for example, during the singing of the *Ausbund.*

An Amish church bench is a plain wooden bench without a seat cushion or a back. Young and old alike sit on these benches during church services, which typically last for three hours.

In an Amish congregation families do not sit together. Instead, women sit with women and men with men, and they section off according to age. Can you picture the disapproving glances from the older ones in the back rows when they witness the younger ones paying more attention to their seatmates than to the words of a hymn?

Many Amish elders complain of the decline of their faith as each generation gathers less to pass on to the next. And that concern isn't exclusively Amish. We can easily point out ways the next generation is growing lazy, but when we consider our own role in guiding those who come after us, it is harder to point out others' faults.

We are raising the church of tomorrow. How are we doing at guiding children and grandchildren to understand God and appreciate the elements of our faith? Here's an idea: consider inviting a young person out to lunch to share what God has meant to you. As a bonus, read the words to your favorite hymn and talk about one reason it's your favorite. Be intentional about passing on your legacy of faith.

If you don't do this, who will?

■ ■ ■

Dear Lord, pointing out the faults of the younger generation is easy, but offering guidance and help is harder. Stir my heart and remind me that I leave an imprint on the future—for good or bad—through those who follow my example. Amen.

Forgiving One Another

Get rid of all bitterness, rage, anger, harsh words, and slander,
as well as all types of evil behavior. Instead, be kind to each other, tenderhearted,
forgiving one another, just as God through Christ has forgiven you.

EPHESIANS 4:31-32

I am often amazed by the number of times I have difficulty forgiving others. When people hurt me, letting go of that hurt is hard. I'm praying for God to cultivate my heart until every stray root of unforgiveness is gone.

My small unforgiveness seems foolish when I think of the forgiveness offered by the families at Nickel Mines in southern Lancaster County, Pennsylvania. In October 2006, the world was shocked and horrified when a lone gunman entered the Amish school, took young girls as hostages, and shot them—killing five and critically wounding five more before taking his own life.

> Forgiveness is as valuable to the one forgiving as it is to the one forgiven.
>
> PROVERB

The world was also amazed by the courage and forgiveness shown by the members of the Amish community. Within hours—not months or years—they visited the widow of the gunman, Charles Carl Roberts IV, and offered forgiveness and grace. This forgiveness wasn't simply a rote response, merely an offering of polite words. The Amish followed up their words with deeds. They went so far as to give a portion of the donations sent to their own community from around the world to the widow and children of Charles Roberts.

Forgiveness can be words we mutter, or it can be actions we take. Yet as we stand in wonder at the forgiveness shown in response to this tragic event, we see that the ability to forgive wasn't a onetime occurrence. The Amish were able to forgive because offering goodwill is a way of life. Their response followed what had already been lived out during the days, months, and years before—a pattern of grace-filled living displayed for generations.

■ ■ ■

Heavenly Father, even now I can see in my mind the face of someone I still need to forgive.
I can't do this in my own power, and I seek Your help and Your strength to do so. Lord,
help me to make a way of life so that my Christian walk will display grace-filled living for
all to see. Amen.

The Least of These

[Jesus] will answer, "I tell you the truth, when you refused to help the
least of these my brothers and sisters, you were refusing to help me."
MATTHEW 25:45

A crystal-white blanket of snow covers the ground outside, but the Amish who sit around the wood-burning stove are thinking about concrete rubble and destroyed lives. Haiti is a long distance from the Amish communities of North America, but prayers cross the distance. More than that, Amish communities have plans—big plans—for sending funds.

If you've been acquainted with the Amish for any length of time, you know about their care for the needy in their own communities. Those who've visited Ohio, Indiana, and Pennsylvania may have been surprised to find benefit auctions providing for the needs of those in developing countries.

Amish communities don't highlight people who have beautiful singing voices or other natural talents, but one true performer is an Amish auctioneer, whose cadence of speech and command of a crowd can build excitement and urgency in the bidding.

Proceeds from these auctions go to various mission organizations, such as those supporting earthquake victims in Haiti. From afar, the Amish bring relief to the sick, the hungry, and the homeless. Auctions are held throughout the year, and as soon as one is over, the Amish families begin working hard on their donations for the next one. Can you imagine the smile on a carpenter's face as he pictures the funds from the chair or table he's making going to drill wells, educate children, and build homes?

It's easy for us to become so consumed with our own needs that we forget about "the least of these." But any time we give to those who have no way of giving back, we will be rewarded: "The King will say, 'I tell you the truth, when you did it to one of the least of these my brothers and sisters, you were doing it to me!'" (Matthew 25:40).

Is caring for our homes, our communities, enough? Yes, but sometimes God asks us to do more. What is He asking you today?

■ ■ ■

Heavenly Father, the times I give to those who cannot give back are the times when my heart is most full. I'm learning that the more I help other people, the more I become like Jesus Christ.

A Buffer of Protection

O God, you have taught me from my earliest childhood,
and I constantly tell others about the wonderful things you do.

PSALM 71:17

During winter, winds howl outside my vehicle as I drive over the snow, and I try to imagine the cold ride inside an Amish buggy. It seems quaint . . . until I remember that Amish buggies have no heaters, let alone heated seats.

Yet the Amish know how to insulate themselves from the cold. First, they dress for the weather. Girls and women wear long stockings and boots. Wool coats and gloves are followed by blankets. Boys layer sweaters and sweatshirts over their handmade Amish shirts. The buggy itself has protection—curtains over the windows and a storm front (windshield) to block the chill. Hot-water bottles also provide heat. Amazingly, children look forward to these buggy rides. Love and togetherness warm them from inside as they're pressed between siblings or held on a parent's lap.

Just as Amish parents dress their children for long buggy rides, they also know to insulate their children's hearts from the outside world. Amish children have little interaction with those outside their community. Their teachers are usually Amish, and children speak Pennsylvania Dutch in the home. They don't learn English until they start school at age six.

Do we take time to insulate our lives? We all need to spend time in God's Word and prayer. We also need to surround ourselves with like-minded believers and put a buffer between ourselves and the harsh winds of society's influence, especially those that blow through the media and music. Our hearts need to be protected—no matter our age. We don't want to block ourselves completely from the world, but we do need to heed the Holy Spirit's still, small voice that says, *This is not for you.*

Although most Amish do not own automobiles, many will hire a car, a van, or a bus if they need another form of transportation. They also will use public transportation where it is available.

■ ■ ■

Heavenly Father, in my life there are things I strive for—connecting with You, reading Your Word, and setting my mind on heavenly things. Help me to be equally diligent about protecting my heart. Wrap Yourself around me as a buffer from the things of the world that threaten to assault me.

Joined Together

Be happy with those who are happy, and weep with those who weep.
ROMANS 12:15

God never intended for His children to live life alone. We read in Romans 12:4-5, "Just as our bodies have many parts and each part has a special function, so it is with Christ's body. We are many parts of one body, and we all belong to each other."

For many years members of the Amish and Old Order Mennonite communities have proved their "belonging" by keeping track of one another through a weekly newspaper called the *Budget*. News is contributed by local scribes and shared in a simple format. Bits of humor and news of everyday moments, interesting events, and tragedies are captured and shared.

The *Budget* serves two distinct purposes: as a national Amish newspaper and as a local newspaper for the Sugarcreek/ Holmes County area in Ohio. In addition to news from Amish settlements around the nation, there is also news from Amish on foreign soil in countries such as Belize, Israel, and Nicaragua.

Sometimes in our ordinary lives it's hard to open ourselves to others, yet as we share our lives, we learn to share our hearts as well. And when we open our hearts to others, we find it becoming easier to open our hearts to God. When we connect our lives on earth, we also gain a glimpse of heaven, where we will commune together with God—and His children—for eternity.

Our physical bodies are joined by flesh, muscles, tendons, and veins, but the body of Christ is joined by words and stories, by laughter and tears. Do you have an interesting event, or maybe a humorous, simple, everyday moment you can share with a believing friend? If so, go ahead and do it. By sharing your life, you are joining with others and building up the body of Christ, constructing connections that will continue for eternity.

■ ■ ■

Dear heavenly Father, sometimes staying isolated is easier than sharing my heart and life with others, and yet You created the body of Christ for a purpose. I'm thankful that I do not have to live this life alone. Show me how to give and share my heart with others, and also how to accept and receive compassionate tears and hugs in return.

In the Way They Should Go

Watch out! Be careful never to forget what you yourself have seen.
Do not let these memories escape from your mind as long as you live!
And be sure to pass them on to your children and grandchildren.

DEUTERONOMY 4:9

My Amish friend Sherry once told me about a special moment that an Amish mother shares with her young daughter in the middle of a busy day. When a mother rolls out a pie crust, she always cuts off the edges; then, with her daughter's help, she rolls out the scraps again in preparation for a special treat. Although the actual pie can't be cut until after dinner, the extra dough is sprinkled with sugar and cinnamon and baked. After it cools, the mother and daughter enjoy the treat together.

I love this picture of mother and daughter "working" side by side. It reminds me of Proverbs 22:6: "Direct your children onto the right path, and when they are older, they will not leave it." Celebrating togetherness and intentionally creating special memories for the little ones in our lives is something we often neglect in our to-do-list-making world.

Memories are made every moment. What your child or grandchild experiences gives him or her a blueprint for living life in the future.

Have you gotten out of the habit of creating a bit of happiness in everyday moments? It's not too late to change that, and I guarantee there are little ones who would love to help you start.

Shoofly pie is a traditional dessert among the Amish and some other cultures. It's believed the name is derived from the flies that have to be shooed away from its delectable sweetness. This layered pie is filled with brown sugar, molasses, flour, salt, and spices and topped with a mixture of flour, butter, and brown sugar.

■ ■ ■

Dear heavenly Father, too often I see the young ones in my life as just another task along with everything else I need to do. Help me to slow down and enjoy the moment. Help me to take the opportunities that everyday moments offer to teach my children through my words and my care.

Pass It On

Here is my greeting in my own handwriting—Paul.

1 CORINTHIANS 16:21

There is nothing like an unexpected letter or package to bring internal sunshine to a long, dreary day. My Amish friend Irene remembers her excitement as a young girl running home from the mailbox with a large manila envelope addressed to her: a circle letter had arrived!

A circle letter is a letter chain sent among family members or friends. Irene was part of a circle made of girls with her same first name and born the same year. With each envelope that arrived there was a letter from all the other members, including Irene's previous letter. After Irene read the letters of the other participants, she'd pull out her old letter, replace it with a new one, and then send the package to the next young woman on the list. The circle letter would be sent to each person, each adding a new letter and continuing the conversation. Through letters like these, friends and family members talked about issues important to them, shared current events, and confessed dreams for the future.

"Circle letters are popular among different groups—spread-out family members, groups of teachers, wheelchair-bound individuals, organic farmers, and Amish bishops, among others."

When Irene told me about the circle letters, I imagined the excitement that letters from Paul, Peter, and other apostles brought when they arrived at new churches. But instead of adding their own words to the revered apostles' letters, the churches studied them, rejoiced over them, and then passed them on.

I'm amazed at how God uses letters and personal experiences to build His body. More than once God has whispered instruction or encouragement to me through a friend's words.

What has God done for you lately? Pass that on to another. What messages has He spoken to your heart? Record and share them. Do you remember the last time you sent someone a handwritten note? Take a moment to write one and send it today. You never know when the words of news or encouragement you offer another person will come back around to you.

■ ■ ■

Dear heavenly Father, thank You for writing a love letter to me through Your holy Word. May Your words of hope flow through me and bless others today. Amen.

He Sees Within

Thank you for making me so wonderfully complex!
Your workmanship is marvelous—how well I know it.

PSALM 139:14

The word *unique* isn't often associated with the Amish. They may be unique from the rest of the world, yes. But unique from each other? No. The Amish dress similarly, follow essentially the same rules, wear the same hairstyles, and order their lives in the same manner. Yet inside—where it counts the most—each person is different. Distinct personalities make a community of similar people. And even as the Amish strive to present themselves in such a way that no one person can claim to be better than another, their individuality is still a reality.

Even those of us who are not Amish often strive to fit in. We may wear certain clothes to gain the approval of others. We may subdue our personalities at times and present ourselves as something we're not. Yet the God who created us sees us differently. Beneath our outer garments He sees the inward soul of each of us. Behind our facades He sees our uniqueness and our potential: "How precious are your thoughts about me, O God. They cannot be numbered! I can't even count them; they outnumber the grains of sand!" (Psalm 139:17-18).

Amish women do not wear bright colors. Because they want to blend in and avoid drawing attention to themselves, they wear colors such as dark blue, dark green, or black.

The closer we get to God in our relationship with Him, the easier it is to see our true selves. We might live in a community that places certain expectations on us, but only when we embrace God's process of molding us into His image can we truly get a glimpse of how our shape, form, and function play a part in His overall plan. To do that, we need to draw near to Him, place ourselves in His hands, and believe the truth of how He sees us—even when to the outside world we appear no different from those around us.

■ ■ ■

Dear heavenly Father, it fills me with awe that as Creator You decided this world needs me—and what I have to offer. Forgive me for the times I question my form or my talents. Help me to live up to the potential You have placed within me. Amen.

Childlike Wonder

Jesus prayed this prayer: "O Father, Lord of heaven and earth, thank you for hiding these things from those who think themselves wise and clever, and for revealing them to the childlike."
MATTHEW 11:25

In my everyday life, ignoring nature is easy. Trees stretching bare branches into a crisp blue sky rarely catch my notice as I zoom down the highway. Around my suburban house, I notice the chirp of a finch hopping along the frost-tipped ground only after my toddler daughter points it out. My daughter notices the branches, too, and the clouds. She reminds me to really *see* these things and to rejoice in our Creator God.

This reminds me of Psalm 8:1-2: "O LORD, our Lord, your majestic name fills the earth! Your glory is higher than the heavens. You have taught children and infants to tell of your strength."

Children praise God when they spend time in creation. Sometimes I wonder if the "entertainment" I provide my children—movies, computer games, and television programs—is actually training *them* to ignore nature too. Perhaps that's why Amish men and women often still have a childlike wonder, awe, and appreciation for God's creation. Television theme songs and flashing graphics haven't captured their attention, drawing their eyes away from the world around them.

The good news is that senses once dulled can be revitalized. When you take time to look around and appreciate God's creation, you begin to see the beauty of ordinary moments. When you listen to the sounds in nature, you find unexpected strains and echoes. Today is the day you can stir your senses once again. And just like children, when you take time to notice the wonders of God's creation and His majesty revealed all around you, your soul will fill with praise!

> Some Amish use modern conveniences such as refrigerators, water heaters, and lamps to light their homes and barns. The difference is that all of these are gas powered. The Amish reject anything that requires obtaining electricity from a power line.

■ ■ ■

Dear heavenly Father, forgive me for spending hours on worthless entertainment. Peace comes when I focus on You and on the world You created. Awaken my senses to Your goodness as I pause and look at the beauty beyond my window.

A Time to Die

For everything there is a season. . . .
A time to be born and a time to die.

ECCLESIASTES 3:1-2

My friends Ora Jay and Irene lost two daughters in a truck and buggy accident. This unexpected tragedy shook their community, yet in the days following their loss, Ora Jay and Irene knew what to expect. Familiar rituals take place when someone passes away, whether that person is a child or an elderly person. Community members come together to prepare the body, attend the service, and dig the grave. They are even present when the simple wooden coffin is lowered into the ground and the men from the community cover it with shovelfuls of dirt.

Yet unlike a typical non-Amish funeral, the focus isn't on the deceased but on God. There is no eulogy. There are no photos (Amish believe taking photographs violates God's commandment to not make an image of anything in the heavens or on the earth or in the sea as we read in Exodus 20:4). Instead, a minister offers a sermon entirely in Pennsylvania Dutch, and Scripture is read in German. Ministers also read the words to a hymn, but these are never sung at a funeral. Even though there is deep sadness, there is an overarching sense of trust in God's plan. The season of one's earthly life is over. *God's will be done.*

After an Amish woman's wedding, she may wear her wedding dress as a Sunday dress. Other Amish women put it away and then are buried in the same dress.

In our society we often don't want to think about death, but it happens to all of us according to God's timing. Just as a field looks barren in the winter, we know spring is sure to come. For followers of God, heaven is that spring. We can look forward to a new life with the Son! It's a season we can count on if we give our lives to Him.

■ ■ ■

Heavenly Father, I often push thoughts of death out of my mind. Remind me that being gone from this earth is being present with You. Thank You for eternity. Thank You for the new life I can look forward to!

Singleness of Heart

"Sing, O childless woman, you who have never given birth! Break into loud and joyful song, O Jerusalem, you who have never been in labor. For the desolate woman now has more children than the woman who lives with her husband," says the LORD.
ISAIAH 54:1

The Amish community is known for large families. It's easy to forget about the single men and women among them. If marriage and children are celebrated, it may seem singleness is despised, but singles often find themselves surrounded with children—and with laughter and joy—in other ways.

Some singles care for elderly parents until their deaths, and many singles find their place within the home or near the home of a sibling. Gifted, talented, loving . . . these singles often find their hearts bursting and their laps overflowing with nieces, nephews, and cousins. This is especially true for single women.

> "Married [Amish] men wear beards, single men do not."

The single Amish woman is loved not only by the little ones who receive her help and attention but also by their parents, who appreciate the extra hand. Many single women are also teachers, and their influence over children in the classroom can continue for years.

In this life, focusing on what we lack is easy, but the Bible reminds us that little is much in the sight of the Lord. With God, a little oil can provide more than enough for a poor widow and her sons. With Jesus, a few loaves of bread and some fish can feed a multitude. Luke 16:10 reminds us, "If you are faithful in little things, you will be faithful in large ones."

Sometimes we believe we know what we want in life, but God has different plans. True joy comes not from looking at what we're lacking but from having a singleness of heart to worship God and to rejoice in His goodness in whatever state we find ourselves.

■ ■ ■

Dear heavenly Father, forgive me for the discontent that stirs within me in the areas of my life that don't live up to my own expectations. Help me to rejoice in the people and relationships You've brought into my life, and give me a singleness of heart that pursues my relationship with You above all else.

True Conformity

Don't copy the behavior and customs of this world, but let God transform you into a new person by changing the way you think. Then you will learn to know God's will for you, which is good and pleasing and perfect.

ROMANS 12:2

Often I like to think of myself as self-sufficient and independent. I make my own schedule. I choose what I want to make for dinner. I make my own entertainment choices, too. But the Amish see "dependence" in another way. They depend on one another, but even more, they depend on God.

One verse commonly used among the Amish is Romans 12:2, above. To them, copying "the behavior and customs of this world" means joining with the outside world by driving cars or buying electricity from a power company. Because they refuse to "copy" what the world does, the Amish are actually able to maintain stability within their community. Not driving long distances or using electricity means they have less contact with outsiders, and that gives them a uniqueness that distinguishes them from the "English."

Where does our dependence lie? Some of us may depend on modern conveniences. Others may depend on their disconnection from those very things. Either way, our true dependence should always be on our God.

Why does God command us not to copy the behaviors and customs of the world? Because God desires that we see life from His point of view. In this world we often long for perfection, but that's possible only in the world to come. And the way we'll find it is by focusing on the One who is good, pleasing, and perfect. As we more and more desire to do God's will, we will find ourselves being molded into God's way.

Most Amish families have a gas range, but a few still use wood-burning stoves to cook and heat food and for warmth. Sometimes coal stoves are used for heat.

■ ■ ■

Dear heavenly Father, too often it's easy for me to focus on all the "don'ts" in the Bible. Instead, help me to live my life in conformity to Your will, Your way, Your Kingdom. Help me to become more dependent on You day by day. Amen.

The Center of Our Attention

A woman dishonors her head if she prays or prophesies without a
covering on her head, for this is the same as shaving her head.

1 CORINTHIANS 11:5

What is the first thing that comes to mind when you hear the word *Amish*? Perhaps you think of buggies, large families, and men with long beards. Prayer kapps no doubt also make that list. Have you ever wondered why Amish women wear prayer kapps? The Scripture above gives the reason. Since all of us are supposed to "pray without ceasing" (1 Thessalonians 5:17, ESV), a woman who loves God never knows when she will wish to pray in private, and running to find a covering would be inconvenient or even impossible. Amish women wear a prayer kapp so they will not be unprepared to pray at any time and so dishonor themselves.

Different Amish communities often have different guidelines for prayer kapps, but these are general rules:

• They must cover as much hair as possible.

• They must be made of a plain, inexpensive material that is also practical.

• The fabric of the kapp must be thick enough that others can't see through it.

• The design of the kapps must follow the rulings of the congregation.

• The kapps must add to a woman's modesty.

This raises the question, how does our faith in God affect how we dress? I've never worn Amish clothes, but the way I dress now is different from the way I dressed before I became a follower of Christ. Years ago I dressed to attract attention and to flaunt my body. Not anymore. Now I try to follow Timothy's teaching: "I want women to be modest in their appearance. They should wear decent and appropriate clothing and not draw attention to themselves by the way they fix their hair or by wearing gold or pearls or expensive clothes" (1 Timothy 2:9).

While we may not choose to dress plainly or wear prayer kapps, the Bible tells us that God is concerned about our outward appearance because it reflects His image. Our dress should not *attract attention*; it should *turn our attention* to the One who loves us unconditionally and wants us to reflect Him to the world.

■ ■ ■

Heavenly Father, I'm often too concerned about how I look and about what others think. May the most outstanding part about my appearance be Your joy flowing through me.

Chasing the Wind

Better to have little, with fear for the LORD,
than to have great treasure and inner turmoil.

PROVERBS 15:16

One of the hardest things about living a busy, modern life is that family members tend to run in their own directions. Parents often have jobs away from home, and younger children spend their days in day care or school. The afternoons of older children are filled with sports practices or other activities, and the evenings and weekends can be filled with sports events or other forms of recreation. Believe it or not, the possibility of the same thing happening in their community is one reason most Amish reject machinery and choose to stay away from modern vehicles as much as they can.

Amish take a critical look at the pros and cons before they are willing to accept a new invention. They consider the effect something new will have on their family, whether it will encourage family members to work together or cause them to drift apart, and whether the cost will force them to take jobs away from the family home to pay for it.

Considering this reminds me of one of my favorite verses, Ecclesiastes 4:6: "Better to have one handful with quietness than two handfuls with hard work and chasing the wind." It makes me think about my own life and about what I often embrace without question: *Will this draw my family closer or move them apart? Will it cause me to work longer hours to pay for it? Am I trying to fill my hands and, in effect, chasing the wind?*

It's easy to think of the Amish as odd for not wanting to make their lives easier, but maybe we need to consider what's truly easier—living a hurried life or working hard with your family by your side?

> The Amish don't shy away from all modern conveniences. They often use disposable diapers, gas grills, skates, and sometimes even cell phones.

■ ■ ■

Heavenly Father, my heart feels heavy when I think of all I've added to make my life easier, when the truth is, those things have become a heavy burden upon me. Give me discernment about what my family really needs. I open my hands to You and ask You to strip away what is not necessary, what is harmful to the contentment of my soul. Amen.

God's Job Description for You

Jesus told [the crowd], "This is the only work God wants
from you: Believe in the one he has sent."
JOHN 6:29

Sometimes I dream about buying a farm, baking my own bread, and sewing my own clothes. The world is noisy at times with television, radio, bloggers, newspaper columnists—just to start the list. Endless information is at my fingertips, and it fills my mind with static. . . . *Oh, to drown out the noise!*

Yet it wouldn't take six months on the farm for me to start buying my bread again, look for a different house without all the extra chores, and dream of living closer to the grocery store. Does that mean I'm lazy? No, it just means I know myself. I also know that the level of my devotion to a particular idea can be seen in the day in, day out of my life.

Not all Amish men are farmers. Some men do woodworking, and others work in factories. Some even run machine shops and fix gas-powered machines.

We may like the idea of quieter lives, but our true devotion is to be serving God in the daily tasks we already have. There is no end to the various ways we can labor. And no matter where we live, each of us has the ability to "turn down the noise." The important thing is to remember that *the work God wants from us is to "believe in the one he has sent."* What an amazingly simple—and very demanding—job description!

Much of the noise around us consists of messages that tell us to do more, be more, and devote ourselves to more of what we can see. Believing means allowing God to still our souls and to tune out the voices that don't matter. We don't have to run away and buy a farm so this can happen. In fact, sometimes our belief is the strongest when we discover Jesus in the midst of the noise.

■ ■ ■

Dear heavenly Father, sometimes I feel as if my belief is not even worth offering up to You. Thank You for reminding me that it's what matters most! Help me in all the ways I struggle with unbelief. I long to believe You more! Amen.

The Gift of Suffering

My heart is troubled and restless.
Days of suffering torment me.

JOB 30:27

Hardly an Amish sermon is given without some mention of the forebears of the Amish and what they suffered. Many an Amish home has a copy of the *Martyrs Mirror*. This thick volume tells story after story of Christian martyrs from the time of Christ to the 1600s, including those of the Anabaptists—their lives, their sufferings, and their deaths. These men and women loved God and believed the gospel of Christ was for all humanity. They preached God's love so persistently—right up until the moments of their deaths—that most judgments against them included the cutting out of their tongues so they couldn't speak. Yet many stories end with descriptions of arms lifted, silent praise, and courageous gazes heavenward in the martyrs' last moments.

The *Martyrs Mirror* is a traditional Amish wedding gift.

Why does God allow suffering? That's a good question. If God loves His children, shouldn't He protect them? Can't we trust that the God who loves us most will do His part to keep us from pain?

The truth is, even when those in the world around us ignore our words during peaceful or pleasant times, they pay close attention to us in our suffering. It's unnatural to praise God in hard times, but that's when our praise rings truest. Others pay attention when they hear us praising God in our pain. They learn to trust Him when we trust Him even on our hardest days.

Often I've prayed that God will use me to reach the world. I've also asked Him to remove my suffering. But often God accomplishes the former through the latter. In my weakness my testimony shines ten thousand times brighter. God's light, reflected on our faces during our dark days of pain, is hard to miss. Turn to God during your trials, and those around you will discover Him in new ways.

■ ■ ■

Heavenly Father, thank You for teaching me that suffering is a gift. It's an open door to sharing the Good News with the lost world. More than that, when I suffer, You draw near, and that is the greatest gift of all. Thank You.

No Looking Back

Jesus [said], "Anyone who puts a hand to the plow and then looks back is not fit for the Kingdom of God."
LUKE 9:62

Do you ever find yourself wishing for the "good old days"? The first Anabaptists were persecuted because of their religious views, so refugees fled from Bavaria (a part of southern Germany) to Moravia, which is now part of the Czech Republic (formerly Czechoslovakia). In 1535 a group of refugees attempted to return home, and in August they traveled up the Danube River. As soon as they stepped into Bavarian territory, they were arrested and imprisoned in the dungeons of the bishop's castle in Passau. Many men and women died in those dungeons, but some survived and were released in 1540. As they exited they carried with them songs they had written while in prison, and these became the foundation for the *Ausbund*, the Amish hymnal.

The Anabaptists were considered radical reformers in sixteenth-century Europe. Today we see the Amish as gentle and peace loving, but for many years their ancestors were opposed and persecuted by religious authorities who disliked their teachings.

I get chills as I read these words from one of the martyrs, Hans Betz: "Let us fight valiantly on, pressing toward the prize. The one who turns to one side or the other will perish with Lot's wife who turned to look back, feeling sorry for the possessions she left behind."

We are tempted to look back when walking along the rocky path of life—a path of hardship. I've never been locked away in a dungeon, but at times, when God led me away from the comfort of my possessions and the people I care about, I've questioned why life has to be so hard.

The apostle Paul says, "I focus on this one thing: Forgetting the past and looking forward to what lies ahead" (Philippians 3:13). Looking ahead beats looking back. And looking beyond to eternity with Christ is where we should focus—even when life is uncertain. *Especially* when life is uncertain.

■ ■ ■

Dear heavenly Father, sometimes it's easier to dwell in the memories of a comfortable past than it is to look forward to an uncertain, or even painful, future. I praise You, Lord, and thank You that the future isn't unknown to You! Eternity with You awaits. Help me to look forward to that!

The Ways of Obedience and Submission

Get all the advice and instruction you can,
so you will be wise the rest of your life.

PROVERBS 19:20

My friend Kendra was eager to begin her first year teaching school. Although she loved children and loved teaching, after the first week of the school year she was discouraged by the attitudes of some of the young children, who preferred to talk instead of listen and to play instead of learn. Kendra thought talking to parents of those children would help, but she received even more disrespect from the parents! After a few years of battling to instruct and guide her charges, Kendra quit. The poor attitudes of the parents influenced the thoughts of the children and made the soil of their hearts resistant to instruction.

Those in modern society are often surprised by the positive attitudes of Amish children. Of course they are not perfect, but Amish children are taught to respect adults. Amish adults live in obedience to their church and community, and they teach their children what it means to follow God and live the Amish way.

While teaching children *is* important, *modeling* correct behavior also goes a long way. The phrase "Do what I say, not what I do" would never be found on the lips of an Amish mother or father. Instead, they know that for good or bad, little ones will follow where they are led.

Are there young ones watching you and following your example? Ask God to guide your steps. Open your heart to the advice and instruction of godly people in your life. Not only will you benefit from the wisdom you attain, but your children will too.

. . .

Dear heavenly Father, submitting to godly leaders and friends and turning to them for advice can be hard to do, yet I know it's where wisdom is found. Soften my heart to receive their instruction. Amen.

Amish churches have no nurseries or children's church. Children are expected to sit with their mothers or fathers during the three-hour service. After a baby is born, instead of having a shower, friends and family bring small toys and gifts that could be used to occupy a child during the church service.

JANUARY 29

Be Reconciled

If another believer sins against you, go privately and point out the offense.
If the other person listens and confesses it, you have won that person back.
MATTHEW 18:15

The Amish live within a relatively small network of people. Churches are organized into districts of a certain number of square miles. The Amish attend church with their closest neighbors, and these are the same people with whom they live and celebrate the events of their lives. Of course, these are also the people with whom they can have the greatest conflict. It may be easy to ignore a problem when a distant friend sins, but it's harder when a neighbor down the road is acting wrongly. The impact of those offenses hits close to home.

Many Amish travel to Mexico, usually by bus or train, to seek medical help there because the costs are lower.

Through the Internet I'm connected with old school friends, former coworkers who have moved across the country, and people I've never met who enjoy the same activities or hobbies that I do. When I have a conflict with a friend far away, I have the option of not answering a call or an e-mail from that person, but the Amish learn to work through their grievances to maintain unity for the good of their community.

Confronting another person can be difficult. Working at reconciliation is challenging. But ignoring a problem is worse. When we turn our backs to fellow believers, we might have less outward conflict, but we also will lose the chance to be used by God in reconciling that person to Him.

Galatians 6:1 says, "Dear brothers and sisters, if another believer is overcome by some sin, you who are godly should gently and humbly help that person back onto the right path." Is there someone in your life with whom you need to be reconciled? Do you need to gently and humbly confront a fellow believer about some sin? Do you need to reconcile yourself to God? It might be easier to ignore these issues, but you can never live in close communion with God and others if you do.

■ ■ ■

Dear heavenly Father, forgive me for the times I've pulled back from the needs of friends instead of drawing closer to those people. Please point out my own faults, and guide me in reconciling myself to You and then to others.

Before You Ask

The King will say, "I tell you the truth, when you did it to one of the least of these my brothers and sisters, you were doing it to me!"

MATTHEW 25:40

In July 1969, a storm brought record flooding in Killbuck, Ohio. Businesses were destroyed, homes were damaged, and the community was in shock. Equally surprising was waking up to discover teams of Amish and Mennonites arriving to help. They responded without receiving a request for aid. They knew assistance was needed, and they showed up. They were not afraid to get dirty—not afraid of hard work. Things have not changed since 1969.

While I was visiting the Amish in Ohio, I heard about tourists who happened to arrive in the small town of Charm after a heavy storm. Even though it was early in the morning, the tourists saw Amish men from nearby towns replacing the roof on a damaged building.

A tourist asked one of them, "Without telephones, how do you get out the word about where to meet and when?"

The Amish man chuckled. "No one needed to call; we just came. We knew someone would need our help."

How wonderful it would be if we all had the same attitude. And shouldn't we? When we see others in trouble, we often tell them, "Call me if you need help." But imagine what a relief it would be if we offered help before someone even asked. I can remember many times help has been offered to me. It's proof that God is at work in the lives of men and women every day.

Jesus declared that when we care for the "least of these"— brothers and sisters in need—we are doing it for Him. Jesus is honored when we put the needs of others above our own, and as the Amish likely know, when God's love flows through us we, too, are blessed.

Amish don't limit their service to their own geographic area. After Hurricanes Katrina and Rita, scores of Amish traveled to the Gulf states to assist with cleanup and reconstruction.

■ ■ ■

Heavenly Father, I thank You for all those You've brought into my life to help me in a time of need. Keep nudging me to do the same. And may You be glorified when I give and serve.

Blanketed in Love

"Who are you?" [Boaz] asked. "I am your servant Ruth," she replied. "Spread
the corner of your covering over me, for you are my family redeemer."
RUTH 3:9

I can't think of anything more comforting than wrapping myself in a thick quilt on a cold winter's day. With the popularity of Amish-made quilts, you might think they were invented by the Amish. But the Amish did not start making quilts until the mid-1800s. They learned quilting from their English neighbors. Yet while many English have given up the practice of quilting, the Amish carry on that skill with fervor.

Amish often make intricate and colorful quilts to sell at benefit auctions, and in their community, making the quilts a significant source of income. Originally, Amish quilts were quite plain; the use of bright colors or large patterns developed over time to make quilts more attractive to people who wanted to buy them. When Amish women make quilts for themselves, they still focus on simplicity and practicality. They make quilts to keep their children warm at night or to place on the lap of an elderly relative. Quilts are evidence of a mother's care and provision for her home.

The average quilt takes approximately 250–350 yards of thread.

Just as Boaz covered Ruth with the corner of his garment to symbolize his commitment to care for her, God used a similar metaphor for His covenant with Israel: "When I passed by again, I saw that you were old enough for love. So I wrapped my cloak around you to cover your nakedness and declared my marriage vows. I made a covenant with you, says the Sovereign LORD, and you became mine" (Ezekiel 16:8).

A quilt communicates a sense of belonging. And although many of us have never learned to quilt, we can bring the same warmth to our families in other ways. A homemade meal, an unexpected gift, a small bundle of handpicked flowers—each can be a symbol of our love for the recipient.

An even greater gift is our prayers. We can provide this special "covering" anyplace, anytime. Lifting the name of a loved one up to God can bring the same warmth as a handmade quilt as we trust Him to wrap our families in His love.

■ ■ ■

Dear heavenly Father, my greatest desire is to cover my family with my love and provision.
I start at this moment with my prayers.

Knit Together

I want them to be encouraged and knit together by strong ties
of love. I want them to have complete confidence that they
understand God's mysterious plan, which is Christ himself.

COLOSSIANS 2:2

Knitting puts form to simple threads. Amish women knit items for their own families and often to sell. Knitting is not as popular as quilting or sewing, but there are still women who come together to encourage one another—to knit their hearts together—as well as to move needles through yarn.

Knitting is like the Amish community itself. The lives of the Amish are interwoven. An Amish man or woman could not live that lifestyle alone, but knit together, the Amish flourish.

Some time ago I was speaking with a banker who had worked with the Amish when she lived in their community. Amish men often came into the bank for loans. Although they had no credit and couldn't put up collateral either, she was still able to give them loans. Why? Because they had one another. The men came to the bank with a simple certificate. It said the bearer was part of an Amish community. If he was unable to settle his debt, the community would cover any default. Many, many people had his back.

Amish women often knit and crochet sweaters, scarves, doilies, pot holders, lap blankets, and baby items. They even use bright-colored yarn.

We may not live in an Amish community, but God has our backs. When we could not pay the debt of sin, God made sure we were covered: "He is so rich in kindness and grace that he purchased our freedom with the blood of his Son and forgave our sins" (Ephesians 1:7).

There is no basis for pride when we are dependent on others. An Amish person cannot boast, "Look what I've done on my own!" Neither can we. True peace is knowing that God covered the debt we could never pay. Even more wonderful, Christ gave us Himself and His righteousness to wear—a garment knit from sacrifice and love.

■ ■ ■

Dear heavenly Father, thank You for having my back—for covering my sins with the blood of Your dear Son, Jesus. I could never pay the debt my sin requires. I'm thankful I don't have to. Today I'm stepping out clothed in Christ. May I display His beauty to those in my community!

Our Inheritance

I pray that your hearts will be flooded with light so that you can
understand the confident hope he has given to those he called—
his holy people who are his rich and glorious inheritance.
EPHESIANS 1:18

A friend and I were discussing frugal living, and she spoke of an elderly family member who'd stored away bags of gold and bank accounts of treasure by living on less. My friend's point was that we'd save a lot if we didn't spend as much, but I also began to think of *my* inheritance. In my garage I have a box of my grandfather's things—his cowboy boots, his plaid shirts, and some of his Western-style jackets. There are no gold coins, no stacks of bills, but those things are treasures to me!

Amish quilts are a cultural inheritance. Quilts of various colors and styles are passed down from one warm bed to another. The precise stitching is often intricate and beautiful—just like the faith passed down from one generation to the next.

I imagine that when an Amish family has an average of seven kids and lives a "plain" lifestyle, there isn't much earthly treasure to pass on—no gold, silver, or bank accounts. Yet when a family passes on Jesus and a community of fellow believers—holy people God has put into our lives—that becomes a much more beautiful inheritance. It's not the *whats* that make us rich but the *whos*, those we can look forward to being with for eternity.

This passage from Acts 3:6 speaks of true treasure: "Peter said, 'I don't have any silver or gold for you. But I'll give you what I have. In the name of Jesus Christ the Nazarene, get up and walk!'" Peter didn't pass on gold. He passed on faith. As I consider my inheritance, I'm thankful for my grandfather's cowboy boots, but I'm also thankful for the memories I have of him sitting at the table, drinking his coffee and reading his Bible. We should never be frugal about sharing that our true treasure lies in our faith in God!

■ ■ ■

Dear heavenly Father, I am overwhelmed with Your inheritance. Thank You for the gift of salvation, and thank You for the godly men and women around the world. Help me to connect at deeper levels with these people of faith and to pass on this heritage to the next generation.

Unfilled Days

*On the seventh day God had finished his work of
creation, so he rested from all his work.*

GENESIS 2:2

Is there a day in an Amish household when work doesn't pile up? I doubt it. Yet the Amish do take a day of rest, just as the Bible directs. Apart from necessary tasks such as caring for animals and milking, they do not work on Sundays. Every other week they meet for church, and after church they eat together. Unlike church potlucks that many of us are used to, this meal is simpler—bread and spread, jams, pickled beets, cheese, and sometimes pie. Women cook ahead on Saturdays so they'll not have to spend time in the kitchen on Sunday.

On Sundays, Amish families visit with others in the community or return home to rest. Sometimes they'll visit the home of an elderly family member or a couple with a new baby. On Sunday evenings the youth gather for "singings," in which they sing hymns and songs from the *Ausbund* and spend time in fellowship. This is a highlight of the week for teens.

On "off Sunday" (when there is no church), families visit another Amish service nearby. They often have devotions together as a family or visit family and friends.

Do you treat Sunday differently from other days? One of the Ten Commandments reminds us, "Remember to observe the Sabbath day by keeping it holy" (Exodus 20:8), but do you set it apart as different? Do you use it as a time to worship God and connect with others, or is it simply another day to get things done?

God could have set up any structure He wanted for our week, but He chose to include a day set apart for rest. What can you do to make your Sabbath more holy? Turn to God and He will show you how.

> "Keep us, Lord, still in communion, Daily nearer drawn to thee, Sinking in the sweetest union, Of that heartfelt mystery."

■ ■ ■

Dear heavenly Father, I thank You for setting up a structure to remind us how to fill our days—or unfill them—and how to keep us focused on You. Help me to remember to fill my Sabbath with ways to quiet and nurture my heart and connect with others and with You.

Let the Light Shine

*Once you were full of darkness, but now you have light
from the Lord. So live as people of light!*
EPHESIANS 5:8

In Amish country of the Midwest, you never know what kind of weather to expect in February. One day a storm could be howling, and a few days later the sun will peek out and raise the temperature above freezing. For many Amish these "warmer" days mean added chores that haven't gotten done during the hard winter months. Laundry doesn't wait for good weather, but when the sun shines, an Amish wife may add coats to her usual wash loads and hang them outside to dry. She might also clean the windows. It's only when the sun shines that the dirt from the snow and rain becomes visible on the glass.

Isn't that like our souls? We don't see how dirty we are until God's light shines in. For many years, before I became a follower of Christ, I considered myself a pretty good person. Once I was a Christian, I had hope and peace like I'd never had before. But at the same time, the light of God's truth revealed my sinful habits. Jesus wants to clean us up so we become people of light!

Romans 13:12 says, "The night is almost gone; the day of salvation will soon be here. So remove your dark deeds like dirty clothes, and put on the shining armor of right living." Once we remove our dark deeds like dirty clothes and live right, we begin to shine as if we are wearing shining armor, which protects us just like right living does.

Has God's Spirit been pointing out sinful habits in you? Ask Him to guide you in right living so that you may shine for His glory.

> Chores in an Amish home are clearly divided. The husband usually works on the farm or at a job outside the home. The wife may help around the farm at times, but her main role is homemaking—cooking, washing, gardening, and cleaning.

■ ■ ■

Dear heavenly Father, shine Your light into my heart, and point out any dirt that You'd like me to deal with. I know this is not to bring condemnation in my life but rather to clean me up so I shine for You!

Perpetual Faith

*Watch out! Be careful never to forget what you yourself have seen.
Do not let these memories escape from your mind as long as you live!
And be sure to pass them on to your children and grandchildren.*

DEUTERONOMY 4:9

From the time most of us were young, we wondered what to do with our lives. Amish girls are raised already knowing the answer to this question. They are to be separate from the world but also live the same as those in their community in both faith and appearance. Because the girls grow up in a closed community, the food, dress, and traditions are all they know. They live as their mothers lived and as their grandmothers lived. Very little has changed for generations.

In an Amish home a mother's role is not only to reflect her values but also to perpetuate them. This means that the same traditions and beliefs are to continue without interruption.

Do you perpetuate your values in the young people in your life? You may value work, but do you work alongside a young person in a mentoring role? You may value community, but do you take food to a sick friend or welcome new families into your neighborhood? You may value family, but do you spend as much time with your loved ones as you do following your own dreams and goals?

> We did not inherit this land from our fathers. We are borrowing it from our children.
>
> **PROVERB**

Proverbs 22:6 says, "Direct your children onto the right path, and when they are older, they will not leave it." It doesn't say, "Tell your children about the right path." It says, "Direct."

Sometimes we worry about the paths our children will choose, and while the decision for which path to take will be theirs, side-by-side teaching and training will build habits that can last a lifetime.

■ ■ ■

Heavenly Father, it's easy to know what I should pass on to the next generation, but actually doing it is hard. Give me the strength and wisdom to pass on my faith to the next generation, and when my time on earth is through, may the seeds of my faith grow and bloom in others.

Come Together

Let us not neglect our meeting together, as some people do, but encourage one another, especially now that the day of his return is drawing near.
HEBREWS 10:25

In many towns across America you can visit at least twenty different churches, and you'll have a different experience in each. Some churches have contemporary worship songs; others use hymns. Some pastors read from their notes. One I know accepts text messages from members of the congregation when he preaches. Unlike the variety you find in non-Amish churches, there is a standard flow to most Amish services.

Old Order Amish usually have church every other Sunday. Families who live in the same district come together on this day. Worship begins with a short sermon by one of the local preachers or the bishop of the district. Scripture reading and prayer come next, and then a time of silent prayer. This is followed by a second, longer sermon.

> "In some Amish church districts, an Alms fund is established and reserved for families in financial need."

The service also includes hymns from the *Ausbund*, sung without instruments or harmony. The way in which the hymns are sung has been passed down from generation to generation. They are written in Early New High German, which is a predecessor to Standard German.

Growing up, I found peace in the order of my church. But the church is the body of Christ, and the most important part of worship isn't the order of the service. The most important part is gathering together to encourage one another and to glorify God.

Do you regularly attend church? If not, consider joining a local congregation. It's good to find one that you are comfortable in, but the most important thing is that the teaching comes from the Word of God and that God is honored there.

God never intended us to walk this Christian life alone. We were created for community, and when we are together, we can get a glimpse of eternity, where we'll be together with all the believers and with Christ.

■ ■ ■

Dear heavenly Father, remind me as I gather with fellow believers that the focus of our gathering shouldn't be on our traditions or hymns or worship style; the focus should be on You. I'm excited for the day when all Your people—no matter what tradition—will join together in worship!

Store Up Goodness

Don't store up treasures here on earth, where moths eat them and rust destroys them, and where thieves break in and steal. Store your treasures in heaven, where moths and rust cannot destroy, and thieves do not break in and steal.

MATTHEW 6:19-20

What do you save? I have boxes of things—old cheerleading uniforms, my grandma's recipes, and crafts and photos from my kids' toddler years. Few Amish collect material goods, but you will often find a cellar filled with pickles, beets, peaches, and apple pie filling. Women usually can together, turning the chore into a time to spend with family or friends. Just imagine the joy when on a long February day you pull out a jar of peaches that taste as fresh as the day you canned them.

Most Amish can hundreds of quarts of food every year, partly because it keeps food costs down. Canning also allows the produce preserved from their gardens to last through the year.

In addition to food from their own gardens, many women buy additional produce from local farmers. Canning may seem like a lot of work, and it is, but it saves money and cuts down on trips to the grocery store.

I know how contented and "stocked up" I feel after a big trip to the grocery store. I imagine the feeling of being rich with a harvest of blessing would radiate within me if I filled my basement shelves with food I had grown and canned for my family.

> "Properly-handled sterilized equipment will keep canned foods in good condition for years. Sterilizing jars is the first step of preserving foods."

Where does your treasure lie? Does your provision come from basement shelves stocked with canned food or clothes you've sewn with your own hands? Those can be wonderful things, but our greatest wealth comes from our faith. Talking about the goodness of God as one cans stores up even more value than the canning itself. Our treasure isn't in what we line our shelves with; it's in our relationship with the Savior and the people we'll enjoy for eternity.

■ ■ ■

Heavenly Father, too often I look at the work of my hands and take pride in all I've accomplished. I enjoy gathering up treasure to feed and provide for my family, but remind me again where my true treasure lies.

Amish Snowbirds

For everything there is a season, a time for every activity under heaven.
ECCLESIASTES 3:1

When I lived in Montana, many of my friends moved south for the winter—mostly to Arizona and Nevada. I knew snow was around the corner when my friends packed their bags and traveled to warmer parts.

In the cold months of winter, some Amish do the same. One popular destination is Pinecraft, Florida. This Amish community is just a stone's throw from the beach.

From December to April, Amish travelers fill charter buses and venture from the snowy hill country to Florida's Gulf Coast. The Amish have been traveling to this area since 1925, mostly during the winter months when farmwork is slow. The small village of Pinecraft caters to the Amish. Even the local self-service laundry has strung up lines outside for air drying—although many Amish do use electricity in their rental homes. Florida is a different type of place, and Amish and Mennonite congregants from "old" to "new" mingle as they wouldn't at home. They enjoy the sun on their faces and remove their sturdy black shoes to walk barefoot on the beach. As they enjoy a respite from their busy days at home, I can imagine them gratefully remembering the words of Psalm 21:2: "You have given him his heart's desire; you have withheld nothing he requested," and Psalm 145:19: "He grants the desires of those who fear him."

Many of the Amish who visit Pinecraft, Florida, visited there as children and return every year.

Does your soul need refreshing? I wish I could offer you a sunny Florida vacation with friends. That would be wonderful, indeed. But we can discover the joy and peace that comes from God no matter where we are. The world outside your window may be a blistering cold storm, but that can't stop the Lord from being with you in a real way. Sometimes we do need a vacation, an escape. But sometimes we simply need to turn to God and allow the warmth of His light to fill our hearts.

■ ■ ■

Dear heavenly Father, some days I desire an escape from the storms outside my window and the storms in my life. I'm thankful that I can turn to You when I struggle with those storms and know that Your presence can bring calm.

A Sacrifice of Praise

They were severely beaten, and then they were thrown into prison. The jailer was
ordered to make sure they didn't escape. So the jailer put them into the inner
dungeon and clamped their feet in the stocks. Around midnight Paul and Silas
were praying and singing hymns to God, and the other prisoners were listening.

ACTS 16:23-25

Some time ago I asked a few friends, "When have you felt closest to God?" I expected to hear answers such as "the birth of my baby" or "when we moved into our new home." But the answers weren't what I expected.

One woman told me it was when she and her children were running away from her abusive husband. Another recalled a cancer episode. Yet another said she felt closest to God when her mother and father died. We want to protect our children from pain and suffering, but often we experience God most in the middle of pain and suffering. That's when we need Him and depend on Him most.

Are you facing suffering now? It may be hard to think about praising God. So if praise is too hard, start with prayer. Ask God to be close to you. To wrap His arms around you. To heal your hurting heart.

We all face hardship during this life, but we don't have to face it alone. The Amish praise God through songs passed down from their ancestors who were persecuted and who died because of their faith. If life presses in like a cold, dark prison cell, then sing songs of praise. God will meet you there. No circumstance—prison walls or a burdened, heavy heart—can keep Him away.

■ ■ ■

Dear heavenly Father, I know that when I pray and praise You in
my painful circumstances You are pleased—and more, others can
see my hope in You. Accept my praise, even in times of hardship.
Especially in times of hardship.

"God, I pray from my heart that You would forgive the sins of those who trouble me. And do keep all Your children safe, wherever they are in this valley of sorrows—driven apart, tortured, imprisoned, and suffering great tribulation."

AUSBUND, 76

Love Thy Neighbor

[The man said,] "Love your neighbor as yourself." . . . The man wanted
to justify his actions, so he asked Jesus, "And who is my neighbor?"
LUKE 10:27, 29

How many neighbors—those who live on the same street or in the same apartment building—do you know by name? Unfortunately, I can't name as many as I would like. I drive past houses every day, not knowing who lives inside and what their lives are like. Things are different in Amish communities.

When an Amish family lives along the same road as familiar family and friends, the word *neighbor* isn't a vague term. The Amish attend church with their neighbors, and their children go to school together. If they don't like the bishop, they can't church hop. If they are at odds with their neighbors, they can't just ignore them. Those people will show up in their lives again and again.

> True humility is neither thinking too highly of oneself nor thinking too little of oneself but rather, not thinking of oneself at all.
>
> PROVERB

If they're permitted to, gossip, grudges, and other conflicts can impact every part of an Amish person's life. Maybe if this were the case with us, we'd do better at conflict resolution. Instead, we tend to ignore those we don't get along with. We walk in the other direction. We don't return their phone calls.

For those outside the Amish community, *neighbor* is a big word. Who are my neighbors? Are they people on my street? Those at work? Those in my town? This question is reminiscent of Jesus' parable of the Good Samaritan, which makes it clear that *anyone* God puts in our path is our neighbor.

It is no coincidence that you live where you do or know the people you know. God's grace is on display when you accept *all* those God brings into your life. Consider the community you're a part of, and ask God to help you be neighborly in ways you never thought of before.

■ ■ ■

Dear heavenly Father, forgive me for the times I've ignored those You've brought across my path and focused instead on people who are easier to be with. Help me to find new ways to love my neighbors.

Songs of Praise

Let the message about Christ, in all its richness, fill your lives.
Teach and counsel each other with all the wisdom he gives. Sing psalms
and hymns and spiritual songs to God with thankful hearts.

COLOSSIANS 3:16

The Amish sing hymns without instrumental accompaniment. They want to keep the emphasis on the words being sung rather than on the music or on musicians, who might become prideful about their skill. The Amish song leader usually sings all but the last word or syllable of the first line, and the congregation joins him at that point.

A song called *Das Loblied* ("Hymn of Praise") is a well-known Amish song. It is the second song sung at every Amish worship service and is often sung at Amish weddings. The singing is slow. Words and syllables are stretched out, and singing a hymn can take fifteen minutes or longer. The Amish consider it singing for the soul rather than singing for the ear.

Here is the English translation of the hymn's first stanza:

O Lord Father, we bless thy name,
Thy love and thy goodness praise;
That thou, O Lord, so graciously
Have been to us always.
Thou hast brought us together, O Lord,
To be admonished through thy word.
Bestow on us thy grace.

"The core songs of the *Ausbund* were formulated by fifty-three Anabaptist prisoners held in the dungeon at the castle at Passau over the years 1535–1540."

Because Amish churches have a set time for services—and a set order—all congregations in a district are singing this hymn at roughly the same time. What joy that must bring to know their voices are rising as one throughout their congregations. It gives us a glimpse of heaven, too. Someday all followers of Christ will be joined in song, gathered in our heavenly home. What a wonderful moment that will be!

Next Sunday when you worship the Lord with your congregation, consider all those around our nation and world who are also lifting songs of praise. What a beautiful feeling of unity as we praise God together!

■ ■ ■

Dear heavenly Father, I thank You that although different congregations have different styles of song, our hearts are lifted in praise to You. Forgive me, Lord, for the times my mind is distracted. Help me to focus on my words—focus my praise!

FEBRUARY 12

Chosen by God

*They nominated two men: Joseph called Barsabbas (also known as Justus)
and Matthias. Then they all prayed, "O Lord, you know every heart. Show
us which of these men you have chosen as an apostle to replace Judas in this
ministry, for he has deserted us and gone where he belongs." Then they cast
lots, and Matthias was selected to become an apostle with the other eleven.*
ACTS 1:23-26

How would you feel if one day you were a farmer, a woodworker, or a factory worker
and the next day you still had that role *and* the additional responsibilities of a minister?

Amish ministers and deacons are chosen by lot, and they serve for life. They have
no formal seminary or college training.

"Some ministers
present their
messages in a
chanting, singsong
manner, in the
Pennsylvania German
dialect, with the
scriptures in High
German."

There are only two reasons a congregation must choose a
minister—if a minister passes away, or moves away, or if the
church district grows and must be split into two smaller districts. When a new minister is needed, church members nomi-
nate married men who exhibit the characteristics described in
1 Timothy 3.

After a communion service, a table holds a row of song-
books—one for each nominee. Inside one of the rubber band–
wrapped hymnals is a piece of paper that reads, "The lot is cast
into the lap; but the whole disposing thereof is of the LORD"
(Proverbs 16:33, KJV). The nominees approach the table one
by one, from oldest to youngest, and choose a hymnal. The
man who chooses the hymnal with the slip of paper is the new
minister of the church.

Although most of us don't live our lives by casting lots, we
all need to ask ourselves, *As a follower of God, am I willing to follow wherever He leads?*
An Amish man may not receive baptism unless he is willing to accept potential nomi-
nation to leadership. May we be willing to do the same—to follow the call of God no
matter the cost.

■ ■ ■

*Dear heavenly Father, I know I don't need lots to direct my future when I have Your Holy
Spirit as my Counselor and Guide. Help me to listen, Lord. And more than that, help me
to be willing to follow You in whatever position You place me in.*

House Amish

He is the God who made the world and everything in it. Since he is
Lord of heaven and earth, he doesn't live in man-made temples.

ACTS 17:24

My kids always know when company is coming because of the frenzy of housecleaning that takes place. The toys get picked up. The floor is swept. The pile of laundry on the couch moves to a bed, and the bedroom door is closed. I can't imagine how I'd respond if instead of just a few friends coming by, my guests were everyone from my local church.

Most Old Order Amish do not meet in special buildings. Instead, they worship together in their homes or barns. (For this reason they are often called House Amish.) These congregations follow the Scripture that declares that God does not dwell in temples made with human hands. It's also possible that they are following the traditions of their Anabaptist ancestors who found it safer to gather and pray in the privacy of their homes than to meet in public and draw the attention of religious authorities.

> **An Amish congregation is made up of twenty-five to thirty families who live in close proximity to one another.**

Each Amish family takes turn hosting a church service during the year. Amish homes are usually built so they can accommodate a large gathering of people. Women sit on the kitchen side, men on the living room side. Congregations don't own a building, but they do own common property—tables and chairs and benches. Wagons transport these to the home where the service is held. After the service, legs are attached to the benches to form tables, and the host family serves a simple meal.

Amish congregations don't fight over the color for the new church carpet or whether the children's wing needs to be painted. Their pooled money goes to provide for the needs of the members.

True followers of God know that Sunday worship doesn't have to happen at a specific place; instead, it's an attitude of the heart. Praise God that He doesn't reside in man-made temples. He's with us *wherever* we gather to worship Him.

■ ■ ■

Heavenly Father, forgive me for the times I've been more focused on the meeting space than on the One I'm joining others to meet. I know You are with me wherever I go. Help me to appreciate that more.

FEBRUARY 14

A Forever Love

*Your children will commit themselves to you, O Jerusalem, just
as a young man commits himself to his bride. Then God will
rejoice over you as a bridegroom rejoices over his bride.*

ISAIAH 62:5

One of my favorite verses is Zephaniah 3:17, "The LORD your God is living among
you. He is a mighty savior. He will take delight in you with gladness. With his love,
he will calm all your fears. He will rejoice over you with joyful songs." Words such as
delight, love, calm, and *joyful* are worth celebrating, and yet they are not what most
people think of when they consider Valentine's Day.

The Amish do not mark Valentine's Day with greeting cards, bouquets of flowers, or boxes of chocolate. Amish children who attend public
school might celebrate by sharing cards and treats, but at home,
the holiday passes almost unnoticed. Romance isn't found in a
flowery poem. The Amish find it in the enduring commitment
between a husband and a wife. When the Amish marry, they
marry for life. There is no thought of divorce. In the same way,
God's love and care for us never end.

Amish inspirational
novels are one
of the fastest-
growing markets in
publishing today.

Public displays of affection are discouraged in the Amish
community. Even at an Amish wedding ceremony, an Amish
couple will hold hands after they are proclaimed husband and
wife, but they do not kiss during the ceremony.

In our modern world, attraction is often shown by physical affection. In most movies, characters show their love by becoming physically intimate. Yet focusing only on
what is physical blinds us to the qualities of a gentler, simpler love.

How will you show your love today? How about with delight, with calm, with your
presence, and with gladness? Maybe even with a song? Love is about far more than
grand gifts or physical attraction. True, lasting love can't be purchased with a card and
flowers. Instead, it comes from a gentle turning of your attention toward the person
who has captured your heart.

■ ■ ■

*Dear heavenly Father, what You created pure, the world tries to counterfeit. I desire to
refocus my gifts of love to others—and to You—on what's given from the outpouring of my
heart, not merely bought with my checkbook.*

Chosen

You are a chosen people. You are royal priests,
a holy nation, God's very own possession.

1 PETER 2:9

What three words would you use to describe your faith? For the Amish, three concepts rise above the others. First is the rejection of *Hochmut,* which means pride, arrogance, or haughtiness. Second is the high value placed on *Demut,* or humility, and third, *Gelassenheit,* which refers to remaining calm no matter what may come. Another way to define this, from a more literal translation, is "letting be."

In our world today, "letting be" seems like a sign of weakness rather than strength. We're told to climb the corporate ladder and to be assertive. In contrast, the Amish are raised to resist the urge to push oneself forward. They trust that God's will is above all things and that the good of the group is more important than that of an individual.

These deep-seated beliefs play a part not only in who the Amish *are* but also in what they *acquire.* Having electricity would foster an unnecessary dependence on those outside the community and make them less dependent on their own community. The Amish believe having photographs, singing a musical solo, or playing an instrument cultivates personal vanity. Instead of feeling as if they are missing out, Amish children grow up with the belief that they were chosen to dedicate their lives to God and live this way.

> The word *Gelassenheit* can be translated "releasement." It means being available for "what is."

We may not choose to forgo technology or to put away our cameras, but rejecting pride and fostering humility are virtues all believers should embrace. We can also take steps toward "letting be" instead of pushing ahead with personal agendas. Imagine how much more peaceful our lives would be if we accepted *whatever* the day held as part of God's plan. God does have His eye on us, you know: "You are a holy people, who belong to the LORD your God" (Deuteronomy 7:6).

Do you have the urge to push ahead and proclaim your worth? You don't need to. You belong to God. What could you ever obtain that would be more wonderful than that?

■ ■ ■

Dear heavenly Father, it's my natural tendency to want approval and appreciation from others. Forgive me for the times I've looked for approval from others rather than from You. I rejoice that I belong to You!

Strength through Weakness

Each time he said, "My grace is all you need. My power works best
in weakness." So now I am glad to boast about my weaknesses,
so that the power of Christ can work through me.
2 CORINTHIANS 12:9

Have you ever felt pushed outside your comfort zone? Moving from the Northwest to the South, I didn't always understand the accents, the values, and the attitudes of those in my new area. I was used to the way things had been, and it was hard getting accustomed to my new world.

While it's true that many Amish spend their lives farming as their ancestors have done for centuries, other Amish men are being pushed out of their typical trades and are being forced to work with outsiders. Amish farmers are having to face two hard realities: farmland has become much more costly, and the Amish style of low-tech farming simply doesn't produce the same level of income it once did. As a result, many Amish men have been forced to work away from their farms at various other trades. It's not uncommon to see Amish laborers working with heavy machinery or even operating computerized systems in their factory jobs.

The Amish do not serve in the military, draw Social Security, or accept any other form of government assistance.

Not only do Amish have to "venture out," in order to provide for their families, other Amish families have opened their doors to the outside world through the tourist trade. Formerly quiet little Amish villages are now vacation destinations. Men engage in shop work and women in crafts for profit. They also open their shops—and sometimes their homes—to "Englishers" who are fascinated by their work and lifestyle.

The only thing certain in life is that change will come; at one time or another we will be forced to venture outside our comfort zones. As things change, we may feel uncomfortable and weak, but the good news is that Jesus meets us in our weakness. In fact, it's through our weakness that His goodness and power shine.

Are you in an uncomfortable place in your life? Jesus will join you there. His power will make up for all your uncertainties. You can trust Him in that.

■ ■ ■

Dear heavenly Father, when I find myself moving to a place outside my comfort zone,
help me to remember that You are already there and that Your power is greatest in all my
weakness. Amen.

Matters of the Heart

When I was with the Jews, I lived like a Jew to bring the Jews to
Christ. When I was with those who follow the Jewish law, I too
lived under that law. Even though I am not subject to the law, I did
this so I could bring to Christ those who are under the law.

1 CORINTHIANS 9:20

In the Amish community there are numerous groups, each with different rules of dress. Within these groups everyone knows "the type of suspenders males are required to wear, if any, or how many pleats there should be in a bonnet, or if one should wear a bonnet at all."

Although getting caught up in such details may seem silly to those of us outside an Amish community, among Christians the same types of rules and arrangements have been going on for centuries. Paul preached to the Jews, and he preached to the Gentiles. Each culture had its own laws, customs, and traditions, but that's not what Paul focused on. He overlooked the outward appearances and focused his attention on the hearts of his hearers. Paul knew he didn't need to dress a certain way or follow various rules to get God's approval, but he respected the practices of those whose customs were different in order to share the good news of Jesus with them.

Who in your life is different from you? Friendship is truest when we offer it to those who aren't exactly the same as we are. Each of us can learn from another and discover something beautiful in that person's heart. Focusing on who people are on the inside can be a challenge, but we honor God when we do: "People judge by outward appearance, but the LORD looks at the heart" (1 Samuel 16:7).

• • •

Dear heavenly Father, it's easier to spend my time with those
similar to me, but what rich friendships I miss out on when I do.
Give me a heart to love others for who they are on the inside.

"White-topped buggies indicate a Nebraska Amish settlement, the only Amish group to use the white top. Nebraska buggies have an open front, lacking any sort of windshield. Nebraska Amish are found at Big Valley, Pennsylvania, and also near Andover, Ohio."

FEBRUARY 18

Deliver Me from Temptation

Temptation comes from our own desires, which entice us and drag us away.

JAMES 1:14

What do you remember of your teen years? Were they "golden years" of fun and friends? Or do you wish (as I do) that you had made wiser choices? Word has gotten out about how "wild" Amish teens can be.

Amish adolescents have a rite of passage called *Rumspringa* (pronounced *room-shpring-uh*). When they turn sixteen, Amish young men and women are released from some Amish restrictions. Some groups allow their teens to explore life outside their Amish communities. In such groups, parents hope their children will face temptation, work it out of their system, and return to the church.

Amish parents understand that there will be a certain amount of misbehavior during Rumspringa, but they neither encourage this nor overlook it.

Some youths indeed reject the secular world and are baptized into the Amish church. Some never return. During Rumspringa some Amish youth smoke, drink, drive cars, and put aside their Amish dress. Some Amish also allow a Rumspringa tradition known as "bed courtship," although this is controversial within the various communities. In bed courtship, an Amish boy is allowed to share an Amish girl's bed for the night (although it is understood that only cuddling and perhaps some kissing will take place). (I can't imagine many other parents of teens being okay with that!)

But current statistics indicate that in spite of what Amish youth may experience during Rumspringa, 90 percent of them eventually join the Amish church. Maybe their time of "running around" does prove to them there is a better, simpler way?

Unfortunately, even beyond the teen years we all face temptation and find our hearts pulled in wrong directions. God doesn't tempt us, but He does use temptation to expose areas of our lives that are not submitted to Him and to show us our weakness in the face of temptation. The good news is that God provides His strength to resist the temptation when we ask Him. And each time we place ourselves in His hands and ask Him to deal with those weak areas, He makes us more like Christ.

■ ■ ■

Dear heavenly Father, many times in my past I've fallen to temptation instead of standing up under it. Today, Lord, let me look to You for strength when I'm tempted to gratify my own desires.

The Object of Your Desire

The woman was convinced. She saw that the tree was beautiful
and its fruit looked delicious, and she wanted the wisdom it
would give her. So she took some of the fruit and ate it.

GENESIS 3:6

How does God's Word influence you? Although the Bible doesn't speak of driving buggies or dressing plain, the beliefs of the Amish have an impact on every part of their lives. They hold diligently to Scripture truths such as 2 Corinthians 6:17: "Come out from among unbelievers, and separate yourselves from them, says the LORD. Don't touch their filthy things, and I will welcome you."

Although I have no intention of adopting Amish customs, observing their faith makes me take a look at my own. Do I read God's Word and strive to live by its principles, or do I simply accept the practices that are the easiest to follow? Do I ever minimize God's Word in order to fulfill my own desires?

"The Amish use the German Martin Luther Bible in church. For an English version, they typically use the King James translation."

When Satan tempted Eve in the Garden of Eden, Eve could have stood strong in what she knew God had decreed. Instead, she minimized the importance of God's Word. In her response to the serpent, she revised what God had said. She questioned His intentions. And she gave Satan room to speak lies.

Each of us must go to God's Word, read it, and ask the Holy Spirit to guide us. As we read, we need to inquire, *What is God asking of me today?* It may not be doing more. It may be loving better, being more present in the moments of our lives, or simply waiting patiently for His guidance. God's Word is alive and active no matter where we are or in what situation we find ourselves. And the more we read God's Word, the more *God* becomes the object of our desire.

■ ■ ■

Dear heavenly Father, it's easy to take Your Word, Your directives, and minimize their importance. Help me to live diligently by Your truth, and may You fully become the object of my desire.

Thankful for Change

From one man [God] created all the nations throughout the whole earth. He decided beforehand when they should rise and fall, and he determined their boundaries.
ACTS 17:26

Do you wish you were born into a closer-knit family or community? We may be drawn to the Amish because we sense they have something we don't. It's true that they have different things, but are they better things? Can we say that their lifestyle is better than our own?

God is the One who chose the time and season in which we were born. He had a purpose in putting us into the families we have. Discontentment is looking to others and wanting what they have. Another word for this is *coveting*, a word used in older

> You are poor only when you want more than you have.
>
> PROVERB

versions of the Ten Commandments. I have to remember that if God wanted me to be born into an Amish community, He could have made that happen. He sets us in nations, communities, and families and determines the boundaries of each of them.

What *is* reasonable is to appreciate someone else's lifestyle and consider how we can make positive changes in our own. I have done this. Because of my connection with the Amish, I've learned how to appreciate my own community more. I have

reached out to my neighbors. I've opened my home more often. I've also learned to be happy with less. I've gone through my closet and given away clothes. I've tried to dress more simply, and I don't worry so much about having just the right outfit and shoes.

God chose me to live an English lifestyle, but He brings people and experiences into my life to help me examine my choices, my heart. How about you? Have you taken time lately to examine your life and your heart? Does God want you to make any changes in your lifestyle? If you haven't taken time to ask Him, today's a perfect day to do it. One prayer God always answers is *Lord, how do You desire for me to change?* You simply need to ask.

■ ■ ■

Dear heavenly Father, forgive me for the times I've been discontented about the life You've given me. Foster in me a thankful heart, and show me the positive changes You desire for me to make right where I am.

Real-Life Holiness

There is one body and one Spirit, just as you have been called to one glorious hope for the future. There is one Lord, one faith, one baptism, and one God and Father, who is over all and in all and living through all.

EPHESIANS 4:4-6

It is easy to look at a group of people such as the Amish and consider them more holy than the rest of us. But holiness comes from daily turning to God in every aspect of our lives. It means being willing to change and become more Christlike. Yes, the Amish choose to follow God in their lifestyle, but I can do the same in my life, where I live.

There are more similarities. We have the same Bible. We have families. (Everyone is born into one.) We have friends, if we choose to make them. We have jobs, food, a home, pets, hobbies. And it's in our attitude toward these things that people see a difference. It's very possible there is an unmarried New York executive living in a sky-rise who is closer to God than an Amish woman who lives with her husband and ten children and bakes her own bread, has her own garden, attends church, and serves the poor. It's what's inside—our personal relationship with Jesus—that counts. The blessing that the Amish have is that the things around them—their community, their church, their ancestors, and their traditions—remind them to nurture the spiritual parts of their souls, whereas someone in a New York sky-rise has to experience God in different areas, in different ways, without being distracted by all the world has to offer.

"Amish began emigrating to North America early in the 18th century, in large part to avoid religious persecution and compulsory military service. They first settled in eastern Pennsylvania, where a large settlement remains today."

If you're a child of God, you should not feel less important to the body of Christ because of where God has chosen to place you. He may have chosen you to change the world in which you live by living out holiness right where you are.

■ ■ ■

Dear heavenly Father, I thank You that the same Holy Spirit who lives in those I look up to and respect also lives in me. Remind me that, as Your Word says, You are "Father of all, who is over all and through all and in all" (Ephesians 4:6, NIV).

Heart Friends

Jonathan made a solemn pact with David, because he loved him as he loved himself.
1 SAMUEL 18:3

We all want to be liked. We want to have friends and feel that we're valued. This is no different in the Amish community. To those in the outside world, all Amish people look the same, but the Amish are still individuals. There is no such thing as a "typical" Amish man or Amish woman; our creative God made each one unique. And as in the rest of the world, when it comes to popularity, there are personalities that are more favored in the Amish community. Some people are just easier to love, no matter where you live.

I have friends whom I love spending time with because I am refreshed by them.

"Amish Friendship Bread is a type of bread or cake made from a sourdough starter that is often shared in a manner similar to a chain letter." There are many recipes online to start your own.

They give to me more than I give to them. I also have friends whom I pour myself into. In those cases, I give more than I get. Everyone has challenging people in their lives, and so do the Amish. One misconception about the Amish is that they don't allow friendships with outsiders. Depending on the community, they may build friendships with neighbors or others who have common interests. These friendships deepen because two people are willing to look past outward differences and focus on the heart.

David and Jonathan should have been enemies because Jonathan's father was set on killing David, but that conflict paled in comparison with their care for each other. When you are considering allowing someone to be your heart friend, the best indicator of that person's character is how he or she reflects God. I have friends who are simple and plain by the world's standards, but their love for God shines. When I'm around them, I want to spend more time with them because I get a glimpse of the Savior when we're together. Those are the types of friends you want to stay close to.

■ ■ ■

Dear heavenly Father, thank You for the special people You've brought into my life. Thank You for uniting my heart with theirs. Please show me how I can become a better friend today. Thank You for Jesus, my truest friend who never leaves me.

Speaking the Same Language

May the words of my mouth and the meditation of my heart
be pleasing to you, O LORD, my rock and my redeemer.

PSALM 19:14

What would you think about an invention that would ensure that your children would listen to and be influenced by only your family and those you trusted most in the world—folks with the same values as yours? Such a tool exists, and it is the Pennsylvania Dutch language. This language comes from a merging of dialects from the first Anabaptist immigrants to the United States.

Amish children learn Pennsylvania Dutch as their first language. It is the primary language spoken within an Amish home, the words of comfort and training. Children don't learn English until they enter school in first grade. They might pick up a few words from hearing their parents interact with the outside world, but the first messages they receive are spoken only by those in their Amish community, those who love God and vow to follow Him.

I didn't know that Amish children don't speak English when I first visited an Amish home. I wondered why the young children watched me with interest and frowned as I spoke. They were trying to figure out what I was saying! It made me consider the words and influences I allow into my own home, with my own children.

"The Pennsylvania Dutch dialect has primarily been a spoken language throughout its history, with very few of its speakers making much of an attempt to read or write it."

Yes, it's important to surround our children with people who "speak the same language" that we do—people who have the same beliefs, interests, and godly qualities. When our children see others in the world around them reading God's Word, serving God, and sharing His truths, they discover a community of Christian fellowship. Following God becomes more than just a "Mom and Dad" thing. It becomes part of their identities.

What language do the children in your life hear? Ask God to help you provide words of comfort and training to the little ones you influence the most.

■ ■ ■

Dear heavenly Father, may my words today be pleasing to You, and may they positively influence the little ones You bring into my life. Amen.

Sweet Sacrifices

Don't forget to do good and to share with those in need.
These are the sacrifices that please God.
HEBREWS 13:16

Our actions and reactions are more the result of training than we may realize. We are used to living within a particular system, and—even for believers—moving outside that system takes thought and conscious effort. For example, in my everyday life, I'm trained to look after the needs of my husband and family. I am also concerned about my neighbors and my community, but it takes time and effort to step outside my comfort zone and care for their needs.

The opposite is true for the Amish. Their eyes are fixed on their community, and the needs of others stand out like neon signs. If someone loses a barn, others provide materials and labor for a new one within days. When illness or death comes to a home, neighbors bring food and help out without being asked. It's the expected thing to do, and they do it with joy.

Amish community members gather to erect a barn in one day, and they finish in time for the owner's cows to be milked that evening. If livestock was lost in a barn fire, people in the community replenish the stock.

Reflecting on this, I've taken steps to train myself to live more like an Amish person. To take a meal to a sick friend. To offer a prayer and send a note to someone who might be discouraged. To check in at the child-care center at church to see if they need an extra hand (many times they do). Doing good and sharing not only benefit others but are also sacrifices that please God.

In the New Testament, a gift or sacrifice offered to another is described as "a sweet-smelling sacrifice that is acceptable and pleasing to God" (Philippians 4:18). No sacrifice is easy. God knows that. But with practice our response can become natural. We can train ourselves to act in this way. When we do, we not only help another but also set an example for others to follow. More than that, we bring pleasure to God's Father-heart.

■ ■ ■

Dear heavenly Father, transform my heart to be more like Yours. Let it become a natural thing for me to give to others and to serve them. May all that I do be a sweet-smelling sacrifice to You!

Train Up a Child

Direct your children onto the right path,
and when they are older, they will not leave it.

PROVERBS 22:6

Do you remember your teen years, when you questioned what you were going to do with the rest of your life? Your parents may have expected that you'd go to college, embark on a career, and make them proud. They may have wanted more for you than they had. Maybe that was your expectation too. Maybe you also dreamed that you'd find a spouse, create a home together, and have a family.

Amish youth have no doubt about their parents' expectations. Even though Amish parents may anticipate a time of "running around" (Rumspringa), they train their children to desire to be baptized into the church as young adults, marry, and continue in the Amish tradition—just as their ancestors have done for generations. Conformity is the goal for the Amish way of life.

The training works. More than three-fourths of all those raised in an Amish community stay Amish. But what about the others? The fact that they leave the Amish community doesn't mean they forget their training.

Deuteronomy 4:9 says, "Watch out! Be careful never to forget what you yourself have seen. Do not let these memories escape from your mind as long as you live! And be sure to pass them on to your children and grandchildren."

> The kind of ancestors you have is not as important as the ones your children have.
>
> PROVERB

Many of my friends have left the Amish community (or their parents left), but they still cling to what they were taught. My friends love God, they are dedicated to their communities, they serve their families and, for the most part, live simple lives in their homes. They may not have fulfilled every one of their parents' expectations, but those I know have clung to the best part—their relationship with God.

We may know people we wish were more like us. But the real test of our training is whether our children still cling to God even if their lives look very different from ours.

■ ■ ■

Dear heavenly Father, I am prone to expecting others to turn out the way I want. I'm often disappointed when they don't live up to what I believe they should. Forgive me, Lord, and help me to point them to You. I pray most of all for their conformity to Your will.

Out of the Comfort Zone

The seeds of good deeds become a tree of life; a wise person wins friends.
PROVERBS 11:30

I received a note from a friend on vacation who found herself in line with an Amish woman at a grocery store. "I wanted to talk to her—to get to know her—but I questioned if it was allowed." Many of us may have the same question. We know that Amish men and women have close relationships within their own community, so we assume the Amish aren't allowed to have friendships with outsiders. Some communities may discourage outside friendships, but many Amish people have great friendships with non-Amish. My friend was happy when I told her that having a neighborly conversation in a grocery store line is fine and could even lead to a new friendship!

Use friendship as a drawing account, but don't forget to make a deposit.

PROVERB

When it comes to friendships, it's sometimes easier to stay within our own circles and spend our time with those who are most like us. We can become uncomfortable when we don't understand others' lifestyles, attitudes, or philosophies. Just as we may question how Amish live without electricity, phones, or other modern conveniences, they may wonder how we live with those things. Our choices seem just as strange to the Amish as theirs do to us.

Jesus is our best example of someone who reached out to those beyond His immediate circles. He ate with tax collectors and prostitutes. He came from an insignificant town but interacted with high priests.

Have you become too comfortable within your own circles? Ask God to open your eyes, open your heart, and open your doors to someone very different from you. You might be stretched beyond your comfort zone, but the joy you experience in a new friend's smile will be worth it!

■ ■ ■

Dear heavenly Father, I often find it easier to spend time with people who are like me. Today, Lord, help me to step out of my comfort zone. Bring someone into my life who needs a friend. And bring someone into my life who needs to hear about our truest friend, Jesus.

Motives of the Heart

As for me and my family, we will serve the LORD.

JOSHUA 24:15

Often the question Amish young people ask themselves isn't *Will I stay Amish?* but *When should I join the church?* Young people aren't prodded into church membership. Parents and church leaders allow each person to choose when the time is right.

Of course, sometimes there are external motivations. Within the Amish community one can't get married until he or she is a member of the church, so the pursuit of membership is usually directly tied to the pursuit of a spouse. It's common for young people to join the church one weekend and send out wedding invitations in the next few weeks.

There comes a time in each of our lives when we must choose if—or when—we're going to follow God. We may have outside motivations, such as wanting to follow our parents' beliefs, wanting to fit in with Christian friends, or—in the case of an Amish young person—wanting to get married. But regardless of those other reasons, our first motivation should be that we desire Jesus as Lord in our lives. He—not any earthly benefits we will receive—must be our hearts' desire.

> The Amish population doubles about every eighteen to twenty years.

The Bible gives us a perfect description of this: "LORD, we show our trust in you by obeying your laws; our heart's desire is to glorify your name" (Isaiah 26:8).

Take a moment to think back to your decision to follow God. Regardless of your initial motivation, consider how your life has changed. What impact has choosing to serve the Lord had on you and your family? Thank Him for the many ways He has guided and protected you. Find some time this week to share your story with someone else. God may use it to encourage another person to follow Jesus too!

■ ■ ■

Dear heavenly Father, choosing to follow You is the best decision I ever made. Today I rededicate myself and my family in service to You. Help me to be confident in sharing my life and my story with someone who may question his or her need for You or who may be considering the Christian life with the wrong motivations. Amen.

To Know and Be Known

As iron sharpens iron, so a friend sharpens a friend.

PROVERBS 27:17

It may seem that it would be impossible to be lonely in an Amish community. The Amish neighbors who live closest to you also attend church with you. Their children attend school with your children. Every local activity involves folks whose faces and personalities are familiar to you and your family. Yet people aren't the cure for loneliness. One of my loneliest moments was at a convention where I was surrounded by five thousand other women, all very similar to me. My loneliness came from being surrounded by bodies but not being seen or known. Sometimes loneliness comes from just being one of the crowd.

For many people the 1985 movie *Witness*, starring Harrison Ford, was their first look into an Amish community. The movie did so well in the box office that some Amish communities worried they would be overrun with tourists.

But when we invite people into our lives, loneliness begins to erode, like a message scribbled in the sand near the ocean. The people in our lives come and go. We either let them approach and wash away our loneliness, or we put up a seawall and hold them back from us. Sometimes we're afraid to let people get close because we're afraid of what they'll think when they discover our real selves. But no one is perfect, and in fact, friends can help us become better people. As our lives rub against the lives of others, our rough edges begin to be smoothed away.

If you're feeling lonely, ask God to show you any walls you need to take down. If you feel as if no one cares to know the real you, think of someone you'd like to connect with. Take a look at the people around you, and take the first step in knowing and being known.

■ ■ ■

Dear heavenly Father, sometimes I feel as if no one even sees me. I'm so thankful that You do. You have brought others into my life to give me benefits I cannot gain on my own. Desiring to be known involves opening myself to change. Please give me the courage to do that.

Jesus, the Way

*Jesus told him, "I am the way, the truth, and the life.
No one can come to the Father except through me."*

JOHN 14:6

The Amish have a slower way of life, but slow and steady isn't *the way*. The Amish build their lives around good morals, including telling the truth, but truthfulness isn't *the way*. The Amish celebrate life. They have large families and commune with others. But living *this way* isn't what saves their souls. The life they enjoy is good but not good enough. Jesus said, "I am the way, the truth, and the life."

Jesus is the Way. The Truth of God, the Word of God, come in the flesh. Following Him is *the way* to live. Dedicating our lives to Him is *the way* to eternal life. And to walk in *the way*, we must read the Word of God and listen to the still, small voice of His Spirit.

It is within Jesus that we will find the life we've longed for. It might be slower paced, but it also might have seasons of outpouring of love and giving of our time and care. In Jesus we find life larger than we expected, both here and in eternity. A life filled with people to walk with, people to circle around us, and people to serve. To gain that life, we need to turn to Jesus—not to human ideas or rules.

Sometimes we are so busy trying to find the *right way*— or we're discontented because we believe that someone else's lifestyle is a *better way*—that we miss out on finding Jesus, *the Way*.

■ ■ ■

Dear heavenly Father, I've spent so much of my life trying to figure out the right way to live, yet I've often pushed Jesus to the side in my pursuit. Jesus, I welcome You today. Thank You for being the Way, the Truth, and the Life. Amen.

> "Listen to me, all peoples of the earth. Listen to me, young and old, great and small. If you want to be saved, you need to leave sin, follow Christ the Lord, and live according to his will. Christ Jesus came to the earth to teach men the right way to go.... He said: 'I am the way the truth and the life, no-one comes to the father except through me.'"

AUSBUND, 82

The Posture of Submission

Come, let us worship and bow down. Let us kneel before the LORD our maker.
PSALM 95:6

Can you remember the last time you knelt before God? For many of us this is no longer part of our lives—not even in church. To the Amish, kneeling is commonplace. Donald Kraybill writes about an Amish church service:

> The congregation kneels twice in prayer. The first prayer, a silent one, follows the opening sermon and lasts several minutes. The congregation waits on God quietly . . . on their knees on a hard floor. . . . The congregation kneels a second time near the end of the service as the deacon reads a traditional prayer.

When you hoe a garden, you are simply cutting off the tops of the weeds. To get to the roots, you have to bend your knee and dig deep.

PROVERB

When a church member has gone against the Ordnung or wishes to be restored to fellowship after being shunned, the member goes forward during the service for a kneeling confession.

When a new minister is selected, candidates kneel as they ask God to direct them to the man He has chosen.

When young people are baptized into the church, the applicants are asked a series of questions. Those who are willing to commit their lives to God and His church kneel before the standing congregation.

Kneeling is commonplace in Amish worship because it is an outward symbol of the quiet humility of the people. It is also something we can incorporate into our daily lives.

Do you have a morning prayer time? Consider kneeling. Does your family have a need? Kneel before God in humility and present that need to Him. Posture is not everything, but it is something. Let us put our knees to the ground and put ourselves in the posture of submission to God's will.

• • •

Dear heavenly Father, I kneel before You now as one who desires Your will above mine. May my heart be as submissive as my posture. May my life display the quiet humility that comes from kneeling before You.

Seeds of Faith

As long as the earth remains, there will be planting and harvest,
cold and heat, summer and winter, day and night.

GENESIS 8:22

Imagine the excitement in the air as rays of spring sunlight stretch over frozen fields and begin to thaw them. Children spend more time outside, even if the wind is cold. Mothers plan their gardens. Farmers, eager for the season ahead, stride through the fields and check the soil. Seeds are still in paper packages, but soon they will be in the ground, taking root and sprouting. Even the animals, eager to nibble on the first fresh green shoots, grow impatient in their stalls after eating hay and feed all winter.

Expectations are good. Farmers would not plant their fields, or their wives a garden, without having expectations of the harvest to come. The sun will shine whether or not the seeds are planted, but sowing the seeds is an exercise in faith. Those who plant, trust that the seeds will take root and grow.

The Amish believe that the outward work—whether it be straight garden rows or neatly hung laundry—is a reflection of the inner person.

Have you ever considered how this applies to the spiritual seeds we plant? Have you looked at the barren soil in the hearts of the people around you and pictured the spiritual harvest that is possible?

God doesn't ask us to force growth. What He requires is for us to plant the seed of His Word: "It is the same with my word. I send it out, and it always produces fruit. It will accomplish all I want it to, and it will prosper everywhere I send it" (Isaiah 55:11).

I mentor teenage mothers. Sometimes months and months go by, and I don't feel as if I see any fruit—any positive changes—in their lives. But producing those changes isn't my job. It's God's job. My job is simply to plant the seed. God will take care of the results, just as He does for the farmer. We can trust Him in that.

■ ■ ■

Dear heavenly Father, thank You for Your Word within me. I'm so glad that I simply need to spread the seeds of Your Word and the rest is up to You. Show me those who need words of hope today. And help me to be faithful in planting seeds in their lives.

Shrove Tuesday

We are made right with God by placing our faith in Jesus Christ. And
this is true for everyone who believes, no matter who we are.
ROMANS 3:22

"Fastnacht Day" is Shrove Tuesday, the day before Ash Wednesday. The translation of *fastnacht* is "fast night," or "eve of the fast," because it precedes the traditional fasting of Lent. Lent is a period of forty days leading up to Easter on the Christian church calendar. It recalls the forty days Jesus spent in the wilderness. Christians have been observing Lent since the early centuries of the church. Even though most Amish do not celebrate Lent, Fastnacht Day is still celebrated today in many Amish communities, including those in Lancaster, Pennsylvania. The traditional food for Fastnacht Day is a doughnut called a fastnacht. In the past this recipe was seen as a way to use up sugar, butter, lard, and other fats before the fasting during Lent.

In addition to fastnachts, Amish families usually have a large dinner Tuesday night and snacks later in the evening.

Originally, on Monday, dough was put in straw baskets to rise, then cut in squares and deep-fried. Served with hot coffee at breakfast, the popular way to eat these doughnuts was to split them in half and spread them with honey. (Today they are often rolled in confectioners' sugar.)

While I wouldn't mind biting into a yummy fastnacht, the important thing to remember is that the reason for Lent—for forty days of sacrifice—is to bring to our remembrance the sacrifice Jesus made for us. During the time leading up to Easter, Amish children learn about Jesus' suffering, death, and resurrection at school and at home. It does us good also to use this season for contemplation. It's not the feasting or fasting that makes a difference but placing our faith in Jesus—believing in Him, trusting in Him with all our hearts.

■ ■ ■

Dear heavenly Father, thank You for the goodness You bring into my life, but thank You
even more for the remembrance of Jesus' sacrifice.

The Holy Kiss

Greet all God's people with a holy kiss.

1 THESSALONIANS 5:26 (NIV)

What do you think of when you read the word *kiss*? Passion, as a kiss for a spouse or a dating couple? Tenderness, as when kissing children?

A kiss was a common greeting in Paul's day. In 1 Thessalonians 5:26, he says, "Greet all God's people with a holy kiss" (NIV). The Anabaptists continue the tradition. In some Amish churches all members greet one another with a kiss; women kiss women and men kiss men.

A kiss is a symbol of love, goodwill, and unity. When one person is in conflict with another, the last thing he or she wants to do is offer a kiss, to be vulnerable enough to allow the other person to get that close. Members of an Amish community are closely connected in everyday life. A holy kiss affirms relationships. But it also can open the door to great hurt: "A crowd approached, led by Judas, one of the twelve disciples. Judas walked over to Jesus to greet him with a kiss. But Jesus said, 'Judas, would you betray the Son of Man with a kiss?'" (Luke 22:47-48).

"The holy kiss is not a peck on the cheek, but a full-fledged smack on the lips. Customarily, Amish men and women don't show much physical affection in public (one reason this practice stands out)."

The closer we are to someone, the deeper the hurt when that person betrays us. Even though Jesus knew His time had come—and knew His betrayer—the sting of Judas's actions still must have gone deep. When someone hurts us, it's easy to put up a wall and not allow anyone else to grow close. But in the Amish church, that's not an option. The holy kiss is not only a greeting and a blessing. It's also a powerful reminder that even though we've been hurt in the past, at this moment we must forgive, release our pain, and trust again.

■ ■ ■

Dear heavenly Father, the pain of betrayal stings deeply, but I hand it over to You. Jesus, Your example of forgiveness—even after being hurt and rejected—is an example to me. Help me today to step forward toward the relationships in my life as a symbol of the love You've given to me.

What's on the Inside

*The Lord said to him, "You Pharisees are so careful to clean the outside of the
cup and the dish, but inside you are filthy—full of greed and wickedness!"*
LUKE 11:39

I got an e-mail some time ago with a subject line that read, "Look important with a
Platinum card." In our society we sometimes buy more to make ourselves look better.
We dress ourselves up. We move into larger homes and fill our lives with more. But
even when we do this, the inside doesn't change.

Life shouldn't be about displaying ourselves or making ourselves look good. It
should be about revealing what's on the inside. Revealing ourselves is lifting the mask
and letting others know our true selves, no matter how much
we want to hide. It's showing our true essence—what we're
really made of. And even if we don't, what's on the inside will
come out in our actions and words eventually.

**Letting go of earthly
possessions enables
us to take hold of
heavenly treasures.**

PROVERB

Instead of trying to cover themselves up, the Amish tend to
strip their lives down. They don't have *things* to hide behind.
Their plain lifestyle and clothes reveal something of who they
have chosen to be on the inside. Then, for good or bad, they are
known for who they are, not for who they display themselves
to be.

Luke 12:3 says, "Whatever you have said in the dark will be
heard in the light, and what you have whispered behind closed doors will be shouted
from the housetops for all to hear!" As humans we can wear a mask or pretend for only
so long. At some point, who we are and what we believe and live for will be shouted
from the rooftops. In addition, God already knows who we really are. We can't hide
our true selves from Him. Is there an area of your life in which you need Him to strip
you of what is not right inside you and then fill you up with His goodness?

■ ■ ■

*Dear heavenly Father, wearing a mask only works temporarily. Show me areas You wish
to transform so I'll no longer have to hide. Then fill me up with Yourself so that I will be
ready to proclaim and display Your goodness in every situation.*

Live to Please the Lord

Our goal is to be acceptable to him, whether we are at home or away from home.
We all must appear before Christ in court so that each person can be paid back
for the things that were done while in the body, whether they were good or bad.

2 CORINTHIANS 5:9-10 (CEB)

If one could briefly summarize the Amish faith, it would be to live as pleasing to the Lord; their Ordnung is a set of rules to help them do that. But Amish men and women are often the first to admit that they sometimes enjoy a little freedom from the rules of their district. My friend Ora, who grew up Amish, remembers the joy of riding a bicycle when he visited his uncle's farm. His uncle lived in a district where bicycles were allowed.

Even today some Amish settlements are known to be more "liberal" than others. Pinecraft, Florida, is considered the Amish Las Vegas, and people joke that what happens in Pinecraft stays in Pinecraft. The Amish there are often seen with cell phones and cameras. There are no horses and buggies, and everyone rides bicycles.

> We pass on our convictions to our children by the things we tolerate.
>
> PROVERB

For us, the idea of using a camera or riding a bicycle is unremarkable, and we don't understand the internal battle some Amish may have over doing so. Yet we have our own struggles with conscience. Some of these struggles may have their basis in religious tradition. But others, those that result in sin, are more serious.

Being away from home should never allow us to feel that we have an excuse for disobeying God's Word. Pleasing the Lord should be the primary aim of *all* believers, something at which we should all seek to excel, and not merely because others are watching. We must strive to obey because we love the Lord and because someday we will stand before Him.

I doubt that when Amish men or women stand before God someday, He'll shake His finger at their use of a cell phone. But being away from home should never be a license to sin, because God is with us wherever we go.

■ ■ ■

Dear heavenly Father, sometimes it gets easy to let down my guard, especially when I'm away from home. Help me to stand firm no matter where I am, no matter who is watching—or not.

The Gift of Children

Children are a gift from the LORD; they are a reward from him.
PSALM 127:3

One of the most important principles that Amish parents live by is to make their children feel as if they belong, they are needed, and they are loved. Many of their life choices revolve around raising children who will love and serve God—and their fellow human beings.

"A family that works together, grows together. Amish families spend a lot of time together and try to keep their work close to home. Children are valued as gifts from God, wanted and enjoyed. They're included in all of Amish life—from barn raisings to three-hour church services," says my friend, Amish novelist Suzanne Woods Fisher.

If you want children to keep their feet on the ground, put responsibility on their shoulders.

SIGN IN THE PINECRAFT, FLORIDA, AMISH COMMUNITY POST OFFICE

In our society, we often show favoritism to our children. Who wouldn't? Amish parents don't spoil or dote on their children. They don't want their children to feel better than others—they want them to feel connected with others. They make children feel special by playing with them in groups, choosing to sit down with their families—their children—at meals, and providing their undivided attention.

Society today often takes a different view. When did we decide that children came with a cost instead of being a blessing? When did they become a bother rather than a joy? When did we decide that loving many children would mean less love for ourselves?

"God blessed them and said, 'Be fruitful and multiply. Fill the earth and govern it. Reign over the fish in the sea, the birds in the sky, and all the animals that scurry along the ground,'" (Genesis 1:28). Following this verse doesn't mean that every family needs to fill a minivan, but we should consider all children gifts from God. We need to do our part to let them know their value in God's eyes and in ours.

■ ■ ■

Dear heavenly Father, thank You for the gift of children. May I always look for the good children bring rather than the cost. Help my love for children to grow and expand.

True Wisdom

Don't be impressed with your own wisdom.
Instead, fear the LORD and turn away from evil.

PROVERBS 3:7

Some time ago my husband and I were driving around an Amish community in Missouri when we came upon a sign welcoming us into an Amish workshop. It was a school day, but I wasn't surprised to see a young man, no older than fifteen, working at his father's side as they crafted handmade hickory rockers. While the majority of Amish education starts in a one-room schoolhouse, it doesn't end there. A son learning his father's trade is just as valuable as any book work.

The goal of an Amish education is not to prepare a child for the workforce; it's to prepare him or her to live in an Amish community. That's why Amish education ends after the eighth grade.

In addition to book education, Amish children learn about caring for animals, farming, carpentry, and home skills by living and working alongside their parents. The Amish believe that school knowledge should never encourage a student to attend college and follow a profession.

How does this apply to non-Amish children? Sometimes schools foster a sense of competition, but God's Word instructs us to show preference for others (see Romans 12:10). Children may be taught about evolution, but God's Word speaks of creation (see Genesis 1:1). Many schools prize individualism, materialism, and secular thinking, which can conflict with the qualities parents are cultivating at home.

On May 15, 1972, the United States Supreme Court gave the Amish the right to maintain community-based Amish education for their children.

Whatever school choice we make for our children, the most important thing we can teach them is to know the Lord. Allowing others to become our children's primary influence or refusing to pass on our knowledge of the Lord's goodness is a recipe for disaster, as we can clearly see in Judges 2:10: "After that generation died, another generation grew up who did not acknowledge the LORD or remember the mighty things he had done for Israel."

Our children need to learn how to thrive in this world, but more than that, they need to learn how to serve God, their families, and their communities.

■ ■ ■

Dear heavenly Father, let me never seek wisdom for wisdom's sake or appear good and wise in my own eyes. I long to know Christ and the wisdom He gives.

A Contrite Heart

The sacrifice you desire is a broken spirit. You will not
reject a broken and repentant heart, O God.
PSALM 51:17

I can't tell you how many times I urged my young children to *confess* when they had disobeyed. The downcast looks and fidgeting told me my children knew that what they did was wrong, but getting the words out was hard. No one wants to admit to disobedience; to confess guilt. "Go ahead and put me in a time-out," a child's actions declare, "but I'm not going to tattle on myself."

The Amish church takes the need to confess one's sins seriously. Members are encouraged to confess their faults to a deacon or minister. In some cases, church leaders request a public confession following a Sunday service.

> "Amish faith is grounded in the teachings of Jesus to love enemies, reject revenge, and leave vengeance in the hands of God."

I have to admit, I'd be more watchful of my own actions if I knew I would need to confess in front of the whole congregation. Then again, I'd be more watchful if I took time to actually verbalize my confession to God with a contrite heart. Like my children, I often offer a downcast look and do a little fidgeting. When I admit my sin and speak it out loud with a contrite heart, asking God to forgive me, it seems to matter more. It also helps me to remember that God doesn't forgive reluctantly. He forgives willingly: "He does not punish us for all our sins; he does not deal harshly with us, as we deserve. For his unfailing love toward those who fear him is as great as the height of the heavens above the earth. He has removed our sins as far from us as the east is from the west" (Psalm 103:10-12).

God delights in hearing our confessions and offering His mercy and forgiveness. All we have to do is ask.

■ ■ ■

Dear heavenly Father, I don't deserve Your great forgiveness and mercy, but I am thankful
for them. Thank You for Your unfailing love!

Learning at God's Feet

I'm asking GOD for one thing, only one thing: To live with him in his house
my whole life long. I'll contemplate his beauty; I'll study at his feet.

PSALM 27:4 (THE MESSAGE)

According to the dictionary, to contemplate means to look at or view with continued attention, to meditate, or to ponder. When did you last take time to contemplate something?

The Amish live a simple lifestyle, which allows them time to interact more with nature. The slow pace of the buggy—without a cell phone, talk radio, or CD player—allows time to view the world God created. Working in a field, a barn, or a garden does the same. When we take time to notice it and to ponder the goodness of God, who created it, we realize that the whole world is a display of God's beauty.

This reminds me of the story of two sisters in the Bible. Martha was busy serving in the kitchen, focusing on caring for Jesus and His disciples. Martha's sister, Mary, sat at Jesus' feet, listening to His words and contemplating Him. Martha let Jesus know she wasn't thrilled about the fact that she was left with all the work. Most of us would have been right there with Martha. Those who live at a fast pace often miss out on the beauty that contemplation brings. But instead of telling Mary to speed up, Jesus told Martha to slow down: "The Lord said to her, 'My dear Martha, you are worried and upset over all these details! There is only one thing worth being concerned about. Mary has discovered it, and it will not be taken away from her'" (Luke 10:41-42).

> "On average, a new Amish community is founded in the United States approximately every three and a half weeks."

Do you get worried and upset over details? Do they keep replaying in your mind? Take time to ponder the world around you, to remember that your loving Creator has everything in His hands, and that sitting at Jesus' feet is the most important thing we can do.

■ ■ ■

Dear heavenly Father, the more I contemplate Your goodness, the more my whole world takes on shades of hope and light. Forgive me for steaming ahead without You. I'm here now, Lord, at Your feet. Help me to see Your beauty.

A Woman of Beauty

I want women to be modest in their appearance. They should wear decent and appropriate clothing and not draw attention to themselves by the way they fix their hair or by wearing gold or pearls or expensive clothes. For women who claim to be devoted to God should make themselves attractive by the good things they do.

1 TIMOTHY 2:9-10

Can you imagine waking up every day and knowing exactly what you were going to wear because it was the same thing you wore yesterday and the day before that? And the day before that?

Most Amish women's outfits have the same four elements: the dress, the apron, the kapp, and a cape. In Lancaster, Pennsylvania, dresses are a dark, solid color. The colors vary in other parts of the country, and in some districts the Amish can even be seen wearing pastels. The apron ties at the waist, and the cape covers the top half of the body.

Whatever the style, many prayer kapps are held on by straight pins or anchored by clips. Some even have double-sided cellophane tape on the underside to help keep the cap in place.

In many districts straight pins rather than buttons are used to fasten the garments. Nothing about what Amish women wear draws attention to a woman's body, and all garments are handmade. Women also bind their hair in a braid or bun and cover it with a black or white kapp (cap). The color and style depend on the district, but most kapps are white or black.

Although it's not necessary to wear Amish dress to be modest or godly, God does say that our adornment should come from the good things we do.

Consider some of the most beautiful women you know. When you think of those women, do you think of what they wear or of the glow of their smiles and the twinkle in their eyes as they love and serve those around them? A runway model can't compare to the beauty of a woman who joyfully serves her family or cares for someone in need. Devotion to God and others is the most beautiful accessory there is!

■ ■ ■

Dear heavenly Father, may my love for You flow out for all to see. May any beauty that others see in me be Your beauty pouring out through my life.

Light. Life. Growth.

The Word gave life to everything that was created,
and his life brought light to everyone.

JOHN 1:4

Amish women spend spring and summer tending gardens. Their schedule changes with the seasons, mostly because of the additional daylight. Light in the spring warms the ground and prepares it for planting. Growth is possible because of the light. Later in the year, the decrease in daylight cools the earth and prepares plants for harvest.

Have you ever considered the impact of light in our lives? The sunrise limits the length of our present night. The moon and stars limit its depth. Yet in our world, it is easy to flood our lives with artificial light. Light gives us a sense of safety. It gives us more time to be active, and we often increase the length of the workday, sometimes beyond what is healthy for us.

The essence of light is both physical and spiritual: "Jesus spoke to the people once more and said, 'I am the light of the world. If you follow me, you won't have to walk in darkness, because you will have the light that leads to life'" (John 8:12).

Just as light brings life to the earth, the light of Jesus brings life into our lives. When we read His Word, the light of His truth enters our hearts and softens them. With Jesus, even the darkest trials don't last forever. Their depth can only go so far.

Do you sometimes look for safety and productivity in places or people other than Jesus? You may be able to keep darkness at bay temporarily, but only the true light of Jesus can produce life and growth in you. Only with Jesus can a harvest of righteousness be birthed within you.

The Amish use oil-burning, gas-pressured, or battery-powered lanterns and lamps for indoor lighting. Some buggies even use lanterns as taillights.

■ ■ ■

Dear heavenly Father, I thank You for Jesus, the Light of the World. Fill me with Your light today. Soften my heart so the seeds of Your Word can take root and grow deep within me.

Deep in the Heart

*The human heart is the most deceitful of all things, and
desperately wicked. Who really knows how bad it is?*

JEREMIAH 17:9

How often does a young person accept a parent's or a leader's rules without question?
Enticed by things beyond their reach, youth often experiment. During Rumspringa,
Amish youth may drive cars, listen to radios, wear English dress, or talk on cell phones.
For some, these choices are just the beginning, and the young people are launched into
harmful activities and damaging sin.

The seeds of sin and the root of rebellion lie in everyone's heart. The first man,
Adam, had two sons. One of them humbled himself before God and offered an acceptable sacrifice. The other one believed he knew better. He offered
less than his best and experienced God's displeasure. Sin took
root in Cain and led to murder. Most Amish youth don't stray
that far, but any rebellion—including ours—is a sign of an
unbowed heart.

Rumspringa is the
time of an Amish
youth's life when
parents allow more
freedom. It's a rite
of passage in which
teens transition from
youth to adulthood.

Many times we attempt to control the actions of young
people. Yet even if we manage to get them to conform, that's no
indication that their hearts are submissive to God. Whenever
we push against God-given boundaries, we're adding another
brick to the walls around our hearts.

Jesus said, "The hearts of these people are hardened, and
their ears cannot hear, and they have closed their eyes—so their
eyes cannot see, and their ears cannot hear, and their hearts
cannot understand, and they cannot turn to me and let me
heal them" (Matthew 13:15). The only conformity that brings true peace is following
Christ and allowing His indwelling Holy Spirit to lead us. The only way we'll be willing
to follow any of God's desires is to humbly bow our hearts and wills to His. As we do,
we gain a better understanding of how helpless we are to change our behavior without
Him. Instead of asking how much we can get away with, we need to ask how we can
honor God, and make ourselves available for greater obedience.

■ ■ ■

*Dear heavenly Father, I have often fought for my own way, but now I ask for the healing
You promise. I'm turning to You and humbling my heart. Make Your desires my desires
today.*

Spring of Your Soul

Forget all that— it is nothing compared to what I am going to do.

ISAIAH 43:18

For an Amish family, winter means chairs circled in front of the coal-burning stove, reading by lantern light, simple board games, and mending and sewing. The warm spring breezes build excitement as activity moves from inside the warm home to outside in the warm sunshine.

Even though there's a chill in the air, an Amish family might have lunch on the front porch or on a blanket spread on the new, green grass. Toddlers pluck the first wildflowers, just as the older kids help push vegetable seeds into the soft ground. Once spring arrives, the chill of winter is just a memory. Dark, cold nights are of no concern. The Amish family knows winter will come again, and that makes spring special; they live to enjoy the moment.

Our own lives have seasons of darkness and cold, both emotionally and spiritually, and also seasons of life, light, and joy. No one's life is always full of sunshine, yet when bright moments arrive, it's important to celebrate them.

If we've faced hard times in the past, we may find worry clouding every moment—even a peaceful one. But worry puts our focus on our circumstances rather than on God. Worry is related to disbelief that our heavenly Father has our good in mind. When we are filled with worry, our minds are busy trying to solve problems and make plans without relying on our Savior. But Jesus told us, "Don't worry about tomorrow, for tomorrow will bring its own worries. Today's trouble is enough for today" (Matthew 6:34).

Do you find yourself worrying about dark days that may be up ahead? Give those worries to God. When spring arrives in your soul, choose to live in the joy of that moment. Live in eagerness and anticipation of what your good God is going to do.

With the spring thaw, farmers prepare the ground for planting. Many modern farmers use no-till techniques, but since the Amish do not use chemical herbicides, they do additional soil preparation to reduce weeds.

■ ■ ■

Dear heavenly Father, thank You for spring. Thank You for life, light, and moments of joy. I open my hands now and release my worries to You. I thank You greatly that they no longer have to be my concern.

MARCH 16

To Publish the Word

The Lord gave the word: great was the company of those that published it.
PSALM 68:11 (KJV)

Imagine singing a hymn in German your whole life and having only a vague understanding of what the words mean. That is how things used to be, until Mary Miller, from Shipshewana, Indiana, compiled a large book that is of great value to any Amish home. *Our Heritage, Hope, and Faith* is a collection of songs, prayers, and Scripture passages that keep the German heritage alive. It takes the High German of the Bible used in Amish services and translates the songs, prayers, and Scripture passages into everyday language.

Here is the summary of the hymn found on page 666 of the *Ausbund*:

Pathway Publishers is an Old Order Amish publishing house in Aylmer, Ontario, with a branch in LaGrange, Indiana. Their books are known for their modest prices, readability, interest, and solid Christian moral teachings.

The author recounts how God saved Israel from Pharaoh, the Philistines, the inhabitants of Canaan, etc. He asks God to help His people today who are prepared to bring their offering, and to help them cross their "Red Sea." He admonishes those who are purified to stay pure.

Line 6 of the hymn reads, "For the Lord alone is my strength; He is become my Helper. For He proclaims His great works up[on] Pharaoh, the corrupt (doomed) one. Therefore He alone is my God, I want to honor Him in my afflictions; His name I want to exalt."

Just as the hymnwriter used songs to connect the biblical story to the Anabaptists who lived under persecution hundreds of years ago, Mary Miller used her talents to make the message available to today's generation of readers. Around the world God is using men and women to share His Good News through the written word. Is He asking you to join them?

Maybe God is asking you to write a note of encouragement to a friend. Maybe He wants you to jot down the prayer He's put on your heart. Words are gifts we give others, birthed from the inspiration of God-within-us. Whether your gift is for one or for many, what words does God desire for you to "publish" today?

■ ■ ■

Dear heavenly Father, too often I worry about spelling, grammar, and other details instead of writing what You inspire in me. Today I sit with my pen and an eager heart. Speak, Lord.

What Really Counts

What do you benefit if you gain the whole world but lose your own soul?

MARK 8:36

Our secular world is run by numbers. How many dollars in a checking account? How many viewers of a television program? How many sales for a product? How many fans for a team? Achieving each set of numbers requires sacrifice: time away from family, the investment of your focus, and the passion of your heart. Yet mere numbers can't bring lasting fulfillment. A big bank account can buy you dinner at the finest restaurant, but often that dinner comes at the expense of a joyful family around the table. Making high sales builds your pride, but consumers are fickle. They're quick to turn toward the next new thing. They aren't committed to you, just for being you. They also have expectations. Fans expect wins. Viewers expect drama.

In the Amish community numbers have different meanings. Parents count noses around the dinner table. Coins are counted up and offered to a needy member of the community. Quilters count stitches. Farmers count rows. Gardeners count the jars of produce they can for the winter months.

There are Amish communities in more than half of the fifty United States.

What kinds of things "count" in our lives? Too often we sacrifice our lives for our work. We may look to the rich and famous as examples, not understanding that their prosperity comes at a great cost.

"Be not afraid when [an ungodly] one is made rich, when the wealth and glory of his house are increased; for when he dies he will carry nothing away; his glory will not descend after him. Though while he lives he counts himself happy and prosperous, and though a man gets praise when he does well [for himself], he will go to the generation of his fathers, who will nevermore see the light," we read in Psalm 49:16-19 (AMP).

Our family, God's Word, and our souls are the only eternal things we have. It's up to you to decide what's going to count for you.

■ ■ ■

Dear heavenly Father, today I long to live in the way that counts. I want my life to add up, Lord, and I know looking toward You, toward eternity, is the only way that can happen.

Death Brings Freedom

Oh, what a miserable person I am! Who will free me from this life that is dominated by sin and death?

ROMANS 7:24

Can you imagine a funeral where there are no photos of the deceased? Where family members sit silently and do not share special memories? Where the summary of one's life is read in just a few minutes, and after that the deceased's name is rarely mentioned?

We read in the Amish guidebook *Our Heritage, Hope, and Faith*, "Through cases of death, we are reminded anew time and again that we must die, that our life has a goal (will end), and that we must depart from here. The funeral sermon shall be conducted accordingly, and not too much be said about the deceased. The good qualities (attributes) of the deceased may be held up as examples and models, but this does not require much time. The most devout (godly) man still has too many weaknesses to allow him to be held up as a perfect example. Christ alone is a perfect example."

The truth of these words humbles me. No one is perfect. Paul proclaims our inner battle in Romans 7:21-24. But as troubling as Paul's words are in Romans 7:24, the answer in the next verse is exciting: "Thank God! The answer is in Jesus Christ our Lord" (Romans 7:25).

While I do appreciate celebrating the life of a person at his or her funeral, I'm also reminded that as hard as death is, it's the only thing that finally rescues us from sin. Our lives will end, and if we have faith in Jesus, our freedom will come. Our story isn't about what we achieved on earth, but rather about what we allowed Jesus to achieve for us and in us—in this life and in eternity.

In an Amish community, there are three times when friends and family can view the deceased. First, at the home a day before the funeral. Second, during the funeral, when the open casket is on display at the home. The third viewing is at the graveside before the coffin is lowered into the ground.

■ ■ ■

Dear heavenly Father, sometimes I think only of the pain of death. Today I thank You for the freedom death brings. I thank You for Jesus, who made a sinless eternity after death possible!

Nipped in the Bud

Other seeds fell among thorns that grew up and choked out the tender plants.

MATTHEW 13:7

Spring is a time of planting. Seed goes into the ground and new plants sprout up, but as quickly as the crops begin to grow, thorns come up with them.

According to Matthew 13:22, "The seed that fell among the thorns represents those who hear God's word, but all too quickly the message is crowded out by the worries of this life and the lure of wealth, so no fruit is produced."

Like anyone else, the Amish have times when worries of this life attempt to choke out their faith. This is addressed in *Rules of a Godly Life*, which is a popular Amish devotional book. It was written in the eighteenth century by a non-Amish author and consists of forty-seven proverbs.

Proverb 11 reads in part, "Never consider any sin as small or of no account, because every sin, though it seem ever so small, is a transgression against God."

Goats are considered the Amish version of weed eaters.

Of course it's easy to mislabel our thorns and thistles. We worry and then claim we are "concerned." We are drawn to things we do not need and have the excuse that when we gain more, we will use it to "bless others." Yet the greatest sin is that these things not only occupy our time but also become idols in our lives, replacing God in the center of our hearts.

A quote I recently read by Tiffany Berry says, "If you're going to worry, there's no need to pray, and if you're going to pray, there's no need to worry."

Like weeds and thistles, "small" sins can grow and choke out God's lordship in our lives. Worry is a sin. It takes our focus off God and places it on the little things. Like weeding a spiritual garden, the best thing to do is nip these sins in the bud.

■ ■ ■

Dear heavenly Father, forgive me for the times I've let sins linger and grow. Sometimes I ignore the "little sins," forgetting how they take root. Point them out to me, Lord. I want to deal with them now. I want You to be the only Lord of my life.

Beauty from Within

When they arrived, Samuel took one look at Eliab and thought, "Surely this is the LORD's anointed!" But the LORD said to Samuel, "Don't judge by his appearance or height, for I have rejected him. The LORD doesn't see things the way you see them. People judge by outward appearance, but the LORD looks at the heart."

1 SAMUEL 16:6-7

God asked the prophet Samuel to travel to Bethlehem to anoint one of Jesse's sons as king. One look at the oldest son, Eliab, and Samuel was certain he had found his man. Yet God hadn't chosen Eliab or the other five brothers who came after him. He had chosen the youngest son, David.

In the Amish community even though everyone dresses alike, there are still those with a more favorable appearance than others. In *Rules for a Godly Life* we read, "Do not be proud and overbearing because you have been blessed with this world's goods, or with outstanding personality features; for God who has given can also take away, and may do so if you through pride or contempt of others make misuse of His gifts to you."

Amish women do not wear makeup.

A desire to appear beautiful to others is something we all deal with, no matter who we are. The difference is that while the Amish encourage those in their community not to be proud or overbearing, often our culture rewards those who focus on their appearance. The media urges us to lose weight, to buy a new wardrobe, or to get a makeover. When we aren't pleased with our outward appearance, we sometimes become jealous of others. Yet these emotions taint our insides, taking away our inner beauty too. And while we can't control our height or physical features, we can allow Jesus to do a daily makeover on our hearts.

God knows who we are on the inside, and He judges our beauty by the condition of our hearts and how well we reflect the beauty of His Son. Love, joy, thankfulness, and gratitude are a beautiful display to Him. Are there any emotions inside that you need God to "make over"? He specializes in that. Just ask Him!

■ ■ ■

Dear heavenly Father, I pray that when You look at my heart, You see the beauty that reflects the image of Your Son. Show me any envy or discontentment that needs to be worked out. May You be glorified!

Trust in His Supply

This same God who takes care of me will supply all your needs from his glorious riches, which have been given to us in Christ Jesus.

PHILIPPIANS 4:19

"Life is messy," my friend Teri wrote on her blog. "Dishes have to be done over and over. Laundry keeps piling up. Furniture needs dusting and floors need vacuuming. Babies need diapers and toddlers spill juice. Children bicker and tweens roll eyes. Spouses disagree. Exhausted and worn thin from emotions spilled over and giving pieces of ourselves to everyone in our lives, we mommas find ourselves drained, empty."

Every time I think about how much work I do, I consider an Amish woman. The average Amish woman has seven children, cooks all the food, makes their clothes, and then has to keep up with the laundry and hang it out to dry!

An Amish man's work is just as challenging. Whether he has a farm or works in a local factory, there is upkeep: animals to care for, a buggy to maintain, and at least one horse to tend to. Both Amish men and women must depend on God's strength to carry them through the day.

More than that, much of Amish families' livelihood comes from what they can provide for themselves. Amish crops and gardens are dependent on favorable weather, which again means trusting God.

The vast majority of Amish housewives use the classic wringer washers, once popular in the post-World War II era in America.

According to Dictionary.com, trust is "confident expectation of something; hope." Do you have *trust* that God will provide? Do you have *trust* that even though life is messy, God will give you the strength to tackle it? Do you *trust* that God will take care of all your needs, whether they involve good weather for your garden or extra money for an unexpected bill?

"Our God is not a faraway God, a character in a fairy tale," my friend Teri continues. "He sees our needs, and He meets them."

Do you have a need today? Jesus is able *and willing* to provide.

■ ■ ■

Dear heavenly Father, thank You for providing for all my needs through the glorious riches of Your Son, Jesus. Today, I lift my eyes beyond this messy world to You.

Darkness Can Lead to Comfort and Glory

The more we suffer for Christ, the more God will
shower us with his comfort through Christ.

2 CORINTHIANS 1:5

Why does life have to be so hard? We may never know the answer to the question, but we do know that when people hurt—*really* hurt—the world pays attention. Maybe it's part of being human. We fear that hard stuff will come to us next. We watch to see how others cope so we can prepare.

We read in *Rules of a Godly Life*, "Beware especially of an uncontented and rebellious spirit. Actually it is through the will and grace of God

When the Amish are asked how they bear up under suffering, many point to their Anabaptist ancestors in sixteenth-century Europe–forebears who were burned at the stake because of their religious beliefs.

that you suffer and are troubled. God has blessed you with unnumbered gifts to supply your needs, and likewise for your own good has meted out trouble and pain that you may remain humble. In the midst of trouble remember that you through your sinfulness deserve much greater punishment."

Life is never "fair," but true fairness means we would have to pay for our own sins. God's supply not only covers our needs during hard times but also comforts us through Christ, who faced great suffering.

Romans 8:17 says, "Since we are [God's] children, we are his heirs. In fact, together with Christ we are heirs of God's glory. But if we are to share his glory, we must also share his suffering." Some time ago, friends of mine lost their son. The situation they were thrust into was a dark one, but light shines brightest in darkness. God is holding them up. Even though they will not hold their son again on earth, they can look forward to sharing God's eternity together and the glory of Christ.

All of us will face heartache in this world, but if we belong to Jesus, we can look forward to sharing His glory in eternity. Turning to Jesus gives us grace, peace, and comfort in the present. It also gives us a future more wonderful than we can imagine.

When darkness comes, there's only one place to turn: Jesus. Sweet Jesus.

■ ■ ■

Dear heavenly Father, I thank You for being the God of all comfort. May I always turn to You first when dark days come.

Have Patience

If we look forward to something we don't yet have,
we must wait patiently and confidently.

ROMANS 8:25

Patience isn't just something the Amish *believe*. It is part of their life that comes from a deep-seated conviction. When it comes to the Amish, what they believe is what they practice. And what they practice is held close with deep affection. Their spirituality is not tacked on to their lives; neither is their patience. It's a thread woven within the very fabric of their community, even among young children.

"The church service is an incubator of patience, a patience rarely seen in most young children," we read in *The Amish Way*. "Amish boys and girls, who can be noisy and rambunctious at play, learn this discipline at an early age. Taught and caught from infancy, patience shapes the character and spiritual disposition of Amish people, becoming the social reality they take for granted."

Reading these words makes me consider whether I make it possible for patience to be "caught and taught" in my home. When a checker at the grocery store is slow, many times I'm impatient. Even if I don't say it, my body language makes it clear. And what does that say about me? That I feel as if I'm better than the clerk? That he or she is wasting my time?

> A handful of patience is worth more than a bushel of brains.
>
> **PROVERB**

Those words also make me consider my day at home. Am I patient with my children? Do I understand that everything takes them longer because they are still growing and learning? Am I patient with my finances, waiting until I can afford to buy something, or do I buy more than I can afford? And what about God's work in my life? Do I try to run ahead of Him to make things happen in my own timing?

The joy of spring is looking forward to the growth to come. The joy of our salvation is waiting patiently and confidently for eternity with God. But we can embrace the same type of joy in everyday life, living in expectation instead of striving to have everything now—and teaching our children to do the same.

■ ■ ■

Dear heavenly Father, forgive me for feeling that my time is more valuable than someone else's. Help me give my time to living patiently and to modeling it for others.

Entwine Me. Free Me. Offer Me.

In my distress I prayed to the LORD, and the LORD answered me and set me free.
PSALM 118:5

My friend Loring and her family are missionaries to Uganda. A hair colorist by trade, Loring wasn't someone I pictured living in a small concrete house with sketchy electricity (at best) and washing her laundry by hand. I never imagined her living in the slums and serving the poorest of the poor. Yet it's amazing what we can do—who we can embrace—when we follow God's call.

Loring isn't Amish, but she has chosen to simplify her life in order to follow Christ. One of Loring's favorite books is a collection of Puritan prayers called *The Valley of Vision*.

Here is a passage from a prayer titled "Humility in Service."

Be life long or short, its completeness depends on what it was lived for.

PROVERB

O give me repentance unto life;
Cement my oneness with my blessed Lord,
that faith may adhere to him more immovably,
that love may entwine itself round him more tightly,
that his Spirit may pervade every fibre of my being.
Then send me out to make him known to my fellow-men.

As my friend Loring knows, when it comes to simplifying our lives, sometimes we need God to set us free from a troubling situation. Sometimes we need to be set free from financial burdens or life worries. Sometimes we need to be set free from the desire to live the great American dream and bask in a life of prosperity and ease. When we focus on what we can acquire or gain, our gaze is inward. But when we focus on our Lord, an amazing thing happens: our vision expands to our neighborhood, our community, and the world.

Amish parents direct their children toward this outward thinking by placing the knowledge of God in the center of their lives. They set their vision on God. They focus on humility and serving others. And by giving themselves away, they discover peace.

Some of us have to move out of our comfort zones to where God will expand our vision. It is there that we can find peace too.

■ ■ ■

Dear heavenly Father, too often I focus on what I can get rather than on what I can give. May my love entwine itself more tightly around You, and then, Lord, expand my vision to care for those You care about.

Strength in Weakness

I take pleasure in my weaknesses, and in the insults, hardships, persecutions, and troubles that I suffer for Christ. For when I am weak, then I am strong.

2 CORINTHIANS 12:10

Some time ago I became aware of a new trend in television—Amish reality shows. *Amish out of Order, Breaking Amish,* and *Amish Mafia* are just three of these, but how true-to-life are these portrayals? Is what they show really how the Amish live, or do the shows simply feature individuals wanting to be in the limelight? While there is some truth to the shows, there is also more drama (much more) than most Amish experience. Some shows are rumored to have been staged. Others are in poor taste. And where does this leave the true Amish men and women?

For hundreds of years people have been "paying attention" to the Amish. They've been persecuted and martyred. They've had to leave home. They've been misunderstood. The challenges they've faced are great. The Amish gain attention because they are different. As an expanded community, they are worth our attention. We want to understand their lifestyle. We pay attention because we believe they have something to offer.

> **Beware of half-truths. You may have hold of the wrong half.**
>
> **PROVERB**

Even though the Amish aren't perfect, they give us an example of what life can look like when a community chooses to center their lives on service to God and one another. Second Corinthians 5:20 says, "We are Christ's ambassadors; God is making his appeal through us. We speak for Christ when we plead, 'Come back to God!'"

When insults, hardships, persecutions, and troubles come—making us feel weak— we can press into Christ and be filled with His strength. Or we can turn away from God and our community, where we find ourselves caught up in troubles and struggles.

The problem with many Amish reality shows is that they focus on the wrong thing. They focus on those who struggle in their weaknesses rather than on those who find strength in Christ during hard times. What about you? When hardship comes, will you be an example of someone who presses into God and finds strength in weakness, or of someone who struggles without God? Either way, the world is watching.

■ ■ ■

Dear heavenly Father, when I press into You, my weakness becomes strength. Today I give You room to work through my weakness. Be strong in me today.

United in Christ

There is no condemnation for those who belong to Christ Jesus.
And because you belong to him, the power of the life-giving Spirit
has freed you from the power of sin that leads to death.
ROMANS 8:1-2

What do you believe? What truths are foundational in your life? How do these truths compare with those around you?

An FAQ page from the Pennsylvania Dutch Country Welcome Center describes Amish beliefs this way: "Both Mennonites and Amish believe in one God eternally existing as Father, Son, and Holy Spirit (Romans 8:1-17). We believe that Jesus Christ, God's only Son, died on the cross for the sins of the world. We believe that the Holy Spirit convicts of sin, and also empowers believers for service and holy living. We believe that salvation is by grace through faith in Christ, a free gift bestowed by God on those who repent and believe."

Amish have expanded beyond North America. There are, or have been, settlements (or attempted settlements) in places such as Bolivia, Mexico, Honduras, Paraguay, Ireland, and England.

When I read this, I believe the same, yet my lifestyle looks far different from an Amish person's. Does one of us have it wrong? Not quite.

Those who believe in the foundational truths of Scripture live a variety of lifestyles. There is a difference between my Christian community and an Amish community, but there is also a difference between African Christians, South American Christians, and Eastern European Christians. These differences are external—dress, traditions, music, and style of church services—but it's what's on the inside that counts.

For those who put their faith in Jesus there is no condemnation. My "laws" might be different from someone else's, but *through Christ Jesus the law of the Spirit of life has set me free from the law of sin and death* (see Romans 8:2). Because of Jesus we are more similar than different. Because of Jesus we can spend eternity together, serving and glorifying Him and communing with one another—members of God's body, each with his or her own part.

■ ■ ■

Dear heavenly Father, I thank You that Your gift of salvation makes me free from sin and death and unifies me with an amazing, varied body of believers.

Be Still

*Be still, and know that I am God! I will be honored by every
nation. I will be honored throughout the world.*

PSALM 46:10

There is nothing more wonderful than taking a walk along a quiet trail on a spring
morning with the air still, one's mind still, and the world around still and at rest. New
buds cluster on previously dormant tree branches. Spots of floral colors can be seen
within the light-green grass. It's easy to feel God in such a place.

I've walked among Amish men, women, and children at a local auction and felt the
same stillness—even in the midst of all the activity. The air stirred slightly from their
voices, but there was no loud uproar. People moved, but not in anxious haste. God
was honored not only by their words but also by the contented
way they interacted.

I don't feel the same way when I'm in a large city, walking
down a high school corridor, or in the middle of a mall. The
blare of machinery or music fills the air. Voices do too. The
hairstyles, clothes, and merchandise scream, "Notice me, notice
me!" The people's actions silently declare the same. Each person
wants to be noticed, to feel valued, to stand out.

**The best things in
life are not things.**

PROVERB

As believers, we know we are special creations, unique and precious to God. So
why do we struggle with comparing our lives, our bodies, our kids, our talents (or lack
of talents) with others'? God didn't create the world to be exalted but to glorify Him.
The same goes for us.

Be still and know that He is God. Be still. Fight against the desire to create idols
of man-made things. Fight against your longing to be noticed and appreciated—to
stand out in a crowd.

Isaiah 37:16 says, "O LORD of Heaven's Armies, God of Israel, you are enthroned
between the mighty cherubim! You alone are God of all the kingdoms of the earth.
You alone created the heavens and the earth." May not only our words but also our
"stillness" in everyday situations make such a declaration.

■ ■ ■

*Dear heavenly Father, when I feel the urge rising to make myself known, I pray I might
make You known. When I feel the desire to gain attention, may I remember to be still and
give You the glory.*

Re-Creation

God, who said, "Let there be light in the darkness," has made this light shine in our hearts so we could know the glory of God that is seen in the face of Jesus Christ.

2 CORINTHIANS 4:6

Just the word *spring* causes a stirring within and brings a bounce to our steps. Spring is a chance for us to get a glimpse of God's creation at a pace slow enough for us to appreciate it. Light comes, and the layers of snow slowly melt away, revealing the form of the land. Day overtakes night, and the waters come in the form of spring rains. Vegetation brightens the landscape, and the air is finally warm enough for us to sit out and appreciate the stars at night. Living creatures emerge from hibernation and birth babies. God's command to "be fruitful and multiply" is seen at every turn.

No winter lasts forever. No spring skips its turn.

PROVERB

The breath—the inspiration of God—enters humanity, too. Something of joy stirs within us, and the changes and beauty of nature connect us with God in a fresh way. But with that our responsibility kicks in too. After a dormant winter, we must once again set out to tend and care for the earth.

My heart stirs as I think of this re-creation, but what I'm discovering is something the Amish and others who live closest to the earth already know. God doesn't re-create simply because He enjoys green sprouts, butterflies, and fresh breezes (although I imagine He does). No, creation is the best preacher and provides the most convincing sermon. When light overcomes darkness—changing everything—we get a glimpse of what Christ accomplishes in our barren hearts.

Do you want to feel renewed? Transformed? Do you desire re-creation within your soul? "God said, 'Let there be light,' and there was light," we read in Genesis 1:3. Turn your face and your heart to Jesus, the Light of Heaven, and new life will grow in you.

■ ■ ■

Dear heavenly Father, I praise You and thank You for the beauty I see in Your creation. I thank You for the re-creation you accomplished in my life when the light of Jesus entered. May His light bringing growth and life within me be a beautiful sermon.

Pull Up a Chair

*Lady Wisdom has built and furnished her home; it's supported by seven hewn
timbers. The banquet meal is ready to be served: lamb roasted, wine poured
out, table set with silver and flowers. Having dismissed her serving maids,
Lady Wisdom goes to town, stands in a prominent place, and invites everyone
within sound of her voice: "Are you confused about life, don't know what's going
on? Come with me, oh come, have dinner with me! I've prepared a wonderful
spread—fresh-baked bread, roast lamb, carefully selected wines. Leave your
impoverished confusion and live! Walk up the street to a life with meaning."*

PROVERBS 9:1-6 (THE MESSAGE)

My friend Suzanne Woods Fisher used to have a radio show called *Amish Wisdom* that
I loved to listen to. The goal of the show was to interview those who interact with
the Amish to discover simple living, everyday joys, and the
greater value of family, community, and church. The Amish
may not know how to Google, drive a car, or install an app
on a smartphone, but they have wisdom concerning the
things that really matter.

The world offers knowledge, but wisdom comes from
God. Wisdom means more than making a right choice; it
involves turning to God to discover the *best* choice. It's not
about trying to figure things out; it's about turning to God's
Word and being willing to partake of the banquet of truth
that God has already spread before us.

When I ponder the word *banquet*, I think about the Bible
stories I heard as a child. I learned about a banqueting table
God has prepared for us. Someday in eternity, we'll be able
to sit down and partake. But the more I seek wisdom—and
listen to those who have it—the more I realize I don't have to
wait until eternity. All I have to do is pull up a chair.

■ ■ ■

*Dear heavenly Father, thank You for providing a banqueting
table filled with truth. I desire wisdom more than knowledge,
for it's there I will find guidance and truth. Thank You for both.*

"The Amish do not
have retirement homes.
The elderly normally
live in an apartment
in a home of one of
their children or in a
Grossdawdy Haus, a
small adjacent house.
. . . Surrounded by
droves of grandchildren,
they pass on the
wisdom, joys, and
secrets of Amish life to
the rising generation."

Way of Life

I ask—ask the God of our Master, Jesus Christ, the God of glory—to make you intelligent and discerning in knowing him personally, your eyes focused and clear, so that you can see exactly what it is he is calling you to do, grasp the immensity of this glorious way of life he has for his followers, oh, the utter extravagance of his work in us who trust him—endless energy, boundless strength!

EPHESIANS 1:18-19 (*THE MESSAGE*)

We make many minor decisions every day—what to wear, what to eat, how to spend our time. Our choices guide us daily.

"Destiny is not a mystery. For better or worse, your destiny is the result of your daily decisions and defining decisions. . . . Those daily decisions add up. . . . We only make a few defining decisions in life, and then we spend the rest of our lives managing them," says Mark Batterson, author of *The Circle Maker*.

The eleven-hundred-page book Martyrs Mirror was first published in Dutch in 1660 and later in German and English. This volume records the religious persecution of the Anabaptist ancestors of today's Amish and influences their values and dedication even today.

So how do we know we are making the right daily decisions? When we know Jesus personally, our eyes gain focus and clarity. When we know Jesus, we can listen to His call. When we know Jesus, we can trust His direction and we can also trust Him to provide the strength to follow it.

Following the lead of their Swiss Anabaptist forebears, the Amish seek to live according to the teachings of Jesus in their daily lives. Their decision leads them to live lives different from most other people. They live "apart from the world." They emphasize the teachings of Jesus, loving their enemies and forgiving insults.

"If your first concern is to look after yourself, you'll never find yourself. But if you forget about yourself and look to me, you'll find both yourself and me," we read in Matthew 10:39 (*The Message*).

Each of us makes choices daily, but when we choose to follow Jesus, we can trust that those choices will transform our lives, and we'll discover lives more bountiful than we ever dreamed.

■ ■ ■

Dear heavenly Father, I thank You so much for not only saving my soul but also guiding my life. When I seek You, I also discover the life that You designed perfectly for me.

Grounded and God-Breathed

The LORD God formed the man from the dust of the ground. He breathed the
breath of life into the man's nostrils, and the man became a living person.

GENESIS 2:7

In 1994, I attended my first writers' conference. While there I met a godly woman named Ethel Herr. Ethel spoke with a soft voice, but there was bright passion in her eyes. "Your life makes your words worthwhile," she urged us. I knew what mattered most wasn't how I crafted my words on paper but how I lived—how I let God live within my dusty frame.

Ethel passed away some time ago, but her memory fuels me, and her words live on:

> *O Great I AM*
> *fix the gentle imprint*
> *of Your perfectly contoured feet*
> *into the moist gray sands*
> *of my earthy being*
> *that all who pass my way*
> *may marvel*
> *at the excellence of Your work of art.*

Demut is the Amish term for humility and submission to God. The Amish understand that when we are prideful, we feel we don't need God and don't ask for help.

In spiritual terms, the word *inspiration* means "breath of God." When we allow God to breathe into our lives by His Spirit, everything will change—our words, our works, our wonder. One of the principles of Amish belief is humility, and realizing who God is and who we are is the only thing that can bring us to a humble state.

According to Dictionary.com the word *humble* comes from the Latin word *humilis*, which means lowly, insignificant, on the ground. Man was dirt—insignificant—until God's breath entered him. And only when God breathes into us and walks with us can we be both grounded and works of art.

"The Spirit of God has made me, and the breath of the Almighty gives me life," we read in Job 33:4. So many times we take note of what the Amish reject. Instead, maybe we should consider what they embrace: humility and the breath of God.

■ ■ ■

Dear heavenly Father, breathe into me today. I am but dust, yet You chose to form me still.
Because of Your breath I have life. Show me today how to live.

Recipe for Fastnachts

    2 cups milk
    ¾ cup sugar
    1½ teaspoon salt
    2 eggs
    1 yeast cake/package of dry yeast
    7 cups flour
    1/3 cup lard
    powdered sugar

Bring milk and lard (shortening can also be used) to the boiling point, but do not boil. Stir in sugar and salt, and let cool to lukewarm. Beat eggs and add to the milk. Soak yeast cake in 1½ tablespoons of warm water and keep warm. Sift and measure the flour. Combine yeast and liquid. Add enough flour to be able to handle easily. Knead well by stretching and folding it over itself. Let rise overnight.

The following day, roll out to ¼-inch thickness. Cut into two-inch squares and make a slit in the center of each. Cover and let rise ¾ of an hour. Deep-fry until golden brown. While warm, roll in powdered sugar.

Words Alone

*The LORD merely spoke, and the heavens were created. He breathed
the word, and all the stars were born. He assigned the sea its
boundaries and locked the oceans in vast reservoirs. Let the whole
world fear the LORD, and let everyone stand in awe of him.*

PSALM 33:6-8

When I pull out my favorite Amish cookbook, I immediately read the ingredients. *Do
I have everything I need?* It doesn't matter if I have the desire or the skill to make the
recipe; if I don't have the right ingredients, I'm not going to get anywhere.

When an Amish wife cooks a meal, she turns to the pantry for supplies. When
Amish men prepare for a barn raising, they order supplies from the hardware store.

**The Amish know
their livelihood
comes from God's
creation. They feel a
part of the unfolding
seasons and see
God's hand in all
parts of their lives.**

We understand how things come from other things, yet it's
hard to wrap our minds around the fact that with God everything came from nothing at all. Words created the world. God's
breath hung the stars: "By faith we understand that the entire
universe was formed at God's command, that what we now see
did not come from anything that can be seen" (Hebrews 11:3).

In our world, many put their trust in science and the knowledge of humanity. They attempt to explain the world without
figuring God into the equation. They ignore the beauty of creation's design. But everything is different when we see the world
as the handiwork of a Creator.

"Peace is seeing a sunset and knowing whom to thank," the
Amish say. What do you see when you look at the world around
you? Whom do you thank?

Today when you step outside your door, look around and let your heart be filled
with awe. Take time to thank your Creator. His Word, the Bible, is something you can
stand on. And the world, created by His words, is something to marvel at.

Let us join together and stand in awe of Him.

■ ■ ■

*Dear heavenly Father, Your words change everything. I'm in awe of the world. Thank You
for all of creation. Thank You for the living Word, Jesus Christ.*

Steps of Faith

Ruth replied, "Don't ask me to leave you and turn back. Wherever you go, I will go; wherever you live, I will live. Your people will be my people, and your God will be my God. Wherever you die, I will die, and there I will be buried. May the LORD punish me severely if I allow anything but death to separate us!"

RUTH 1:16-17

You may be familiar with William Penn, a Quaker who appealed to the king of England to establish a Quaker settlement in the New World. The king offered Penn "an extraordinarily generous charter," and he became the New World's largest private landowner, controlling more than forty-five thousand square miles, and created the province of Pennsylvania in 1681. Within months Penn had parceled out land to mostly rich London Quakers, but soon Lutherans, Catholics, Jews, Huguenots, and Mennonites joined them. The first sizable group of Amish arrived in America around 1730 and settled near Lancaster County, Pennsylvania.

William Penn's "holy experiment" in religious tolerance changed the settlement of our nation. Because of their religious beliefs, men and women left their homeland and crossed oceans. In the Bible, Ruth, who was from Moab, declared that she would follow her mother-in-law, probably because of both their friendship and her faith in God.

What values do you hold deep in your heart? Are any of those values strong enough that you would cross seas and travel into foreign countries for them?

Three years ago God asked my husband and me to leave a good job and our beautiful home in order to move two thousand miles away for a ministry job. We traveled in a U-Haul rather than a ship or buggy, but the journey was still hard—not only for the distance but because of the life we left behind. Yet God was with us.

"[William] Penn first called the area [around Lancaster] 'New Wales,' then 'Sylvania,' (Latin for 'forests or woods'), which [King] Charles changed to 'Pennsylvania' in honor of [William's father]."

Because of the faith of their ancestors, the Amish found a place to flourish. The faith they live today is made possible by the steps of faith their ancestors took long ago.

■ ■ ■

Dear heavenly Father, show me any area in my life where I need to take a step of faith to follow You. I'm thankful, Lord, that You go with me.

Remember

It was there at Gilgal that Joshua piled up the twelve stones taken from the Jordan River. Then Joshua said to the Israelites, "In the future your children will ask, 'What do these stones mean?' Then you can tell them, 'This is where the Israelites crossed the Jordan on dry ground.'"
JOSHUA 4:20-22

For as long as I can remember, I have collected memories. I have my second grade report card, my junior high basketball schedule, my megaphone necklace from my cheerleading years, and the monogrammed napkin from my wedding. I collect trinkets in shoeboxes, dresser drawers, and memory jars. In the 1970s and '80s of my childhood, having photographs required money for film and developing. Photos were only for special occasions, but trinkets could be slipped into one's pocket and saved.

A happy memory never wears out.

PROVERB

I used to think that one of the most unfortunate parts of the Amish lifestyle was the lack of photos. Don't they wish they could remember what their children looked like as babies? Wouldn't a wedding photo be something nice to tuck away? Of course, even though we can appreciate photos, who hasn't looked at one and first noticed the ten extra pounds, the bad haircut, or the dated outfit? Photos move our focus to what we see, whereas mementos turn our attention to the moment, the experiences, and how we felt.

Has the focus of our memories of God's work in our lives changed in the same way? We ask God to give us faith for the future. We want to grow in our knowledge of Him, but maybe we're missing the point. "Sometimes you don't need to learn to trust God," says Pastor Steven Furtick. "You just need to remember."

Have you, like Joshua, set up stones of remembrance in your walk with God? Think back to transforming moments. Then find a journal to write down your remembrances of God's goodness in your life. If you have mementos, collect them in a jar. Photographs are great, but the memories are what count. As you remember God's work, you'll be amazed by how much is already captured in your heart!

■ ■ ■

Dear heavenly Father, thank You for all You've done in my life. Forgive me for forgetting all the ways You've blessed me. Remembering reminds me to trust You more.

My Song and My Strength

*Rejoice in the Lord always [delight, gladden
yourselves in Him]; again I say, Rejoice!*

PHILIPPIANS 4:4 (AMP)

One of my favorite things about spring is the songs of the birds. Joy fills my heart when I hear the music of a birdsong. The winter is past. A new season has come! Gratefulness to God is heard on every chirp and warble, and hearing that makes my heart rejoice too.

There is nothing more beautiful than a smile reflected from a thankful heart. Many an Amish mother will set about her tasks singing hymns of praise, and when one of her children whines or complains, she will simply sing louder!

Rejoicing in the Lord isn't something you need to wait to do at a church service. You can rejoice any moment of your day, in the middle of any task. Rejoicing doesn't need to happen when you "feel like it." I have many, many days when I'd rather complain. But when I sing praises to God, my heart and my attitude begin to change. The circumstances and situations that had been troubling me a moment before are still there, but something is different. When I rejoice, my heart acknowledges the goodness of God—and all the good in my life—and my

> **Some may see a hopeless end, but as believers we rejoice in an endless hope.**
>
> **PROVERB**

attitude changes: "God has come to save me. I will trust in him and not be afraid. The LORD GOD is my strength and my song; he has given me victory" (Isaiah 12:2).

Sometimes God shows you His strength or His power, as in the coming of spring, and through that you find a song. But sometimes, when you make Him your song, you discover strength that you didn't have before.

The most beautiful songs are those that rise above the whining around us—or the whining in our own hearts. What song of rejoicing can you sing today?

■ ■ ■

Dear heavenly Father, I rejoice in You. I will sing a song of praise, no matter what the circumstances. I thank You for the strength that returns to my gladdened heart.

God's Good Plan

GOD-of-the-Angel-Armies speaks: "Exactly as I planned, it will happen. Following my blueprints, it will take shape."
ISAIAH 14:24 (*THE MESSAGE*)

When I was young, I used to wish I was born in the days when the American prairie was being settled. It seemed to be such a simple and exciting time. I believed that families spent more time together. Maybe the seeds of that longing are the reason why I'm so interested in the Amish today. Yet if God had wanted me to be born Amish, He could have made that happen. God makes the blueprints for our lives, and then He constructs them into our reality.

No matter where you live or what challenges you face, this is the life the Lord has constructed for you, for me. Not the bodies, health, or circumstances we wish we'd had, or the perfect lives we can never attain, but the blueprints by which He is constructing us.

Amish see themselves as travelers heading to eternity. If earth were their home, it would make sense to accumulate things. If life were about enjoyment, they would enjoy earthly comforts.

Why did He choose me to be born to a single mom? Why did He choose my grandmother to be born to an immigrant family and live in a boxcar during her growing-up years? Why are others born into lives of privilege? According to Acts 17:27, "His purpose was for the nations to seek after God and perhaps feel their way toward him and find him—though he is not far from any one of us."

The challenges the Amish face lead them to the place where they realize they cannot live this life without God. It is the same for the rest of us. The challenges we face bring us to the place of surrender, of acknowledging our need. Because of who God created us to be—and the families and places He set us in—we will need to seek Him. God is not far from any of us. He wants to make sure we look for Him until we find Him.

■ ■ ■

Dear heavenly Father, my longing for You and needing You are not signs that I'm weak. Instead they are indications that Your plan for me has worked after all.

Mutual Aid

Love your neighbor as yourself.

MARK 12:31

Where do you turn when you need help? When there is a natural disaster, do you turn to your insurance company? When you go into the hospital, do you worry about how you'll handle the bill?

The Amish believe in mutual aid. Their faith is centered on God, and they also depend on the church community. Church members are expected to help one another in times of difficulty or disaster. Within a family, members take care of one another, and they do not depend on Social Security.

Yet when given the command to "love your neighbor as yourself," the Amish often give beyond their church community, too, as this news story reports:

> It took just a few moments one chilly January afternoon for Wes and Tammy Barr's Valley View home to burn to the ground. It's taken nearly a year for Wes, a roofing contractor, to rebuild with the help of a couple of friends. But last week, the Barrs got some much-needed help from some friends they didn't even know they had.
>
> Wes got a phone call from Tim Schrock of Seal Proof Roofing in St. Ignatius with an unexpected offer no one could refuse: a group of carpenters from the Mission Valley's Amish community wanted to donate their time to get the Barrs' new roof built. And on Friday morning, 10 men showed up ready to spend a frigid day helping a neighbor.

Amish people help those within their community. They also sometimes travel outside their community to assist non-Amish families who are victims of tornadoes, hurricanes, or other natural disasters.

Neighbors loving neighbors. Isn't that what the Jesus-life is all about? It is *expected* when we do good to those we are close to. It's *unexpected* when we reach out to others—those who do not have anything to offer in return. The world takes notice when we care for others. People pay attention, and they get a glimpse of the God we believe in. Jesus knew this.

How can you show the love of Jesus to some "unexpecting" person today?

■ ■ ■

Dear heavenly Father, show me someone I can love with a great, unexpected love. Help my actions point others to You.

God's Concerns, My Concerns

Watch out for people who cause divisions and upset people's faith by teaching things contrary to what you have been taught. Stay away from them.
ROMANS 16:17

Some wonder about the difference between the Amish and the Old Order Mennonites. Both live and dress plain. Both have the same Anabaptist origins. The "split" happened in 1693, when Jakob Ammann, the founder of the Amish, thought that shunning should be taken more seriously. He believed only hook-and-eye fasteners would do on clothing. When Swiss Anabaptists refused to shun excommunicated members (those who'd gone against the rules of the church), Jakob Ammann and his followers broke away from and formed their own "Amish" community. Amman was also a tailor who thought the others "too worldly" with their new buttons and button holes.

A member might be shunned for not observing religious and lifestyle practices, marrying a non-Amish person, or socializing with a shunned individual.

Today, Old Order Amish women still do not use buttons, but some segments of the Amish church use snaps on clothes and buttons on coats or outerwear. The Amish also still practice social shunning when members of their community break their rules for daily living (the Ordnung) and have experienced church excommunication. (This is also known as being in the *Bann*.) The Amish believe that members who openly sin must be removed from the church, lest others fall into the same sin. When members are shunned, they are also avoided in social and business circles. Shunning (and excommunication) happens only when church members refuse to repent. They are always welcomed back if they choose to change their ways.

The Amish base the practice of shunning on the discipline prescribed in the New Testament church in 2 Thessalonians 3:14: "Take note of those who refuse to obey what we say in this letter. Stay away from them so they will be ashamed."

While most of us do not practice shunning in our daily lives, we should be wary of spending too much time with people who go against our beliefs because we may become comfortable with their sinful behaviors and eventually start behaving in the same way.

■ ■ ■

Dear Lord, give me courage to confront those who know better but are still living against Your standards. And help me to be wise enough not to be concerned about small differences that are of no concern.

Open Your Hand and Give

Don't worry about these things, saying, "What will we eat? What will we drink? What will we wear?" These things dominate the thoughts of unbelievers, but your heavenly Father already knows all your needs.

MATTHEW 6:31-32

Recession has hit our country in recent years. Friends have lost their homes. Others have whittled down their savings. Many are out of jobs. But the Amish are a segment of society that has hardly been touched with financial trouble. When the world around us uses advertising and promotion to urge consumers to buy more, the Amish raise their children to get by with just enough. "Waste not, want not" is a common saying. Amish are consumers, too, but they consume in a different way. They don't purchase products to make them look good or to bring comfort, ease, or beauty to their lives. They purchase food, clothing, tools, or other supplies because they have a specific need.

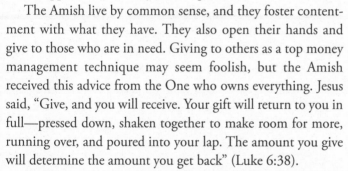

The Amish live by common sense, and they foster contentment with what they have. They also open their hands and give to those who are in need. Giving to others as a top money management technique may seem foolish, but the Amish received this advice from the One who owns everything. Jesus said, "Give, and you will receive. Your gift will return to you in full—pressed down, shaken together to make room for more, running over, and poured into your lap. The amount you give will determine the amount you get back" (Luke 6:38).

The Jura Mountains of Switzerland have a cave called the Goat Cave, which was used by early Anabaptists as a place of worship and refuge.

If you want to live in peace, throw away your long shopping list and learn to live with less. Do you want to be unruffled and content? Cease focusing on what you don't have, and instead consider what you can give to someone who has less.

Those who don't believe that God is there—and that He cares for them—have reason to worry and fret. But our heavenly Father not only knows our needs but also brings others into our lives to help meet them. He also brings people in need into our lives because He knows *we* will be blessed when we open our hands to give.

■ ■ ■

Dear heavenly Father, thank You for all You've provided—in unexpected ways and through the care of others. Show me someone who needs something I have to offer. I open my hands today.

Tapped In

The fact that you are now fed by that rich and holy root gives you no cause to crow over the pruned branches. Remember, you aren't feeding the root; the root is feeding you.
ROMANS 11:18 (*THE MESSAGE*)

Even when the air is still cold and the days are dim, good things come from nature. In early spring, sap begins flowing from maple trees. With the chilly nights, water from the soil is absorbed into the maple trees. During the day, the rising temperature creates pressure that pushes the water back down to the bottom of the trees, making it easy to collect the precious maple sap. The sap is gathered over twelve to twenty days, usually between early March and late April, depending on the region.

During maple syrup season Amish women will take their children to the sugar shack, where water is evaporated from the syrup. They make pancakes and ladle fresh, warm syrup over them, demonstrating that hard work has sweet rewards.

In the Northeast, many Amish farms have maple trees, and they are tapped for sap. It takes twenty-five to sixty gallons of raw sap to make one gallon of pure maple syrup. As you can imagine, this requires many labor-intensive hours.

When we look at a tree, we are drawn to its trunk, branches, and leaves, but without the sap feeding it all, there is no life. During maple syrup season, each tree can be tapped one to three times, but each tapping draws only 7 percent of the sap from the tree. There is still plenty of sap left to feed the tree.

As Christians, we have a holy root feeding us. When we are connected to God, our souls are nourished, and we grow. When Jesus is our root, we can be sustained even when others "sap" our strength. We have no worry of withering and dying because Jesus is a never-ending supply of strength, peace, and relationship.

What things are drawing your strength from you? They might even be good things, like ministry, family, or friends. If you sink into Jesus, you will have enough life and nourishment to share with others.

■ ■ ■

Dear heavenly Father, I thank You for being my holy root and for feeding my soul. I'm feeling empty today, Lord. Fill me up to overflowing so I can feed others.

All Things New

Since our friendship with God was restored by the death of his Son while we
were still his enemies, we will certainly be saved through the life of his Son.

ROMANS 5:10

"The Amish are keen menders, going to great lengths to fix what is broken, patch what is torn, and repair what is repairable," writes Lorilee Craker, author of *Money Secrets of the Amish*. "I like the dictionary definition of mend: 'to restore something to satisfactory condition,' or 'to improve something or make it more acceptable.'"

Mending is great for socks, fences, and farm equipment, but when it comes to our souls, there is no mending. Our efforts cannot cut out sin or repair the damage it has caused. Our good works do not stitch together the broken pieces. Since we are born sinners, we can't ever do enough to repair our relationship with God. Jesus didn't come to patch together our good parts with His great parts so we'd be sufficient. No, He takes all sin so there is not a stitch left within us to bring condemnation.

An Amish bishop once said, "We don't prepare our children for the future; we prepare our children for eternity."

I like how 2 Corinthians 5:17-18 puts it: "We look inside, and what we see is that anyone united with the Messiah gets a fresh start, is created new. The old life is gone; a new life burgeons! Look at it! All this comes from the God who settled the relationship between us and him, and then called us to settle our relationships with each other. God put the world square with himself through the Messiah, giving the world a fresh start by offering forgiveness of sins" (*The Message*).

How have you looked at your life: as something you need to fix, to mend, to make do with? No matter how you try, you'll never, ever be able to restore yourself to a satisfactory condition. Sinful human beings can never make themselves good enough for eternity.

How have you looked at Jesus: as Someone who helps you have a better life or as Someone who *is* your life? If you are still battling that question, settle it now. Hand over the frayed mess that you've been trying to put back together, and accept the fresh start, the new life, that only He can create within you.

■ ■ ■

Dear heavenly Father, I'm so grateful that instead of mending, You make new. I offer the
tattered mess I have made and rejoice at the new life You have to give!

Come Close

Come close to God, and God will come close to you. Wash your hands, you sinners;
purify your hearts, for your loyalty is divided between God and the world.
JAMES 4:8

People are drawn to the Amish because they believe the Amish are close to God, and many non-Amish long for that. It's true that many Amish *are* close to God, but some are not. Being Amish doesn't automatically sign a person up for a front-row seat.

There are elements in the Amish lifestyle that make it easier to find God. Their quiet lives allow them room to listen. Their lack of material things makes God's gifts more evident to them. Their dependence on one another reminds them what the body of Christ is supposed to look like.

If God is not first in our thoughts in the morning, He will be last in our thoughts all day.

PROVERB

The Amish believe that worldliness can keep them from being close to God, and that's a possibility, yet there are also those who have everything the world has to offer and still seek God. King David is a great example. Acts 13:22 says, "God removed Saul and replaced him with David, a man about whom God said, 'I have found David son of Jesse, a man after my own heart. He will do everything I want him to do.'" David had everything, and although he stumbled at times, sometimes seriously, he returned to God always—he drew close.

No matter who you are, what you have, or the messes you've made, at this moment you, too, can draw close to God. You don't need to become Amish. You don't need quiet and simplicity (although those can help). Drawing close to God means taking time to approach Him, to acknowledge your sins, and to focus your mind on the Creator rather than on His creation. Your loyalty will be divided only as long as you let it be.

Do you want to be a man or a woman after God's own heart? Then seek it out. Chase after God as if finding Him is worth more than anything, anyone else, because the truth is . . . it is.

■ ■ ■

Dear heavenly Father, I desire You more than anything else. The world doesn't hold a
candle to You. The riches of this world are like dime-store trinkets compared to what You
have to offer.

The Waiting Game

Blessed are those who wait.

ISAIAH 30:18

The Amish look favorably on someone who is living a modest and simple life. We may gaze with approval on someone with a new home, but the Amish would appreciate someone with a more modest existence. They approve of items that are well used. They don't rush to spend money. They are accustomed to waiting.

We often think of waiting as a bad thing. We dislike waiting rooms and get frustrated when we have to wait in line. But the ability to wait is a virtue. In fact, we'd do well to add more waiting to our lives: wait to get a pair of new shoes. Wait before you trade in your old car for a new one. Wait to take the vacation you've been wanting, and explore your own town first. Wait to buy more food until you've used up the food you have stored in your pantry and freezer. Wait before you purchase a new house.

Waiting isn't easy, and it's not passive. Waiting takes preparation.

How do you wait? Wait in prayer. Wait with expectation. Wait in faith that the Lord sees your need and can bring anyone to help provide. Isaiah 30:18 says, "The LORD must wait for you to come to him so he can show you his love and compassion. For the LORD is a faithful God. Blessed are those who wait for his help." Waiting is a two-way street. The Lord is waiting for us to come to Him, and He asks that we wait for His help.

The normal speed of an Amish buggy is five to eight miles per hour.

Waiting is also a matter of attention. Are you willing to turn your attention away from the "thing" or "action" you desire and instead turn your desire to God? If you do, you will be blessed, not because of what God will provide but because you will be discovering Him in your increasingly modest and simple life.

■ ■ ■

Dear heavenly Father, help me to wait on You. Help me to wait for You. Help me to look to You instead of to things.

To Become Yielded

We work wearily with our own hands to earn our living. We bless those who curse us. We are patient with those who abuse us.

1 CORINTHIANS 4:12

We drive slowly past a yield sign, watching to see if we have the right-of-way, but to the Amish the word *yield* means something completely different. They choose to give up what they want—to yield their desires—for the sake of others. They see life on the farm as being interdependent on others (which it is). They believe God has called them to a life of hard work. They also believe their work on the family farm is a redemptive tradition: each season there is life, harvest, and then death—which leads to life again. They know seasons of our lives are the same. We can't have a 100 percent harvest, a 100 percent life.

Swiss Anabaptist Peter Fankhauser built his barn with a trapdoor that led to a secret space where Anabaptists could hide from the authorities who were persecuting them.

The Amish are raised to die to their own wills. They believe the truest form of love is found in being powerless—in giving over power to God. Isn't this the example of Christ? He was patient with those who cursed Him and abused Him. He had all power, yet He yielded still, for God's—and our—greater good.

The lives of the Amish are symbols of the same. Although many of us do not have Amish friends, the lives of the Amish speak, making their words unneeded.

While I'm sure no Amish person claims to be perfectly yielded and accepting of hard work, curses, or abuse, the difference lies in their attitude. They know that life in this world brings pain and heartache, and they aren't surprised when it does. And they choose to yield to whatever God hands them.

In contrast, many of us are stunned and shaken when challenging times come. We are caught off guard. We want to know why. We question God.

Jesus gives us the answer in John 15:20: "Do you remember what I told you? 'A slave is not greater than the master.' Since they persecuted me, naturally they will persecute you. And if they had listened to me, they would listen to you." Would we look at life differently if we believed that, as the Amish do? How would life look if we became yielded to all God brought, in every season, trusting Him always as the Right-of-Way?

■ ■ ■

Dear heavenly Father, I offer myself, my life, to You. I yield my will to Yours. I know that whatever comes into my life comes from Your hand. And, Lord, in my powerlessness, I trust I will experience Your power as I never have before.

Spring Cleaning

I scrub my hands with purest soap, then join hands with the others in the great circle, dancing around your altar, GOD, Singing God-songs at the top of my lungs, telling God-stories. GOD, I love living with you; your house glows with your glory. When it's time for spring cleaning, don't sweep me out with the quacks and crooks.

PSALM 26:7-10 (*THE MESSAGE*)

I remember as a child watching my grandmother open all the windows and doors and clean every inch of her house in the spring. Her house had been sealed up tight for the winter, and now a breath of freshness filled the rooms. For the Amish, spring cleaning is a way to have fun while tackling a big job.

"In the Amish society cooperative work provides opportunity for socialization," blogger Loretta Coblentz writes.

> When we moved back to Ohio, my Amish sister-in-laws invited me to "Ladies Day." In other circles, this might be tea and crumpets. When I asked about Ladies Day, I learned it was a day that all of the sister-in-laws go to one of the sisters' house[s] and wash her windows, walls, floors, and whatever deep cleaning might be found to do. Each lady takes a dish of food. A lot of fun and fellowship is had while getting a big job done. Recreation and socialization combine in such a way that it doesn't seem like work.

Boiled rice water makes an excellent starch for dainty collars, cuffs, and baby dresses.

AMISH LAUNDRY TIP

When we join with others to clean or build or cook, or even to come before God, we gain new energy. Worship explodes when we hear those around us worshiping. Chores seem less like work and more like play with others beside us. But allowing others into these activities brings us to a place of transparency. We humble ourselves before others as we join them in praise. We have to admit the windows, walls, and floors need a good scrubbing. When we join with others, we can no longer hide. We also consider what things in us God wants us to clean up.

Is there something in your heart that needs a good scrubbing? Submit yourself to God, and trust Him to get the big job done. Invite others to do the same.

■ ■ ■

Dear heavenly Father, clean me out. I desire to worship in Your presence, and I don't want any hindrance. Open up my heart and my life to others and to You.

What Belongs to Caesar

[Jesus said,] "Here, show me the coin used for the tax." When they handed him a Roman coin, he asked, "Whose picture and title are stamped on it?" "Caesar's," they replied. "Well, then," he said, "give to Caesar what belongs to Caesar, and give to God what belongs to God."

MATTHEW 22:19-21

Tulips open their blooms in the April air, and the world around us bursts with new life. But for those of us in the United States, the arrival of April also brings feelings of dread . . . *Tax Day.*

Many people think the Amish don't pay taxes, but they pay taxes like anyone else. Because they do not use computers, they do taxes the old-fashioned way, with paper and pencil. My friend Moriah, who lives near an Amish community, does taxes for many Amish families. They always check her work, and sometimes they even find mistakes!

Since all of us have to pay taxes, the question isn't *if* we pay but *how* we pay them. What kind of heart attitude do we have? Do we trust that God is in charge of everything, including our taxes, and that He will provide?

Romans 13:1 reads, "Everyone must submit to governing authorities. For all authority comes from God, and those in positions of authority have been placed there by God." Do we trust these words? Can we be thankful for those in authority over us? Can we accept what we have to give up in the same way we receive the gifts given to us—gifts like sunshine and rain, the tulips and new grass, the joy of family and friends, and our incomes?

There are many things in life that we can't change, but we can change our attitudes. We can rejoice that God has everything under control and that no matter what, we can always rejoice in Him!

■ ■ ■

Dear heavenly Father, I'm thankful that all authority is under Your control. Help me to hold loosely the things on this earth and to turn my attention to what can never be taken away from me, here or in heaven.

The Good Shepherd

He will feed his flock like a shepherd. He will carry the lambs in his arms, holding them close to his heart. He will gently lead the mother sheep with their young.

ISAIAH 40:11

One of the most wonderful parts of spring is all the baby animals. There is nothing more precious than new colts taking wobbly steps or new lambs hurrying after their mothers. Lambs are usually born in late winter, and by the spring they are running behind their mothers in the pastures. Many Amish farmers raise sheep and goats, which are another way to provide for their families. Like all shepherds, they tenderly care for their lambs. As a mom, I appreciate this picture of a shepherd holding a little lamb close, but my favorite part in Isaiah 40:11 is this: "He will gently lead the mother sheep with their young."

I can't count the number of times I've turned to this verse for inspiration when raising my own children. "Lord, thank You for leading me with my little ones, just as You lead the mother sheep with her lambs."

The picture here is one of knowing and security. It's one of provision. To have security, we must trust that Jesus has our best interests in mind. To be provided for, we must stay close to Jesus. To be led, we must recognize His gentle voice: "I am the good shepherd; I know my own sheep, and they know me" (John 10:14).

In the winter the Amish often hang their clothes in the house to dry, but in the spring the clothes hang outside to dry, and they gain a fresh, clean smell.

Maybe you do not have children at home, but no matter who you are, you still have influence over others. Whom do you need guidance to lead?

More than that, do you ever have a time when you need to be especially close to God—to feel close to His heart? Trust Jesus. Draw near to Him. Listen to His voice. He is there to carry you in His arms!

■ ■ ■

Dear heavenly Father, I thank You for always being here to lead me. Help me to be a godly influence over those You bring into my life.

APRIL 17

Go Forth to Sow

He told many stories in the form of parables, such as this one:
"Listen! A farmer went out to plant some seeds."
MATTHEW 13:3

A connection with nature is a natural part of the Amish church service:

> Since the Amish have bi-weekly worship services, their liturgical calendar . . . is divided into twenty-six parts that reflect both religious holidays and agricultural seasons. . . . While many of their scripture readings and studies are connected with holy days, quite a few are associated with the agricultural seasons. Sometime in April, when the farmers are sowing clovers and oats, Matthew 13 and John 15 (Aemann Schriften) are read: "[A] sower went forth to sow."

The Amish *Ausband* dates back to the 1500s, and its hymns are related to the times and seasons of year as well:

The Amish still tend to pay attention to the signs of nature as a planting guide rather than relying solely on the date on the calendar.

> While most of these songs tell stories of Anabaptist ancestors imprisoned for their faith in Europe in the fifteenth and sixteenth centuries (particularly in a prison in Passau, Germany), there are some that express an appreciation and knowledge of nature. For example, the Sunday the Aemann Schriften are read, hymn 47 is sung. In this beautiful song several stanzas are about the European skylark, which sings his wonderful courtship song as the farmers sow their seeds in early spring. . . .

The lark wings through the clouds,
With sweet voice and melody.

Jesus also used many natural elements in His parables. And He wasn't teaching in an air-conditioned sanctuary with stained-glass windows. Jesus proclaimed truth to the crowds gathered on the hills or along the seashore.

Consider taking God's Word out into the elements. How does reading your Bible in a grassy field or on a park bench change the way you take in the words? How does the beauty of spring connect God's Word to your heart?

■ ■ ■

Dear heavenly Father, thank You for the gift of nature that speaks Your truth in unexpected ways. Open my eyes to see Your messages of the season.

Good Friday Prayer

You do not belong to yourself, for God bought you with a
high price. So you must honor God with your body.

1 CORINTHIANS 6:19-20

Amish men are off work on *Kaofreidawk* (Good Friday). It's a quiet day to remember Jesus' hours on the cross. No work is done that day, and the time is given to fasting and prayer. A common Good Friday prayer includes this passage: "Oh Jesus, Thou eternal good, who hast on this good, quiet Friday held still before Thy Father, and for my sake hast obediently born His wrath even unto death, grant that I also today may observe this fitting, good, quiet Friday with suitable thoughts and quiet devotion. Yea, that I might keep, observe, Thy great day of sacrifice and through true faith make myself partaker of Thy sacrifice and great payment, atonement."

Good Friday is a time to remember—to remember Christ's sacrifice and to remember that we are bought with a price. We don't belong to ourselves. Second Corinthians 6:16 says, "We are the temple of the living God. As God said: 'I will live in them and walk among them. I will be their God, and they will be my people.'"

When was that last time you remembered all that Jesus has done for you? When you remembered that you belong to God? When was the last time you took time to be quiet? To be still? You might not have the day off work on Good Friday, but could you carve out time to sit quietly before God, to consider what Christ has done?

> "Gruna Dunaschdawk, to those well-versed in Pennsylvania German folklore, means Green Thursday, the day before Good Friday. It was an occasion to eat something green to insure good health for the coming year."

In our busy lives it's hard to sit still. It's hard to take time to remember. But if we don't take time to remember, we won't appreciate all that's been given. Then we'll walk through life as if Jesus should appreciate all we're doing for Him instead of the other way around.

■ ■ ■

Dear heavenly Father, I thank You for the Lord Jesus, whose perfect obedience saved my soul. Take my mind and heart to the foot of the cross. Help me never to take such a costly gift for granted.

Spring's Abundance

Yes, there will be an abundance of flowers and singing and joy!
. . . The Lord will display his glory, the splendor of our God.

ISAIAH 35:2

When fresh spring air blows through my open windows, my thoughts turn to planting flowers in the front flower beds and hanging pots near the door. Spring abundance brings beauty and joy. And for the Amish, spring also means looking forward to an array of fresh, healthy food for their tables. Food they don't have to cultivate. One Amish woman writes:

"Just like rhubarb, asparagus will come up year after year in the same patch, so its arrival is always a signal that winter is through."

Nature provides the first taste of spring with perennial plants that grow "wild" around here: rhubarb, dandelions, asparagus, and onions, to name a few favorites. Rhubarb begins spreading its big leaves, ready to be used in shortcakes, pies, jams, and other family favorites. Wild asparagus begins peeping through in patches, and green onions, with their flavorful taste, are a sure sign of spring. Bright red strawberries, which thrive in the coolness of spring, also begin blooming. But perhaps the most exciting signal is when our favorite foods finally find their way onto our supper plates. Perhaps the most eagerly awaited is the arrival of young, tender dandelions.

Because I live in the suburbs, I see dandelions as weeds that I need to poison. I'm more concerned about cutting grass than harvesting fresh rhubarb and asparagus. I enjoy the beauty of spring, but I'm missing out on the abundance. This makes me consider how much of the Lord I'm missing out on. Do I barely glance at His beauty in my subdivision life? With a lawn instead of a garden, do I miss really seeing all He provides? It takes more effort to look for God's bounty, but it can be done. Isaiah 61:10 says, "I am overwhelmed with joy in the LORD my God! For he has dressed me with the clothing of salvation and draped me in a robe of righteousness. I am like a bridegroom in his wedding suit or a bride with her jewels."

Most of the time I enjoy the Lord's beauty without rejoicing over my clothing of salvation and robe of righteousness. May spring's abundance remind me to praise God for *all* He has provided!

■ ■ ■

Dear heavenly Father, thank You for the abundance of what You've provided! You are a good God who gives both beauty and bountiful blessings!

The Greatest Gift(s) on Easter

Jesus told her, "I am the resurrection and the life. Anyone
who believes in me will live, even after dying."

JOHN 11:25

Amish children gather around the living room to listen to the familiar Easter story. Their father shares how Jesus died on the cross. He explains how the saddest day turned into the happiest when the women and the disciples discovered Jesus had risen indeed! The story of Jesus' resurrection is the most important part of Easter in the Amish home.

If you step into most American homes on Easter mornings, you'll find gifts, candy, baskets, and bunnies. The Amish do not bow to this commercialization. Their celebrations are simple. If Easter falls on a "church" Sunday, the Amish attend church, but they do not have a special celebration marking Easter. The sermon that day does include Scripture that speaks of Jesus' resurrection. If Easter Sunday is an off-Sunday, they celebrate together as a family at home.

Easter dinner is no different from any other Sunday meal, except that boiled eggs and horseradish are added to the menu. Later in the day some Amish families may color eggs. Food coloring and vinegar are used. It's an exciting time with a dozen small hands dipping and turning the eggs and a multitude of voices speaking at once. Dozens and dozens of eggs are decorated, and some are peeled almost as soon as they are colored.

"Psalms 133 is sung in [Amish] communion services which are held twice [a year]: in the spring at Easter and in the fall at the end of harvest."

Where do you put your focus on Easter? Do you spend more time considering a new Easter outfit than you do the gift of eternity in heaven? Because of Jesus, death has no hold on us. If we believe in Him, we get two great gifts—His presence with us here on earth and eternity with Him in heaven. Consider how you can transform your thoughts from the celebration of a day to rejoicing in these gifts from the Savior.

■ ■ ■

Dear heavenly Father, today I center my heart on Jesus. He not only provided this greatest gift through His death and resurrection, He is my greatest gift!

God Grants Rest

It is useless for you to work so hard from early morning until late at night, anxiously working for food to eat; for God gives rest to his loved ones.
PSALM 127:2

Can you remember the last time you rested—really rested—during the day? On Sundays we often spend time taking our family to church and visiting with friends. On holidays there is often a lot more "entertaining" than there is rest. Yet rest is a part of God's design for us. It is not something we should push off but, rather, is a practice we need to embrace.

Easter Monday is another day off for many in the Amish community. It's a day of buggy rides, spring picnics, and visiting family. It's another day to contemplate Christ's resurrection before rushing back into a busy life. You may not celebrate Easter Monday, but is there another day you could choose to rest? Maybe you can set aside an upcoming weekend. Or maybe you can use one of those "personal" days at work to sleep in, read a good book, and take a walk or a long bath.

> He is the happiest, be he peasant or king, who finds peace at home.
>
> **PROVERB**

I've noticed that when I'm pushing myself to constantly do more, I often accomplish less. My body doesn't do well when I "just keep going." I have no peace because my mind is weary too. Yet when I allow myself to have some downtime, I often come back to my tasks with renewed energy.

Taking time to rest is a way of saying that not everything in life is up to you. It's remembering that God holds all things in the palm of His hand. He provides everything, yet our busy work puts our attention back on what we do instead of on what He's done. As Job 11:18 says, "Having hope will give you courage. You will be protected and will rest in safety."

When we rest, we are placing ourselves back in God's hands and having hope in His provision. Won't you set aside time to do that today?

■ ■ ■

Dear heavenly Father, thank You for the rest You provide. Forgive me for the times I feel my busy work is accomplishing more. Thank You for giving me all that I have.

APRIL 22

Working for the Lord

Work willingly at whatever you do, as though you were
working for the Lord rather than for people.

COLOSSIANS 3:23

Have you ever known someone who loves work? My eighty-three-year-old grandma lives with me, and she said the hardest thing she's ever had to do is sit still. She can't cook and clean the way she used to, but she can load stray dishes and plates into the dishwasher—and she does. I can't leave a half-full glass on the counter for five minutes without worrying that it'll be dumped out and loaded by the time I return to the kitchen.

My husband is a hard worker too. He started college after we were married, and he was a pizza delivery guy in the evening after his classes. I've never had to worry about John not having a job. There's a certain peace to that. It's a sweet thing knowing that even though times are tight, my husband is willing to work hard and he does his best to provide.

An idle mind is the devil's workshop.

PROVERB

An Amish person doesn't understand the world where we spend time taking our kids to music lessons, sporting practices, and other extra-curricular activities. Members of Amish communities value work and shun idleness. The Amish teach their children to work hard, to enjoy their work, and to appreciate a job well done. Children aren't given sticker charts to motivate them. They don't earn allowances. Instead, they see their father, mother, and older siblings working hard, and they do all they can to pitch in.

Of course, part of the Amish work ethic is that they know all their work is done for the Lord. They know that their lives have purpose and that they are valued and needed.

"Whatever you do, do well. For when you go to the grave, there will be no work or planning or knowledge or wisdom," we read in Ecclesiastes 9:10. Think about the work you've done over the past week. Do you feel as if you're truly working for the Lord and not only for other people? What would you need to do to change your attitude about your work?

■ ■ ■

Dear heavenly Father, in a world that values entertainment, may I focus on serving You. Help me to put my self-interest aside so that I might care for others as You desire me to do.

Looking to Oneself First

They kept demanding an answer, so he stood up again and said, "All right, but let the one who has never sinned throw the first stone!"
JOHN 8:7

My friend Elizabeth's parents left the Amish lifestyle when she was just a child, but her family was able to maintain a close relationship with her Amish relatives. Recently Elizabeth was visiting her Amish grandmother when she learned a good lesson in humility. Elizabeth writes:

It was probably May, and I was visiting with her in her small apartment on my Uncle David's property. My girls were playing, and Mammie and I were putting away her laundry and hanging up her dresses in her closet. My mom had folded everything perfectly the night before because she knows exactly how *her* mom liked it done.

As we were putting it all away she begins to tell me how she just can't believe the way in which some people hang their clothes on the line to dry. She said how if you do it properly, you'll avoid wrinkles or misshapen clothing. She'd tried her best not to be prideful with how well she hung and folded clothing, she told me. She even said she prays she won't be so judgmental toward others on how they do their laundry.

> It is better to give others a piece of your heart than a piece of your mind.
>
> PROVERB

It's amazing how pride can sneak up on us, isn't it? We can look at how we do laundry or cook or care for our children, and it's easy to compare our way with someone else's way. The first step in solving that problem is noting, as Elizabeth's grandmother does, when pride is moving in.

It's the same way with other sins. Our tendency is to compare our sins with those of others. It's easy to see someone else's sin as worse than ours, but Jesus makes it clear that no one can point a finger at another's sin without being sinless. Do you feel pride or a judgmental attitude sneaking in? Turn that pointing finger back around, and ask God to help you take an honest look at your own heart before you judge someone else.

■ ■ ■

Dear heavenly Father, it's easy to compare ourselves with others and find them lacking. Help me to look at myself first. Work in me, and help me to be an example to others of grace and goodwill.

Our Greatest Treasure

Keep me safe, O God, for I have come to you for refuge. I said to the LORD,
"You are my Master! Every good thing I have comes from you."

PSALM 16:1-2

What are some of your most cherished possessions? If you had to evacuate your home and could grab only three things to take with you, what would they be?

One of my favorite things is a shadow box I created. Inside is my favorite baby picture of my husband, some black-and-white photos from my grandfather and grandmother, and my grandma's baby T-shirt from 1929. There are other "treasures" around my home—my children's baby photos, marionettes I've collected from mission trips in the Czech Republic, a copy of my novel *From Dust and Ashes* that has been signed by many of the World War II veterans I interviewed. These treasures do not have large monetary value, but they have memories attached. Each represents relationships I cherish, none of which I've deserved or earned. Instead, they are gifts from God, as all good gifts are.

One of an Amish family's greatest gifts is each other. They have no family photographs, no overseas vacation souvenirs. But they do have people who love them, people who fill their lives. More than that, their—and our—greatest gift is God Himself. He is our refuge and strength, and even if we lost everything else, we would still have Him. We'll always have His love: "No power in the sky above or in the earth below—indeed, nothing in all creation will ever be able to separate us from the love of God that is revealed in Christ Jesus our Lord" (Romans 8:39).

> The dearest things of life are mostly near at hand.
>
> PROVERB

All our earthly possessions can turn to dust and ashes, but our treasure in eternity will never be taken away. No fire, no flood, no tornado can strip us of what's most important. All else can be lost, but He is our greatest treasure. Let's cling to that.

■ ▪ ■

Dear heavenly Father, You are my greatest treasure. Nothing I have in heaven or earth compares to You. Thank You for all the good gifts You have given me—especially Yourself.

Communion

*Every time you eat this bread and drink this cup, you are
announcing the Lord's death until he comes again.*

1 CORINTHIANS 11:26

Amish churches observe Communion twice a year. Communion days are filled with solemnity as the members of the community remember Christ's sacrifice in the Lord's Supper. In some Amish communities everyone wears black.

The first sermon of the day reflects on the Anabaptist ancestors who were martyred for their faith. Then, at some point in the middle of his message, the preacher clears his throat and begins the retelling of the gospel story, starting with Adam and Eve. One by one all the major Bible stories are retold. As one preacher finishes a story, the next

In 1693–1697 the Amish (led by Jakob Amman) split from the South German Anabaptists-Mennonites. Amman forbade attendance at state churches and initiated the practice of observing Communion twice yearly (instead of once a year, the Mennonite practice).

preacher picks up where the first left off. The service lasts most of the day, and around noon members of the congregation go out in small groups to eat a simple meal before returning. Only after all the stories are shared does the congregation partake of the elements of Communion.

As the bread is passed and the cup is shared, the preachers describe their relation to the Amish lifestyle. Each member is like an individual kernel crushed and made into flour and then kneaded together to make bread—many joined together to become one. Likewise, with the wine, each grape gives up its individual identity to become wine.

Part of the Communion prayer reads: "And, so that we do not doubt Thy grace, Thou hast not only revealed it in the holy gospel, but also Thou does particularly assure us of forgiveness of sins through Holy Communion, which thou has desired to establish for the strengthening of our weak faith, through the remembrance of Thy beloved son Jesus Christ as a visible pledge and seal of Thy grace, so that we can thereby be assured of the great benefit of our redemption, likewise also of the saving communion with His body which was crucified and His blood [which] was shed for us."

May each of us approach our observance of Communion with a true realization of what we have—salvation, community, eternity—because of what Jesus has done.

■ ■ ■

Dear heavenly Father, my thank-you is not enough, but I thank You again.

Washing One Another's Feet

[Jesus] got up from the table, took off his robe, wrapped a towel around his waist, and poured water into a basin. Then he began to wash the disciples' feet, drying them with the towel he had around him.

JOHN 13:4-5

One part of the Amish Communion service that is not common in many other denominations is foot washing. Chairs are set up in front of the church and buckets of warm water and towels are provided. Older men wash the feet of older men. Younger men wash the feet of younger men. Women do the same; those close in age are matched up.

Since the Communion service and foot washing are solemn observances, even afterward, people are subdued. They leave quietly and contemplate how what they have just experienced can apply to everyday life.

During the time of Jesus, men and women wore sandals and walked dusty roads. When people had guests, they provided water so the guests could wash their feet. In Genesis 18:4, Abraham offered water for his guests, who were visiting angels. In Genesis 43:24, Joseph's steward provided water for his brothers before their banquet. Yet Jesus not only provided the water, He also washed His disciples' feet. His example showed His willingness to humble Himself and serve us in unconditional love. He desires that we do the same: "Since I, your Lord and Teacher, have washed your feet, you ought to wash each other's feet. I have given you an example to follow. Do as I have done to you" (John 13:14-15).

Foot washing is a symbol of harmony among Amish church members. If there is discord in the church, Communion will not take place until the matter has been resolved.

Chances are, unless you're a mom of little ones, you aren't going to wash someone's feet today, but are you willing to serve unconditionally in other ways? Think of something you can do for someone you love today. Now think of something you can do for someone else, someone who won't even expect it. As Jesus did, go and do.

■ ■ ■

Dear heavenly Father, so many times I come before You as if You're a stern Father who is annoyed by my presence. Thank You for Jesus' example, which gives me a glimpse of Your extravagant, giving love.

Ordnung Sunday

This plague of death will not touch you when I strike the land of Egypt. This is a day to remember. Each year, from generation to generation, you must celebrate it as a special festival to the LORD. This is a law for all time.
EXODUS 12:13-14

What rules do you live by? Did you learn them in church? From your family? Did you learn them in school or on your job? When I got married, I was surprised that some things I considered rules were more like options. Bedtime rituals, church attendance, and how one interacts with neighbors varied between my husband and me. The Amish live by a set of rules, and many people are surprised to discover that those rules aren't always set in stone either: "The *Ordnung* vary from community to community, district to district . . . and they specify prohibitions and restrictions on modern technology, job options for Amish men and guidelines for everyday living, such as dress codes and how to interact with non-Amish people. When an Amish person is baptized, they are promising to uphold these rules of their church and to never break from them."

Ordnung is a German word that means rules, regulations, and order.

Author and blogger Saloma Furlong writes, "Every spring and fall, two weeks before Communion Services, there is Ordnungs Church, a service in which the bishop of the church reviews the ordnung, or set of church rules. This is a service that lasts until about 2:00 p.m. It always seemed to me this was in preparation for the mega-long Communion Service."

Even before God sent the angel of death to kill the Egyptians' firstborn sons, He was telling the children of Israel to *remember*. He commanded that a special day be set aside for parents to tell their children the good deeds of the Lord. Is there a time you can set aside to share with your children or grandchildren or other young people why you believe what you believe and do what you do? Although you don't need to make it a law, you could use the opportunity to help the next generation remember the deeds of the Lord.

■ ■ ■

Dear heavenly Father, I know the rules You establish are for my good. I'm thankful for the way Your Word guides me and that I can turn to You to learn how to live.

Like Morning Fog

Your life is like the morning fog—it's here a little while, then it's gone. What
you ought to say is, "If the Lord wants us to, we will live and do this or that."
Otherwise you are boasting about your own plans, and all such boasting is evil.

JAMES 4:14-16

In our American society we value order, organization, planning. We create systems and charts. We fill in calendars and create schedules. We create five-year plans, set life goals, and make bucket lists. We believe in "doing" for the sense of accomplishment we get. Even though we may not admit it, our plans help us to excel—to compete with others—and even compete with the goals we've established for ourselves. And sometimes we've become prideful in our sense of self-sufficiency.

We may not boast outwardly, but our deeds speak loud and clear. We are so certain of what we have planned for tomorrow that we become discouraged and overwhelmed when unexpected sickness, injury, natural disasters, and loss force us to change our routines. The Amish are not immune to trouble. Like the rest of us, they make plans and then find themselves disappointed too. What the Amish understand, though, is the beauty of sacrificing *time* to the Lord. Everything they do takes more time, but that means they have more time to spend with God as they do it.

Do you feel as if your life is a morning fog, here and then gone? Only the things we do for God will last for eternity. Everything else will fade to nothing: "You have made my life no longer than the width of my hand. My entire lifetime is just a moment to you; at best, each of us is but a breath," says Psalm 39:5.

This is a good reminder to slow down and cherish the time we spend with loved ones. Put aside your five-year plans, life goals, and bucket lists, and instead, refresh your soul and cherish family and friends. Do not boast about what you think is to come. Instead, be thankful for the moments you have today with those you love and with God by your side.

■ ■ ■

Dear heavenly Father, thank You for Your plans for me. Help me to realize that my life
is short. I invite You to walk with me today.

APRIL 29

Praying Together

Our Father in heaven, may your name be kept holy. May your Kingdom
come soon. May your will be done on earth, as it is in heaven.
MATTHEW 6:9-10

In *The Amish Way,* author Donald Kraybill discusses Amish prayer practices:

The Amish rely primarily on written prayers in a book titled *Die Ernsthafte*
Christenpflicht ("The Prayer Book for Earnest Christians"). First published in
the early 1700s, the prayer book's resources are only slightly more contemporary
than the hymns of the *Ausbund.* The collection, written in German by both
Anabaptist and non-Anabaptist authors and intended for private devotional

**Amish women never
cut their hair, and
they cover their
heads with prayer
kapps because
of the words of
1 Corinthians 11:5:
"A woman dishonors
her head if she
prays or prophesies
without a covering
on her head, for
this is the same as
shaving her head."**

reading, includes prayers for morning and evening, a
prayer for "devout parents for their children," a traveler's
prayer, a pre-sermon prayer, and "a reminder of several
points for which we should rightly sigh and pray to God."
Christenpflicht is now used by the Amish in church services
and for family devotions. For the Amish, these prayers are
second in importance only to the Lord's Prayer, the model
prayer that Jesus taught (Matthew 6:9-13).

The Lord's Prayer is the most well-known prayer for all
Christians, but there are many other written prayers in the
Bible. The Psalms contain many of them. Colossians 1 is Paul's
prayer for the saints and faithful brethren in Christ at Colosse.
In the book of Numbers God spoke to Moses, giving him a
blessing to pray over the children of Israel. John 17 is Jesus'
intercessory prayer for His followers.

There are times in our lives when we cannot think of what
to pray on our own. In those times we can turn to these Bible
prayers for guidance. Connecting our hearts with the written
words can be a great springboard to our own prayers. We can
read the words of others written long ago and share their same
thoughts, same emotions. With written prayers, hearts can be
connected across miles and across history as the shared words glorify our same God.

■ ■ ■

Dear heavenly Father, I thank You for Your Kingdom on earth. I thank You for the prayers
of the saints. May my words mingle with theirs before Your throne!

To Trust and Obey

The Lord said to him, "You Pharisees are so careful to clean the outside of the cup and the dish, but inside you are filthy—full of greed and wickedness!"

LUKE 11:39

I once knew an elderly woman who was complaining about "children these days." She shared how her children always dressed in nicely pressed clothing, always sat quietly at meals, and never complained. I listened, but I didn't comment. I know her children, who are now grown. They learned to "display" themselves well as children, but as adults they've struggled with holding down jobs, with relationships, and with life in general. While there may be some Amish who believe that presenting themselves well is enough to receive God's approval, most of them realize that the outside should be a reflection of what's in the heart. An anonymous Amish man writes, "We wear plain clothes, but we know plain clothes do not save us. We give alms, but our good works cannot earn the grace of God. We partake in communion, but know that the emblems in themselves are just bread and wine, with no power to sanctify us. We pour water at baptism, and know the water cannot wash off a single sin. We obey because God said so. Is that not, after all, the best reason, the most important reason in all the world?"

The right to do something doesn't always make it the right thing to do.

PROVERB

Obedience to God's commands is the source of the Amish lifestyle. Everyone is expected to obey the will of God. To the Amish, obedience is a joy, not a burden. They don't believe that having their children "look good and act right" is enough.

How do we look at obedience in our own lives? Do we come to God's Word with moldable hearts that are willing to obey? Often we teach our children the "how" of obedience without instructing them in the importance of heart motivation. Sometimes we need to remind ourselves of the same thing. We obey first, and as we do our hearts are transformed. Obedience alone is never enough, but it's the first step toward developing a faithful heart.

■ ■ ■

Dear heavenly Father, there are times I ignore the voice of Your Spirit urging me to obey. At this moment, soften my heart. I long to follow Your ways, and I know that as I do, I'll be faithful inside and out.

MAY 1

Planting God's Word

*Plow up the hard ground of your hearts! Do not
waste your good seed among thorns.*

JEREMIAH 4:3

The way the Amish farm today is very similar to the way farmers farmed for hundreds of years. Instead of using motorized plows, cultivators, and fossil fuels, Amish farmers use horses and horse-drawn plows. These Amish plows are similar to those with two wheels, designed during the time of the Civil War. The plows are designed to allow farmers to sit while plowing.

When it comes to plowing the ground, Amish farmers have an intimate knowledge of their land. Their farms are more diversified than non-Amish farms. They plant different crops during different years so as not to deplete the soil of necessary nutrients. They also know when the ground is ready for planting. Amish farmers monitor the weeds that grow on their land to determine soil deficiencies.

Many Amish buggies are pulled by former race horses. Draft horses are used to pull Amish plows.

What would happen if we had such an intimate knowledge of the soil of our own hearts? Each of us needs to plant God's Word in our hearts daily, but are we taking time to prepare our hearts to come to His Word? Maybe you need a little diversity. Instead of writing in your prayer journal, sing a familiar hymn. Instead of reading from your favorite devotional book, consider meditating on a Scripture passage that God has put on your mind. Do you have other deficiencies? Ask God to point them out.

Hosea 10:12 says, "Plant the good seeds of righteousness, and you will harvest a crop of love. Plow up the hard ground of your hearts, for now is the time to seek the LORD, that he may come and shower righteousness upon you."

We do need to plant the seed—God's Word—in our hearts, but let us not forget to prepare the soil first.

■ ■ ■

Dear heavenly Father, plow up my heart, and prepare it for Your Word. Show me any hard ground that needs to be softened by Your Spirit. May the seed of Your Word go deep and grow strong within me!

Reaping a Harvest

Let's not get tired of doing what is good. At just the right time
we will reap a harvest of blessing if we don't give up.

GALATIANS 6:9

It is not uncommon for Americans to go through what is referred to as a midlife crisis. Men and women realize their mortality more clearly as the years tick by, and they desire a change in their day-to-day situation. Some may make good choices, such as turning away from selfish pursuits to serve other people. Others focus on self-indulgence and pursue things they wish they had had before, whether it be a new place to live or a different kind of work.

For the Amish, the work they do as teenagers is most likely the work they'll do all their lives.

Dedication and perseverance can be said to characterize an Amish worker. Writing about the Amish, David Luthy says, "A person's devotion to an idea is not measured until the newness has worn off, until the challenge has lost its initial excitement, and the fun and glamour have faded. Then, when only the hard work remains—the daily tasks, the mundane labor—that is when a person's commitment to a project is truly tested."

In Shipshewana, Indiana, bells on windmills are used to call Amish men in from working.

It's not uncommon for those who believe in God to have spiritual midlife crises too. Maybe they had expected that life with God would turn out differently. Yet the level of their devotion to God—their commitment—becomes evident when doing good is hard. Aren't you glad that God does not leave us alone in our efforts?

Isaiah 40:31 says, "Those who trust in the LORD will find new strength. They will soar high on wings like eagles. They will run and not grow weary. They will walk and not faint." When the last day comes and we finish with our earthly work, what will God say about us? Were we committed to His cause? Did we turn to Him during every crisis that came?

■ ■ ■

Dear heavenly Father, there are days when I become weary in doing good. I give, I serve, and it seems that more gets poured out than put in. I thank You, Lord, that You can give me strength. I need it—I depend on You—now.

Last Is First

Some who seem least important now will be the greatest then, and
some who are the greatest now will be least important then.
LUKE 13:30

A large Amish family may have fourteen or more children. One by one, the children grow. The older sons learn trades, and the daughters marry and start families of their own. In most cultures it is common for the oldest son to receive the majority of an inheritance, but in the Amish culture it's typically the youngest son who takes over the farm from his father.

Amish land stays within the family, and when the youngest son prepares to start his own family, he usually takes over his parents' home, and his parents move to an attached apartment or adjacent house called a Dawdy Haus, or a Grossdawdy (granddaddy) Haus. In effect, the last son—the youngest—receives the most. He will also have the responsibility of caring for his parents for the rest of their lives.

A man who gives his children habits of industry provides for them better than by giving them a fortune.

PROVERB

You will never find an Amish rest home, and perhaps the greatest inheritance isn't the property the youngest son receives but the joy of having the extra time with his parents. It is often during people's latter years—when they don't have the strength to go full speed ahead in busy lives—that their relationship with God really has time to flourish.

As Psalm 92:12-15 says, "The godly will flourish like palm trees and grow strong like the cedars of Lebanon. For they are transplanted to the LORD's own house. They flourish in the courts of our God. Even in old age they will still produce fruit; they will remain vital and green. They will declare, 'The LORD is just! He is my rock! There is no evil in him!'"

In God's economy, it's often the youngest and the weakest who receive the most. In God's economy, it's the elderly who flourish and grow in their faith and relationship with Him. In a world that exalts the first and the fittest, it's important to remember that in God's economy, those who give are as blessed as those who receive, every time.

■ ■ ■

Dear heavenly Father, I love how Your economy works. We don't gain by grasping. Instead we gain by opening our hands and hearts. Help me to do more of both today.

Faith like a Radish Seed

[Jesus said,] "The Kingdom of Heaven is like a mustard seed planted in a field. It is the smallest of all seeds, but it becomes the largest of garden plants; it grows into a tree, and birds come and make nests in its branches."

MATTHEW 13:31-32

The Amish give much thought to what goes into their gardens. The border is rimmed with flowers—zinnias, marigolds, and huge spider plants. One might think they are simply for looks, but marigolds keep moles out of the garden. The vegetables vary, depending on what space permits, but among those commonly planted are lettuce, carrots, celery, cooking and sweet radishes, onions, beets, tomatoes, cantaloupe, watermelon, and much more. The Amish are raised with a garden being part of their lives, and they can't imagine anything different. They often spend time during the winter poring over seed catalogs and dreaming of the growing season to come.

Some of the first produce to be ready includes lettuce, radishes, and green onions. Later in the summer, children can be seen sneaking out to the garden with a salt shaker in hand to snack on fresh peas. A number of Amish families sell their produce at roadside stands. Not only does it help raise money, it gives the children something to do and an opportunity to learn business sense. And to think all of this produce started with little seeds.

The seed of faith is small when it is first planted in the heart. It must be protected and watered and nurtured, and only then will it grow. But seeds, though small, have something wonderful within them. And faith—when it grows—turns into something wonderful, too—a harvest of goodness in our lives.

Some Amish communities host community quilt gardens. Flowers are planted in the pattern of a beautiful quilt. Every quilt garden and quilt mural has its own intricate pattern, and many are original designs.

■ ■ ■

Dear heavenly Father, thank You for the seeds of faith that were first planted in my life. Lord, I pray that those seeds will continue to grow and flourish and nurture others in wonderful ways.

Weeding Out Harmful Cultural Influences

The seed that fell among the thorns represents others who hear God's word, but all too quickly the message is crowded out by the worries of this life, the lure of wealth, and the desire for other things, so no fruit is produced.
MARK 4:18-19

I traveled to Europe this summer, and other than the ancient cathedrals and cobblestone streets, I was amazed how similar things were to where I live. People dressed fairly similarly, ordered the same coffees, listened to the same music. With the Internet, television, and music, once-varied societies seem to be merging into one.

It's a hard life for those who choose to leave the Amish community. Often they have only an eighth-grade education, and they no longer have the support of their families.

Because the Amish have set themselves apart, their culture, customs, and values have stayed the same for hundreds of years. They've not only held on to what matters most; they've also built an invisible fence between themselves and globalization. Many Amish today have relationships with coworkers and tourists, so modern living is familiar to them. They simply choose not to join in.

Resistance to computers, electricity, and automobiles restricts the Amish in some ways, but it has also freed them. They are able to live as they believe, in simplicity, obedience to God, and peace—without comparing themselves with others.

As Christians we have the ability to choose what influences we allow into our homes. It's our job to "weed out" those that are harmful. If we don't, then too easily the worries of this life, the lure of wealth, and the desire for other things will choke out the Christian teaching we're trying to impart.

We read in Romans 12:2, "Don't become so well-adjusted to your culture that you fit into it without even thinking. Instead, fix your attention on God. You'll be changed from the inside out. Readily recognize what he wants from you, and quickly respond to it. Unlike the culture around you, always dragging you down to its level of immaturity, God brings the best out of you, develops well-formed maturity in you" (*The Message*).

■ ■ ■

Dear heavenly Father, help me to weed out any ungodly influences that have a way of creeping into my life. Help me to see that "different" is good if I'm different because of You.

The Amish Carpenter

Unless the LORD builds a house, the work of the builders is wasted.

PSALM 127:1

Amish-made furniture. Just the name evokes images of finely crafted products. There are numerous Amish businesses that take a piece from tree to showroom. Amish lumber mills and woodworking shops are also growing in popularity. Instead of using electricity, many of these workshops run simple tools with hand power or even bicycle power! More progressive Amish workshops use hydraulic power, and some even use diesel generators to run their tools. If you drive through Amish country, you'll commonly see Amish workshops in buildings a short distance from Amish homes, with signs posted welcoming visitors.

In addition to furniture, the Amish have a good reputation for their carpentry and construction skills. They are known to work hard and do an expert job for a reasonable wage. There are trade catalogs and business directories that highlight Plain companies. Some Amish businesses even hire other businesses to sell their products online.

No matter what jobs we work in—or what our reputation is—we must remember that all knowledge, ability, and strength come from God. First Corinthians 1:24 says, "To those called by God to salvation, both Jews and Gentiles, Christ is the power of God and the wisdom of God."

We can set to work at our tasks. We can have a fine reputation and a history of fine products, but the truth is, unless the Lord builds a home—or a home-building business—we labor in vain.

It's easy to focus on our education, our training, or our experience, but we must always turn our attention back to God. We do all things through Him, with Him, and for Him. To think otherwise is only vanity.

Amish carpenters and other local volunteers saved the day for a water wheel at the historic Volant Mill in Lawrence County. When weather and age broke it down, Amish carpenters revitalized the town icon within a day.

■ ■ ■

Dear heavenly Father, I know the very breath I breathe is from You. Thank You for the strength I have to handle my daily work and daily tasks. Build Your house through me today, Lord.

The Shelter of God

Those who live in the shelter of the Most High will
find rest in the shadow of the Almighty.
PSALM 91:1

Amish prayers have been passed down for generations. There are prayers about the storms of life and for the spring storms outside one's door. Here is one such prayer:

Guard (preserve) us, Lord Christ, all together,
From fire, hail, and thunderclaps,
Protect all who are in the field,
So that the storm does not set them on fire.
Preserve cattle, men and grain,
Then young and old will praise and glorify Thee.

When storms in cities take out electricity and cripple neighborhoods, the Amish tend to fare well. Even during large storms they bounce back quickly.

It's a beautiful prayer, but how often can we relate? When one lives in a solid brick building, can work on the Internet without leaving one's home, or simply has to jump into a car in a warm garage, physical storms can seem no more than minor inconveniences. But when, whether hundreds of years ago or today, one works in the fields and comes face-to-face with the elements, storms take on a new meaning.

Isaiah 25:4 wasn't just for our ancestors; it's for us, too: "You are a tower of refuge to the poor, O LORD, a tower of refuge to the needy in distress. You are a refuge from the storm and a shelter from the heat. For the oppressive acts of ruthless people are like a storm beating against a wall."

Faith is seeing a storm rage outside your window and believing that the Lord is able to protect all that you've worked so hard for. Hope is seeing the darkest clouds and knowing that the storm will not last forever. It will rage only for a time. True praise happens, when hail pounds and the rain pelts, as you thank God for being with you in the storm . . . and for the sunshine to come.

The same is true in the storms of our lives, when our livelihood hangs in the balance, or when our safety or that of our family is at risk. The bigger the problem, the harder it is to praise God, but our purest praise comes in the midst of those storms.

■ ■ ■

Dear heavenly Father, thank You for being my shelter. Thank You for the rest I find in Your shadow, no matter what storms are raging.

My Meditation

May the words of my mouth and the meditation of my heart
be pleasing to you, O Lord, my rock and my redeemer.

PSALM 19:14

Do you have a prayer list? If so, what does it look like? Is it filled with requests? Needs? One Amish saying goes, "Prayer is not asking. Prayer is putting oneself in the hands of God, at His disposition, and listening to His voice in the depths of our hearts."

God *does* tell us to ask. Matthew 7:7 says, "Keep on asking, and you will receive what you ask for." But there are numerous other places in the Bible where we are called to meditate. *The Message* version of Psalm 19:14 says, "[These words in my mouth] are what I chew on and pray. Accept them when I place them on the morning altar."

Meditation is a simple way of saying you're listening to—or chewing on—God's voice in the depths of your heart. To be able to meditate, you need three things:

1. *Quietness.* Turn off the television, your music, your computer. Let your mind ponder your favorite Scripture verses and think of God.

2. *Discipline.* What are your values? What activities do you want to fill your day? What does God want you to cut out so you can have more of Him? Discipline yourself to allow into your life only what's best for your day. You don't have to limit yourself to driving a buggy, but you can uphold whatever values you deem fit.

3. *Structure.* The Amish have definite structure to their days. When our bodies work in an ordered way, we can turn our minds back to God. When we take time to ponder God's goodness, our meditations rise to Him in sweet prayers. God desires that we fill our days with thoughts of Him. He wants to be our constant companion, and we can find that companionship when we take steps to allow room for His presence.

> If you admire our faith, strengthen yours. If you admire our sense of commitment, deepen yours. If you admire our community spirit, build your own. If you admire the simple life, cut back. If you admire deep character and enduring values, live them yourself.
>
> PROVERB

■ ■ ■

Dear heavenly Father, what joy we bring to You and to ourselves when we "chew on" Your goodness in our hearts. May structure and quiet and discipline be the pillars to allow more room for You within me.

Godly Interdependence

Take note of those who refuse to obey what we say in this letter. Stay away from them so they will be ashamed.

2 THESSALONIANS 3:14

Those who make a commitment to be members of the Amish church do so for life, but there are reasons they can be excommunicated. These offenses can include owning automobiles or computers, drinking alcoholic beverages, wearing English clothes, or refusing to kneel during religious ceremonies.

Those within the community must acknowledge the authority of the church. Excommunication does not happen lightly or quickly. It is done as a last resort.

"Jacob Ammann, a young Anabaptist leader from the Alsace region of modern-day France, strongly believed that the Bible mandated that excommunicated members should be avoided at all costs. He cited the Anabaptist Confession of Faith as authority for the practice of shunning. When the Swiss Anabaptists refused to shun excommunicated members, Jacob Ammann and his followers broke away and formed the Amish movement in 1693."

When Amish people come close to excommunication, church leaders attempt to persuade them to repent and return wholeheartedly to the church. They offer the wayward members a few months to reform. If they do not do so, they are excommunicated, and are also shunned, which means that all active members must avoid those people in all social activities. Active members also may not conduct business with shunned members.

The Amish believe excommunication is a loving act, designed to bring the wayward members back to repentance and fellowship with the church. The shunning also acts as a warning to active members not to fall into others' sins. Since one of the Amish's greatest values is family and community, the fear of being shunned goes deep.

Most of us live by different rules, but God has put us in the body of Christ to encourage one another to remain faithful. God has also given us Himself. When we share in His divine nature, we can stand strong. God doesn't want us to become independent. This may look different in our world than it does in an Amish community, but the truth remains that we were made to serve God together in this world.

■ ■ ■

Dear heavenly Father, everything within me fights to do things my own way. But I long to draw nearer to You and to work in close fellowship with other believers. May Your desires become stronger in me, and may my own desires weaken.

Learn It. Live It. Share It.

Commit yourselves wholeheartedly to these words of mine. Tie them to your hands and wear them on your forehead as reminders. Teach them to your children. Talk about them when you are at home and when you are on the road, when you are going to bed and when you are getting up.

DEUTERONOMY 11:18-19

Growing up Amish reminds me of what it would have been like to live in the days of Laura Ingalls Wilder. When I was a fifth grader, the Little House series of books was my favorite. I loved the passages about Ma making simple oil lamps of buttons, scraps of calico, and axle grease. Or about Pa hanging a wild boar in the smokehouse. I liked the idea of waking at dawn, riding in a horse-drawn wagon or buggy, and sitting as a family by lantern light.

History—the kind Laura lived—is still being lived out in some ways. Today, Amish families not only sit around the living room at night, sewing and reading by lantern light, they also live by many values modern progress has forgotten. What lessons from the past are worth embracing? Sometimes the best person to ask—it seems—is an Amish man or woman. In some ways, our past is their present.

Here are some values to consider: common courtesy, family togetherness, neighborliness, service, and putting others before yourself. These values are based on the Scriptures, and the reason they don't get passed down is that parents neglect to teach and train their children by them.

Teaching scriptural values should be even more important than teaching our children to brush their teeth, turn off lights when they leave the room, or recycle. Do we forget to teach these values because we've forgotten their worth?

Spend time reading God's Word. Ask Him what values He desires you to live out in your own life. Ask His Holy Spirit to work through you. And then pass those values on to the children and young people in your life.

> The ideal environment for the Amish is that everyone–except for the children in school–works close enough to gather around the table for meals. School-age children eat lunch at school, but they eat breakfast and dinner with their families.

■ ■ ■

Dear heavenly Father, living by Your Word displays often-forgotten values. May I be a diligent student of the way You desire for me to live. May I depend on Your Holy Spirit to "work out" the truths Your Word "works in."

A Celebration of Mothers

My child, listen when your father corrects you.
Don't neglect your mother's instruction.
What you learn from them will crown you with grace
and be a chain of honor around your neck.

PROVERBS 1:8-9

On Mother's Day, children gather flowers or purchase potted plants as gifts for their mothers. Some teachers have their students make cards at school. Not every Amish community celebrates Mother's Day, but every community does honor mothers and women in general.

In the Amish church, everyone has a place. Even the seating reflects this. As the church service begins, Saloma Furlong writes, "the oldest women . . . file in and take their places, followed by the middle-aged women, and on down to the younger married women. Then the unmarried women . . . file in and take their places, again by age."

Many Amish consider Mother's Day to be the time when they no longer worry about frost and they can start preparing their gardens.

In Amish society, women are their children's caregivers. They are their children's first teachers. They provide food, clothes, and affection. Older women are looked up to for their wisdom. And although mothers are honored with flowers, when we follow wisdom, we're the ones who wear wreaths and crowns: "If you prize wisdom, she will make you great. Embrace her, and she will honor you. She will place a lovely wreath on your head; she will present you with a beautiful crown" (Proverbs 4:8-9).

It's possible that you weren't raised by a godly mother, but there may be an older woman in your life to whom you can turn for advice and support. None of us will ever outgrow the need for loving mentors. Each of us needs instruction and advice. When we can learn from the experiences of others, we don't need to learn things the hard way.

If you do have a wise, caring mother, you are blessed, for every time you follow the guidance and instruction of loving parents, you become someone who will be effective in leading the next generation toward God. You can also be a godly mentor to girls and younger women. Your own life experiences can make another person's life easier.

■ ■ ■

Dear heavenly Father, I thank You for wise, godly women, for those who are faithful guides to future generations. I pray that You will give me someone to look to, and also someone to lead toward You.

Nourishing Souls

My child, listen to me and do as I say,
and you will have a long, good life.
I will teach you wisdom's ways
and lead you in straight paths.

PROVERBS 4:10-11

It is easy to consider dinner just another thing to add to the to-do list. Dinner comes *after* washing, mending, canning, scolding, embracing, tending, weeding, reading, and numerous other additional tasks.

Dinner comes *before* baths, bedtime, chores, and tuck-ins. It's easy to think of dinner as just another thing "to do." And for an Amish woman, it's a *big* to-do. She must not only think of what to make but also make a lot of it for many hungry mouths!

Amish parents know that the most important part of the meal isn't the food itself but family togetherness. In the American culture many are rediscovering the joy of shared mealtimes, when family members gather around the table to eat together and talk about their day and what's going on in their lives. Dinnertime reunites family members after a busy day. Each person feels part of the family unit. They work together on the cooking and cleaning up. And because we have our family's undivided attention as they sit and eat, mealtime is also a perfect time to share something from the Scriptures or tell stories about our own faith walk.

> Some tours of Amish country advertise dinners at the homes of Amish families. You can share your life with them as they share theirs with you.

Proverbs 3:1-2 says, "My child, never forget the things I have taught you. Store my commands in your heart. If you do this, you will live many years, and your life will be satisfying."

Just as the food we eat brings health to our bodies, gathering together regularly brings health to our souls. Do you want to nourish your family? Then try not to consider dinner just another thing on your to-do list. Instead, turn it into a focal point of your day, and then make God the focal point of the conversation!

■ ■ ■

Dear heavenly Father, often in my quest to be productive and effective, I miss out on connecting with the hearts of those in my life. Please, Lord, help me to put the focus on You in everyday moments.

Strains of Faith

Faith is the confidence that what we hope for will actually happen; it gives us assurance about things we cannot see.
HEBREWS 11:1

In the Amish church service, the songs that are sung are the same ones that have been sung for hundreds of years. Saloma Furlong writes, "One of the 'foresingers' (leaders in song) announces a number, and everyone opens their black songbook (The Ausbund) to that page. The foresinger will begin the first word of the first line of the chant, and then as he begins the second word, the other men join in. The women join in with their voices and the song goes on for fifteen or twenty minutes."

The songs are ones of joy and ones of pain. Yet strains of faith carry through the words. Here are a few lines from *Ausbund* 55: "The lamb is eaten with sorrow and bitter herbs, for he who will not suffer with Christ, and he who keeps himself back from eating his flesh and his blood—he who worries about the cross or tribulation—cannot find the body of Christ. The Lamb must be eaten completely. Nothing shall be left, from the beginning to the end. In all distress and need, we dare not turn away from the Lamb. We are to stay in closest unity with him, not allowing our faith in him or our love for him to grow cold."

Faith is the bridge over which we can cross all the unknown waters of tomorrow.

PROVERB

The faith of the Anabaptists is carried on every vocal strain. They did not know if their words would travel beyond the prison walls. They couldn't envision a new land, a strong people, and their seeds of faith still growing and blooming.

What do you need faith for today? Faith takes the smallest hope and dares to believe. It trusts that even if you can't see the future, God can. Ephesians 3:20 says, "All glory to God, who is able, through his mighty power at work within us, to accomplish infinitely more than we might ask or think." Because of God, the future—which belongs to Him—is more wonderful than you can believe.

■ ■ ■

Dear heavenly Father, I thank You that Your plans for me and for my future, which I can't see, are something wonderful. Take my faith and use it, spread it, for Your glory.

Barefooted Joy

He has shown you, O mortal, what is good. And what does the LORD require of you? To act justly and to love mercy and to walk humbly with your God.

MICAH 6:8 (NIV)

Some time ago I was driving around an Amish community when I passed by a school during the afternoon break. Twenty or so children were running around the playground. There was a volleyball game. There was a game of tag. Some of the children laughed as they spun on the ancient merry-go-round, and all of them were . . . barefoot.

I smiled when I saw them racing around on the spring grass without a shoe in sight. One Amish man I spoke to told me that as a child he knew summer was just around the corner when he could kick off his shoes. Shoes are needed for chores and school, but summer is a time of barefooted play.

There is nothing more humble than running around barefoot. There is no pretense. No one's looking to impress others. There's a simple sense of abandon that comes with being free of shoes and socks. There's an appreciation for God's good earth and the warm season He's brought.

In a time when modern teens are complaining they don't have the newest iPhones or are demanding the latest expensive sneakers (two conversations I've overheard recently), Amish children enjoy the simple things in life. If anything, they share the goodness of God through their laughter, their simple games, and their barefooted ways. That reminds me of Isaiah 52:7: "How beautiful on the mountains are the feet of the messenger who brings good news, the good news of peace and salvation, the news that the God of Israel reigns!"

Do you want a reminder that God is good? Watch children at play. They are unexpected messengers who remind us that life doesn't have to be as hard as it seems. Their laughter gives us hope for the day and hope for the future.

Amish children don't just take their shoes off at school. Sometimes they walk to school barefoot. During the warm days their feet get as tough as leather, and they enjoy the freedom of not wearing shoes.

■ ■ ■

Dear heavenly Father, thank You for the messengers of good news You bring into my life. They remind me to find joy in You. May my heart fill with laughter and bubble over.

In His Steps

Jesus grew in wisdom and in stature and in favor with God and all the people.
LUKE 2:52

One of my all-time favorite people in the Bible is Joseph. When God chose the man and woman who would be Jesus' earthly parents, He chose not only Mary but also Joseph. Joseph was the spiritual leader, a mentor, and a role model. Jesus learned the carpentry trade by Joseph's side.

The interaction between Joseph and Jesus is the same type of relationship we see in many Amish homes. Joe Eicher describes an example of that interaction from his own life:

Amish girls learn how to be wives and mothers. Amish boys learn how to work a trade, handle finances, use tools, and drive a horse and buggy.

Dad took me along as a child to hunt mushrooms. He showed me which ones are okay and which ones aren't. We always went mushroom hunting after a thunderstorm in warming spring weather. Those seemed to be the best conditions for finding some good ones. Dad taught me that flat mushrooms that grow on or around trees are the poisonous ones. The main ones we hunted for when I was a boy were the spikes and the yellow sponges that grow around stumps. We didn't take any tools with us to gather them, just a bag to put them in.

Each of us can look back at people who influenced our lives. In addition to my godly grandparents, I also had a Sunday school teacher who was an encouraging example to me. She spent time with me, invited me into her home, and made me feel special.

We can read books and hear sermons to learn to do what is right, but the best way to learn is to follow the footsteps of another. Just as Jesus was led, He reached out to others. When gathering His disciples, He spoke these familiar words, "Come, follow me, and I will show you how to fish for people!" (Matthew 4:19).

Were you influenced for good in some way? The best way to say thanks is to turn around and reach out to another person.

■ ■ ■

Dear heavenly Father, thank You for bringing people into my life who model the right way to live. May my life be an example to others today, and may You be glorified in the process!

May Flowers

The flowers are springing up, the season of singing birds has come.

SONG OF SONGS 2:12

In late spring and summer you can find many auctions in Amish communities. In Hazleton, Iowa, flower and produce auctions are held on Tuesdays and Fridays. In Lancaster County, Pennsylvania, the term for the annual auction is "mud sale." This is an appropriate name since the ground is thawing after winter and the thousands of people who attend, looking for bargains, make their imprints.

People attend Amish auctions looking for quilts, lumber, produce, flowers, antiques, and used items. Some of these auctions make money to benefit the local town. On the second Saturday of June every year, the small Amish community in Rexford, Montana, has an auction that raises money for their Amish school. They're also raising money to put a fire station in their area.

When flowers bloom in Amish gardens, they are bundled into bouquets and sold at auction. The quilts that have been stitched and the cupboards that have been built in warm homes and shops during the winter months now are out in the warm spring air, waiting for bidding to begin.

> In Rexford, Montana, the quilt auction portion of the sale has a large variety of quilts made locally and sent from Amish homes around the country.

What do you look forward to in spring? Not only does spring bring new life blooming in the world around us, but spring also brings freshness and new hope to our hearts. The season is a reminder that even though some days are dark, sunshine and flowers will come again, as we read in Song of Songs 2:11: "Look, the winter is past, and the rains are over and gone."

Are you going through a dark time in your life? Remember that God can bring light into your darkness as surely as He brings the light of springtime after the dark days of winter. Thank God for the answers and hope that will come in His perfect timing.

If you're finding joy in a bright season of your life, don't take it for granted. Use this time to reach out to someone else. Share a bouquet of flowers with a friend who's having a hard day or going through illness or some other difficulty. Share with your friend what God has done in your life.

■ ■ ■

Dear heavenly Father, I thank You for the spring flowers that come after seasons of cold, darkness, mud, and rain. Show me someone with whom I can share a bit of Your sunshine today.

Powerful Proverbs: Nuggets of Wisdom

If you stop listening to instruction, my child, you will turn your back on knowledge.
PROVERBS 19:27

Are there some popular sayings that have been passed down through your family? My mother-in-law always says, "Many hands make light work." My stepfather would always say, "What goes around, comes around."

Sharing proverbs isn't so common in our modern society, but they are still popular with the Amish. Suzanne Woods Fisher, author of *Amish Proverbs*, writes,

The Amish *Budget* now has a Facebook page: www.facebook.com /theamishbudget.

The *Sugarcreek Budget* is a weekly newspaper for the Amish-Mennonite community that began in 1890. Scribes from all over the world send in a weekly letter to the Ohio headquarters. At the end of most letters, a proverb is added, like a benediction. "The trend began about five to eight years ago," explains editor Fannie Erb-Miller. "We started to allow a saying on the end of a scribe's letter, and then it just caught on. Now, almost all of the letters have one. Early on, letters didn't include them. Mostly, they're sayings that pass from generation to generation."

Here are some of the proverbs that have appeared in issues of the *Budget*:

Time spent with God is well spent.
Only Jesus, the Living Water, can satisfy the thirsty soul.
The Bible does not need to be rewritten, but reread.
Today's prices often indicate that the best time to buy something was last year.

These proverbs say a lot about the people who include them. As they write about farm life, births, deaths, and visiting guests, they also offer a bit of truth. What truth do you embrace? The more willing we are to ponder others' wise words, the more wisdom we'll have to pass on to the next generation.

In fact, here's one that I'll end with: The best gift for the younger generation is a good example from the older generation.

■ ■ ■

Dear heavenly Father, give me a heart willing to listen to instruction. Help me to embrace these truths so I can pass them on.

Caring for Our Neighbors

*A despised Samaritan came along, and when he saw the man, he felt
compassion for him. Going over to him, the Samaritan soothed his wounds
with olive oil and wine and bandaged them. Then he put the man on his
own donkey and took him to an inn, where he took care of him.*

LUKE 10:33-34

If you were in an automobile accident in Lancaster County, I'm certain the last thing you'd expect to see is an ambulance pulling up and an Amish man jumping out to help you. Yet that's exactly what you might see. Lancaster County has as many as three hundred Amish and Mennonite volunteer firefighters, both men and women. Amish have been volunteering for generations. And some are even certified as emergency medical technicians.

Some Old Order Amish responders arrange with their neighbors for transport or live close enough to the fire station to get there by scooter. Many of the Amish believe this is a way to "love your neighbor as yourself." In this community and others, Amish also help with disaster relief, blood donation, and hospice care.

They take seriously the words of Isaiah 58:7: "Share your food with the hungry, and give shelter to the homeless. Give clothes to those who need them, and do not hide from relatives who need your help." There are some who respond to hundreds of calls each year and come upon heartbreaking scenes. Yet they also discover that God helps them in their weakness. Their faith keeps them strong and helps them to serve.

Shouldn't we all be so diligent? Shouldn't we serve where it is hard and reach out to help those who need it most? It's the hurting who need to feel God's love through our care.

■ ■ ■

*Dear heavenly Father, help me to step up to help instead of
looking away. It's hard leaving my comfort zone, but I'm
thankful that when I do, You're there waiting for me.*

"The state requires [EMT] trainees to be clean-shaven so protective masks seal tightly against their faces. That's a catch for Amish men, who . . . let their beards grow after they wed. 'It's not a deal breaker,' said John Stoltzfus, . . . who is an EMT and assistant fire chief. . . . 'The majority of them are getting (training) done before they're married.'"

Steps to Godly Living

Supplement your faith with a generous provision of moral excellence, and moral excellence with knowledge, and knowledge with self-control, and self-control with patient endurance, and patient endurance with godliness, and godliness with brotherly affection, and brotherly affection with love for everyone.

2 PETER 1:5-7

Just as an Amish child or a non-Amish child grows and matures, we must grow into mature children of God. Why must we do that? To make ourselves look better? To treat others in a more positive way? No, the ultimate reason is so our excellent character will reflect our excellent God.

God sets a high standard—perfection. That means that none of us can ever reach it, not completely, and not in our whole lives. Did God set this standard just so we'd fail? No, He gave it to us so that we will turn to Him.

> If you hear a bad report about someone, halve it and quarter it, and then say nothing about the rest.
>
> PROVERB

No matter what society we live in, no matter how we are raised, no matter what heritage of faith we carry, none of us can be godly without God's Spirit in us. We may be good in some ways. We may be kind sometimes, but godly character is from Him: "The Holy Spirit produces this kind of fruit in our lives: love, joy, peace, patience, kindness, goodness, faithfulness, gentleness, and self-control. There is no law against these things!" (Galatians 5:22-23).

This fruit isn't "produced" by working harder, trying more, or living in a Christian community. The only way the fruit of the Spirit will flow out from us is for God's Spirit to flow in.

How can we do that? First, we must understand our shortcomings. Genuine character starts with facing the reality that we are sinners in need of a Savior. Jesus saved our souls and allowed us to enter into eternity. But He also rescues our character on a daily basis as we turn to Him. With every step, let us praise God for where we've come and also submit to our Father's leading and to where He wants to take us.

■ ■ ■

Dear heavenly Father, I'm thankful that I'm not where I used to be. You have begun a good work in me. Now, dear Lord, I submit myself to where You want me to go from here.

A Gentle Answer

A gentle answer deflects anger,
but harsh words make tempers flare.

PROVERBS 15:1

Unlike the bustling areas of Lancaster, Intercourse, and Bird-in-Hand, Somerset County, Pennsylvania, is a quiet place. It was especially quiet when a friend and I visited one Sunday morning. Only a few vehicles were on the road, and every house was still. I guessed it was a church Sunday and all the Amish families were gathered in a local home. Imagine my surprise when I noticed a cluster of buggies gathered around a meeting house! I didn't know that the Amish in this area held church services in meeting houses instead of in homes.

As we drove by, I imagined the Amish families sitting on wooden benches and raising their voices to hymns from the *Ausbund.* What a joyful moment that was for me, and it was even more special to share it with a friend. Only a few Amish communities have meeting houses.

A wholesome tongue is a tree of life.

PROVERB

One region where the Amish built meeting houses but kept the Old Order way of life in other respects was Somerset County, Pennsylvania. In 1880 and 1881 two districts voted favorably on having one meeting house. After the meeting house was built, the question remained as to what kind of seats to install. There was a difference of opinion: some thought backless benches were sufficient; others felt that the benches should have backs. During the week a few of the carpenters quickly but quietly built seats with backs and put them in the church. When the people arrived on Sunday an opponent said: "We have to do something." With a sense of humor the bishop replied: "*Ich denk sie hen uns gebodde*" ("I think they have beat us to it"). A division was avoided.

What a difference a soft (and humorous) answer made. It makes me consider how we use our own words. Today that meeting house still stands, and many gather there often to worship God. The right answer at the right time not only has an impact on our current situation, but it can also influence generations to come.

■ ■ ■

Dear heavenly Father, even now my harsh words—and the harsh words of others—come to mind. May Your Holy Spirit fill me today, empowering me to answer even unkind words with grace and love.

Chores

*She gets up before dawn to prepare breakfast for her household
and plan the day's work for her servant girls.*
PROVERBS 31:15

Sometimes it's the alarm that beeps first. Other times it's a baby's cry that splits the air, but there is never a time an Amish mother gets to sleep in. She's usually out at the barn by four o'clock, working by her husband's side. There's milking to be done, and if things go well, Mom's back in the kitchen in time to greet the children when they wake.

By four in the afternoon, after a full day of dishes, cooking, washing, cleaning, and sewing, it's back to the barn. In the winter it's nearly dark by then, and she takes a lantern for light, but in the spring and summer the sun is still bright, and the children can run and play near the barn as she milks. There are times when a fussy baby has to wait for attention. There are times when the weeds in the garden have to wait too. While large Amish dairy farms now bring in power equipment and refrigerated bulk tanks to meet safety standards, on small Amish farms, metal milk buckets and three-legged stools are still used.

Whatever happens, do not lose hold of the two main ropes of life—hope and faith.

PROVERB

I'm sure there are exceptions, but it often seems that those who work the hardest complain the least. Instead of moaning about their many chores, members of an Amish family roll up their sleeves and set to work.

Do you give the same dedication to what fills your day? God has given each of us unique roles. Some of us may be at home serving family. Others may work in a business. And still others may do both. Hard work helps us accomplish tasks, but our attitudes as we work are what draw others to God.

"Never be lazy, but work hard and serve the Lord enthusiastically," says Romans 12:11. Our work for God and others will always be a part of our lives. The question is *how* will we serve.

■ ■ ■

Dear heavenly Father, give me the strength to do even the smallest tasks well. Even more, give me a thankful heart so that I may work with joy!

Fed

He escorts me to the banquet hall; it's obvious how much he loves me.

SONG OF SONGS 2:4

What memories do you have of mealtimes when you were growing up? When I was younger, my family sat around the dinner table, but by the time I was school age, we usually ate in front of the television.

An Amish family gathers around the dining room or kitchen table, and everyone grows quiet. Before the food is served, Dad bows his head in silent prayer. After a minute, he clears his throat, signaling that the prayer is over. Only then are platters of meat or a casserole, potatoes, vegetables, and salad passed. Dinner isn't the only time Amish families gather for the meal. Whoever is home gathers in similar fashion for breakfast and lunch.

Everyone—children included—is expected to finish all the food on their plates. They are given enough to satisfy, and sometimes seconds are available. There is usually more eating than talking.

Many meals are served up in an Amish home, but one thing that's always served up is love. This reminds me of the banquet table we'll have in heaven someday. Matthew 8:11 talks about this very thing: "I tell you this, that many Gentiles will come from all over the world—from east and west—and sit down with Abraham, Isaac, and Jacob at the feast in the Kingdom of Heaven." In heaven we will have no physical need for food; we'll gather for fellowship and celebration.

In our busy world, coming together to eat is a reminder that our need is great. Gathering for a meal also reminds us that we're not alone. Tonight, when you gather with your family or with friends, express what it means to you to sit down with the people who fill your heart and life. And if you're single, then take time to meet for meals with others. It's around the table that our souls—as well as our bodies—are fed.

"A Pennsylvania Dutch saying is *Allemol as an Schof blatt, verliert's en Maulvoll.* Translated to English, it would be 'Every time a sheep bleats it loses a mouthful.' This is sometimes given as a reminder to talkative children."

■ ■ ■

Dear heavenly Father, I cannot wait for the day when I'm gathered with You and Your family around Your banquet table to celebrate and rejoice for eternity. Thank You for all Your provisions, Lord!

Music from the Heart

*If I could speak all the languages of earth and of angels, but didn't
love others, I would only be a noisy gong or a clanging cymbal.*
1 CORINTHIANS 13:1

You will never find a band or any sort of musical instrument inside an Amish church, and most likely not inside an Amish home, either. Some Amish have been known to play a harmonica or accordion, but it is not common practice. Brad Igou, author of *The Amish in Their Own Words*, says, "'Instrumental music tends to draw attention to itself through its natural beauty, distracts our thoughts from the meaning of the words we sing, and entertains us rather than glorifying God,' writes one Amish man. 'Also, instruments of music are an expensive luxury. Much money is wasted that could be put to better use.'"

In some Amish schools a song is sung before daily lessons begin.

There is another reason why the Amish don't play instruments. They believe that no one person should be set above the others. They believe that those who play instruments will be tempted toward pride.

During the years of Rumspringa, Amish youth might install stereo systems in their buggies—much to the disapproval of their parents. Teens may also have radios, stereos, cell phones, or iPods. Amish do hear popular music at stores and at other public locations, and they might enjoy (and even learn) the songs.

Amish church members are not allowed to listen to music. More than one female church member has had to go to the front of the church to confess to listening to music while cleaning house for the English.

Although we may never be so concerned about our freedom to listen to music, we do have to pay attention to the music's message and the words. As the Amish know, music can have a powerful influence. And as the apostle Paul wrote, if we act without love, our actions can be like clanging cymbals—senseless music.

If your life were a melody, how would it sound? People are tuning in and listening. For good or bad, they will hear the music coming from your heart.

■ ■ ■

Dear heavenly Father, music stirs my emotions. Help me to choose music that steers me toward faithfulness to You in all things.

Voices Lifted in Song

Don't let anyone think less of you because you are young. Be an example to all believers in what you say, in the way you live, in your love, your faith, and your purity.

1 TIMOTHY 4:12

When you were a young person, where did you go for fun or to meet other young people?

"Sings" or "singings" are Sunday evening gatherings attended by young people who are approaching marriageable age. These consist of an evening of hymn singing and are considered an acceptable part of Amish courtship. They are usually held in barns or homes, and the young participants chat between hymns.

Depending on the community, these Sunday night youth singings can have a positive or negative influence on young people. In some larger communities they are an excuse for teens to get together. As the night goes on, they turn into parties with alcohol. But in most Amish communities these are wholesome events for diligent young people to get to know each other. Some of these singings are chaperoned by adults, and snacks are served.

One of the goals of a youth singing is to spend time with other youth and to worship God together. Since youth above age fourteen don't attend school together during the week, they don't get to see each other on a regular basis. Another goal is to find a life partner.

Amish teens are expected to "go with the youth" and attend youth singings when they turn sixteen.

During the singings the Amish youth do not sing popular hymns. Instead they sing the same songs from the *Ausbund* that they sing at church, but they often sing them to a quicker tempo. They often sing other Christian hymns in English, but they never sing popular or secular songs.

Similar to adults, young people can choose either to follow God or to follow their own desires. When it comes to knowing God, age is not as important as maturity of heart. Remember this when it comes to the young people in your life. Be an example to them. Encourage them and support them in their wholesome efforts, but also watch them, and you might discover ways they can be examples to you.

■ ■ ■

Dear heavenly Father, I'm thankful that You are no respecter of age. Help me to grow in maturity at the pace You've set for me.

MAY 25

God Goes with You

May the LORD bless you and protect you. May the LORD smile on you and be gracious to you. May the LORD show you his favor and give you his peace.
NUMBERS 6:24-26

I was having dinner with an Amish couple who told me they'd taken a trip to Europe. They'd gone sightseeing and had a wonderful time. Since most communities don't allow members to use air travel except for medical emergencies, they went by ship instead—cruise ship.

"But we didn't partake of the luxuries," they quickly explained.

Many Amish live their whole lives within a few miles of where they were born, but that doesn't mean they don't travel and see the world. Since they speak Pennsylvania Dutch, a form of German, the Amish have a relatively easy time communicating in Germany and Switzerland, but their travel takes them all over the world.

Amish communities are the vacation destinations of millions of people each year. They visit each year to enjoy Amish baked goods, buggy rides, and even tours of Amish homes.

As the spring air warms with summer's approach, the Amish may consider summer vacations. While those who live and work on farms may need to stay close to home, others find this a perfect time to visit friends in other communities. Some Amish let their friends know they're coming, but sometimes they simply show up as surprise guests.

Vacations are a time to see the world and enjoy Christ's creation. How have you discovered God better when you've been away from your daily routine? Vacations often allow us to find peace. To settle our minds and bodies from work. To enjoy the company of family members and friends, and maybe meet new friends too.

When was the last time you went on vacation? Did you invite God on the journey? If you had been intentional about "inviting" God on that vacation, how might that have changed your itinerary?

God wants to be part of our everyday lives—and our special vacations, too. His peace, His grace, and His protection are with you wherever you go.

■ ■ ■

Dear heavenly Father, there are times when my mind mistakenly segments what things are "godly" and what things are "ordinary." I am thankful that You are with me wherever I go!

Strength under Control

Blessed are the meek, for they will inherit the earth.

MATTHEW 5:5 (NIV)

What do you think of when you hear the word *meek*? Do you picture someone frail, fearful, and timid? My husband, John, is one of the meekest people I know. He is tall, strong, intelligent, and wise. John is a former Marine, and his meekness has blessed me as we've parented our children together. In twenty-three years of marriage there have been many things that made John angry, but there have been very few times I've heard him raise his voice. Meekness is strength under control.

Meekness is not a character trait we hear much about. We hear more about assertiveness, optimism, and drive. Jesus was an example of meekness. In a time in history when the Romans ruled by domination, Jesus limited His power for our sakes. He wept over the lost. He gathered children around Him. And even Jesus' act of turning over the money changers' tables in the Temple was a sign of meekness. He could have called on a host of heavenly angels to destroy them instead.

Like any other people, the Amish are prone to anger and frustration, but their faith reins them in. Psalm 149:4 says, "The LORD taketh pleasure in his people: he will beautify the meek with salvation" (KJV).

Asking for help is not a sign of weakness but a sign of wisdom and maturity.

PROVERB

Meekness is required if we are to find salvation in Christ. We must acknowledge that God is holy and submit our human condition to His authority. We lay our egos on the altar and depend on God's strength instead of our own. The meek understand that the greatest weakness is losing control of their emotions and themselves.

Do you know someone who is meek? Take time to let that person know how much you appreciate this less-honored trait. And next time you're angry, instead of losing control, pray and ask God to help you. There are some things we should be angry about, yet with meekness a watching world will see us shine rather than sin.

■ ■ ■

Dear heavenly Father, thank You for giving Your Son as an example of infinite strength under control. Thank You, Lord, for all the times You've held back Your anger at things I've done wrong. Thank You for offering love when I don't deserve it.

Faith Journeys

The LORD had said to Abram, "Leave your native country, your relatives, and your father's family, and go to the land that I will show you."
GENESIS 12:1

When we think of "traveling across the plains" to start a new community, we think of pioneer settlers long ago. But it's not unusual today for the Amish to pack up everything, join with other families, and start new communities all over the United States.

With large Amish families there is only so much land to go around, and new farms are needed. Late spring is a good time to begin a journey to a new settlement. Families from Pennsylvania and Ohio move to places such as Kentucky, Florida, and Texas. Sometimes whole church districts pack up and move. Other times only one or two families go. But when a new Amish community is settled, other Amish from around the States soon join them.

One of the conflicts that may arise when Amish families move into a new town is the misconception that the Amish use city services but do not pay taxes.

When looking for a new community, they search for good farmland in a place that's not too crowded. For the most part the Amish are welcomed into a community, but one has to get used to watching out for horses and buggies, horse droppings on the road, and misconceptions about the Amish.

While there is a sense of adventure about these moves, there are also worries and questions. Like Abram, these families pack up and leave everything they know to follow God's desire for them. They leave behind a familiar place. They leave behind family, too—fathers and mothers, aunts and uncles, sons and daughters.

Sometimes faith calls us to do hard things. Hebrews 11:8 says, "It was by faith that Abraham obeyed when God called him to leave home and go to another land that God would give him as his inheritance. He went without knowing where he was going."

God went with Abraham, and He always goes with those who love and serve Him. No matter where we travel, we always have our heavenly Father as our traveling companion. Following God, wherever He may lead us, may take huge steps of faith, but He is our guide and our great reward!

■ ■ ■

Dear heavenly Father, the first step is always the hardest. Give me faith to follow where You ask me to go.

Faith Walks

Don't just listen to God's word. You must do what it says.
Otherwise, you are only fooling yourselves.

JAMES 1:22

In every community there are expectations. In my neighborhood it's expected that we keep our lawns mowed. It is expected that we wave when passing a neighbor on the street or chat for a few minutes when passing each other on a walk. The expectations are different in an Amish community. When a neighbor has a loss in the family, you show up with food and help with chores. When there is a hospital bill, the cost is split between all church members. And when a sermon is preached, the words aren't simply something you should ponder. Instead you must do your part to give and serve, to fast and pray.

Here is an English translation of an excerpt from an Amish prayer offered up after the sermon: "Beseech Thee, beloved and merciful Father, that Thou wouldst let Thy Word, which we have heard and received, be powerful and genuine in the heart of each one of us, and be fruitful, bearing fruit that remains until eternal life. May we through it be not only born again, but completely turned about, changed, and renewed."

The Amish do not keep phones in their houses, though some have phones in their barns.

Being born again is being in a state of acceptance with Jesus Christ. It is also a call to action. It would be foolish to an Amish person to accept the gift of salvation without acting upon it. Or, as we read in James 2:17, "Faith by itself isn't enough. Unless it produces good deeds, it is dead and useless." Amish people know that they are saved by grace alone, but they are also expected to act as those who are saved.

How do your actions prove your faith? Do you care for others differently because of the gift of eternal life God has given you? It's easy to hear God's Word, but it's much harder to do what it says. Yet when you do, your faith shines and people take notice!

■ ■ ■

Dear heavenly Father, I thank You for Your Word, and I thank You that Your love shines so clearly through people living out their faith. I long to do the same, walking and talking what my heart believes!

Ascension Day

When the Lord Jesus had finished talking with them, he was taken up into heaven and sat down in the place of honor at God's right hand.

MARK 16:19

The Amish don't celebrate many English holidays, but forty days after Easter, on the day before Pentecost, they celebrate Ascension Day, which remembers Christ's ascent into heaven. The morning is spent fasting, and during the afternoon families visit or perhaps fish together. It's a good time to pause from the bustle of spring planting and schoolwork to enjoy time together.

There is much meaning to be found in the understanding that Jesus reigns with God in heaven. The following translation of an Amish Ascension prayer gives evidence of that:

"Apart from twice-a-year collections at communion, the deacon or other appointed men may visit each home to solicit voluntary contributions when special financial needs arise."

Oh, Lord Jesus Christ, Thou majestic Victor and almighty victorious Prince, allow me to praise Thy joyful ascension, let me glorify Thy blessed ascent—for now all our enemies are conquered, because Thou has risen on high and hast led captivity captive—who would not sing praises about this? For now neither the world nor hellish Satan, neither hell nor death, shall be able to triumph over us, because Thou hast made an open display of them and hast made a triumph of (over) them—who would not wish to extol (exalt) this?

Although we know that one day we will be in heaven with God, it's easy to forget what God has already done for us now. He is victorious. He has triumphed and will triumph at the end of time. Just as the disciples lifted their eyes to watch Jesus ascend into the clouds, today let us lift our gaze to Him in awe of what He has already done.

■ ■ ■

Dear heavenly Father, I lift my eyes to You. I thank You that You reign for eternity and that You are always watching out for me. I extol You, Lord, for all You've done!

A New Song

He has given me a new song to sing, a hymn of praise to our God. Many will
see what he has done and be amazed. They will put their trust in the LORD.

PSALM 40:3

Song leading is a tradition in Amish churches. The ancient hymns are part of tradition, and they are simple and humble. There is something special about singing with a hundred others in a full house, voices lifted to God. And there is a specific style of leading and singing in Amish churches: "When it is time to sing a song, a couple of the older men announce the song to sing by its page number in the *Ausbund* and who is to lead the song. So, the 'Loblied' is announced as 770, instead of 'Loblied' or 131. . . . When the Amish sing a song, the leader sings the first syllable of the line, the rest join in on the second syllable. The last syllable of a line is much shorter than the rest."

I've heard from some Amish friends that because of the long, drawn-out syllables in singing, being worshipful takes work. It's easy to miss the words when one is focused on the sounds. It's hard to focus on the message when one is focused on the individual words. It takes a prepared heart and listening ears to discover treasure in musical tradition.

No joy is complete unless it is shared.

PROVERB

Have you been only going through the motions in your faith lately? Have words of hope and life become dull syllables in your ear? Ask God to put a new song in your heart. Have you ever experienced one? Maybe you've been singing along to a familiar hymn, and then suddenly the words hit you, touching your heart in a powerful way. Or maybe a familiar verse unexpectedly stirs your praise.

Ask God to give you a fresh sense of awe in every aspect of your life. Every song we sing—even those that are hundreds of years old—can be a new song from our mouths.

■ ■ ■

Dear heavenly Father, may all that's old to me become new as Your Spirit flows through me. May a new song fill my heart and flow from my lips.

MAY 31

Beautiful Seasons

God has made everything beautiful for its own time. He has
planted eternity in the human heart, but even so, people cannot
see the whole scope of God's work from beginning to end.
ECCLESIASTES 3:11

When a young man or woman decides to join the Amish church, he or she usually does so with a group of other young people. Once the bishop is informed of those desiring membership, instruction classes begin. The classes teach the foundations and Scriptures of their faith. Lessons begin in late spring and continue through the summer.

Baptism is an outward sign of an inward conviction to believe in the Lord Jesus Christ and to join the church. There comes a point in each of our lives when we must make the decision about Christ for ourselves. In the Amish church seasons come and seasons go, but with the coming of late spring, mothers and fathers pray that their young adult children will choose to do so *this* season.

There is no beauty without purpose.

PROVERB

The questions "Why do bad things happen to good people?" and "What happens after we die?" show that our souls yearn to know God, yearn for His redemption of ourselves and of this dying world. Job 5:9 says, "[God] does great things too marvelous to understand. He performs countless miracles." Out of all of creation—the seas and skies, the fields and creatures—the most beautiful miracle is when humans, born into sin, choose God—choose to give up their own lives for God's life and their own wills for God's will.

How is God working in your life? It may be hard to see now, but if you've chosen to follow Jesus Christ, He has a good plan. Where is the beauty in your life? It may be outside the window as spring blooms. It may also be inside your heart, as hope blooms.

What choice is God asking you to make today? Do you need to find more instruction in the Scriptures? Do you need to join with friends to seek God together? God will be waiting for the moment you take another step toward Him.

■ ■ ■

Dear heavenly Father, thank You for putting eternity on my heart, and thank You for creating something beautiful in my life. Your work from beginning to end amazes me!

Boys Will Be Boys

There's a young boy here with five barley loaves and two
fish. But what good is that with this huge crowd?

JOHN 6:9

A horse-drawn wagon rolls by with three boys sitting on the bench seat. They're wearing homemade clothes and wide-brimmed straw hats. Fishing poles of various lengths stick out the back of the wagon. This scene could have happened two hundred years ago, one hundred, fifty, but in Amish communities all over the United States it's commonplace today. For Amish boys, summer means helping Dad, fishing, doing chores, climbing trees, and lying under apple trees when the work is done.

"Boys will be boys," people say, but Amish boys are different from English boys today. Amish boys do not have video games, and every person in an Amish family, including the children, is considered a productive member. Before an Amish boy can head to the fishing hole, there are chores to be done. Morning chores include making beds, feeding farm animals, and collecting eggs. Amish boys learn how to use farm equipment and tools.

In the evening, after the chores are done, Amish boys will spend time making wooden toys, playing board games, or sitting on the porch. Because the sun is in the sky longer, Amish children stay up later in the summer. In the winter months bedtime comes soon after dark because the Amish rely on lantern light instead of electricity. Since Amish children go to school only through eighth grade and then join the workforce, they tend to savor childhood.

Similar to the young boy who offered his basket of lunch to Jesus' disciples, Amish boys are asked to give only one thing—whatever they have available.

What do you expect from the boys in your life? Do you expect them to be trouble or to be helpful? Do you expect them to be draining or productive? Or all of the above? Children tend to live up to our expectations.

Today encourage a boy in your life to "give what he has." As you do, you'll help prepare him to serve his family and God.

"Safety games are played in order for the children to learn how to safely live on a farm. . . . With large equipment moving and farm animals roaming around, Amish children need to learn early how not to get hurt. These safety games are an important part of life in an Amish community."

■ ■ ■

Dear heavenly Father, thank You for Your work in the boys in my life. Thank You for asking us to give only what we have.

Sweet Fragrances

The Holy Spirit produces this kind of fruit in our lives: love, joy,
peace, patience, kindness, goodness, faithfulness, gentleness,
and self-control. There is no law against these things!
GALATIANS 5:22-23

The sweet whiff of an apple orchard is enough to take some of us back to our childhood summer days. Numerous Amish families have apple orchards. Hillcrest Orchard, in Sugarcreek, Ohio, is one. They have fifty acres of apple and peach trees, and you'll also find other fresh produce, including squash and pumpkins as well as honey, maple syrup, jams, and jellies.

Ohio produces around forty varieties of apples. The apples grow during the summer and are ripe and ready to pick at different times, from the end of August to the end of September. Some apples are sweet and others are tart. Some are best for baking, and all are delicious right from the tree.

In addition to apple pies, Amish women make apple cider, apple rolls, apple dumplings, apple butter, apple doughnuts, and numerous other treats.

It would be foolish to believe that an apple could grow out of the ground without being part of a tree. But we often expect to be loving, joyful, peaceful, patient, kind, etc., in our own effort, and then have little success. Just as an apple tree produces apples, it's the Holy Spirit who produces spiritual fruit in our lives. And just as there are many different varieties of apples, the fruit we produce is different—unique to each of us.

Amish apple orchards fill summer nights with a sweet fragrance, and the fruit that is produced by the Holy Spirit in our lives does the same. Second Corinthians 2:14-15 says, "Thank God! He has made us his captives and continues to lead us along in Christ's triumphal procession. Now he uses us to spread the knowledge of Christ everywhere, like a sweet perfume. Our lives are a Christ-like fragrance rising up to God."

Do you have a desire to seek God and ask for more of His Spirit? As you do, the fruit that is produced will be fragrant and beautiful to those around you. Sometimes we try to act better and then don't get far with our efforts. But God-in-us will produce more and better fruit than we have ever dreamed.

■ ■ ■

Dear heavenly Father, fill me so that the fruit of love, joy, peace, patience, kindness,
goodness, faithfulness, gentleness, and self-control grow in my life!

Daily Strength

*LORD, be gracious to us; we long for you. Be our strength
every morning, our salvation in time of distress.*

ISAIAH 33:2 (NIV)

One iconic symbol of an Amish community is the clothesline hung with dresses, shirts, and pants fluttering in the breeze. In winter months it takes longer for laundry to dry indoors. In the summer months it can be washed, dried, folded or ironed, and put away in a single day.

The fact that the Amish believe in simple living doesn't mean they do their laundry in the creek. Most Amish housewives use wringer washers that were popular post–World War II. These are power washers, but since the Amish do not get their electrical power from public services, they are usually hooked up to a generator. Once washed, "spinners" remove most of the excess water before the clothes are hung to dry.

Can you imagine how long it takes to do laundry when you have seven, ten, fourteen, or more children? All the folding and ironing and putting it away only to have it get dirty again! Of course, there are always little ones who "help" by wrapping clean socks and underwear around their heads.

> A woman's work
> is not seen unless
> it's not done.
>
> PROVERB

The thing about most household tasks is that they are so *daily*. They seem never-ending. They aren't projects we can mark off our lists and say, "Done." The same thing is true about seeking God's strength. We can't fill up once a month or once a week; we must turn to Him every day for more: "God's desire is for us to encounter His Word truth by truth until there isn't a folded piece left," writes author Jen Hatmaker. "He wants to find us covered in Scripture and loving every minute of it."

"I am counting on the LORD; yes, I am counting on him. I have put my hope in his word," reads Psalm 130:5. Just as you can count on laundry always being there, you can count on God's showing up to help you with every task you face.

■ ■ ■

Dear heavenly Father, even though my daily tasks never end, I'm thankful that You are always there to provide strength. I am counting on You today, Lord.

The Gift(s) of Children .

Children are a gift from the LORD; they are a reward from him.

PSALM 127:3

Many Amish mothers look forward to summer. In the evenings there is no homework. In the mornings there isn't the hustle and bustle of getting the children up and ready for school. The children can spend the day at play and spend longer nights staying up, playing games, and watching the stars.

According to *The Amish Cook at Home*, "Play mirrors reality for many Amish children. Games that imitate real-life situations like 'school' or 'farmer' are a fun way that Amish children prepare for adult life." You'll often see Amish children playing with wooden farm animals, playing "tractor," or playing house with dolls. They play the same sports that other children do, but games like baseball and soccer are often played noncompetitively. The goal is to play for exercise and fun.

Age is a question of mind over matter. If you don't mind, it doesn't matter.

PROVERB

It made me smile to discover that Amish children aren't very different from other children. My children, too, often model what they see. They don't model driving a tractor or farm play. Instead, they model talking on a phone and slipping a casserole dish into the microwave—a little different!

I often see myself better when I see my child following suit. How I act, what I say, and what I believe are displayed in the little ones who fill my days. When I get frustrated with my daughter's childishness, God often points out mine. When I see my son's lack of trust, God reminds me how I fret too. Children are gifts. They are gifts of laughter. They are gifts reminding us that we need to take time to play. They are gifts that allow us to see the world in new ways. As our children play around us, preparing for adult life, we can use what we see to discover more about ourselves.

Do you have a moment to spend some time playing with little ones? Do it. You may be surprised how much you'll learn.

■ ■ ■

Dear heavenly Father, sometimes You use the simplest moments to change me the most. Thank You for the gift of children, and thank You for the gifts they provide me.

No Easy Solutions

Anyone who listens to my teaching and follows it is wise,
like a person who builds a house on solid rock.

MATTHEW 7:24

Can you imagine a hot, muggy day in an Amish home, where there is no air-conditioning?

Because Amish don't choose to accept the luxury of electricity, traditional air-conditioning is simply not an option. One way to keep the house cool is to build their homes with basements that are built into the bank of the hill, at least as much as possible. The soil around the basement is cooler than the air temperature and helps insulate the basement, keeping it cooler in the summer and warmer in the winter.

In old farmhouses particularly, Amish will "move into the basement" during the summer. They even equip the basements with kitchens so they don't even need to cook upstairs. The extra kitchen also comes in handy when they host church and hold weddings where they need to feed many people. The floors are concrete, both for easy cleaning and because they feel cool on bare feet!

The world has too many cranks and not enough self-starters.

PROVERB

This makes me consider how often I fall back on an "easy solution" because I didn't put in enough time preparing. When five o'clock rolls around and I don't have dinner plans, I order pizza. When I wake up late and don't have time to read my Bible and pray, I make plans to read and pray later. In fact, much of my life happens haphazardly because I didn't take time to plan.

If you have easy solutions, are they hurting you in the long run? It's probably too late to draw up house plans so your house will be more energy efficient, but are there other areas of your life that you can revise? Ask God to show you parts of your life that you can run more effectively. Read God's Word. His guidance can impact all areas of your life. Then even when storms—or the blazing heat of summer—come, you'll have a plan in place. You'll have a solid rock to stand on.

■ ■ ■

Dear heavenly Father, I know that waiting until the last minute doesn't give me peace in my heart, nor does it give me time to read Your Word and hear from You. Help me to sit and learn, to listen and wait.

JUNE 6

Special Moments

You must commit yourselves wholeheartedly to these commands that
I am giving you today. Repeat them again and again to your children.
Talk about them when you are at home and when you are on the
road, when you are going to bed and when you are getting up.
DEUTERONOMY 6:6-7

Do you have a favorite family vacation memory? Author Suzanne Woods Fisher writes:

Mine was at Pine Island at Lake Winnipesaukee, New Hampshire, where my family would stay in a rickety old cottage for a week or two. It was back-to-the-basics kind of living, small and simple, but I have such fond memories of those vacations. I can still get a whiff of a certain tree and I am transported back to the lake as a ten-year-old with perpetually skinned knees.

If you want to feel rich, just count the blessings that money can't buy.

PROVERB

My very favorite memory was a rainy night when my entire family was in the living room at the cottage, reading or playing a game of checkers or stroking the dog. I'll never forget the buttery glow of the lamp light and the sound of the rain on the roof. It was that rare for my entire family to be together, relaxed. No place to go, no phone ringing, no pressures.

The thing we often like about family vacations is togetherness, but it's not necessary to wait for family vacations! Turn off the television and clear off your schedule (and ask family members to clear off theirs). Then eat a simple meal together and share what God has been doing in your life. We usually make family time around "events," but there is nothing wrong with making time for one another in the middle of every day, as the Amish do—when we sit, when we rise, when we're getting up, or when we're on the road.

How can you create a special memory for your family today? Who knows? The simple, special moment you create may become one of their favorite memories and one that will last for a lifetime.

■ ■ ■

Dear heavenly Father, I thank You for the family You've given me. Help me not take this for granted. Guide me as I share You with my family in the everyday moments and in the special ones too.

Step Away to Step Toward

You're cheating on God. If all you want is your own way, flirting with the world
every chance you get, you end up enemies of God and his way. And do you suppose
God doesn't care? The proverb has it that "he's a fiercely jealous lover." And what
he gives in love is far better than anything else you'll find. It's common knowledge
that "God goes against the willful proud; God gives grace to the willing humble."

JAMES 4:4-6 (*THE MESSAGE*)

In 1972, the United States Supreme Court ruled that the Amish could not be forced to attend public high schools and sanctioned the Amish system of one-room schoolhouses. The Amish feel this is important because bookwork is only half of the learning that is needed for life.

During the school years Amish youth also spend time on the farm, and after the eighth grade young men learn a trade, while young women learn to care for a home. To the outside world the Amish are sheltered—in their homes and in their one-room schoolhouses. We only think they're "missing out" because we put value on other things, such as knowledge, possessions, and life experiences.

Some Amish have three to four generations living under one roof.

In truth we appreciate what we *learn* to value, and the more we put up boundaries between the world and ourselves, the more we appreciate the simple things in life. The further we walk away from what the world has to offer, the less we miss it.

Sometimes we may wish we could become Amish to shelter our children, but each of us can be more diligent about blocking outside influences. Even though we're careful, we can be more careful. Even though we watch our tongues to keep from saying wrong things, we must also remember to speak life and hope to our children.

The more you strive to set yourself apart, the more joy you'll find. Matthew 5:6 says, "God blesses those who hunger and thirst for justice, for they will be satisfied." What could be more worthwhile than that in saying "back off" to the world?

■ ■ ■

Dear heavenly Father, sometimes I forget that You are a jealous God and that You care when I'm flirting with the desire for pride, possessions, and power. Help me to step away from those things because that will mean I'm stepping toward You.

Eyes Fixed Ahead

*[Jesus said,] "Anyone who puts a hand to the plow and then
looks back is not fit for the Kingdom of God."*

LUKE 9:62

I once spent time mentoring a young woman who at age eighteen was living with her boyfriend and had two children when God transformed her life. She and her boyfriend got married, and the next day they attended church and dedicated their lives to the Lord. They've never looked back. Nearly nine years have passed, and they are active in church. They also reach out to other young parents. They know what it's like to be lost—and to be found. They are working on earth to share the Good News while also trusting their lives—and their eternities—to God.

Many Amish farms are now uniting in cooperatives with other Amish and conservative Mennonite farms to engage customers. The goal is for the Amish to continue to work on small farms yet join together to make a profit.

If you've ever visited an Amish community, you may have seen farmers preparing the soil for sowing seed. They still plow behind a team of horses and mules. This is not an easy task. It takes focus, perseverance, and manpower in addition to horse power. To obtain a straight row, one must fix his gaze on a distant object and keep looking ahead.

Jesus knew that to be His followers, we could not continue forward as His disciples while looking back to our old religious practices and ways of life. The apostle Paul spoke of the same thing: "No, dear brothers and sisters, I have not achieved it, but I focus on this one thing: Forgetting the past and looking forward to what lies ahead, I press on to reach the end of the race and receive the heavenly prize for which God, through Christ Jesus, is calling us" (Philippians 3:13-14).

Keeping our gaze fixed ahead is not easy. There is nothing sensational or awe-inspiring about the simple steps of daily faithfulness—at least not to us. We want fireworks and dazzle, but God desires simple, daily, obedient steps. We want to rush ahead, but God longs to lead us one step at a time. Desires to lead *you* one step at a time. Will you follow Him?

■ ■ ■

Dear heavenly Father, thank You for Your transforming power. Help me to fix my gaze ahead and never look back.

One in Purpose and Speech

On the day of Pentecost all the believers were meeting together in one place. Suddenly, there was a sound from heaven like the roaring of a mighty windstorm, and it filled the house where they were sitting.

ACTS 2:1-2

Just as the Amish celebrate Easter Monday, they also set aside Pentecost Monday (Whit Monday) as a time for family togetherness or family visiting. The observation of Pentecost, when the Holy Spirit descended on the believers ten days after Jesus' ascension, comes the seventh Sunday after Easter. On Pentecost, 120 of Jesus' disciples received the Holy Spirit. They had gathered together and waited on God, and the Holy Spirit came to them and worked through them powerfully. Experiencing the Holy Spirit in our lives isn't just something that happened two thousand years ago but something that can have an impact on our lives today.

Acts 5:32 says, "We are witnesses of these things and so is the Holy Spirit, who is given by God to those who obey him." How did the disciples obey? They came together, and they waited in humility.

Thousands of years before Pentecost another group of people gathered. Genesis speaks about the tower of Babel. "They said, 'Come, let's build a great city for ourselves with a tower that reaches into the sky. This will make us famous and keep us from being scattered all over the world'" (Genesis 11:4).

In Genesis, the men and women sought their own fame. In Acts, they waited in unity and in obedience to God. In Genesis, the language was confused and the people were scattered. In Acts, they joined together, they could understand each other, and the world was changed.

Can you plan a time for family visiting soon? Do you have an opportunity to gather with others to seek God? If not, can you make one? When you do, God will be lifted up, and His Holy Spirit will bring you and others together and help you understand one another in new ways!

Historically the "every other week" worship service was established so the Amish could attend church services in other districts too. This gave families opportunities to connect with others beyond their district.

■ ■ ■

Dear heavenly Father, show me ways that I can join with others to lift You up. May humility—not pride—guide my conversation whenever I gather with those You love.

More God, Fewer Things

Instruct those who are rich in this present world not to be
conceited or to fix their hope on the uncertainty of riches,
but on God, who richly supplies us with all things to enjoy.
1 TIMOTHY 6:17 (NASB)

We read about the lives of the rich and famous. We watch television programs that take us on guided tours of their homes. We also watch as they move from partner to partner, struggle with addictions, and spiral downward as they battle all types of personal demons. Money doesn't bring happiness.

Where do true riches come from? The Amish probably have fewer material things than most people.

No house without a mouse, no barn without corn, no rose without a thorn.

PROVERB

Those who have money too often put their faith in this world, in things, and in looking outward in an attempt to solve what's inward. They are robbed of trusting Jesus and finding peace in Him alone. They stockpile what won't last and miss out on what will last forever. In the words of Jesus, "Beware! Guard against every kind of greed. Life is not measured by how much you own" (Luke 12:15). Those of us who have accumulated things soon discover that the things we think we own begin to own us as we dust them, manage them, sort them, store them, and sometimes insure them.

If we have only God, we have everything, but with each thing we purchase, it becomes easy to feel that we need God less. Getting a few of our "wants" is fine, but, like the Amish, our focus should always be on the deeper gifts God gives us: our church families, our friends, our homes, and our talents.

As today's verse reminds us, it's God "who richly supplies us with all things to enjoy." True enjoyment comes from Him alone, no matter what marketing people and retailers say. Do you want to be happy? You won't find happiness chasing what the world offers. Do you want to be joyful? Look to God, pay attention to what He values, and stock up on those things.

If you were to look inwardly and outwardly, where would you say you are placing your dependence? Are you guarding your heart against every kind of greed? If not, today is a good day to start!

■ ■ ■

Dear heavenly Father, if I spent less time managing "stuff," I'd have more time for You.
And when I spend more time with You, I'll need less stuff. Fill my heart-hunger, O God!

Open Hands, Open Heart

*Do not withhold good from those who deserve it when it's in
your power to help them. If you can help your neighbor now,
don't say, "Come back tomorrow, and then I'll help you."*

PROVERBS 3:27-28

I know an Amish couple whose infant son was having seizures after birth. He was hospitalized for many weeks, yet the couple did not worry about medical bills. They knew that all their needs would be cared for because the Amish believe—and live—mutual care for each other.

In Lancaster, Pennsylvania, there is a local organization called the Amish Aid Society. This organization of the Old Order Amish and Mennonites has been assisting Plain communities since 1890. When one member of the Amish community has a bill, the cost is split between all members. In fact, the concept of informal hospitalization insurance exists in all Amish communities. This makes me consider *my* expectations for giving and receiving within my own neighborhood.

When I first moved to Little Rock and started working with teenage mothers, I was overwhelmed with their needs for advice, for clothing items for their babies, for diapers, and for food. Although it took me time and money, over time I found community resources and other ways to help them.

> The grand essentials of happiness in this life are something to do, something to love, and something to hope for.
>
> PROVERB

Sharing doesn't come naturally. Just ask any mother of a toddler. Yet God is glorified when we give . . . not just live our own, independent lives. Unlike the Amish, most of us don't live in communities where our money is pooled to take care of each other's needs, but that shouldn't stop us from doing what we can on our own.

When it comes to giving, there are two godly principles to consider. First, what can I give? Second, what can I give *today*? Often we have good intentions of giving, but time slips away from us. "Whenever we have the opportunity, we should do good to everyone—especially to those in the family of faith," reads Galatians 6:10. I love that word *whenever*.

Who do you know in need? Open your hands, open your heart today. *You* can be an answered prayer for someone in need.

■ ■ ■

Dear heavenly Father, stir my heart concerning the need of a special person today, and may I give cheerfully.

165

Limitless

How precious is your unfailing love, O God! All humanity finds shelter
in the shadow of your wings. You feed them from the abundance of
your own house, letting them drink from your river of delights.
PSALM 36:7-8

We live in a world of limits. There are limits to how much we can do, how much we can bear, and how far we can go. We can be only so patient, so understanding, and so strong. And depending on who we are, those limits vary. I can drive three hundred miles a day, but an Amish friend may be limited to ten miles with a horse and buggy. In the Amish community, limits enforce and support values. Home is valued—so stay close. Contemplation and quietness are valued—so go slow.

Don't brag; it isn't the whistle that pulls the train.

PROVERB

The problem comes when we apply our view of limits to our view of God: God can love only "this type" of people. God can forgive only "these types" of sins. God cannot tolerate "that type" of lifestyle—a busy, fast-paced, modern one. Or, God must be displeased by those who live with so many rules and laws.

Yet God is not affected by our view of limits. Nor is He limited by anything. Psalm 145:3 says, "Great is the LORD! He is most worthy of praise! No one can measure his greatness." Psalms such as this one remind us how great God is, yet mere words cannot fully describe His love and faithfulness, righteousness and judgment.

Think about the limits you've set up. They may be for your protection and safety, but maybe they're rigid walls that need to be taken down. Ask God's Spirit to show you what adjustments you need to make.

Limits help us conform, but may we never be more concerned about keeping within them—or with stretching them—than we are concerned about dwelling with our limitless God.

■ ■ ■

Dear heavenly Father, my mind cannot grasp Your greatness, and my words cannot explain Your glory. Remove any unhealthy limits I've placed around myself. Build up any healthy limits I need to set. But mostly, fill me with the joyful knowledge of Your limitlessness!

A Heart of Obedience

Because of [God's] glory and excellence, he has given us great and precious
promises. These are the promises that enable you to share his divine
nature and escape the world's corruption caused by human desires.

2 PETER 1:4

I remember standing before my mother with tears welling up in my eyes. "Don't you trust me?" I asked. I wanted to take the car to the football game. She was afraid I was going to stay out too late and drive friends around. At my question, my mom handed over the keys. She told me she did trust me, but she wanted me to obey. Even as I took the keys, plans for *dis*obedience filled my mind.

Amish church members are taught to humbly obey those with authority over them. Children obey parents, students obey teachers, wives their husbands, and members their leaders. Even younger ministers learn to humbly obey their bishops. This obedience is based on trust. Both the ones giving the rules and the ones accepting them must trust one another. When I didn't obey my mother, it was because I placed more value on having fun with friends than on my mom's desire for me to stay safe. It seems as if I often do the same with God. I disobey Him because I believe what I want for myself will be a greater benefit for me than what He wants. I'm usually looking at temporary satisfaction while God has a bigger picture in mind.

Though branches and leaves make a beautiful tree, our lives will be known by the fruit people see.

PROVERB

A truly obedient heart comes from trusting in the promises—whether spoken or unspoken—of another person. Children trust that their parents have their good in mind. Students trust their teacher's directives. A wife trusts that her husband is guiding her in a loving and godly manner. Amish ministers understand that their bishops must stand before God.

Do you struggle with obedience? Do you obey with your actions but not with your heart? Take your struggles before God. One of His good and precious promises is that He'll be there for you, loving you, guiding you, and sharing His divine nature along the way.

■ ■ ■

Dear heavenly Father, obedience is hard for me. Most of the time I feel as if I know best. May Your good and precious promises transform my heart so that my obedience to You is a joy rather than a chore!

Taking Sin Seriously

*The Lord isn't really being slow about his promise, as some people
think. No, he is being patient for your sake. He does not want
anyone to be destroyed, but wants everyone to repent.*

2 PETER 3:9

How seriously do you take God and His statements of both promise and warning?
God sets standards, but we often become slack at following them. God warns what
will happen if we choose to walk away from His path, but we treat the warnings as
"suggestions" instead. The Amish, on the other hand, do not treat those who fall from
their standards lightly.

**Even a humble
man of God has the
potential to become
proud and to rebel
against the Lord.**

PROVERB

Although the Amish community is reluctant to use legal
or political force against those who violate Amish practices, they do excommunicate or shun transgressors. Based
upon religious scriptures, the Amish believe that members
who openly sin against traditional church doctrines must
be purged from the church as a warning and safeguard to
maintain the purity of the church.

Members who are excommunicated and shunned
are avoided by active members in all social and business
activities. However, the offenders are always welcomed
back to the community if they repent.

Shunning is considered a way of protecting faithful members. To continue in a
close relationship with someone not living by Amish standards risks becoming defiled
by the person's sin. Within the Amish community if a member refuses to shun the
offending individuals, he or she risks excommunication. That means friends must
shun friends, and parents must shun children. Shunning doesn't mean total avoidance
but rather restricted interaction. At family gatherings a shunned individual eats at a
different table.

While we might not adhere to the practice of shunning in our own lives, how we
treat sin matters. God desires repentance. He is patient with us, but our time on earth
will come to an end. Then we must stand before Him and answer for the story we
wrote with our lives. May our stories speak most of His grace and goodness! May we
be quick to repent of every offense.

■ ■ ■

*Dear heavenly Father, thank You for Your patience. I trust in that. Thank You that I can
also repent and come back to You, and You'll never turn me away.*

A Father's Love

The LORD *disciplines those he loves, and he punishes each one he accepts as his child.*

HEBREWS 12:6

I once read the memoir of a woman who had an incredible, loving, sacrificing, giving father. I wept on every page—for two reasons. I cried because that wasn't what I experienced growing up and I still don't have that type of relationship. I also wept because seeing a living, breathing example of the care a father can provide to his daughter made me understand God better.

This time of year there are greeting cards and television commercials that show images of fathers spending time with their children: roasting hot dogs and marshmallows, playing catch in the yard, or sitting side by side on the couch watching the big game. If there were a greeting card for an Amish father, it might show father and son tilling a field, or father and daughter pitching hay together. But whether he's Amish or English, the greatest gift a father can give his children is time and attention. These are the gifts children remember most. They go straight to the heart. If you have a father who spends time with you, consider him one of your greatest gifts in life.

> A wooden spoon compels even the strangest of ingredients to get their acts together.
>
> PROVERB

An additional gift you might not expect is discipline. In an Amish home, parents stress obedience and submission. These characteristics are instilled at a young age. Most Amish use spanking and corporal punishment to teach good behavior: "Amish recognize the importance of proper discipline to their children's future development. Yet it is generally recognized that spanking should not be done in anger, but out of love with the goal of teaching the child."

When it comes to giving time and attention to our children, it's not just the Hallmark moments that will last a lifetime. The character-building moments do too. The time and attention we give to providing our children with discipline will shape their lives through all their years. This, too, is a beautiful, loving thing.

• • •

Dear heavenly Father, thank You for Your love, Your attention, and Your discipline. Thank You for being a loving Father I can always count on. Thank You for all the loving fathers in our lives.

Out of the Mouths of Babes

They asked Jesus, "Do you hear what these children are saying?"
"Yes," Jesus replied. "Haven't you ever read the Scriptures? For they
say, 'You have taught children and infants to give you praise.'"
MATTHEW 21:16

When one of my children was two, she often sang about the itsy-bitsy spider and other animal antics. She enjoyed Bible songs, too, and I found that was a great way to introduce her to the goodness of God throughout the day. The more she sang, the more she learned about God. And the more she learned about God, the more she would sing! "In der Stillen Einsamkeit" is a children's song in Pennsylvania Dutch. Here are the words in English:

In the still isolation
You find my praise ready
Greatest God answer me
For my heart is seeking you.
You're always here
Never still though silent
You rule the yearly seasons
And you set them in order.

This cold winter air
Calls with mighty feeling.
See what a mighty Lord,

Summer and Winter He makes. My favorite part of this song are the words "You find my praise ready." Is your praise ready? Do you wake up with a song of praise on your lips? Do you tune into hymns or praise music throughout the day and find yourself singing along?

Nancy Lee DeMoss writes, "Gratitude is learning to recognize and express appreciation for the benefits we have received from God and from others." Our praise is ready when we take note of our benefits. When we consider that it is God who rules the seasons. And when we sing from the joy building within!

Children and infants give God praise because nothing they have is achieved by their own efforts. May we realize the same. And as we do, may we lift our voices in praise.

■ ■ ■

Dear heavenly Father, I am thankful—help me to be more thankful. And like a child, may
I lift my voice in praise and gratitude to You!

Be My Disciple

Jesus said to the people who believed in him, "You are truly
my disciples if you remain faithful to my teachings. And you
will know the truth, and the truth will set you free."

JOHN 8:31-32

What does it mean to be a disciple of Christ? It means to believe what He says, to trust in His Son Jesus, to accept His presence, and to follow His way. To be a disciple takes discipline. It means no matter how old you are, you're still a pupil and, like the Amish, still passing on what you believe. Author Steven Nolt writes,

With their rejection of automobile ownership, public utility electricity, and the fads and fashions of Madison Avenue, they annually attract countless tourists and academics who see in Old Order people everything from images of nostalgic conservatism to icons of postmodern environmentalism. Yet the Amish are really none of these things. They are not timeless figures frozen in the past, nor the poster-children of political activists. Taken on their own terms, the Old Order Amish are a living, dynamic church—a committed Christian community whose members have taken seriously the task of discipleship and group witness.

"Shunning, or *meidung,* means expulsion from the Amish community for breaching religious guidelines—including marrying outside the faith."

How seriously do you take discipleship? Do you consider yourself to be a pupil of Christ? The purpose of discipleship is to replicate the one you are following. It's to embrace truth in order to share it. The Amish live within the confines of their community, and as Christians we live within the confines of what can seem like "rules and laws." Yet when we choose to follow God's way, we discover unexplainable freedom. We can live pure lives, and we are free from guilt, shame, and painful consequences. And when we live with frugality and simplicity, we can get free of debt and clutter.

Discipline takes commitment and focus, but the reward is freedom and right living. Only a good God could come up with something as balanced and wonderful as that.

■ ■ ■

Dear heavenly Father, the more I follow, the more I walk in freedom. Thank You for not leaving me alone but for allowing me to follow in Your steps and be filled with Yourself for the journey.

Believers' Baptism

Go and make disciples of all the nations, baptizing them in the name of the Father and the Son and the Holy Spirit.
MATTHEW 28:19

In the fifteenth century, Europe had essentially one church. During this time the church baptized infants, thus making every baptized citizen a member of the church, regardless of his or her interest or commitment. In 1524 in Zurich, a new movement arose, initiated by a group of people who desired a radical return to New Testament beliefs:

"It might seem hard to believe but it is because of such divergent concepts such as adult baptism that led the Anabaptists to suffer severe persecution. . . . During the 16th and 17th centuries in Europe, adult baptism became a criminal offense punishable by death."

For them the church was a community of Christians voluntarily committed to imitating Christ and to each other. Baptism—the sign of church membership and commitment—was only for adults or those old enough to choose the path of discipleship. The state could have no part in controlling or directing the activities and doctrines of the church. The church must be free of government control.

From these first "free church" radicals Anabaptism was born. The name *Anabaptist* means "rebaptized" or "twice baptized," since the first Anabaptists had already been baptized as infants under the Roman Catholic Church and then later were rebaptized as confessing adults. Both Mennonites and Amish branched off into their own Anabaptist groups. Today adult baptism is still one of the most important principles of the Amish religion.

Baptism is a step of faith. It's an outward symbol of an inward choice. Baptism isn't something to be taken lightly. It's letting others know of our life change, and it's a symbol of the change in our eternal status.

If you have trusted Jesus, have you been baptized? If not, consider taking this step of obedience to Christ. Talk to a pastor in your local church. If you have been baptized, what does it mean to you to follow Jesus' command to make disciples of all nations? How can following Jesus in this command bring peace to yourself and to others?

■ ■ ■

Dear heavenly Father, thank You for those believers who have taken a stand for You. Help me to do the same and to share Your truth with new generations.

Good News Scattered

Saul was one of the witnesses, and he agreed completely with the killing of Stephen. A great wave of persecution began that day, sweeping over the church in Jerusalem; and all the believers except the apostles were scattered through the regions of Judea and Samaria.

ACTS 8:1

In Switzerland, the Zurich Council demanded a unified church and state. The free church radicals not only refused to let their children be baptized, they met on January 21, 1525, and baptized one another. It was the birth of the Anabaptist movement, and it symbolized the need to be baptized upon a confession of faith in Christ. These men also decided to form a church apart from the state:

In rejecting infant baptism, the Anabaptists separated that political tie between church membership and citizenship. By challenging the unity of the church, the Anabaptists shredded the social fabric. In rejecting the state's authority in matters of religion, the Anabaptists threatened anarchy, and, by refusing military service, the Anabaptists made the city vulnerable to foreign attack. Anabaptists were imprisoned and exiled, fined and threatened. Meanwhile their ideas, already present in the rural countryside around Zurich, spawned a number of fellowships beyond the city walls.

"Within several years [of 1525], Anabaptist groups emerged elsewhere in Switzerland and in southern Germany, the Austrian Tyrol, and Moravia."

A similar scattering happened in the early church. Because of the persecution of Christians, many families left Jerusalem. With parcels on their backs, they carried faith in their hearts. Like dandelion seeds on a summer's wind, they splayed out in many directions. In Acts 8:4 we read, "The believers who were scattered preached the Good News about Jesus wherever they went."

So many times we question why persecution comes. We might not personally face punishment or death for our beliefs, but in this world there will always be those who oppose Christ and those who follow Him. Peace comes when we find Jesus in the midst of everything we face and point others to His saving grace.

■ ■ ■

Dear heavenly Father, it's so easy in retrospect to see Your plan in the spreading of Your Word in history. Help me to know that I am part of Your plan too. Help me to open my mouth and share Your goodness, even when doing so is costly.

A Dividing Line

We are here for only a moment, visitors and strangers in the land as our ancestors were before us. Our days on earth are like a passing shadow, gone so soon without a trace.
1 CHRONICLES 29:15

In the years following 1525, Anabaptists were jailed, tortured, and burned at the stake. They hid from authorities, met in secret, and grew to distrust society:

In addition to fostering a tendency to withdraw, the fierce opposition further encouraged values of simplicity and piety that the Anabaptists already saw in the Bible. The line dividing the suffering church and the cruel world became all too clear. The world was arrogant, wealthy, proud, and violent. The Anabaptists saw themselves as meek, simple, humble, and nonresistant. While some of these characteristics may have been typical of rural Swiss and south German people generally, the experience of persecution accentuated them among the Anabaptists.

Not everyone who joined the Anabaptists stayed true to them. Some returned to the state church and even betrayed their former friends to the authorities.

No matter who we are or where we live, if we choose to follow Christ, there will be a dividing line between us and others. Numerous Scripture verses refer to God's children as visitors, strangers, and aliens in this world. Abraham, the father of the nation of Israel, lived in tents as he migrated to the land of Canaan. During Jeremiah's time the children of Israel lived in exile. Throughout history there has hardly been a time when believers have been able to completely take root. It's impossible to be completely settled in a world that believes the opposite of what God believes.

Each of us must make a stand for Christ. We also must walk away from the pursuit of wealth for the sake of wealth and pursue lives of simplicity. Walk away from striving and walk toward abiding. Walk away from arrogance and pride and walk toward humility.

Take a few minutes to think back on your life and write down key moments when God has asked you to walk away from the world's opinions or pursuits. Where did this obedience lead?

Now ask God if there is anything else He may desire for you to walk away from. Taking those steps is hard, but God's peace is on the other side.

■ ■ ■

Dear heavenly Father, thank You for forming a dividing line between Your ways and the world's ways. I choose You today.

Spiritual Leadership

Brothers, select seven men who are well respected and are full of
the Spirit and wisdom. We will give them this responsibility.

ACTS 6:3

Who we grow up to be is set in motion from infancy. We have personalities, habits, and character traits that point back to those who raised us. Equally important are the conditions in which we live. My grandmother, who grew up during the Depression, is very frugal. She has never used a credit card. She believes you shouldn't buy something unless you have the cash to pay for it. Likewise, the way Amish churches are run today can be traced back to the infancy of the Anabaptist movement:

> Local congregations were self-standing, each with its own ordained leadership who preached and provided pastoral care, as well as looking after the material needs of members and collecting and distributing money for the poor. Swiss Anabaptists allowed lay members to lead worship and teach if no ordained leader was available, though performing the rites of baptism, communion, ordination, and marriage was reserved for senior ministers called "elders" (later, in North America, they came to be called "bishops"). However, the most important roles for Anabaptist leaders—elders or junior ministers—were modeling daily Christian discipleship and guiding church discipline.

During the sixteenth century, several thousand Anabaptists were executed.

Amish today follow the same model. Laymen are called into leadership. Deacons oversee the material needs of members and the collection and distribution of money for the poor. Ministers (also called preachers) are responsible for delivering the messages on Sunday and spend a lot of time preparing for that by reading God's Word in both German and English. Bishops are the spiritual leaders over one or two church districts. All those who hold these positions are untrained and unpaid.

Who are the men or women God has called to ease your spiritual and emotional burdens? Take time today to pray for them. It's not easy caring for others and leading them toward God. Pray God will give them a fresh joy and strength as they face the responsibility.

■ ■ ■

Dear heavenly Father, I often find it easier to point out others' faults than to appreciate
their hard work. Thank You for those You've brought into my life to lead me closer to You.

Serve One Another

God has given each of you a gift from his great variety of spiritual gifts. Use them well to serve one another.
1 PETER 4:10

The Amish know that serving one another brings interdependence, which is what God intended when He created us to work together as the body of Christ. Nancy Sleeth, author of *Almost Amish*, writes:

> The Amish understand that the key to a joyful life is simple: serve God and serve your neighbor. Interdependence can be more holy than independence. But how does that play out?
>
> The Amish serve their children by doing the hard work of parenting, teaching them the skills and habits that will make them healthy spouses, colleagues, and neighbors. Instead of short-term distraction or coddling, they aim for long-term character and strength.
>
> Through example, they show how caring for grandparents is a joy, not a burden. Likewise, service to neighbors and coworkers is treated more as an opportunity than an obligation. And service to one's own faith community is a chance to follow the example of Jesus, one act of compassion at a time.

You only live once, but if you work it right, once is enough.

PROVERB

Nancy also offers these *Almost Amish* service tips:

- Join a small faith group, not for what you can get but for what you can give.
- Adopt an elderly neighbor, single mom, or jobless friend, and look for ways you can help fill the gaps.
- Gladly lend tools, sports equipment, and other little-used items. If it comes back in less-than-ideal shape—or not at all—consider it a donation to a good home.

Take a moment and write a list of your own service projects. Consider things you naturally like to do, and figure out a way that you can do those things to bless another person.

■ ■ ■

Dear heavenly Father, I'm amazed how blessed I feel when I give. You pour in as I pour out.

JUNE 23

Through Him

All things were made and came into existence through Him; and without
Him was not even one thing made that has come into being.

JOHN 1:3 (AMP)

I have a beautiful quilt that lays over the back of my sofa. My aunt Sandy made it for me, and every time I wrap it around my shoulders I consider her creative design. What was once imagined in her mind now keeps me warm. What took form under her fingers is a beautiful display. It would be foolish for a visitor at my home to walk in and believe the quilt took shape on its own, that fabric scraps in a store pressed against each other randomly and by chance became the intricate design.

As I read through this week's *Budget* newspaper, evidence of God's creation is on every page. Amish scribes from all over the country write about warm weather forecasts, the rain, the crops, and vegetable auctions, among other things. Like an intricately designed quilt, a week on an Amish farm is a beautiful display of God's design. An Amish couple are the threads that stitch together the bounty of nature and the needs of their home. It would be foolish to say that they do this without God's plan, God's design, and God's hand. Inspiration and creative thought are intangibles, but they are seen in what is tangible. Proverbs 8:29-31 says: "I [Wisdom] was there when he set the limits of the seas, so they would not spread beyond their boundaries. And when he marked off the earth's foundations, I was the architect at his side. I was his constant delight, rejoicing always in his presence. And how happy I was with the world he created; how I rejoiced with the human family!"

You don't advertise your religion by wearing a label, you do it by living a life.

PROVERB

Do you hear Jesus' love for His creation in those words? Ask Him to open your eyes to how He's stitching together *your* world today.

■ ■ ■

Dear heavenly Father, I thank You that You who are unseen are so beautifully seen in all that's seen. May I see You more clearly as the great Architect in my life.

177

Filling the Earth

[God said,] "Fill the earth and govern it. Reign over the fish in the sea, the birds in the sky, and all the animals that scurry along the ground."
GENESIS 1:28

Have you lived in one place or many? Have you discovered that wherever you live, God is there providing for you? The Amish experience this when they move to a new area.

With a church doctrine that prohibits birth control, Amish families are predictably large. When you combine big families with a culture that still makes an attempt at agrarianism (you won't find Amish families living in the Bronx or suburban Chicago), you can end up with land shortages in some settlements. Lancaster County, Pennsylvania, was once home to the largest population of Amish in the United States. Holmes County, Ohio, has since surpassed its Keystone neighbor, but Amish populations in Pennsylvania still have limited room to grow. One solution is simply to move someplace far away and start a settlement from scratch. Late spring is a good time to journey to a new destination, so that families can have the summer to settle in before the arrival of a new school year.

"The Amish have settled in as many as twenty-four states, Canada, and Central America, though about 80 percent are located in Pennsylvania, Ohio, and Indiana."

Sometimes it's easier to look at the problem—more people than available land nearby. Instead, we need to look at what God has done in the past and trust Him for the future. He is the giver of life, and when we have a place of our own to flourish on—no matter where that is—it is a gift from God.

I've made two cross-country moves. Each place has been a gift, and I've discovered a unique beauty in the seasons. There have been varied local cultures, and my family has made lifelong friends.

"With my great strength and powerful arm I made the earth and all its people and every animal. I can give these things of mine to anyone I choose," we read in Jeremiah 27:5. Where are you currently living? God has a plan for you there—a place for you. He has chosen to plant you where you are for a reason.

■ ■ ■

Dear heavenly Father, sometimes I feel that situations out of my control have moved me where I am. I'm thankful, Lord, that even during the times I can't see the plan, You always have one, and that the place where I lay my head is a gift from You.

Never Revoked

God's gifts and His call are irrevocable. [He never withdraws them when once they are given, and He does not change His mind about those to whom He gives His grace or to whom He sends His call.]

ROMANS 11:29 (AMP)

Even though the percentage is small, there are those who leave the Amish. The culture shock can be hard. All they've been raised to believe comes under assault. Those who choose to leave must weigh every value as they decide what to hold on to and what to discard. They now dress differently; they must think differently too. Yet no matter what age they are when they leave, or how long they are gone, the foundation of being Amish is with them for life. They will continue to view much in the world through the Amish frame of reference.

It's the same for those whom God has loved and called. Romans 11:28 says, "From the point of view of the Gospel (good news), they [the Jews, at present] are enemies [of God], which is for your advantage *and* benefit. But from the point of view of God's choice (of election, of divine selection), they are still the beloved (dear to Him) for the sake of their forefathers" (AMP).

"[Failure to enforce] the practice of shunning is the main reason that the Amish broke away from the Mennonites in 1693."

Former Amish may live completely different lives from those they were raised in, but for the Amish who love them and care about them, the calling to be Amish is never revoked. Those who choose to leave could return at any time if they were willing to submit to the Ordnung, the church, and the community.

If the Amish can believe—and depend on—such grace, how much more can we as children of God? Do you feel far from God today? Realize that your point of view may have changed, but God's never does. He is never further away than a heartbeat. Do you know someone who feels rejected by God? The best way for that person to understand God's love and grace just might be for you to fully extend your love and grace first, praying that these will point the other person toward the Eternal One.

■ ■ ■

Dear heavenly Father, I thank You that I am forever Yours. Help me to understand that deep in my heart. And may the way I view everything in my life change because of Your amazing grace.

Lifted High

God also selected (deliberately chose) what in the world is lowborn and insignificant and branded and treated with contempt, even the things that are nothing, that He might depose and bring to nothing the things that are, so that no mortal man should [have pretense for glorying and] boast in the presence of God.

1 CORINTHIANS 1:28-29 (AMP)

We think we are so smart. We have technology. We have our gadgets. Through our smartphones we can know what's happening anywhere in the world in a matter of minutes. From the same phone we can read the latest bestseller, written, no doubt, by a very educated person.

Yet even though we know so much, my guess is many of us don't know the right time to plant. We have not taken time to study the stars, only to stare up at them in wonder. We've missed being aware of the cool morning breeze, and we can't tell by looking at a billowy cloud if it's going to rain. We think we're smart, but are we really smart about what matters?

The Amish have less education than most of the people in our country, yet they live debt-free and know how to be part of a thriving community. How do they know so much about the right things? This Amish prayer explains:

FULFILLMENT

Help me, Lord, to meet this day—
its challenges,
its changes,
its opportunities
to speak of Thee
whose loving care
arranges
each transient hour
I live upon this great
(though troubled) earth,
that when I kneel
at eventide
I'll have been for Thee—
some worth!

God chooses those who are the lowest, those who get on their knees before Him and who trust Him more than their education. He chooses those who understand His workings more than they understand the workings of a smartphone.

We have no room for boasting once we understand that only turning to God will carry us through the challenges of the day. And coming before Him—seeking Him—at the start of the day brings more wisdom than any college scholar can obtain.

■ ■ ■

Dear heavenly Father, with You in me, the knowledge of the universe resides, and I have no doubt that though I am lowest, with You I have more than those who are considered greatest on earth.

A Song for Children Lost

Jesus said, "Let the children come to me. Don't stop them! For the Kingdom of Heaven belongs to those who are like these children."

MATTHEW 19:14

When I was writing this, a horrible tragedy was being reported on the news. The innocent young children who lost their lives in a school shooting in Connecticut reminded me of the Amish school shooting in 2006 at Nickel Mines, Pennsylvania. I often come across reports of the deaths of Amish children, including some killed in accidents with drunk drivers.

The Amish believe that God sets a child's time of death soon after he or she is born. The following is "A Child's Funeral Song" from the book *Lieder Sammlung* ("Song Collection"):

I was a little child
Born into this world;
But my hour of death
God has quickly sent.
I had nothing to say
About the world and its doings
I have in my days here
Needed nothing of that.

He receives me up unto grace,
To an inheritance in His kingdom,
Death can not harm me,
I am like unto the angels;
My body shall live gain
In rest and eternal joy,
And soar with my soul
In great splendor, glory.

My most beloved father,
Who begot me into the world,
And my sweetheart mother,
Who has taken care of me,
These follow me to the grave,
With inward, heartfelt sighs;
Yet I was God's gift,
Which He now takes to Himself.

Farewell, my loved ones,
You father- and mother-hearts,
Why do you sorrow?
Forget this pain
It is very well with me,
I live in bliss and joy,
You shall see me again
There in God's glory.

I am so thankful that because of Jesus we can look forward to eternity. Jesus loved the little children on earth, and He loves them—welcomes them—into heaven.

Even years after losing a child, parents remember and grieve. Send a note to let those parents know that you still care and remember. It will mean more than you can know.

■ ■ ■

Dear heavenly Father, I grieve for those who've lost a little one. May You bring Your sweet peace to those families, no matter how many years have passed.

A Cheerful Heart

A cheerful heart is good medicine.

PROVERBS 17:22

According to author Suzanne Woods Fisher, the Sugarcreek, Ohio, *Budget* has been published since 1890 and serves the Amish and Mennonite communities around the world. The national edition consists primarily of letters from mostly Amish and Mennonite "scribes" who write in on a weekly basis (more or less) to report on local happenings: births, deaths, weddings, visitors, the weather, the state of crops, and so on. Here are some humorous stories Suzanne pulled from its pages:

Every family tree has a little sap.

PROVERB

A baby boy was born to William and Roseanne Miller on June 24th, weight 9 lbs. 4 oz., length 23½", named Daniel. This makes boy number eight with no girls. They were thankful for a healthy boy, but a little disappointed it wasn't a girl. The same week the baby was born, the Millers hatched fifty-four guineas in their incubator. William said they are probably all roosters.

Recently Luke came in the house, flopped himself on the loveseat and said, "Mom, I want a whiskey." "A what?!" I asked. "A whiskey," he repeated. Keeping a straight face I said, "Are you sure you know what you are asking for?" "Yes," he said. "It's one of those things that you throw," giving his arm a fling, "and it sails through the air." "Oh," I said with relief and much laughter. "Maybe you mean a Frisbee." "Yes, that's it," he said.

Did those bring a smile to your face? Many people wrongly assume that the Amish are stoic and stern simply because they are meek and mild, but they do have funny bones, and they find moments of humor in everyday life. They observe, laugh, and share funny stories with friends and in places like the *Budget*.

Do you need some cheerfulness in your life? Carry around a small notebook and write down humorous things you see during the day. Then share your observations with family members or friends. Not only will you start seeing life in a brighter light, but you'll also put a spark in someone else's day.

■ ■ ■

Dear heavenly Father, You've given us so many gifts, and today we thank You for the gift of laughter. I'm so glad that serving You doesn't mean we have to put away our smiles!

Like Apples of Gold

Like apples of gold in settings of silver is a ruling rightly given.

PROVERBS 25:11 (NIV)

I have received many gifts in my life. Some were wrapped in newsprint. Others in fine papers and ribbons. Some gifts were simple and handmade, but none have been as cherished as encouraging words. I can still remember my grandmother saying, "What a beautiful picture. When you grow up, you can design your own line of greeting cards." I remember tips shared by my favorite writing mentor. I still think of his wisdom years later when I sit down to write. Encouraging words—wise words—not only have an impact on a moment but also can influence a lifetime. The Amish often use proverbs to share messages and lessons that they want their children to carry with them for life:

> **Silence should not be broken unless it is improved upon.**
>
> PROVERB

These time-tested proverbs—such as "God has two dwellings, one in heaven and the other in a meek and thankful heart" or "You can't keep trouble from coming, but you needn't give it a chair to sit on" or "Many things have been opened by mistake, but none so frequently as the mouth"—become like small lights along a path, guiding a child (adults too) toward wise behavior and choices. They have a way of clearing away the gray fog, distilling an issue down to black or white clarity, simplifying the decision. And helping a child remember simple but piercing wisdom.

What helpful advice have you been given? Pass it on. What encouragement have you received? Think about how you can encourage someone else.

Take time to write a note to someone whose words have made a positive difference in your life. He or she will appreciate knowing how your life was influenced by those comments.

Finally, share God's Word with others. Luke 1:37 says, "No word from God shall be void of power" (ASV). The kind, loving, wise words we speak into the lives of others have some impact, but when we share God's Word, it goes forth with greater power and purpose.

■ ■ ■

Dear heavenly Father, I thank You for all the people in my life who have shared wisdom and pointed me to You. Thank You for Your good and powerful Word, which will never fail to accomplish Your purpose.

JUNE 30

God's Training Ground

I, a prisoner for serving the Lord, beg you to lead a life worthy of your calling, for you have been called by God. Always be humble and gentle. Be patient with each other, making allowance for each other's faults because of your love. Make every effort to keep yourselves united in the Spirit, binding yourselves together with peace.
EPHESIANS 4:1-3

When I was first married, I thought I had the perfect man, but I soon discovered his faults, just as he discovered mine. When I had children, I imagined that with my guidance and training they could be molded into kind, gentle human beings. While they are good kids, they test my patience. More than anything else, my four kids cause me to depend on God's strength. Yet it's the daily molding toward humility, gentleness, and forgiveness that prepares us for the storms of life.

> Keep your words soft and sweet, just in case you have to eat them.
>
> PROVERB

"The traditions surrounding birth, Communion, worship, baptism, marriage, and death reinforce Amish values. These values bear fruit in daily life, particularly through the practices the Amish are best known for—forgiveness and peace," writes Nancy Sleeth. "The most public example of Amish forgiveness took place after the schoolhouse shooting in Pennsylvania. . . . The true test of any value system is how we act under duress. Forgiveness, like anything else we value, must be practiced on a regular basis. If we do not forgive the small infractions—the cranky response of a tired spouse, the tool a neighbor forgets to return, the missed appointment with an overworked friend—how can we forgive the bigger wrongs?"

Any right response I have during a large test results from the training and character God has built into me during the dailyness of life. I learn to forgive because of the people in my life who need forgiveness and who have given me forgiveness. I become humble because I fail often with my family and learn to confess those failures. I become patient because living with others shows me that I can't have everything I want when I want it. We face large challenges in this life, but God prepares us for them in the course of everyday living.

■ ■ ■

Dear heavenly Father, help me to see small annoyances and frustrations as the training ground of life. Thank You for being there to provide wisdom and strength whenever I turn to You.

Recipe for Happiness

2 heaping cups of patience
1 heart full of love
1 dash of laughter
2 hands full of generosity
1 head full of understanding
1 teaspoon of courtesy

———————————— ∎ ————————————

Mix well with humility. Sprinkle generously with kindness and plenty of faith. Spread over a lifetime, and serve to family and friends.

JULY 1

For the Season to Come

*Take a lesson from the ants, you lazybones. Learn from their ways and
become wise! Though they have no prince or governor or ruler to make
them work, they labor hard all summer, gathering food for the winter.*
PROVERBS 6:6-8

My grandfather, one of eleven children, grew up on a farm in Kansas. When Kansas
became a dust bowl in the previous century, the family sold the farm and moved to
California. I hope to travel to Kansas someday and find their land. My hope is that
it's still being farmed. There's something satisfying about the continued cycle of life,
of seasons.

Summer is a busy time as farmers gather the hay that will feed their cattle and

**Pray for a good
harvest but continue
to hoe.**

PROVERB

horses. Even when the sun is bright overhead, good farmers
think of the winter to come. Amish farmers prepare not only
outwardly but also inwardly. Many of their Scripture readings
are connected to the agricultural seasons: "In summer, John 4
and Revelations 14 (Ernd Schriften) is read, and then toward
the end of summer when the grains have been gathered into
the barns, appropriately the harvest scriptures (Einsammeln
Schriften), Luke 12 and 13 will be used. Oftentimes the services
are held in barns where the well-worn boards of the threshing

floor are lightly covered with new hay and the granaries bulging with summer's bounty
of grain."

Summer is a good time for tending your soul, too. Are you in a bright spot right
now? What can you do to plan and prepare for a challenging season you will face in
the future? Some men and women tend to bask in the sunny moments and never
tend the soil of their interior lives. What farmers teach us—what ants teach us—is the
importance of planning ahead.

Do you desire to grow closer in your relationship with God? Do you want to be
more diligent in prayer? Listen to what God is speaking to you, and remember that
any soul work you do now will pay off when a challenging season comes.

■ ■ ■

*Dear heavenly Father, I thank You for seasons of sunshine that give me a reprieve. Let me
not waste these moments; rather, show me today how to tend my soul and draw closer
to You.*

Confess

If you confess with your mouth that Jesus is Lord and believe in your heart that God raised him from the dead, you will be saved.

ROMANS 10:9

People assume that every Amish person has a personal relationship with Jesus Christ. That's like believing that every person in the Bible Belt is a believer and a follower of Christ. But for the Amish, like in any other community or church, showing up, participating, and having your name on the membership roll don't get you God's saving grace. In fact, sometimes it might be hard to realize you're missing a personal relationship with God when everything in your life is set up for you to serve God and know about Him: "Although the Amish profess salvation by grace, many of their congregations practice salvation by works. They believe God decides their eternal destiny by weighing their lifelong obedience to the rules of the church against their disobedience."

Mission to Amish People is a ministry dedicated to evangelizing and discipling Amish and former Amish people.

But saving faith is more than just "knowing." It's understanding that we are lost and in need of a Savior. It's confessing with our mouths that Jesus is Lord. We can strive our hardest to live good lives, but nothing changes until we take care of our sin problem. We may trifle with our sins or excuse them, but God hates sin.

How seriously do you take God's holiness and His hatred of sin? Do you grieve over the things that grieve God's heart? We can discuss the benefits of living simpler lives. We can speak about having peace in our day-to-day routines, but true peace comes when all our sins are taken away and they are no longer counted against us.

1 Corinthians 15:3 says, "I passed on to you what was most important and what had also been passed on to me. Christ died for our sins, just as the Scriptures said." Do your rest, peace, and security come from Christ? Salvation comes by grace alone, in faith alone, by Christ alone. Trust in that today.

■ ■ ■

Dear heavenly Father, I thank You for the sacrifice of Your Son that leads to my salvation. I'm thankful that the only act that is necessary is for me to confess with my lips and believe in my heart that Jesus is Lord.

Transparent

Confess your sins to each other and pray for each other so that you may be healed.
JAMES 5:16

In our society the age at which a person is considered an adult differs with each family. Yes, from a legal perspective, eighteen is considered adulthood, but in some families a mother is still providing for all her child's needs when he or she is twenty-five. In other families, a young person is leading a mostly independent life at the age of fifteen. In Amish society, sixteen is the turning point for Amish youth. At fifteen you are a child; at sixteen you are an adult. It's then that Amish youth can make many of their own decisions, and some of them choose the way of the world for a time.

Rumspringa, or "running around," is expected in the Amish culture, but the degree and extent of this behavior vary. In small communities many youth stay closer to the straight and narrow. In large communities, some youth live wild lives. Even among some Amish families, there is no escaping the "wild teen years." In fact, some of that has been happening for generations.

During Rumspringa, some Amish young people, particularly boys, may acquire a driver's license and a vehicle, which they might park at their parents' home.

Many Amish youth grow up assuming their parents wandered in the ways of the world for a time. Yet like most adults, Amish parents often don't take time to discuss their own choices or the consequences of those choices with their young-adult children. After all, it's hard confessing one's own mistakes. But as hard as it may be, transparency is a better way. It's easy to lecture and scold. Harder to kindle a relationship—a friendship—with a young person and speak from one's own experience.

"People who conceal their sins will not prosper, but if they confess and turn from them, they will receive mercy," we read in Proverbs 28:13. When we confess our sins to our God, we find forgiveness. And when we confess our sins to our children, there is a chance we can protect them from making the same mistakes.

It's not easy to admit we were wrong, but healing comes—both in our hearts and in our relationships—when we do.

■ ■ ■

Dear heavenly Father, give me courage to open my heart to those who need to know the truth of my past. And may sharing my mistakes save someone else from making the same ones I did.

Freedom in Christ

You have been called to live in freedom, my brothers and sisters.
But don't use your freedom to satisfy your sinful nature.
Instead, use your freedom to serve one another in love.

GALATIANS 5:13

How will you be celebrating Independence Day? For the most part Amish do not celebrate the day as we do. There are no fireworks, barbecues, or parades. Some Amish—especially those who work for factories and have the day off—spend the day with family and go on picnics. A few others participate in English celebrations. Each year, Topeka, Indiana, holds a buggy-pull race following the town's Fourth of July parade. Both Amish and English participate in this race.

One article says, "Though Amish appreciate being able to live in a democratic nation, the liberties and privileges they are allowed and the protection they receive from the state, they rarely if ever engage in explicit displays of patriotism." It is rare to see an American flag displayed at an Amish home. (They don't display crosses or other Christian symbols either.) They believe their lives should be the evidence of where their allegiance lies.

Is that true of you? Can people tell where your commitment and loyalty lie? It's easy to shoot off fireworks or wear red, white, and blue one day a year, but true patriotism is shown by how you live. It's easy to buy Christian T-shirts and hang a cross on your wall, but true freedom in Christ will be displayed in everything you do. When you use your freedom to serve one another in love, your unselfish display will be as bright as fireworks on a dark summer night. When we are following Christ, we serve Him not because we must but because we can, and when we do, we are rewarded with His smile.

■ ■ ■

Dear heavenly Father, may my life display You in a dark world.
Thank You for the freedom You give! And thank You for my
country, which allows me to worship in freedom.

"Amish businesses employ both Amish and non-Amish workers. . . . Since different holidays are observed, this requires flexibility in granting time off." Instead of celebrating Memorial Day, July Fourth, and Labor Day, the Amish will celebrate Ascension Day, Pentecost Monday, and Fall Fast day.

Peacemakers

God blesses those who work for peace, for they will be called the children of God.
MATTHEW 5:9

The Amish are pacifists and conscientious objectors. They avoid all violence, including angry words. They refuse to sue in a court of law, and they do not believe in participating in military service. They do not believe in personal physical violence either. The Amish believe that Jesus called us to be peacemakers, and they follow Jesus' instruction in Matthew 5:39: "I say unto you, That ye resist not evil: but whosoever shall smite thee on thy right cheek, turn to him the other also" (KJV). They see the violent approach to solving problems as un-Christian.

The Amish follow the commands of the Bible, and both the Amish and Mennonites believe the New Testament takes priority over the Old. Yes, the Old Testament records numerous instances of warfare, but the Amish believe that Jesus came to show us a different way:

> If you had never tasted the bitter, you wouldn't know what is sweet.
>
> PROVERB

Amish follow a very strict interpretation of "two kingdoms" doctrine. Two Kingdoms doctrine is the belief, held by numerous Christians, that there is a spiritual kingdom with its own set of rules, and a worldly one. The worldly kingdom and its authorities is seen to be instigated by God. Amish respect and follow the rules of the worldly kingdom, so long as they don't interfere with God's dictates.

Mandatory military service or using force as a police officer, or indirectly as a government official or agent of the state, is in the Amish view un-Christian and in violation of the rules of the spiritual kingdom.

Can others consider you a peacemaker? You may not hold the same beliefs on pacifism or military service, but do you lean toward being peaceful or do you stir up tension and trouble? Working for peace starts in your own heart. It's admitting that God is in control, and allowing Him to have ultimate justice in all areas that concern us. When peace is in our hearts, it has a way of filling our homes and our lives, too.

■ ■ ■

Dear heavenly Father, I bring my thoughts and attitudes to You because I know that my words and actions flow from them. Help me to be a peacemaker today.

Thunder and Lightning

When he speaks in the thunder, the heavens roar with rain. He causes the clouds to rise over the earth. He sends the lightning with the rain and releases the wind from his storehouses.

JEREMIAH 10:13

Few things are as awe-inspiring as summer storms—the kinds that uproot trees. With them come hail, high winds, and rain. A peaceful world turns violent overnight.

Living in the South, we aren't out of reach of a hurricane's wind. And when storms come, I have my radio tuned in and my television turned on, waiting to hear news of tornadoes.

The Amish have no such ability. It's bad enough to have a storm hit when they're at home, but even worse when they're away. The rain pounds, making it impossible to see their way in open buggies. And even in a closed buggy, the simple frame rocks and shakes. When storms come, our sense of our need for God is greater. We understand He controls the storms, and our prayers become more fervent.

A cheerful heart and a smiling face put sunshine in the darkest place.

PROVERB

Where do you turn when the storms of life hit? Do you see God's hand in them? Do you turn to Him in your troubles and trials?

The first Amish immigrants to America in the early 1720s settled in Berks, Chester, and Lancaster Counties in Pennsylvania. Indian raids in Berks County in the 1760s caused those early Amish settlers to move to other areas. New immigrants and Lancaster-area Amish seeking more land settled in Somerset, Mifflin, and Union Counties in the mid- and late-1700s. Holmes County, Ohio, was first settled in 1808.

Those early settlers might have felt uprooted by the storms of life, but through their "scattering," new communities were established, and they still thrive today.

When have you felt shaken? Do you feel shaken today? Trust that God will bring something good—even from the storms. You may be able to see the end result some-day, but in the meantime you'll trust more deeply that God is the Keeper in the storms.

■ ■ ■

Dear heavenly Father, I thank You for holding me tightly when the storms of life come. And I thank You that the storms bring a greater good I cannot always see, especially a closer walk with You.

Example of Faith

Abel's offering gave evidence that he was a righteous man,
and God showed his approval of his gifts. Although Abel is
long dead, he still speaks to us by his example of faith.
HEBREWS 11:4

During July, winter grains are threshed and oats are cut. Corn has tassels and hay crops are harvested. This is the ideal lot for an Amish man. The Amish don't believe you need to live and work on a farm to be godly, but they do believe the two are related:

In the past, most children learned to be Amish in the context of the farm. Farming reinforced the core values of hard work, simplicity, and separation from the world. "Besides," said an Amish farmer, "cities are dangerous and destructive. After Cain killed Abel, the Bible says that he went and founded a city. The country is the place to live and raise a family."

"Time will tell how we Amish will do as a society," said a young business owner. "This generation is the first in which most of the children and youth have grown up off the farm." Kraybill contends that the occupational shift to business poses the most serious challenge to historic Amish values and visibility.

What are your concerns for the next generation? You may worry about violence, inappropriate media, or a lack of respect. No matter where youth live today, they are dealing with the challenge of constant change—they just don't realize it. What we see as a downward shift in values and beliefs, they see as normal.

Names the Amish use for non-Amish people include Englishers, Yankees, or High People.

What do young people need most today? Is it to live on a farm? Is it better media, better schools, or better examples? No, what they need is a better faith. Abel is the example of that. His right living speaks long after he's gone.

We may long to shield our children—to tuck them away and surround them with the values of old—but it's faith that will guard their hearts. When the youth of today have faith in God, they will set appropriate boundaries and pursue right living. As with most issues, what's on the inside is more important than what's on the outside.

■ ■ ■

Dear heavenly Father, I pray for the young people in my life. I pray for a greater faith.
I pray that You will give them inner strength that is able to overcome all that's without.

For the Lord

[Hannah said,] "I asked the LORD to give me this boy, and he has granted my request. Now I am giving him to the LORD, and he will belong to the LORD his whole life." And they worshiped the LORD there.

1 SAMUEL 1:27-28

An Amish mother sinks heavily onto her rocking chair, the unborn baby heavy within her. It is her eighth child, and she is weary to the core. She wonders how she will care for one more child.

The Amish consider children special blessings, but that doesn't mean caring for them is easy. Fortunately, when Amish children are born, they are born into a community as well as a family: "One cannot raise Amish children alone. It is the effort of a whole community, intently devoted to a way of life. Nurturing children is one of the strongest factors in Amish fathers and mothers choosing to work at home; it is the reason for the Amish community's investment in its school system."

Datt is the Pennsylvania Dutch word for Dad, and *Mamm* the Pennsylvania Dutch word for Mom or Mother.

Yet as helpful as it is, a loving community is not enough. One Amish Proverb says, "When you come to the end of your rope, God is there to take over."

Do you trust God to help you when you don't have the strength to carry out your tasks? God will strengthen you when you are weak. If you have children, He has given them to you, and He asks for one thing in return—that you give them back to Him.

Jesus' parents did this very thing. Luke 2:22 says, "It was time for their purification offering, as required by the law of Moses after the birth of a child; so his parents took him to Jerusalem to present him to the Lord." Like Jesus' parents, and like Hannah in 1 Samuel, you must have the mind-set that your children belong to the Lord. They are His for their whole lives. When God gives children, He has a plan for them, and He will strengthen you to bring that plan to life.

■ ■ ■

Dear heavenly Father, what You want from us is our everything. I'm thankful that in exchange You give us Your everything.

Eternal Rewards

All athletes are disciplined in their training. They do it to win
a prize that will fade away, but we do it for an eternal prize.
1 CORINTHIANS 9:25

Amish youth may be raised to be noncompetitive and humble, but in some places—such as Holmes County, Ohio—most of them know the best way to have fun is with a game of softball. The following is a true story by John Schmid from Common Ground Ministries in Berlin, Ohio.

In Holmes County, the Amish love baseball. . . . When I played fast-pitch softball, the best teams were always made up of Amish boys who had quit school after eighth grade and hadn't joined the church yet. Several of those teams won the State and then the USA National Softball Title in their respective divisions! At the annual Ft. Wayne softball tournament the last few years, the girls champions have been local Amish girls whose uniform is their everyday dresses. The local Amish businesses will sponsor them but only if they dress appropriately. It sort of tickled me to see a team of girls from Florida who had expensive flashy spandex uniforms and who looked like a mixture of professional athletes and Hollywood movie stars get beat by our local Amish girls wearing dresses and head scarves.

Every spiritual investment will bear eternal interest.

PROVERB

The truth is, it doesn't matter what you're wearing if you don't follow the rules. First Corinthians 9:25 says, "Everyone who competes in the games goes into strict training. They do it to get a crown that will not last, but we do it to get a crown that will last forever" (NIV).

How are you preparing for the good fight of faith? Do you discipline yourself? Do you give intentional time and attention to your faith? Does peering ahead to that eternal prize urge you on? The training we put into our feats on earth lasts only for a season, but the training and devotion we put into building our faith earns a reward we can claim for eternity!

■ ■ ■

Dear heavenly Father, may my pursuit of You and my desire to build my faith, urge me on against every temporary struggle.

Let Those Who Glory

Let him who glories glory in this: that he understands and knows Me
[personally and practically, directly discerning and recognizing My character],
that I am the Lord, Who practices loving-kindness, judgment, and
righteousness in the earth, for in these things I delight, says the Lord.

JEREMIAH 9:24 (AMP)

What do we boast about? There are things we are all proud of, and maybe we don't speak them aloud or brag about them, but we do tend to make sure we bring them up in our conversations. In reality, there is only one thing that is worthy of our boasting—that we know the Lord. Not just know who He is, but that we also understand His character.

To boast about God—or give glory to Him—is to make others aware of Him. We naturally want other people to give us praise, but instead, we point a flashing neon sign in God's direction. When we share God's Word, we are also raising awareness of God's truth. When we practice loving-kindness and live in unity with others, people see that God is the center of the union and the source of our unity. Our actions delight the Lord. The *Ausbund* says: "God's commune, washed in the blood of Christ, is to be holy and pure. He who wants to be in it must purify himself by giving all that he has to be used for the glory of God. He gives to his neighbour as he has freely received. . . . Oh how pleasant it is in Jesus Christ where brothers live together in unity and have all their property in common!"

Hans Betz, one of the Anabaptists imprisoned for their convictions in Passau castle, was among those who did not survive the imprisonment. He died under torture in 1537.

In what do you boast? To whom do you give glory? Anytime we practice the loving-kindness of God, we point to a goodness beyond ourselves. Are you making others aware of God's Word? Of God Himself? As you do, you will offer the Lord much delight.

■ ■ ■

Dear heavenly Father, forgive me for the times I take personal credit for what You do
through me. May any glory I receive be immediately lifted to You.

Traditions, Traditions . . .

*The Pharisees and teachers of the law asked Jesus, "Why
don't your disciples live according to the tradition of the elders
instead of eating their food with defiled hands?"*

MARK 7:5 (NIV)

Families huddled together in the barn. Even though the hay was clean, the odor was strong. A noise outside caused everyone's hearts to pound a little harder. Even the littlest children looked to the door, worry evident in their gazes. Any day officials could come and arrest them or their family members. Hundreds of years have passed, but the Amish still hold their church services in members' homes or barns, a practice carried over from Europe centuries ago.

The higher a man gets in divine grace, the lower he will be in his own esteem.

PROVERB

But the Amish aren't the only ones who hold fast to traditions. Many of us live the way we do because that's just the way it is. From the way I fold my towels to the way I put sheets on beds and even organize my pantry, I do those tasks in a certain way because of how I was taught.

When it comes to following church traditions, it's important to distinguish between God's moral laws and human traditions. Sometimes where we gather to worship, when we sit or stand, or what particular style of worship is followed is based on traditions, not on specific biblical references. One day, when we meet God in eternity, He will not want to discuss the moral implications of benches versus padded pews.

In Mark 7:5, the Pharisees weren't necessarily worried about dirty hands. Their bigger concern was that Jesus and his disciples were not following the "tradition of the elders." This sounds similar to a comment we've often heard: "That's the way we've always done it." The Pharisees took it one step further. They considered anyone who didn't follow their traditions "unclean," which denied those people access to God.

Jesus told them, "'You ignore God's law and substitute your own tradition.' Then he said, 'You skillfully sidestep God's law in order to hold on to your own tradition'" (Mark 7:8-9).

There is nothing wrong with traditions, but you need to be careful not to hold firmly to traditions at the expense of other people. Ask God to focus your heart on what's most important to Him.

■ ■ ■

*Dear heavenly Father, help me to focus my heart on what's most important to You.
May I be firm only on what You truly desire.*

Fear of God

He grants the desires of those who fear him; he
hears their cries for help and rescues them.

PSALM 145:19

What does the phrase "fear of God" mean to you? Respect? Reverence? It means this for many Amish, but for some it means more.

"I desperately wanted to leave the Amish, but I didn't want to pay with an eternity in hell by an angry God," writes Malinda Detweiler, author of *I Was Amish: A Personal Story of an Amish Girl and Her Life.*

A dream came to me, one night. I was lying out in the meadow feeling peaceful, knowing I was going to die. I was lying there when suddenly a terrible feeling of guilt overpowered me. The intensity of guilt urged me to frantically pray for forgiveness. I prayed obsessively but regardless of my constant praying, I felt worse. . . . Finally I began to have a sense of peace.

Yet I woke up sweating and tense, distrustful. I contemplated my dream. I knew I had a terrible fear of God as a young Amish girl, after hearing many horror stories about hell. The Amish taught me that God might approve of me if I dressed plain enough. He might extend favor to me if I followed the Amish rules. I might have hope of getting to heaven, but only if I tried hard enough. And yet, it seemed hopeless.

> **When fear knocks on the door, send faith to answer!**
>
> **PROVERB**

Do you fear that you aren't good enough to earn God's love? No one is good enough. Nothing you can do will ever be enough. Ephesians 2:8 says, "God saved you by his grace when you believed. And you can't take credit for this; it is a gift from God." Salvation is a gift, not a paycheck for good things we do to try to earn God's love.

A simple, heartfelt prayer confessing your sins and asking God to forgive you is all you need. Go before God now. Read His Word. Pay attention to His Spirit's nudgings in your heart. God desires to rescue you from sin. Turn to Him!

■ ■ ■

Dear heavenly Father, thank You for the gift of salvation, which is free to us because Jesus paid the full price. May I cling to You until You carry me home.

Contentment

True godliness with contentment is itself great wealth.

1 TIMOTHY 6:6

When I was growing up, a perfect summer day meant riding my bicycle to the library. I would also set up a "house" for my dolls under the tall bushes near the back fence. There were trips to the lake, where I'd float on my back and stare up at the blue sky. There were no video games in the 1970s. No malls near me. No all-day cartoons to keep me entertained, and yet life was good. The same can be said of an Amish childhood.

These children's days are not given shape by a lineup of soccer games, piano lessons, camp, or play groups. Instead, the morning sun, chore-time twice a day, and the coming of evening set a structure for their time. So, too, do the days of the week and the seasons. In this largely rural, soil-anchored world, life follows the lead of the weather and the promise of productive fields and gardens. The children are not removed from this daily interplay with nature. They learn it, they begin to sense it and read it alongside their parents, who interpret what is happening while they go about their jobs, who point out the signals as they come, who invite their children to join them in responsive work.

Ninety-five percent of Amish women said they enjoy life most of the time, compared to 80 percent of non-Amish women.

Not dulled by television or computers, not distracted by telephones, these children grow to be keenly alert both to the natural environment and to the interests of their church community. They are fully occupied but not frenzied. They learn a contentment still available to those who focus their energies on the earth and its requirements, who devote themselves to giving and receiving from others.

When you were growing up, where did you find the most contentment? Has your life grown easier or better from all the wonderful things you added? Or do you sometimes realize that *more* is really *less*?

With God, it's possible to be content wherever we are, with whatever we have. Sometimes it takes looking back at our childhood to realize that simpler is better—for ourselves, our children, and our whole lives.

■ ■ ■

Dear heavenly Father, strip me down. Transform my heart so that it becomes easy to hand off all the unnecessary elements of my life that draw away my focus from the simple things.

It's Time to Plant Celery

The time has come for the wedding feast of the Lamb,
and his bride has prepared herself.

REVELATION 19:7

If you want to start rumors in an Amish community about who's going to be marrying in the fall, take a peek into an Amish garden. If it's filled with sprouting stalks of celery, a fall wedding is a good possibility.

A wedding is a particularly joyous occasion, for two baptized members of the church are joining in marriage, continuing the faith, and starting a new family together. While parents do not select who their children will marry, approval must be given, and the deacon usually acts as the go-between. At a church service after fall communion, the couples planning to marry are "published," announced in front of the congregation. But much preparation, mainly by the bride's parents, has already begun, including the planting in early summer of several hundred stalks of celery, an important part of any Lancaster Amish wedding feast.

> It is better to rejoice that our purse is half full than to fret that it is half empty.
>
> **PROVERB**

Why celery? Celery is used in the stuffing served with the fowl. It is also cut up and used as an appetizer. Jars of celery are set out on tables for decoration.

Celery sprouting in the garden is a sign of hope. It's a sign of a young woman's faith that she will soon have a home of her own and then a family. It means that she, above all others, is the chosen bride. And since there is no divorce in the Amish community, her dreams are focused on a forever commitment.

Christians have a forever Groom. His name is Jesus, and He has gone to prepare a place for us. The wedding to come isn't simply wishful thinking. It's as real as the chair we're sitting on, and yet often we tend to focus only on today's issues. We forget to plant spiritual celery! We forget to look forward with eagerness to the marriage feast to come. It's wonderful to know that Christ is eager for that coming moment when He and his bride are reunited forever.

■ ■ ■

Dear heavenly Father, I cannot wait for the moment when I see the Bridegroom face-to-face. My heart is overwhelmed when I think of it. May each day find me more eager than the last.

The Wrong Side of the Tracks

God does not show favoritism.

ROMANS 2:11

Is it possible to live on the wrong side of the tracks in an Amish community? You may be surprised that the answer is yes. While the goal of every parent is to model and teach what a good Amish man or woman is like, each Amish child grows up with both an individual and a family identity. The truth is, some Amish families are just more popular than others.

Although youth are not officially Amish until they join the church as adults, their Amish identity begins to form in infancy. Identity emerges from intentional training and instruction combined with the cultural influences that surround a person. Some aspects of Amish identity are achieved, such as their approach to work, and some emerge from relationships and associations.

Loving does not empty the heart, nor giving empty the purse. The boy who gave the loaves and fishes didn't go hungry.

A teenager's family of origin is an important source in defining self-identity. Children and youth from highly esteemed families are likely to form positive self-identities since they benefit directly from the accomplishments and status of their grandparents and parents. Family success is usually measured by hard work, thrift, good management, and the outcome of their children. Young people whose parents fail to meet the community ideals may struggle more with identity issues, both personally and socially because of these family liabilities.

It seems no matter who we are or where we live, the popularity game is present. What a blessing that God shows no favorites! Deuteronomy 10:17 says, "The LORD your God is the God of gods and Lord of lords. He is the great God, the mighty and awesome God, who shows no partiality and cannot be bribed."

Do you find yourself showing favoritism to people in your life? Do you have a better relationship with one child than with another? Do you favor certain friends because of their accomplishments or because you deem them more "worthy"? Thank God that He doesn't compare you with others. Then ask Him to transform your heart. Work on doing your part to show all those you interact with that they are loved by God.

■ ■ ■

Dear heavenly Father, I am thankful that You do not have favorites. Help me to see those people around me as You see them. Help me to focus on hearts first—and not show favoritism.

Quest toward Quietness

Better to have one handful with quietness than two
handfuls with hard work and chasing the wind.

ECCLESIASTES 4:6

Amish have been referred to as "the quiet in the land." Their refusal to rely on modern conveniences such as radios, televisions, and various appliances prevents a great deal of noise in their lives. But the Amish also have quiet hearts and minds.

Advertisers spend billions of dollars to send thousands of messages into our minds every day. The Internet connects us with an endless stream of friends and associates who have something to say. There is an increasing flood of information, facts, and advice. We get tired of sorting through it all. We pay big money to go on summer vacation. To get away. To find quiet.

Is it possible to discover quietness in our everyday lives, too? To work less, not more? To turn off the electronics and listen to the still, small voice of God's Spirit? *Better to have one handful with quietness. . . .*

It's up to us to stop chasing the wind. To say no to more commitments and yes to more peace. But we can't do it on our own. Jesus said, "Come to me, all who labor and are heavy laden, and I will give you rest" (Matthew 11:28, ESV). He knows the realities of this world are too hard to face if our minds are too full and our backs are too burdened. We must turn to Him. (And being attentive to Him may mean turning off a few electronics.) We must confess that we're trying to do too much and ask Jesus to take our burdens.

"Though the rules vary widely from district to district, many technological items are allowed in Amish homes and farms, including calculators, flashlights, manual typewriters, gas grills, chain saws, inline skates, and more."

Sometimes God answers us by giving us strength. But sometimes He answers us by asking us to lay down burdens He never asked us to carry in the first place. Will you hand over those burdens today?

■ ■ ■

Dear heavenly Father, I thank You that the way You've chosen for me is a quiet path. Here are my burdens, Lord. Thank You for speaking to my heart and guiding the release of things I don't need to carry.

Together under Him

All the believers met together in one place and shared everything they had.
ACTS 2:44

My teenage daughter and I had a discussion about tattoos recently. Although she didn't necessarily want one, she approved of her friends' choices to have them.

"Don't they realize what they'll look like when they're seventy years old?" I asked her.

"They'll look like everyone else," she answered. "The nonconforming ones will be those who don't have a tattoo!"

So true. Each generation of young people has its own definition of "normal." In our society we focus on individualism, which may lead to group acceptance. The Amish focus on the group itself. The better a person casts off individualism, the better he or she fits in.

The Amish use the term *English*, or *Englishers*, for those who are non-Amish, because they speak English rather than Pennsylvania Dutch.

Choice is appropriate only within group-approved options and only if it maintains and strengthens the group. Understanding this difference is central in comprehending the heart of Amish identity.

The task of Amish young people is not to distinguish themselves from others by their uniqueness and achievement but rather their willingness to conform to the group. They are expected to strengthen the cohesion of the community through "giving up the self," as they term it.

This reminds me of 1 Corinthians 12:27: "All of you together are Christ's body, and each of you is a part of it." As followers of Christ we would do well to see ourselves as part of collective society. Yet instead of focusing on the well-being of the group, it's our job to worship Jesus, to follow Him as the head of the body. As we worship, walk, and work, He will bring everything together.

Have you ever felt God asking you to give up some of your individuality for His sake? The more claim you give Him to all of yourself, the more joy and peace you'll experience!

■ ■ ■

Dear heavenly Father, I thank You that You are the head of Your body, the church. Remind me again today that it's not up to me to figure out my part. Instead, I simply need to look to You and follow where You lead.

Unchanging

This is what the LORD says—your Redeemer, the Holy One of
Israel: "I am the Lord your God, who teaches you what is good
for you and leads you along the paths you should follow."

ISAIAH 48:17

How different is your life today than it was five years ago? Ten years ago? Though my job as a writer is the same, I go about it differently because of technology.

Most of us embrace technology, but what do we lose with the constant change? When our eyes are consistently focused on the "next thing," we can lose our contentment. When we are constantly upgrading technology that still works perfectly well, we lose our dollars. When we spend time connecting with others "out there," we lose our connection with those who are physically present. When do we say, "Enough is enough" and mean it?

The Amish take the long view. They ensure that family togetherness, community support, and faith are the cornerstones of their daily lives. They aren't concerned about what the world says is important or necessary. They look back—not forward—to establish their way.

Peace comes when you are thoughtful about what you choose to change. When you ask yourself, *Do I really need an upgrade?* and *What will I be sacrificing if I get one?*

We can be thankful that God is available to teach us and lead us. He wants us to turn to Him instead of running to keep up with the fast-paced world.

Isaiah 30:21 says, "Whether you turn to the right or to the left, your ears will hear a voice behind you, saying, 'This is the way; walk in it'" (NIV).

"Most districts permit the use of public transportation, though some have restrictions against air travel. Bicycles are used by some groups but not others. In Lancaster County, the simplest way to get around is on a scooter."

There are some aspects of our lives that need to change, but two things should hold true: (1) that we seek the Lord and let Him direct our paths, and (2) that we don't get swept away with the changes of life but instead allow God to set the pace.

■ ■ ■

Dear heavenly Father, I am thankful You are my unchanging God! I turn my life over
to You to guide my steps and set the pace.

JULY 19

Sight

He told them, "The man they call Jesus made mud and spread it
over my eyes and told me, 'Go to the pool of Siloam and wash
yourself.' So I went and washed, and now I can see!"
JOHN 9:11

I remember when I first heard about Amish fiction. People would make comments like, "The book was good, but the author didn't do her research." "I read other Amish novels, and the characters were different." I haven't heard that in a while. Readers now know that the Amish are as varied as any other segment of society.

It is risky to talk about THE Amish and to make generalized statements about all Amish groups in North America based on one Amish community. Typically, most Amish groups forbid owning automobiles, tapping electricity from public utility lines, using self-propelled farm machinery, owning a television, radio, and computer, attending high school and college, joining the military, and initiating divorce. Members are expected to speak a German or Swiss dialect and to adhere to the dress standards of their group. Most groups have battery-powered lights on their carriages but the most conservative affiliations use kerosene lanterns. . . . In some regions of the country power lawn mowers are permitted but not in others. The women in one affiliation are permitted to use only treadle (foot-powered) sewing machines, but those in another group may power their sewing machines with batteries. Some communities are wealthy and others are rather poor. Clearly, diversity abounds even within affiliations and local church districts.

If you wish to be happy, we'll tell you the way: don't live tomorrow till you've lived today.

PROVERB

The diversity we see in the world reminds us that sometimes there isn't only one right way. This is a lesson Jesus made sure we paid attention to. Just look at how Jesus healed the blind: sometimes He healed with words. Sometimes He healed by touch. Jesus also healed by mixing spittle with mud and placing it on a man's eyes. These instances show us that it's not the method that's important but rather faith in Him that matters.

■ ■ ■

Dear heavenly Father, we like systems. We want check-off lists, but You have shown us there isn't always only one right way to do things or fix things. But when it comes to salvation, I thank You that You are the Way!

Faith Foundation

God so loved the world that he gave his one and only Son, that
whoever believes in him shall not perish but have eternal life.

JOHN 3:16 (NIV)

What is the basis for all that we believe as followers of Christ? We can sum it up in three words: *God so loved.*

What is the basis for all that Amish followers of Christ believe? The same three words. One bishop explains, "When seekers from the outside come to us wanting to be Amish, they are often attracted for the wrong reasons. They could have fallen in love with one of our *Youngie.* Or they may have fallen in love with what they think is a simpler way of life. What they fail to recognize is that our faith in Christ is at the center. Horses, buggies, and kerosene lanterns will quickly grow stale without the faith foundation."

"God so loved the world that he gave his one and only Son." This is the faith foundation on which everything else we believe is set. We have great hope, but even hope needs a firm footing. The acceptance of God's gift will anchor us, enabling us to hold strong through every storm, every flood of trouble. It's this simple truth that can transform the darkest soul and fill it with light.

"In some communities young women in a 'buddy bunch' wear identical colors to Sunday evening singings."

We may want a different lifestyle, a simpler way of life. But even if we seek that and find it, we will never be truly satisfied. If we try to become Amish—or anything else for that matter—the results of our attempts will last only as far as our determination. But when we turn our lives over to Jesus Christ, it's His gift—not our reliability—that we can count on!

If people know only one Bible verse, John 3:16 is usually the one, and that's okay. It's the verse on which a foundation of faith is built. If they start there, they start off right!

■ ■ ■

Dear heavenly Father, thank You for reminding me that in the long run, sometimes what is simplest matters the most. May You whisper the truth of all today's verse means over and over in my heart today!

Open Hearts, Open Lives

You must worship Christ as Lord of your life. And if someone asks about your Christian hope, always be ready to explain it.
1 PETER 3:15

Every year millions of tourists add a new destination to their summer vacation travels. It's not the Grand Canyon or Yellowstone but Amish country. Amish friends have told me many stories about tourists who behave as if the Amish are characters in a play rather than real people living out their lives. Here is one woman's point of view:

> To Linda, personal privacy is an important consideration. She knows that who she is and how she lives is an increasing curiosity. Visitors stream into Lancaster County to learn about the Amish. Many do not believe what they see, sometimes thinking they have stumbled into another version of Colonial Williamsburg. So they ask questions, sometimes thinking they are interrupting a costumed interpreter, not a real-life person with work to do and places to go. Many visitors know better but still cannot help themselves.
>
> Who are you?
>
> How do you live?
>
> What can you tell us about yourself?
>
> Because Linda likes to talk to people and enjoys making new friends, she often opens herself to the questioners. And finds it frustrating. For even a bit of openness means she may be inundated with requests.

"Usually the Amish give the first initial of the father's name as a middle initial for their children's names. This is done out of respect for the father."

Do you ever feel like Linda? When you live differently from others—when others see your peace and joy—people will want to know about that. God's Word says we should always be ready to explain our hope. And Colossians 4:6 says, "Let your conversation be gracious and attractive so that you will have the right response for everyone."

Do you want your life to have an impact? You don't need to travel the world to make that happen. Sometimes God brings the right person—with the right questions—right to your backyard.

■ ■ ■

Dear heavenly Father, words have power. Give me words that speak truth of You, and may the impact of my life extend further than I ever imagined possible.

Never Forget

My child, never forget the things I have taught you.
Store my commands in your heart.

PROVERBS 3:1

No doubt you've heard this popular quote from philosopher George Santayana before: "Those who cannot remember the past are condemned to repeat it." At one time the Anabaptist history was nearly lost, but one man changed all that.

In the late sixteenth century the Dutch government took a tolerant stance toward Anabaptists. Socially accepted Mennonites gradually moved into mainstream culture and eventually became economically prosperous. By the mid-1600s they had achieved a "golden age" and filled the ranks of wealthy merchants, physicians, artists, and artisans.

Dutch Mennonite minister Thieleman Jansz van Braght feared his people were acculturating. . . . He began collecting stories of Anabaptist martyrs from court records and other books. In 1660 he published them in a 1,478-page tome entitled *The Bloody Theater,* or *Martyrs Mirror.* . . . Today the *Martyrs Mirror* is found in Amish homes, and references to it are common in Amish circles.

The stories in the *Martyr's Mirror* became more graphic in the 1685 edition when Jan Luiken, a Dutch artist, provided more than a hundred copper-engraved illustrations.

Have you become forgetful about what God has done? It's easy to do that. We become lulled by ease. Yet it's important to remember both times of pain and times of blessing. When we see God's faithfulness to his people in history, we will be more likely to trust Him in the present.

"Praise the LORD, my soul, and forget not all his benefits," we read in Psalm 103:2 (NIV). Quiet your heart for a moment, and consider some of the pains and the joys of your past. Then take a few minutes to write out some of those moments. Consider coming back to them over the coming weeks and months and adding more detail. You might want to share them with a family member or a friend. When we take time to remember God's goodness, our faith will grow. Who knows, our story may be one that people will remember even after we're gone.

■ ■ ■

Dear heavenly Father, thank You for all Your benefits. My history is Your history—my soul knows that. Help me to study the past so I can share the stories of Your faithfulness in all life's situations.

Fifty Years from Now

Direct your children onto the right path, and when
they are older, they will not leave it.
PROVERBS 22:6

One of my treasured possessions is an aged book from 1947 titled *Meet the Amish: A Pictorial Study of the Amish People*. Looking through it, I'm thrilled to say that not much has changed! When discussing the clothing, the culture, and the beliefs, the basics discussed in 1947 are still the basics today. Here is an example: "Unlike most of the other Pennsylvania Germans, the Amish have no activities which can be classified as folk arts. No attempt may be made to decorate any article with colors, flowers, pictures, or other devices. There are no dances of any sort. Musical instruments are banned, part singing is discouraged, solo singing is unheard of, and only a simple form of group singing, without instrumental accompaniment, is permitted."

The values we leave our children are more important than the valuables we leave them.

PROVERB

As I read through the pages, one thing is certain: the Amish have done a fine job of passing down their beliefs. They know what matters to them, and they pass it on to the next generation. Deuteronomy 4:9 says, "Watch out! Be careful never to forget what you yourself have seen. Do not let these memories escape from your mind as long as you live! And be sure to pass them on to your children and grandchildren."

What matters most to you? Jot down your top three values (or three characteristics you would most like your life to display). If you could ensure that fifty years from now your children or grandchildren or others you knew as young people were living by the values and beliefs you had established, what would that look like?

Now look at your life today. How well are you living out these values? More than that, how well are you passing them on—not just to your children but also to others you mentor or those in your church?

There are many *good* things to build our lives around, but we lose much ground unless we focus on the *best* things.

■ ■ ■

Dear heavenly Father, help me to live today in a way that I would be proud to see my children and grandchildren modeling fifty years from now.

Making Disciples

My child, don't reject the LORD's discipline, and don't be upset when he corrects you. For the LORD corrects those he loves, just as a father corrects a child in whom he delights.

PROVERBS 3:11-12

I remember a call I received from the police. My son had gotten in a bit of trouble, and they needed me to come to the station. I was confused and burdened. I also wondered what I'd done wrong. The Amish are no different:

> Recently complaints were registered by residents of the New Holland [Pennsylvania] area that several hundred Amish buggies were being raced along public roads at dangerous speeds (for such vehicles). When State police officers investigated, it was found that Amish young bloods congregated in large numbers and challenged one another to speed contests. Excellent horsemanship was demonstrated, but, because of the ever-present danger of collision between buggies or between buggies, and automobile, the practice was discouraged. Several young Amishmen who lost their heads over the matter were charged with disorderly conduct. A few days later they appeared in alderman's court, promptly and courteously paid their fines, and apologized for their conduct. . . . The Amish elders did not enjoy the publicity, however, and apparently took their young charges to task over the matter.

"It is said when an Amishman buys land he is more likely to build a barn than a house, and the longer he lives, the more barns he builds."

Everyone needs to be disciplined, or corrected, at times, but parents also need to consider how they discipline and why. The word *discipline* comes from a Latin word that means to teach or instruct, or from the noun form, which means student or disciple. Parents should never discipline out of anger. Any discipline that comes as the result of parents' embarrassment will just frustrate children. There is a better way: "Fathers, don't exasperate your children by coming down hard on them. Take them by the hand and lead them in the way of the Master," we read in Ephesians 6:4 (*The Message*).

If you are a parent, prayerfully consider how God can better use you to guide and instruct your children in being disciples of our Lord Jesus Christ.

■ ■ ■

Dear heavenly Father, I hate to think where I'd be without Your loving discipline. Thank You for patiently and consistently correcting me when I make wrong choices. Thank You for Your loving guidance, which is always available to me.

JULY 25

Trustworthy

If you are faithful in little things, you will be faithful in large ones.
LUKE 16:10

An Amish friend once told me, "The Amish don't believe in their photos being taken, but if someone—like a newspaper photographer—happens to catch them in a shot, they don't mind. In one older book about the Amish, it is noted that the "photographer" took the pictures with the camera hidden under his arm. While most Amish don't like to be photographed, some allow it.

Bill Coleman is an internationally acclaimed photographer of the Amish. The photographic legacy he deems his Amish Odyssey is four decades long, a goodly number of years to document the lives and landscapes of the Old Order Amish sect in a hidden valley somewhere in Pennsylvania. But forty years is scantly time to portray a people whose ancestors immigrated to the area in the eighteenth century.

If you live an honest and upright life, there is no need to "talk the talk." Your life speaks for itself.

The Amish have a love affair with life and simplicity, with preserving ages of innocence and respect, with teaching responsibility and the joys of tradition. These very private people are reluctant to reveal themselves to outsiders.

Bill, albeit knowing he will always be an outsider has, charmingly, respectfully cajoled his way into the hearts and homes of a number of Amish families willing to allow him to document their lives from birth to death, generation after generation. His determination to keep their location secret, their lives private, equals their determination to maintain their way of life.

Do you have a friend like Bill? Someone you can trust no matter what? Are you a friend like that? Can those in your inner circle trust you without reservation? Do you uphold their trust?

Do you see Jesus as a friend like that? That's the way He sees you: "I no longer call you slaves, because a master doesn't confide in his slaves. Now you are my friends, since I have told you everything the Father told me" (John 15:15).

When you turn to Jesus, He knows that you may find it hard to open your heart, but He's completely trustworthy. Above all else, know that.

■ ■ ■

Dear heavenly Father, I am amazed that You call me friend and long for me to trust You. I do trust You, Lord. Help me to trust You more!

Remember

Remember your history, your long and rich history.
ISAIAH 46:9 (*THE MESSAGE*)

Is there any way to track your spiritual growth? Faith is not something you can weigh. You can't measure hope with a ruler. Truthfulness may be something you can feel inside, but you can't bag it up.

I reread my journals to gauge my personal growth. When I look back, I can see the ways God is transforming my life. I'm also able to witness how many prayers God has answered!

Although all Amish have limited formal education and a limited knowledge of popular culture, most Amish, young and old, have some interest in history, both oral and written. . . . For the Amish, recalling their stories helps define who they are and gives them a standard for judging whether or not they are drifting into mainstream worldliness or following the biblical description of "keeping the faith once delivered to the saints" (Jude 3). . . . The Amish constantly negotiate with the press of modernity, and now post-modernity, by weighing present realities with their historical core values.

Without our written history, we have no way to compare our "now" with "then." How many lessons are learned as we can sit around the dinner table and say, "Dat, tell me a story"?

When my grandmother tells my daughter about growing up during the Great Depression, we begin to realize how wealthy we are. When an Amish grandfather shares about his growing-up years, youngsters can see how different their lives are and weigh whether they're heading in the right direction.

If you keep a journal, take time to go back over your own history and thank God for the ways He's "shown up" in your life over the years. If you don't have a journal, consider starting one to record your prayers, your thoughts, and your important "history." Someday the record you've kept will stand as a monument to God's faithfulness!

"Amish adults who require further learning on a particular topic, such as bookkeeping, will teach themselves, learn from a coworker, or take a correspondence course. In some communities, when a high school diploma is required for a job, Amish youth may be allowed to get a GED."

■ ■ ■

Dear heavenly Father, I thank You that You are part of my history, part of my present, and part of my future. May the words I write and share be monuments to Your faithfulness.

A Recipe for Success

I've learned by now to be quite content whatever my circumstances. I'm just as happy with little as with much, with much as with little. I've found the recipe for being happy whether full or hungry, hands full or hands empty. Whatever I have, wherever I am, I can make it through anything in the One who makes me who I am.
PHILIPPIANS 4:11 (*THE MESSAGE*)

Amish recipes have become popular in recent years. People enjoy them because they are often simple (no fancy ingredients), hearty, and quick. (Amish mothers do not have time or money to create a gourmet meal for a dozen hungry bellies.)

When we hear the word *recipe*, we often think of food, but according to one definition, a recipe can also be "a formula or procedure for doing or attaining something," such as a recipe for success. Paul found the recipe for contentment and joy. No matter where he was or what he had—or didn't have—he turned to Jesus. He knew that Jesus made him who he was. Recipes are only as good as the ingredients that go into them. Contentment comes from mixing heavenly focus, more than a smidgen of patience, and a lot of trust in God.

> Good deeds have echoes.
>
> PROVERB

Recipes are meant to be shared. One of my treasured possessions is a resealable bag filled with my grandma's handwritten recipe cards. They mean something to me because she made the dishes—and shared them—with love. If you have learned a method for achieving something, don't you want to share it? When you share how you've learned to trust God, others can try it for themselves.

The best recipes are simple. If you want to achieve joy or contentment or peace in your own life, consider taking doable steps. If you make things too complicated, you'll end up with nothing more than good intentions.

Finally, the best recipe starts with turning to God: "The LORD protects the unwary; when I was brought low, he saved me" reads Psalm 116:6 (NIV). No matter what recipe for success we're trying to follow, nothing will work without God as the main ingredient. When we come before Him with our needs and desires, He will not fail us.

■ ■ ■

Dear heavenly Father, whenever I am in need, You are the answer. Whenever I have a need, turning to You is the first step. I take that step again, at this moment, with all my heart!

To Gather, to Offer

God doesn't miss anything. He knows perfectly well all the love you've
shown him by helping needy Christians, and that you keep at it.
HEBREWS 6:10 (*THE MESSAGE*)

Have you ever been to a place where as soon as you stepped through the door, you knew you'd come back and knew that this place would be a forever deposit in your memory bank? That's how it felt when I walked through the doors of the West Kootenai Kraft and Grocery. It's a store in northwest Montana, not far from the Canadian border. It's not a place you would stumble upon. It's so far off the beaten track that you must make it a destination to get there. It's a place centered in the middle of a small community composed of both English and Amish. It's part store, part bakery, part restaurant, and part gift shop. I thank God that He brought me to this community and allowed me to be a tour guide of sorts to those who are unfamiliar with the Amish lifestyle in Montana.

> **If you give your love away, it will multiply each day.**
>
> PROVERB

What I loved about the West Kootenai when I first discovered it was the sense of community I encountered. It truly is a picture of neighbors helping neighbors. Approximately twenty Amish families live among the English. They work together, too. And when there is a need—such as for a local firehouse—everyone pitches in. What an example to all of us!

One of my favorite verses that focuses on having giving hearts is Matthew 10:42: "If you give even a cup of cold water to one of the least of my followers, you will surely be rewarded." Is there someone in your life who needs a cup of cold water from you? If so, what does this cup look like? What do you have to pour out with love? The person may be as different from you as the English are from the Amish, but God isn't concerned about *whom* you extend grace to, just that you do it.

■ ■ ■

Dear heavenly Father, I thank You that wherever we are gathered, You are there in our
midst, and that when we offer help to others, You are pleased.

Reaffirm

Two people are better off than one, for they can help each other succeed. . . . A person standing alone can be attacked and defeated, but two can stand back-to-back and conquer. Three are even better, for a triple-braided cord is not easily broken.
ECCLESIASTES 4:9, 12

There is no community without conflict. Whenever you have a variety of people, you'll also have a wide range of ideas and opinions.

Limitations on Amish life are dictated by the *Ordnung*, which is what the Amish call the unwritten set of rules and regulations that dictates their day-to-day life. The *Ordnung* deals with a wide variety of topics, such as clothing, transportation, technology, education, and much more.

> We must pick our friends but not pick them to pieces.
>
> PROVERB

Rules in the *Ordnung* can vary widely from affiliation to affiliation and can even vary somewhat from district to district within the same affiliation. As districts grow and divide into new ones and as new technologies and issues arise, the *Ordnung* necessarily changes and adapts as well. Minor regulations are updated by church leaders as needed, but major decisions usually involve congregational input and can cause debate in member meetings.

Regardless of how intensely various issues are debated, all matters of contention are laid to rest at the twice-yearly council meetings that precede the communion services. Once the group is at peace with each other and the rules, members reaffirm the commitment they made when they were first baptized to follow the *Ordnung*. In this way, they remain united as a people.

Have you had a conflict with someone or with a group of people lately? Is the conflict ongoing? If so, maybe you need to make new beginnings in your relationship with those family members or friends. Maybe you need to reaffirm the commitment you first made to God, and then reaffirm your commitment to others.

Our gracious God has offered forgiveness, strength, and unity, even after we fall short. Perhaps it's time for you to share those qualities with someone else.

Two people are better than one. Joined they are stronger, and when they come before God together, that's a triple cord that can't be broken.

■ ■ ■

Dear heavenly Father, I'm so thankful that we have the opportunity to fix our mistakes. Turn my heart toward those with whom I have conflict. Soften my heart toward them as only You can.

Watching Fireflies

"My thoughts are not your thoughts, neither are your ways my ways," declares the Lord.

ISAIAH 55:8 (NIV)

An Amish father and his son study the twilight sky. The father is searching for clouds gathering in the distance. His corn is waist high, and he's waiting for a "million dollar rain." If rain comes in time, the crop will continue to grow and will feed his family. If rain comes too late, the corn is cut for silage, a fodder for animals. It is still useful, but the food and money the family counted on will be lost.

As they stand there, the son also sees the stalks of corn. He sees the horizon. But the boy's eyes are on something else. He's focused on the fireflies. They dance and flash, bringing him joy.

In everyday life we see things from our own perspective. The physical view is the same, but our minds translate the view differently. Worry clouds the thoughts of a farmer. Simple joy fills the mind of a child.

Do you ever wonder how God sees things? He gazes at the horizon, already knowing not only whether the rain is coming but also how much. We allow worry to cloud our vision. God doesn't worry. He knows His plans and His power to accomplish them.

> Every moment of worry weakens the soul for its daily combat.
>
> PROVERB

God longs for us to come to Him with childlike faith instead of allowing worry to fill our minds. Mark 10:13-15 reads, "One day some parents brought their children to Jesus so he could touch and bless them. But the disciples scolded the parents for bothering him. . . . [Jesus] said to them, 'Let the children come to me. Don't stop them! For the Kingdom of God belongs to those who are like these children. I tell you the truth, anyone who doesn't receive the Kingdom of God like a child will never enter it.'"

What is on the horizon of your life today? Are you waiting for rain? Do you have a heavy heart? Worries about the future? Allow thoughts of God to fill your mind. Remember that He holds your future in the palm of His hand. And take time to focus on the fireflies.

■ ■ ■

Dear heavenly Father, thank You so much for holding my future in Your hands. Forgive me for all the times I worry. Help me to delight in the small joys today brings.

Get Wisdom

If you need wisdom, ask our generous God, and he will
give it to you. He will not rebuke you for asking.
JAMES 1:5

If you could sit down with a young couple for thirty minutes on their wedding day, what would you tell them? What wisdom would you impart? To love God and each other? To find a good community? To surround themselves with like-minded people? To diligently train any children they may have to love God? To not get caught up in the trappings of the world? When we choose wisdom, everything in our lives—our relationships, our homes, and even our health—is affected.

Suzanne Woods Fisher writes,

Medicine and advice are two things more pleasant to give than to receive.

PROVERB

The fastest growing population in North America, the Amish have held strong to enduring traditions for over four hundred years. They have a much lower rate of heart disease than do average Americans. Lower depression rates, lower cancer rates. They maintain one of the strongest and most stable family systems in our country. The elderly are highly esteemed, cared for in the home. Over 85 to 90 percent of the youth remain in the church, choosing baptism as young adults. The Amish . . . seem to be doing something right.

God's wisdom will never lead us astray, and He never withholds it from us when we ask for it. God wants you to turn to Him—turn to His Word. The Amish are great examples of what it looks like to live in light of the wisdom that comes from above: "The wisdom from above is first of all pure. It is also peace loving, gentle at all times, and willing to yield to others. It is full of mercy and good deeds. It shows no favoritism and is always sincere" (James 3:17).

How often do you ask God for wisdom? What would happen if you did so more often? Seek God and listen to Him speaking to you through His Word. You'll be amazed at how the wisdom from the Word can improve every part of your life.

■ ■ ■

Dear heavenly Father, You created all things, and I know You can guide me in every detail of my life. I seek Your wisdom today.

Kitchen Garden Service

Do you see someone skilled in their work? They will serve before
kings; they will not serve before officials of low rank.

PROVERBS 22:29 (NIV)

When the first of August rolls around, you and I might see summer as winding down, but the Amish gardener has different things on her mind. She picks onions by August 1 because she knows they'll rot if they stay in the ground. Once the onions are picked, she hangs them on a string in the basement to dry. When they are free of moisture, they are laid out on newspapers and tied off.

In Amish homes, "kitchen gardens" are used to produce fruits and vegetables for the family's own use. Produce is essential to the Amish way of life, and onions, like a lot of other produce, will be stored and used throughout the winter months.

There is something beautiful about a simple garden that reminds us of God's intricately designed creation. We read in Genesis 2:15, "The LORD God placed the man in the Garden of Eden to tend and watch over it." Tending the garden allows us to join with God in His act of supplying the earth. Gardening allows us to organize and create as we tend and watch. We also use our skill to serve our families and communities. God could have designed the produce of this earth to grow without our effort, but as with so many areas in life, He chose to involve us in the process. He no doubt knows and understands the joy and satisfaction we gain from using our skills.

> Gardening is a way of showing that you believe in tomorrow.
>
> PROVERB

You may not have a garden to tend, but the way you do your work each day provides the best outward reflection of your commitment to serving the Lord. When you work with skill and dedication, you honor God. When you are committed to Him, that shows in the work you do for others.

How do you serve others in real, physical ways? Know that God is pleased by your efforts. He sees the tending and watching you do in others' lives. He sees the impact. He sees how your service nourishes others' hearts and souls.

■ ■ ■

Dear heavenly Father, sometimes work seems like just work. Thank You for the reminder
that You are pleased by my service. May my whole heart serve You today.

Humility before Honor

Before a downfall the heart is haughty, but humility comes before honor.
PROVERBS 18:12 (NIV)

I once had an Amish friend tell me that one of the hardest things he faced was not to become prideful in his lifestyle, and especially in his dress. He felt as if he had "got it right," and it was easy to become proud when the world took notice of him too.

An Amish seventh grader named Emma wrote, "We wear plain clothes because the Bible says we should. Sometimes the English stare at you but they never have said anything to me about my clothes. We can be a witness for others by being plain. . . . I read in the last Family Life that just wearing plain clothes doesn't make you a Christian. I think sometimes we forget that."

In Farmerstown, Ohio, hundreds of Amish workers erected a barn in one day after it was damaged by a tornado.

Emma was talking specifically about the pride that comes from wearing plain clothes, but I admit to feeling this way about my life at times. I see unchurched people around me making bad choices. They seem to pay attention to my life, and I'm pleased I can be a witness with my life and my choices. And even through that thought, pride seeps into my heart.

"Seek the Kingdom of God above all else, and live righteously, and he will give you everything you need," we read in Matthew 6:33. But sometimes we're too busy building our own kingdoms—focusing on our own right living—to seek His Kingdom first. Jesus made himself nothing. He surrendered Himself and humbled Himself to the point of death on the cross.

Some of my biggest stumbles have come after I've examined my life and thought I was doing a pretty good job. Humility is realizing that I can do no good thing without Christ. It reminds me that I'm accountable to Him, and to others. If Christ humbled Himself to allow God to lift Him up, I can do no less.

■ ■ ■

Dear heavenly Father, forgive me for the times I become prideful in my own right choices. I know that I'm able to do good—to be an example—only because You are living out Your life through mine.

Be Rich

*A person is a fool to store up earthly wealth but
not have a rich relationship with God.*

LUKE 12:21

Fifty years ago it would have been rare for Amish people to enter a grocery store. Even today the majority of what they fill their shelves and cellars with comes from their gardens, from canning and butchering. Even when Amish people do go to the store, they most likely do not fill their carts as we do. What they do buy is simple and cheap, but if you ask them, they would say they consider themselves blessed. In fact here is a note from an Amishman titled "I Am Rich."

For real excitement on the farm, there's nothing like gathering in the first eggs from a flock of chickens you've raised from baby chicks. Nor is there anything as tasty as vegetables you've hoed and cultivated till you're hot and tired. When we stop to consider, it's nothing short of a miracle when we behold how much God provides for us to eat, all from one little dried-up dead-looking seed.

You're never too old to learn.

PROVERB

No, we have no so-called modern conveniences, but we are blessed with an abundance of life's necessities. We don't have an over-flowing grocery cart, or beautiful clothes or a big bank account to fall back on.

But I do have a family and friends, and many people I meet on life's highway. I have good eyesight, a healthy mind and body. I AM RICH.

May I remember to be as rich with gratitude as I am rich with gifts which God has bestowed upon me.

When do you feel rich? When you can fill a grocery cart or shop in the best stores for the best clothes? Or, like the writer of the note above, do you see your family, friends, health, and relationship with God as your true riches?

Proverbs 13:7 says, "Some who are poor pretend to be rich; others who are rich pretend to be poor." You can pretend to be anything you like, but real riches can't be tossed into a grocery cart and paid for. They come only from God.

■ ■ ■

Dear heavenly Father, thank You for all that I have that cannot be bought. Thank You for paying the price so that I am able to receive what I have.

Focused on God, Not on the World

Don't love the world's ways. Don't love the world's goods.
Love of the world squeezes out love for the Father.
1 JOHN 2:15 (THE MESSAGE)

Do you consider yourself "worldly"? If you drive a car, have a phone, and enjoy modern conveniences you are—at least according to the Amish. They believe that worldly things take our time and attention away from godly things. When we're driving in our cars, we're not spending time at home. When we're talking on the phone, we're not talking to the people who are with us. When we're focused on gadgets, we can miss the opportunity to connect with others in our community.

How can we live in the world without loving the world? It all comes down to focus. Everyone has focus. But the question is, Are you focused on getting more, having more "things," or are you focused on using all that you have to glorify God? Are you making Him the main focus of your life and your days?

Times of Trial: Poem Stories of Anabaptist Martyrs for Children by Amy Schlabach starts out: "Long ago and far away / In lands across the sea, / A faithful band of followers / Of Jesus came to be."

"Life works better when we know how to glance at things but gaze at God," writes Welsh minister and author Selwyn Hughes. "Seeing Him clearly will enable us to see all other things clearly."

The first Anabaptists chose to change their lifestyles in order to draw closer to God. Even though they faced persecution, what they chose to focus on continued for generations. And that's really the point, isn't it? The world is always changing, but God never changes. There will be new cars, new phones, and new gadgets every year, but as Hebrews 13:8 says, "Jesus Christ is the same yesterday, today, and forever."

Here's something you may want to consider: Are you worldly focused, or are you heavenly focused? As you focus on the second part of that question, the first part will begin to take care of itself.

■ ■ ■

Dear heavenly Father, please cleanse my mind and heart of the concerns this world uses to try to trap me. Instead turn my mind—my focus—to You.

Finding Rest

*Jesus said, "Come to me, all of you who are weary and
carry heavy burdens, and I will give you rest."*

MATTHEW 11:28

Do you find yourself ready to get off of your feet at the end of the day? According to the *New York Times*, the average American takes 5,117 steps a day; the average Amish man takes 18,000 steps a day, and the average Amish woman takes 14,000 steps! If anyone needs rest it's the Amish . . . and they take it. The Amish community considers Sunday a day of rest. They eat simple meals, prepared the day before, and give their bodies time to rejuvenate. They may read, sit and visit with family, or write letters. Their feet do not have to worry about all those steps!

For many people Sunday isn't so different from any other day. They shop, they cook, and they even squeeze in work. I can't tell you how many times I've told myself, *Answering a few e-mails won't hurt*. But it does.

Most Amish homes have a special Sunday night treat—popcorn!

In Matthew 11:28, above, God tells us He will give us rest. The question is, do we take it? Do we rest on the Sabbath? More than that, do we go to God—every day of the week—and ask Him to lift our burdens? Isaiah 28:12 adds, "God has told his people, 'Here is a place of rest; let the weary rest here. This is a place of quiet rest.' But they would not listen."

I don't know about you, but sometimes I find it easier to complain about my burdens than to take them to the Lord. Sometimes it's easier to feel overwhelmed with my work than it is to push it all to the side for an hour and just relax with my family or a friend.

The question is not whether we have burdens and weariness. The question is, will we take them to God and still our minds and our hands for Him to do His refreshing work?

. . .

*Dear heavenly Father, I admit it: I need rest. I need You to come and lift these burdens.
At this moment I'm not too proud to say so.*

Shared Bread

As they sat down to eat, [Jesus] took the bread and
blessed it. Then he broke it and gave it to them.
LUKE 24:30

On church Sundays typical Amish families don't rush home because there is a roast in the oven. Instead they participate in an after-church meal. When I first asked my Amish friends about this, I expected them to describe something similar to a church potluck but with Amish whoopie pies, fresh cinnamon rolls, and homemade sausage on the menu. My jaw dropped when I learned that the most common items were bread, Amish spread (peanut butter sweetened with marshmallow or molasses), and pickled beets! The drinks are black coffee and water, and a social time usually follows the meals.

"When ladies neared the end of the canning . . . they often had odd amounts left over from their gardens. So, everything would get combined as chow chow–carrots, onions, cauliflower, cucumbers, cabbage, celery, corn, peppers, and assorted beans. Chow chow is sometimes referred to as 'End of the Season' relish."

When did you last take time to break bread with those in your church community, at church potlucks or in some other way? While the point of gathering around the table is to nourish our bodies, connecting with others feeds our souls, too. The Bible talks about this in Acts 2:46: "Day by day, attending the temple together and breaking bread in their homes, they received their food with glad and generous hearts" (ESV).

In almost every other generation except the one in which we live, bread was seen as the mainstay of life. To share your bread was to give a piece of your daily living to another. It meant that you weren't keeping everything for yourself but rather depended on God to provide what you needed.

Whether Jesus was multiplying the contents of a young boy's lunch basket or gathering with His followers in an upper room, He set the example of feeding the soul by feeding the body first.

Have you shared lunch with a church friend recently? What you eat doesn't have to be anything fancy. Amish-style works just fine!

■ ■ ■

Dear heavenly Father, too often I plan where to eat after church,
but I fail when it comes to planning get-togethers with others.
Thank You for showing me that I need to feed my soul with
friendships as well as feed my body with food.

Gut Words

*[Jesus said,] "These things I have spoken to you in figurative
language; an hour is coming when I will no longer speak to you in
figurative language, but will tell you plainly of the Father."*

JOHN 16:25 (NASB)

In one of my daughter's college classes, her teacher shared the true meaning of good communication. To my daughter's surprise, he didn't launch into a discussion of gerunds and prepositional phrases. Instead he said, "Any communication that can be understood is good communication." This is true for the Amish, too.

Many Amish people still speak the same language as their forefathers, who came to America in the seventeenth and eighteenth centuries. The dialect varies a bit from county to county in Pennsylvania and in other states, but the differences are not many and most Dutchmen can understand each other. Expressing themselves in English, however, is another matter, and the results are amazingly funny. They often use the German word order and idioms in speaking our language. Here are some *ferhoodled* phrases:

"Mom's layin' over the dough—she's got to get her bakin' caught after."

> **Ve grow too soon old
> and too late schmart.**
>
> PROVERB

"We walked the town all over and looked the windows thru—ach, such wonderful pretty things for a body to see."

"As soon as I first see him, I fall myself in luff."

Those phrases are cute, but could you imagine trying to carry on a conversation like that for any length of time? The disciples who first listened to Jesus talk of the Kingdom of Heaven might have experienced the same kind of confusion. Was Jesus a poor communicator because so many people walked away scratching their heads? No, just as Amish ancestors molded their own language, so did Christ. When He spoke of His death, resurrection, and the Kingdom to come, He was introducing a new dialect, a new vocabulary, so to speak. Christ spoke not just to those who were present but to all those to come who would fully embrace His message.

If you were to spend the day with an Amish person, you would begin to understand the lingo. And the more time you walk with Jesus, the more you will understand His messages to humanity. And for those who follow Him, His messages are very *gut*!

■ ■ ■

Dear heavenly Father, I'm so amazed that the words You spoke thousands of years ago were given for me today. Thank You for Your Spirit, who helps me understand what You have said.

Called to Protect

[Love] always protects.

1 CORINTHIANS 13:7 (NIV)

The old woman sat across from me, her face a map of wrinkles. Her concerns weighed heavily on her. "It's time for my children to care for me," she said with a sigh. "But when I talk to them, they have such busy lives."

In everyday life there are things we protect. We protect our credit cards from identity thieves. We protect our homes with locks. We protect our pets by taking them to the veterinarian. But what about the elderly people in our lives? How well do we protect those who have cared for us in so many ways? Nursing homes are filled with men and women who feel alone and abandoned. And while there are many elderly people who need constant care, many others still have much to offer to those who need their wisdom and guidance.

> Time is a great healer but a poor beautician.
>
> PROVERB

In the Amish community, caring for the elderly is considered biblical and appropriate. The elderly are respected for their knowledge and traditional values. There is also an advantage to having Grandma or Grandpa living in your home. They are joyful participants in their grandchildren's lives and help to provide stability in Amish society.

What if the Amish didn't take their commitment to fulfilling this role seriously? In an extended-care facility, Amish seniors would encounter modern conveniences such as television, phones, and electricity. They would not be able to spend significant time with their families. Building a relationship requires face-to-face contact, and the Amish understand this! While we work to protect the elderly, Amish communities are also protecting their customs, values, and traditions. I know this from personal experience. My grandmother has lived with our family for the last ten years, and my children have grown up knowing her and learning from her. It's a beautiful thing to watch them interacting and sharing life together.

Proverbs 2:8 says, "He guards the paths of the just and protects those who are faithful to him." And sometimes God calls us to be His physical hands of protection.

■ ■ ■

Dear heavenly Father, although it would be easier to step back from my responsibilities to the elderly in my life, help me to step forward and be Your hands and feet of protection today.

God Is Able

The LORD says, "I will guide you along the best pathway for your life.
I will advise you and watch over you."

PSALM 32:8

I've never seen a more beautiful picture of God's care for us than a father or mother caring for a disabled child, or a brother or sister showing gentleness toward a sibling with special needs. God is always there to guide and protect us, and sometimes He calls us to guide, protect, and watch over others.

Every culture and group has members with disabilities. How do the Amish care for the disabled among them? Just as members of other cultures do, the Amish learn the needs of the disabled in their community and do their part to help. If someone can't walk, they make a ramp for his wheelchair. If someone can't hear, they write out the church messages for her. The needs of a family with a new baby who has medical problems are no different from a family's need for a new barn or for help with a harvest.

> "Kindness is a language which the deaf can hear and the blind can see."
>
> ATTRIBUTED TO
> MARK TWAIN

Being hard workers is a worthy pursuit for the Amish, and disabled children are expected to participate as members of the family, to the extent they are able. Chores are doled out, and each person does his part—even blind children are taught to garden or cook. Adults with special needs have their own shops or create items to sell. Their part in the community is embraced like everyone else's.

The Amish believe that disabilities are part of God's plan. They feel God's will is revealed as people love and care for others. This reminds me of when Jesus was asked the reason for a man's blindness: "'It was not because of his sins or his parents' sins,' Jesus answered. 'This happened so the power of God could be seen in him'" (John 9:3).

God is always there for you when you turn to Him. And He just might use you to be the one that another can count on.

■ ■ ■

Dear heavenly Father, I thank You for those whom this world labels "disabled" but who are able to bring glory to You through the abilities they do have and through our ability to serve them.

History of Obedience

Remember the days of long ago; think about the generations past. Ask your
father, and he will inform you. Inquire of your elders, and they will tell you.
DEUTERONOMY 32:7

One true story that every Amish child is bound to know is about Dirk Willems, a
young man on the run from the authorities after escaping from prison, where he was
incarcerated for his Anabaptist faith. According to the story,

> *He safely slid across the river*
> *And turned around to see*
> *The leader plunge down through the ice*
> *Now was his chance to flee!*
>
> *But wait! What words did Jesus give*
> *About our enemy?*
> *Show love and pray they'll turn to God*
> *For all eternity!*

The story continues with Dirk's turning back and rescuing his pursuer. The official
wished to set Dirk free, but the others refused because the Anabaptists went against
the established church and the government. Dirk Willems was again imprisoned and
later tortured and burned. It's a story that's repeated to remind
the Amish that God asks each of us to remain strong to the end:
"Remember your history, your long and rich history. I am GOD,
the only God you've had or ever will have—incomparable, irre-
placeable—from the very beginning telling you what the end-
ing will be, all along letting you in on what is going to happen,
assuring you, 'I'm in this for the long haul, I'll do exactly what
I set out to do'" (Isaiah 46:9-10, *The Message*).

Prayer is the
greatest wireless
connection.

PROVERB

History such as this story is evidence that heroes aren't necessarily those who achieve great victories but those who follow God in obedience, even
if it means all in this life is lost. A relationship with God doesn't guarantee a life filled
with happiness and blessings, but the blessings we will receive in eternity will be greater
than any hardship we face in this life.

■ ■ ■

Dear heavenly Father, I pray that You will give me strength and courage for whatever
I face. May my life and obedience always be a testimony to You.

Strength to the Powerless

No one can measure the depths of [God's] understanding.
He gives power to the weak and strength to the powerless.

ISAIAH 40:28-29

Have you ever felt powerless? I remember feeling that way when my youngest son was hospitalized with pneumonia. I couldn't do anything to help. My heart ached. I also felt powerless when I saw two cars crash in front of mine on the highway. In both cases the situation was out of my hands.

It may seem that living in an Amish community would bring the same feeling of powerlessness. The Amish function on the premise of unity . . . but what if you don't agree with the rest of the group?

Every Amish community has members who hold different opinions about what is right, but the community is not swayed by the opinions of a few. This might be hard for us to imagine. If we want to dress a certain way, we do. If we want to decorate our house in neon or send our son to college, there is no one to stop us. Yet in both of these cases, if you lived in an Amish community, someone else would have final say.

> Experience tells you what to do. Confidence allows you to do it.
>
> PROVERB

It may seem as if being Amish takes all decisions out of the hands of individual Amish people, but the biggest decision is still in their grasp: individuals choose to remain in the Amish community. Their decision is toward reticence—the ability to restrain themselves. They choose not to oppose. They choose unity. They choose not to follow their own ideas and plans.

To submit to others in an Amish community is to understand their position as children of God. It's also to understand that when we do right and attempt to live right, God will strengthen us, give us understanding, give power to the weak and strength to the powerless. When we look to Him and submit to our fellow followers, He is glorified. We show His power when we don't try to claim it for ourselves.

■ ■ ■

Dear heavenly Father, I thank You for being my strength and my power. Help me to be willing to give up some of my own power and control so You can exhibit Yours.

AUGUST 12

When I Am Weak, Then Strength Comes

Those who trust in the LORD will find new strength. They will soar high on wings like eagles. They will run and not grow weary. They will walk and not faint.
ISAIAH 40:31

When do you feel the strongest? For me, it's not when I have someone giving me a helping hand, but when I'm offering help or hope to others. Sometimes I've been completely weary, and then someone—a child, a friend, a neighbor—asked for help. My first inclination has been to decline, but I've discovered that when God's strength flows through me to help another person, I benefit. This is true in the Amish community, too:

> Intrigued. That's the word to describe how Dr. Bryan Cloyd, Professor of Accounting at Virginia Tech in Blacksburg, Virginia, felt when he learned that a busload of Amish from Nickel Mines, Pennsylvania, was coming to honor the victims of the April 2007 school shootings. Dr. Cloyd's only daughter, Austin, age eighteen, was one of thirty-two victims who lost their lives in the rampage. . . .
>
> The purpose of the Amish visit was to bring the Comfort Quilt to Virginia Tech. After the 9/11 terrorist attacks in New York City, a school in Ohio created a simple patchwork quilt for children whose parents had been killed in the attacks. A school in New Jersey hung the quilt, and there it stayed—until four years later, when Hurricane Katrina hit New Orleans. The Comfort Quilt was sent to a school in Mississippi that had taken in many displaced New Orleans students. When the Nickel Mines School shooting occurred, the Comfort Quilt moved again . . . this time to bring comfort to the Amish families of Nickel Mines. After the Virginia Tech tragedy, the Amish made a decision that the quilt should be moved again.

Those who delivered the quilt were the very ones who had lost their daughters in the Nickel Mines shooting. Instead of allowing their weary grief to burden them, they spread hope to others who had recently faced tragedy.

You can find the same to be true. When you give out of your weariness, not only will you help others, but also God will strengthen you in the process.

■ ■ ■

Dear heavenly Father, when I'm weakest, the last thing I want is to give. But I know that when You flow through me, I also benefit!

A Place Called Home

While he was still a long way off, his father saw him coming. Filled with love and compassion, he ran to his son, embraced him, and kissed him.

LUKE 15:20

My daughter Leslie, now in her twenties, had planned to spend a year in the Czech Republic doing mission work. While leaving her parents was hard on her, even harder was leaving her younger brothers and sisters. A year is a long time for anyone, but it's especially long in the life of a toddler. And while we approved of Leslie's decision, parenting is much harder when a young person leaves and his or her parents don't agree with that decision. This is especially true for those young adults who choose to leave the Amish faith. As you can imagine, this grips Amish parents' hearts with fear, not only because they are losing one of their children but also because many other sets of eyes are watching every step, every choice. Here is part of a letter an Amish parent wrote to his child:

Kindness, when given away, keeps coming back.

PROVERB

> Now that you are grown up, think of those little feet that follow yours, your little brothers and sisters. . . . How can we tell them why you've gone away? How can we explain so they will understand, that you have gone of your own free will? You turned your back on all you once held dear. Your chair is empty at the far end of the table, and no one can take your place.
>
> Sometime there well may come a day when the enthusiasm of your newfound life will wear away. Perhaps the day will come when all this glitter will vanish from your life. Then you may see your highest hopes were nothing, and all the things you sought were vain. . . . Don't be afraid to turn your steps and come on home.

Wherever older siblings go in life, their leaving will have an impact on younger brothers and sisters. There will be times in our lives when we personally don't approve of the choices family members make, but like the father in the letter above, we must let them know that we will always be there with arms open wide on their return, just as our heavenly Father waits and watches for us to come to Him.

■ ■ ■

Dear heavenly Father, I thank You for always being available to me and reaching out with open arms.

From the Inside Out

Put on your new nature, created to be like God—truly righteous and holy.
EPHESIANS 4:24

Growing up I learned the "wrongs" and "rights" of being a follower of God. It was wrong to steal, to kill, to lie, and to covet another person's belongings. It was wrong to disobey my parents and to worship idols. There were many wrongs, and as a kid I tried to do the best I could to obey. The problem was that for many years I knew the rules, but I didn't understand the meaning behind them—which was to help me to have a pure heart and grow in my relationship with Jesus Christ.

The Ordnung covers a whole realm of biblical principles and teachings on how the Amish are to conduct their lives in the home and church, on relationships, courtship, marriage, business life, youth activities, and how they respond to being treated wrongfully.

In any religion this is a concern. Rules are easy to learn and memorize, but they are harder to live. Rules are easy to break and even easier to walk away from. Because we get tired of trying to live by rules, it becomes easy to walk away from God. Many Amish are seeing this to be true in their faith, too, as noted by a letter from a bishop in the Amish magazine *Family Life*:

> One danger I see among our "plain" churches is the tendency to focus on our plain ways and hold to them successfully, but meanwhile become lax in other areas of the Christian life. . . .
>
> A church that gives us separation from the world is a church that will apostatize from the outside in. But a church that successfully maintains a separate lifestyle but fails to apply other Bible principles will apostatize from the inside out.
>
> We must put forth an honest effort to follow Christ in all His ways if we are to maintain a true church for the coming generations.

When it comes to your own life, are you more focused on the rules or on a relationship? Allow God to transform you from the inside out so that His life flourishes within you.

■ ■ ■

Dear heavenly Father, it's easy for me to look at rules and obey them, but today I ask You to help me focus on my relationship with You that renews me within.

End of Summer Visitors

Work willingly at whatever you do, as though you were
working for the Lord rather than for people.

COLOSSIANS 3:23

When my kids see me put my shoes on, they look at me and ask, "Where are we going?" Likewise, when my kids see me (quickly) cleaning the house, they ask, "Who's coming over?" If you've ever grabbed a handful of toys and shoes and books and raced out of the main living area in search of an out-of-the-way spot to hide them, you'll understand. Why are we more concerned about how the house looks for those who visit it than for those who live in it?

In this, the Amish are no different from us. In August, the Amish often get many visitors. It's a last chance for friends and family to go visiting before the busyness of harvest begins. Sometimes this means hosting visitors from all over the United States for weeks straight, which can be tiring, especially for those who attempt to play hostess and keep the house looking neat while also providing meals and fellowship. It can be enough to weary even a hardworking Amish woman!

One thing I read in the Amish magazine *Family Life* gave me something to ponder. A woman named Hannah Zimmerman wrote, "I like the saying a friend shared, 'I have learned in whatsoever state I am, therein to have company!' Things don't need to be in top shape, nor grand meals served. Just do your best, give your best, and enjoy your visitors!"

Do what you do with all your might. Things done by halves are never done right.

PROVERB

Romans 12:13 says, "Always be eager to practice hospitality." Paul didn't say that we had to have a perfectly clean house or serve a fine meal. The only requirement is an open door, a cheerful attitude, and a willingness to share whatever is on hand.

Have you opened your home lately to friends and family? If not, today's the perfect day to extend an invitation.

■ ■ ■

Dear heavenly Father, when I strive to make my home look nice for others, I know it makes me look good. But when I open my home with a generous and giving heart, it makes You look good. Help me to do that today.

Wisdom to Live Life in Control

Fools are headstrong and do what they like; wise people take advice.
PROVERBS 12:15 (*THE MESSAGE*)

I have raised three children through their teen years, and I have three more to go. The hardest part about having teenagers isn't trying to *lead* them in the right direction; it's getting them to follow that leading and listen to your advice. There is a fine balance between helping your children become well-functioning, independent adults and also setting boundaries to keep them safe.

During the teen years Amish youth enjoy a season of Rumspringa in which some of the usual boundaries are lifted. Yet even as the young people "explore the world," their parents are often there to give advice. And although most youth believe they are

Wisdom enables one to be thrifty without being stingy, generous without being wasteful.

PROVERB

the ones in control of their decisions, some of them come to realize that their decisions are taking control of them. If they choose to drink, they are "under the influence." The same is true of the movies and music they may watch and listen to, which also influence their thoughts and beliefs. And if they choose to be sexually active, their freedom can often turn to confining responsibilities as they enter into an unhealthy relationship or find themselves pregnant out of wedlock. What they initially tried to control soon ends up controlling them.

I like the way one Amish father discussed the issue of cars: "Many people have asked me, 'Why don't you have cars?' I found no one who was unable to understand when I said, 'We do not feel cars are wrong in themselves. It is the misuse of them that is wrong. How many sixteen-year-olds do you know who own a car? Is it not usually that the car *owns them*?'"

We don't have to be teenagers to believe that we can control the world around us—and then fail to do so. While it's not necessary for us to give up cars or music or other outside influences, one question all of us can ask is, "Is this habit controlling me, or am I controlling it?" And then we can turn to God and to others for wisdom to find the answer.

■ ■ ■

Dear heavenly Father, open my ears to the wisdom of caring people in my life. And help me to soberly judge the things that I mistakenly believe I'm controlling but are actually controlling me.

A Designed Life

You have decided the length of our lives. You know how many
months we will live, and we are not given a minute longer.

JOB 14:5

In 1991, aspiring newspaper editor Kevin Williams convinced Elizabeth Coblentz, an Old Order Amish wife and mother, to write a weekly cooking column called "The Amish Cook." For more than ten years Elizabeth shared family recipes and discussed daily life on her Indiana farm with her husband, Ben, and their eight children and thirty-two grandchildren. When she passed away in 2002 from an aneurism, her daughter Lovina Eicher took over her column. *The Amish Cook's Anniversary Book* is a compilation of columns that appeared through the years. Here is an excerpt from Elizabeth's first column:

This has been a rushy morning, but enjoyable. We still have five girls here at home yet. Four went to work as usual. They all leave 6:00 to 6:30 A.M. The girls were all busy doing all my cleaning before they left. Working all together like this is what I call real family life. With no boys at home, the girls do the milking and other chores around the barn. We have one daughter and two sons married, and feel lucky to have five grandsons and five granddaughters. Guess we just don't appreciate all our good health enough. The kitchen has the smell of freshly baked pies.

"As an 18-year-old college sophomore journalism major, Kevin 'discovered' Elizabeth, and an unlikely duo was created."

It was no coincidence that Kevin Williams met Elizabeth in her driveway that day. It was part of God's plan for her life—for the lives of her readers. The circulation of Elizabeth's column grew from one paper in 1991 to being distributed in more than one hundred at the time of her death.

Our days, too, are numbered. God alone knows the paths we'll take. Sometimes our love is meant to be poured out over family and community, and sometimes God desires that our love be spread further than that. There's no way to know where God will take us, but like Elizabeth, we'll find joy in simply taking note of what God is doing in our daily lives and magnifying Him in the middle of it.

■ ■ ■

Dear heavenly Father, there is so much in my life that I take for granted. Help me to pause, look around, and find joy in daily life.

A Bride Prepares

When everything is ready, I will come and get you, so
that you will always be with me where I am.
JOHN 14:3

I can clearly remember the weeks leading up to my wedding day. As I was taking care of all the details of the wedding ceremony and reception, John, my future husband, was preparing our first place—cleaning it (yes, really), hauling furniture, and making the place ready.

Before every Amish wedding there is also a time of preparation. Here is Lovina Eicher's description of the days leading up to her Amish wedding:

"Old Order Amish women in Pennsylvania wear the same type/style/pattern of dress and the same type of material for their wedding as they do for everything else. . . . They don't wear a veil."

The days before our wedding were busy days of washing walls, ceilings, cleaning closets, cabinets, windows, and everything that goes with a thorough cleaning. Mom would have us girls helping her make homemade noodles for the big event. Another job was collecting Mom's many plates, glasses, bowls, silverware, pots, and pans needed for the wedding meal. . . . The day of our wedding was one of the coolest days in July. I am sure the cooks were glad for this, since they fried three hundred pounds of chicken for the noon meal. As always, God has sent his blessings from above.

Preparation is the outward manifestation of inward anticipation and eagerness. We prepare because we're excited, because we've been waiting for something for so long. There is no way we can sit still with all that nervous energy inside!

A wedding, whether Amish or English, tops the list of things to get excited about. Brides focus on all the details because they want everything just so. Yet sometimes we forget that we still have the most amazing wedding celebration waiting for us: "Let us be glad and rejoice, and let us give honor to him. For the time has come for the wedding feast of the Lamb, and his bride has prepared herself" (Revelation 19:7).

How are you preparing for your reunion with the Son of God? What can you do today to make yourself ready?

■ ■ ■

Dear heavenly Father, so many times I focus on the dailyness of life and forget that the most amazing wedding feast awaits me. Thank You for Your Word, which gives me a glimpse of what's in store.

A Time to Prepare

For shoes, put on the peace that comes from the Good
News so that you will be fully prepared.

EPHESIANS 6:15

This time of year, Amish folks are gathering their harvest or are attending vegetable auctions where they can get food in bulk to put up for the winter. The women are busy canning vegetables, including tomatoes, to use for soups, sauces, relishes, and so on for months to come. The Amish value preparation, which means they understand the benefits of delayed gratification. Hard work in the kitchen *now* means great meals *later* this winter. For the Amish, peace comes from knowing that God watches over them and that they are doing the hard work of preparing for the winter to come.

The Bible talks about the peace that comes from the Good News, which makes us prepared. Christians are to be prepared with the gospel of peace in the same way that ancient soldiers prepared to meet attacks they might face. They were to be ready for action. Peace meant they were on firm footing for what was to come.

The Amish spend time, energy, and knowledge to prepare. They know winter is coming, and they start getting ready months ahead of time. They expect the worst and stockpile needed items. Yet I can imagine the peace that comes when they see their pantries and cellars full. Even as the sun shines around him, an Amish man can picture the stacks of firewood needed to heat his home.

The Amish often build cold frames to extend the beginning and end of the growing season.

Do you expect that there will be "winter seasons" in your spiritual walk? What are you doing to prepare yourself for those seasons? Do you look to God's Word to stockpile truth and strengthen your faith? Do you continue to grow closer in your relationship with God so that it will be a natural thing to turn to Him during hardship?

We make a mistake when we simply enjoy the sunny seasons of life and do not see them as a time of preparation. Whatever season you're in, turn to God and ask Him to help you prepare for the next one.

■ ■ ■

Dear heavenly Father, it's so easy to see these sunny days as picnic weather and not remember that they are also a time of preparation. Help me to stockpile Your Word and Your truth in my heart.

Known by God

Have you comprehended the vast expanses of the earth? Tell me, if you know all this.
JOB 38:18 (NIV)

One of the results of modern technology that amazes me is Google Earth. Through this computer application, I can zoom down and view towns, streets, and even individual lots with ease from the comfort of my couch. I love viewing places I've already been and checking out places I'd like to go. But even with all I can see, do I really know the earth? I can locate familiar streets, but those are simply pixels on the screen. Knowledge is not the same as understanding.

Job 28:24 speaks of God saying, "He looks to the ends of the earth and sees everything under the heavens" (ESV). But God doesn't see only pixels; He sees all of life. He can walk along with that person in Paris or with an Amish farmer in Ohio, just as He walks with me.

A happy memory never wears out.

PROVERB

Isaiah 41:10 says, "Don't be afraid, for I am with you. Don't be discouraged, for I am your God." He is with each of us, and He longs for each of us to know Him just as we are known by Him.

My friend Elizabeth shared this illustration: "When I was a child I remember my mom telling me a story of her dad returning from a trip into town to buy groceries and other supplies. He bought each of the kids candy bars; there were nine of them. This was a personal touch that made each child feel loved and thought of. As a large Amish family, buying anything extra, like candy bars, was a big deal . . . but still it was a simple way to show love."

We may not all get a candy bar from God today, but if you turn to Him, He will certainly connect with you in a personal way. It doesn't matter where you live or what corner of the earth you inhabit. God sees you, God knows you, and God loves you more than you can imagine. And you don't need a computer application to give evidence of that.

■ ■ ■

Dear heavenly Father, I'm overwhelmed by the thought that You can see across the earth and yet Your heart is fully present with me. Help me to know You better at this moment than I did a moment before.

A Believing Heart

It is by believing in your heart that you are made right with God,
and it is by confessing with your mouth that you are saved.

ROMANS 10:10

The Amish people in general do not believe that a person who has not been baptized is a true believer. During Rumspringa many youth worry about being killed and question where they will spend eternity. It's often in the backs of their minds.

The following is a piece by John A. Hostetler titled "God Visits the Amish," written in 1954.

Traditionally the Old Order Amish have not had revival meetings. The present spiritual awakening found in well over half of the fifty settlements in the United States, however, shows that there is exceptional hunger for new religious life. In Ohio last year, for example, [Evangelist David] Miller was booked up for thirteen days straight. He preached Sunday and weekends, in the morning, sometimes afternoon, and occasionally after an evening hymn sing—in brooder houses, in barns and on lawns.

There are dozens of other Amish preachers like Miller who are getting "new light." They preach "biblical" messages stripped of the usual Amish singsong delivery and the old terminology. While this newer preaching has brought deep satisfaction to many who have been praying for release from the power of sin and overbearing traditions, it has also brought stress and worry to those leaders who hail it as *eppes neues* (something new).

> "The Amish practice adult baptism, or what they call 'believer's baptism,' because the person is old enough to choose what they believe in."

Of course this "new thing" isn't new at all. The gospel preached thousands of years ago is the same that applies to us today: "If you confess with your mouth that Jesus is Lord and believe in your heart that God raised him from the dead, you will be saved" (Romans 10:9).

The verse above tells us that only two things are required: believing and confessing faith in Jesus. Sometimes God brings someone into our lives to remind us of this truth. And sometimes He asks us to share this truth with others.

■ ■ ■

Dear heavenly Father, I thank You for Your gift of salvation. I believe, and I will continue to believe!

Actions Follow Thoughts

Fix your thoughts on what is true, and honorable, and right, and pure, and lovely, and admirable. Think about things that are excellent and worthy of praise.

PHILIPPIANS 4:8

What have you been thinking about today? Have you thought about your schedule, your plans for the coming week, or even your hopes? What you think has an impact on how you live in your home and in society as a whole. But how society thinks also has an impact on who you are and what you believe. Those who surround us influence how we treat children, a spouse, and one another. Those who believe in the Bible—and think about what is true, honorable, right, pure, lovely, and admirable—will live differently from those who put their own interests first.

"In Lancaster County, Pa, there are many people of German or Dutch descent, called Pennsylvania Dutch. However, being Pennsylvania Dutch does *not* automatically make you Amish. . . . The Amish are a religious group that make certain lifestyle choices, not a nationality."

The care of the elderly in the Amish society points to this:

The way the Amish care for their elders helps preserve the communal society, or *gemeinschaft*, they continue to value. This communal society stands in stark contrast to the individualism of the twentieth and twenty-first centuries, in which each person calculates what is in his or her best interest. . . . In contrast, the Amish seek to preserve cooperative relationship and informally agreed-upon rules, most of which are unwritten and sometimes even unspoken.

Today our social changes have made us an individualistic society in which people no longer automatically help one another or share freely what they have. Instead, each individual's main concern is over his or her own possessions and time. We may not want to open our homes to an elderly relative. We may not want to visit someone who repeats "the same old stories."

Yet positive change can happen within us, and it all starts with our thoughts. We don't have to be Amish to strive for *Gemeinschaft* (community) relationships that are "intimate, personal, and cooperative." When we fix our minds on what is true and honorable and excellent and worthy of praise concerning God and the people He has placed in our lives, our actions will soon follow.

■ ■ ■

Dear heavenly Father, cleanse my thoughts. May they reflect only what honors You, and may my actions follow.

Separate for Love's Sake

If anyone comes to you and does not bring this doctrine [is disloyal to what Jesus Christ taught], do not receive him [do not accept him, do not welcome or admit him] into [your] house or bid him Godspeed or give him any encouragement.

2 JOHN 1:10 (AMP)

Have you ever heard of the Amish shunning someone who has left the Amish faith? Shunning is a foreign concept to most Christians. During Amish baptism, a man or woman promises to live within the community of the church and follow its decrees—all of them. To walk away is to break that promise, and the Amish believe walking away is symbolic of a man or woman's soul wandering away from God. To them there is no difference.

Shunning, to the Amish, is a way of showing love. They believe that putting separation between themselves and the other person will cause that person to reconsider his or her ways.

Saloma Furlong is a former Amish woman, and she explains shunning this way:

> If a church member does not stick to the rules of shunning, that person must confess his deeds before the church.

> In my home community, some time (usually several weeks) after a person has left, the community will hold a "fast and pray" day, hoping that it will bring the person back. Two weeks later, if the person has not returned to conform to the Amish "Ordnung" he or she is then placed in the "Bann" (pronounced 'Bawn'), which means all rules of permanent shunning apply. There are four basic rules:

1. Amish members of the church may no longer eat with a former member.
2. Members may not do business with a former member.
3. Members may not ride in a car driven by a former member.
4. Members may not receive gifts from a former member.

Even though we may not practice shunning as part of our own church doctrine, God does tell us to separate ourselves from those who choose to walk away from Him. Of course, this is a serious matter and should always be considered with prayer. God, who knows all people's hearts, will give us wisdom about whether to reach out to that person or to step away from him or her for a time.

■ ■ ■

Dear heavenly Father, my heart aches for those who truly choose to walk away from You. Guide me in dealing with those people so that the result will be their turning back to You.

Welcome the Stranger

*You shall treat the stranger who sojourns with you as the
native among you, and you shall love him as yourself.*
LEVITICUS 19:34 (ESV)

How would you like to attend an Amish church service? My friend Amy had a chance
to do that, and here are some of her observations:

> Janet and I sat in the back of the barn with the grandmothers when the service
> began at 9 a.m. The service started with the congregation singing hymns very
> slowly in German. A male song leader began the first syllable of each line, and
> then the rest of the congregation joined in.
>
> The married men sat on one side of the barn, facing the
> married women. Young unmarried men and women sat
> in separate sections, as well. Many of the youth were gone
> during the hymn singing while they met with the bishop for
> their baptism class.
>
> Since the barn doors were open, it was like having church
> with nature. Pigeons roosted in the rafters, and their musical
> cooing filled the barn. A cow wandered by mooing loudly.
> A barn cat also came to visit, and since I'm a cat lover, I
> gestured for the feline to come to me. I rubbed its chin before
> it continued to the back of the barn to take a leisurely bath
> before falling asleep in a warm sunbeam. Later in the service,
> a dog joined us and fell asleep at Janet's feet.

**Believing that formal
education leads to
pride, the Amish
end their formal
education after the
eighth grade.**

What an impression the community made on Amy and her friend Janet. It reminds
me of the impact we can have on the strangers who live among us. My daughter Leslie
attends a conversation club for international college students. She once told me that
most of these students never enter an American home, even though they may attend
college in the United States for many years. In the past we've opened our home to
students, and we're looking forward to doing so again in the future. We never know
what impact we'll have on others when we allow them to enter our world and hear
about the God we serve.

■ ■ ■

*Dear heavenly Father, for so many years I've supported those who've gone out to spread
the Good News of Jesus around the world. Forgive me for ignoring the "foreigners" in my
own community.*

Youth Singing His Praises

Don't let anyone think less of you because you are young. Be an example to all believers in what you say, in the way you live, in your love, your faith, and your purity.

1 TIMOTHY 4:12

When I was growing up, I attended my church youth group for just one reason—to see my friends and to see what cute guys were there. In Amish communities young people do that, too, but they spend the majority of time singing hymns and songs.

The singing is a venue where young members of the community socialize. When an Amish teen reaches the age of 16, he or she will be expected to "go with the youth," and select a youth group to join. . . . Groups are "higher" and "lower"—I was at the singing of a particularly "low" group, which is another way of saying more conservative when it comes to guidelines. All youth in this group, for example, use open carriages. . . . This group is adult-supervised, with adults attending the day's events, though that is not the case with all of them.

"The Sunday evening gathering is a key event in the social life of Amish youth."

The youth singing usually starts off with a game, such as volleyball. Then there is a time to eat and chat. In addition to socialization, the young people are also looking for future husbands or wives. The teenagers sing hymns from the *Ausbund*. They take turns leading the songs, and they sing for two hours and then have more snacks.

Not all Amish youth behave properly, but reading about these youth singings gives me encouragement. It also reminds me that young people will rise to the standards we set for them. I've personally set high standards for my children as teenagers, and although they have fallen short at times, they've at least learned to set their sights high.

Whether we are setting standards for ourselves or for others, we should always aim for God's standard. When we focus on living with love, faith, and purity, God will strengthen our efforts, and we'll be shining reflections of Christ to the world around us.

■ ■ ■

Dear heavenly Father, the world puts no trust in young people. Help me to lift up, inspire, and encourage the young people You put in my life! And may I live my own life by a standard they can follow.

AUGUST 26

Sweet-Smelling Sacrifices

At the moment I have all I need—and more! I am generously supplied with the gifts you sent me with Epaphroditus. They are a sweet-smelling sacrifice that is acceptable and pleasing to God.

PHILIPPIANS 4:18

Not too long ago our family welcomed two new children into our home through adoption. It was a huge adjustment adding a five-year-old and two-year-old, especially when we already had a two-year-old at home! To help out, my church family posted a sign-up sheet asking people to volunteer to provide meals for us. I ended up not having to cook one meal in three weeks, and that gave us more time to focus on our transition.

Paul wrote about the gifts the church at Philippi sent to him through a believer named Epaphroditus. He said that to God, those gifts were a sweet-smelling sacrifice. And as the recipient of many wonderful gifts from others in the recent past, I can attest to the fact that sometimes they really do smell sweet!

Amish clothing reminds those in the community that they are part of something—not individuals. Dressing alike is a symbol and reflection of their unity.

My friend Sherry Gore is a member of the Sunnyside Amish Mennonite Church in Sarasota, Florida. In her book *Simply Delicious Amish Cooking*, she describes another such sacrifice:

Daughter Shannon and I were walking up to the door of the fellowship hall Friday evening when she looked at me and said, "I didn't know they were having a singing." They weren't. It was Lester Hostetler, sitting in as auctioneer for the night. The youth brought in a little over $2,000 that night. . . . Most of the funds raised came from services auctioned off to the highest bidders. Among those offered were sewing, baking, cleaning, car repair, lawn work, a Dominican dinner for six to eight people, prepared by Kris and Rebecca Knepp, and a four-hour water-skiing excursion by Tim Gingerich.

God tells us to give to others and to share what we have. This can happen in so many ways, but when we offer up our best, it becomes a fragrant offering to God. Not only do those you bless and serve appreciate it, but He does too.

■ ■ ■

Dear heavenly Father, I thank You so much for all those who have given me good gifts that required their time and sacrifice. Bless them for their efforts, and show me whom I can pour my best into next.

Call on Jesus

In my distress I cried out to the LORD; yes, I prayed to my God for help.
He heard me from his sanctuary; my cry to him reached his ears.

PSALM 18:6

I have a love-hate relationship with my telephone. I love the fact that I can use it to talk to family and friends, most of whom live thousands of miles away. What I dislike is the ringing. It interrupts my thoughts. And even worse, it wakes sleeping babies! Here is a passage from a sociology textbook where the use of a phone in an Amish home is discussed:

> The telephone has been the source of intense controversy among the Amish since the 1920s. Eventually, the telephone was accepted because it could be used to call doctors, veterinarians, and merchants. But this did not mean that one should have a phone in the home. Rather, the phone should be in a communal location where it could be used by many people. . . . Think about the number of times a phone call has interrupted a conversation. Have you ever left a family meal to take a phone call? Now that the cellphone can follow us to most locations, it also can interrupt all kinds of social encounters. Relegating the telephone to some communal spot outside of the home sends the message that telephone conversations are much less important than those taking place in the community or the home. Keeping the telephone at a distance is a symbolic way of making it your servant rather than the other way around.

A task takes as long as it takes.

PROVERB

One thing I try to remember when it comes to the use of my phone is to focus on the people in my presence first. It's silly to talk on the phone when there is a child in the room who would love time to talk to you.

Do you have something worrisome that you'd like to talk to a friend about? Go to God first. He's waiting, the line will never be busy, and He'll *always* answer when you call.

■ ■ ■

Dear heavenly Father, please forgive me for the times I've called others about my problems instead of calling on You. You not only have all the answers but also are the source of peace!

Words for Wise Living

[Solomon] composed some 3,000 proverbs and wrote 1,005 songs.
1 KINGS 4:32

My friend Suzanne Woods Fisher used to have a radio show called *Amish Wisdom*, and one thing she always said was, "If you want to know a people, understand their proverbs." While these days the use of proverbs in our everyday life is not common, it is very common among the Amish. They share them, repeat them, and scribes even include them at the ends of the letters that they send to the *Budget*.

Proverbs help point us toward wisdom, toward good judgment, and toward God's teachings. They're for anyone who seeks guidance for everyday circumstances. Here are some Amish proverbs that I like:

Good character like good soup is usually homemade.
It is better to give others a piece of your heart than a piece of your mind.
A child can read a parent's character before he can read the alphabet.
Bibles that are coming apart usually belong to people who are not.

The use of proverbs for teaching and training isn't new. The book of Proverbs describes their purpose at the beginning of the first chapter: "to teach people wisdom and discipline, to help them understand the insights of the wise. Their purpose is to teach people to live disciplined and successful lives, to help them do what is right, just, and fair. These proverbs will give insight to the simple, knowledge and discernment to the young. Let the wise listen to these proverbs and become even wiser. Let those with understanding receive guidance by exploring the meaning in these proverbs and parables, the words of the wise and their riddles" (Proverbs 1:2-6).

If you haven't spent time in the book of Proverbs lately, dig in. One way to do it is to read one chapter of Proverbs every day for a month (there are thirty-one chapters). Also, as the Amish (and Solomon) remind us, truth is meant to be shared. If we do not fill our minds and hearts with God's Word and with wisdom, the world will be quick to fill the void.

■ ■ ■

Dear heavenly Father, thank You for sharing Your truth. Thank You for Your promise that when we pray for wisdom, You will always answer our request.

Faith That Shows

This Good News tells us how God makes us right in his sight. This
is accomplished from start to finish by faith. As the Scriptures
say, "It is through faith that a righteous person has life."

ROMANS 1:17

I love reading the Amish newspaper the *Budget* because it not only shares what is happening in the lives of the Amish but also explains much about their values and beliefs. Here is an excerpt of an update by Martha Zimmerman from Rutledge, Missouri:

> This morning at 3:30 we had a rude awakening with Bertha telling us that Marietta had another "spell." By the time we got over there she was okay, as they don't last long at all, although her speech was a little slurred yet. But I know what we will be doing tomorrow, if our plans hold out. We will be running to a doctor somewhere to do blood tests or something. I'd really like to know what's going on. We didn't think we need this stress yet, but I guess we must take what's given. Abe said we've made it through before, surely we will again this time. And so by faith and God's grace we move on.

Those who fear the future are likely to fumble the present.

PROVERB

I'm not sure what was wrong with Marietta, but I can read the concern and weariness in Martha's words. I've never met this family, but their faith and their commitment to one another shine through this passage.

How can this woman's words be a testimony to you today? You don't need to have all the answers to know that you will make it through to the other side of your problems. The middle of weariness and questions is a wonderful place to exercise your faith. And with God's grace, you can continue to walk forward.

Faith carries us from start to finish. Faith pushes out fear. It centers our minds and our hearts on the One who is always with us, even when someone we love is hurting and when we don't have answers. Faith makes life bearable. No, more than that, faith makes life hopeful.

■ ■ ■

Dear heavenly Father, there are so many areas in my life for which I have no answers.
I thank You that faith gives me hope in You in the midst of my questions and concerns.

Have Patience

If we look forward to something we don't yet have,
we must wait patiently and confidently.
ROMANS 8:25

As a mom of three preschoolers, one thing I often find myself saying is, "Have patience." Sometimes I even sing part of a song about patience that I learned in Vacation Bible School when I was a child.

If there is one virtue that rises above the others when it comes to the Amish, it's patience. This story is an example of that:

> Linda sat with her son in the emergency room of their local hospital, waiting to be seen by a doctor. Her son had twisted his ankle playing a game of basketball and she worried he might have caused serious damage to it.
>
> After ten minutes, her son grew fidgety and impatient. "This is going to take forever," he moaned.
>
> Seated across from them was a young Amish couple. The wife had taken a spill and hurt her shoulder. They sat calmly, though Linda noticed the wife wince in pain whenever she shifted in her seat. Finally, the nurse came out and motioned to the Amish man. He jumped up to help his wife rise to her feet. Linda heard him say to her, "Now, Katie, that wasn't too bad a wait. Only an hour."

A handful of patience is worth more than a bushel of brains.

PROVERB

To the Amish, being patient, waiting, and yielding to others are marks of maturity. But first, they must decide whether they want to be mature. Growing in maturity requires a choice to wait and to yield and an understanding that God is the One who is ultimately in charge of meeting their needs.

To wait is to trust. It's to believe that our needs will be taken care of, that God is worthy of our confidence. He is also the One who will help us be patient with others.

■ ■ ■

Dear heavenly Father, patience is the hardest thing to pray for because it goes against my nature, but right now, I'm praying exactly for that.

As the Spirit Leads

All who are led by the Spirit of God are children of God.

ROMANS 8:14

In the Amish culture there is no discussion about whether or not God is real. Everything in their lives is focused on the reality of His existence. Youth are taught to believe without question. They are surrounded by those who also believe without question. But how deep does that belief go? It's one thing to believe a chair is a chair; it's another thing to sit in it—to trust it completely.

Today, some of the modern terms that non-Amish Christians use are making their way into the Amish culture too. Many Amish are concerned about this because the more things change, the more their tradition is challenged:

> More and more Amish talk about "a personal relationship with Jesus" and the "assurance of salvation and forgiveness" while attending Bible studies, sing-alongs and revival meetings. Alarmed Amish leaders have banned large-group prayer meetings and Bible readings as dozens of Amish families consider joining other churches. This closer walk with the outside world and emphasis on individual experience challenges the traditional Amish understanding of faith, said Donald Kraybill, a professor at Lancaster's Elizabethtown College who has written widely on the Amish. "People may say, 'The spirit led me to do this.' And that becomes a new challenge against tradition, heritage and the authority of church leaders," he said.

If you sense your faith is unraveling, go back to where you dropped the thread of obedience.

PROVERB

Sometimes the hardest part of being a Christian is believing what we cannot understand. We often want all the answers, but if we have them, then there's no need for faith, is there? Sometimes God's Spirit guides us to places that aren't comfortable and to truths we don't understand. The only way to know if what we are doing is from God is to compare it with His Word. We know we are God's children when we follow where His Spirit leads us and trust that our lives are something God has planned for us all along.

■ ■ ■

Dear heavenly Father, I thank You for not leaving us alone. Thank You for Your Spirit. Thank You for Your guidance.

Whoopie-Pie Prayers

If you sinful people know how to give good gifts to your children, how much
more will your heavenly Father give the Holy Spirit to those who ask him.
LUKE 11:13

If you've never eaten a Whoopie Pie, imagine a large Oreo cookie made of two soft cakes with fluffy cream in the middle. "It's believed that Whoopie Pies were first made from leftover cake batter, and Amish legend has it that, when children and even farmers would find the delicious treat in their lunch pail, they'd yell out, 'Whoopie!'"

Whoopie Pies are typically chocolate cakes with vanilla cream, but many flavor variations for both the cookies and the cream have appeared in recent years. Like all good gifts, a Whoopie Pie is an unexpected yet appreciated treat. It is a reminder of how much the recipient is loved.

Whoopie Pies are also known as Hucklebucks or Creamy Turtles.

Do you feel loved by God? Really loved? Do you anticipate His good gifts in your life? Gifts that will make you stand up and shout, "Whoopie!"? If you've had a good-natured and generous parent, it may be easy to see God like this. But maybe you had a parent who was ill-tempered or even stingy. Is it hard to ask for or expect much because you're afraid you'll be disappointed?

God generously gives good gifts to His children, yet we must also trust His timing. Even though Amish children would like to find Whoopie Pies in their lunch pails every day, good parents know that special treats should be reserved for specific times. When God doesn't give us what we desire when we desire it, we must trust His timing. And as we wait, we can also pray with confidence, knowing that God will answer with *what* is best, *when* it's best. Or, as John Newton wrote, "Thou art coming to a King, / large petitions with thee bring; / for His grace and pow'r are such, / none can ever ask too much."

■ ■ ■

Dear heavenly Father, I thank You for the good gifts You've given me. I also thank You for not always answering my prayers as I think You should but as You know is best.

"Fair" According to God's Word

The word of God is alive and powerful. It is sharper than the sharpest
two-edged sword, cutting between soul and spirit, between joint
and marrow. It exposes our innermost thoughts and desires.

HEBREWS 4:12

I can't tell you how many times as a teenager I told my mom, "That's not fair!" Or how many times I've heard the same words from my kids' mouths. Fair to a teenager is watching the movies the other kids watch, listening to the same popular music, and wearing similar clothes—no matter what values or lyrics or body parts are compromised. The Amish hear the same things from their kids—and from the world around them. There are those who believe that without television, popular music, and the Internet, Amish children are deprived of happy childhoods. I love how one Amish father, Isaac R. Horst, responded:

> We also "deprive" our children of the evil influence of the TV, the exposure to crime, violence, immorality, liquor, and drugs. We deprive them of the addictive pursuit of pleasure, of becoming sports or entertainment fanatics.
>
> Instead of all manner of public entertainment, our children find enjoyment in nature on the farm: the baby chicks, cuddly kittens, and playful puppies. They learn to know and appreciate the wild animals and birds abounding in woodland and meadow. They swim and fish in pond and stream. Above all, they enjoy learning and doing.

A lot of the trouble in this world wouldn't bother people if they weren't always looking for it.

PROVERB

I'm reminded of times when I've declared, "That's not fair," when I've seen the success of an unbeliever or thought of the "fun" I'm missing out on by choosing to live a righteous life. God's Word cuts through "fairness" and moves straight to issues of our hearts.

Some may think that God's Word deprives us of what looks like fun. The truth is, it protects us. It exposes our innermost thoughts and desires, and points us to a Savior who died unfairly for our salvation.

■ ■ ■

Dear heavenly Father, if all things were fair, I would have to die for my sins and spend eternity apart from You. I'm thankful that You didn't stick to what's "fair"!

Amish Romance

*There are three things that amaze me—no, four things that I don't
understand: how an eagle glides through the sky, how a snake slithers on
a rock, how a ship navigates the ocean, how a man loves a woman.*
PROVERBS 30:18-19

Amish romance novels have been on the bestsellers lists for years, but many Amish
women I know chuckle over the fact that they cause such a stir. Like the rest of us, the
Amish often get married and then wonder, *Where's the romance?* It's hard to be romantic
when one is caring for a half dozen children, tending a farm, and doing all the household chores without the benefit of electricity. One Amish person wrote:

**People who care
about each other
take care of each
other. It's not a
duty; it's a pleasure.**

PROVERB

It is hard to look around the plain churches today and not get
the feeling that we have far too much courtship *before* marriage,
and not nearly enough *after* marriage. Young people who make
every effort to win each other's love before marriage, often do
not put forth much effort after marriage. . . .

Ah, if only we could get a little more courtship into
marriage, how much happier would be many of our homes.

Marriage, to be worthwhile, requires intelligent thought
and continued effort. Good marriages do not just happen.
They do not result from having married the "right" one as
much as from the blessings of God, persistent work, and
loving labor to make ourselves the "right" one.

If you are married, how are you doing in the romance department? What can you
do to bring some courtship back into your relationship? God is the creator of men, of
women, of love, and . . . of romance.

First John 3:16 says, "We know what real love is because Jesus gave up his life for
us. So we also ought to give up our lives for our brothers and sisters." God might not
be asking you to literally give up your life for your spouse today, but could you give up
part of what's on your own list of tasks to care for the other person? Make this your goal.

■ ■ ■

*Dear heavenly Father, forgive me for the times I've acted selfishly in my marriage. Pour
Your love into me, and fill my mind and heart with ways I can bless my spouse.*

Tried-and-True Truths

Hold on to the pattern of wholesome teaching you learned from me—a
pattern shaped by the faith and love that you have in Christ Jesus.

2 TIMOTHY 1:13

These days it seems that every business is trying to come up with something newer, better, and faster. This may work with computers, but with some things—like farming—the best is achieved through tried-and-true methods, as one Amishman shares:

> In the past, our European forefathers faced formidable obstacles, too. In spite of their hardships, they became known for their resourcefulness as farmers, developing new and better methods in agriculture. They were thinkers and trend-setters, not blind followers of the crowd. I am convinced their initiative still lives in their descendants—but not by outdoing the big time farmers at their own game, or by adopting their goals. Not at all!
>
> Rather we need to return to the time-proven principles of past centuries, and apply them to the agriculture of today. We must not be afraid to try a "new" idea, improve it, develop its potential, yet also in the context of "a quiet and peaceable life in all godliness and honesty" (1 Timothy 2:2, [KJV]).
>
> Instead of relying on big machinery, a million dollar investment, and mass production, our strengths must be in a good work ethic, family togetherness, integrity, church fellowship, a simple lifestyle, and the blessings of God.

Many of us follow principles passed down by our ancestors, but the best ones to follow are those passed down by God-followers in the Bible: "Work brings profit, but mere talk leads to poverty!" (Proverbs 14:23). "The wicked borrow and never repay, but the godly are generous givers" (Psalm 37:21). "Honor the LORD with your wealth and with the best part of everything you produce" (Proverbs 3:9).

What time-proven principle could you share with someone today?

■ ■ ■

Dear heavenly Father, I thank You for not leaving us to our own devices but instead
for guiding us to Your truth.

SEPTEMBER 5

Becoming a Timekeeper

Make the most of every opportunity in these evil days. Don't act
thoughtlessly, but understand what the Lord wants you to do.
EPHESIANS 5:16-17

We all have only so many hours in a day, and the Amish know how to fill them to the brim. Here is a portion of a "Daily Diary" column from September 1998.

4:00 A.M. Time to get the day started off. Rainy-like outside in these early morning hours. We could use rain. . . .

4:45 A.M. Breakfast is ready and we're seated at the table. Fried potatoes and eggs, bacon, cheese, toast, peaches, marshmallows, sliced tomatoes, hot peppers, coffee and tea. . . .

Things that steal our time are usually the easiest to do.

PROVERB

5:10 A.M. My husband is off to the dairy farm and Susan and I wash dishes and Verena starts ironing the laundry. Plenty of it. . . .

7:30 A.M. Girls getting ready for work. Verena quits ironing. Yesterday, they assisted daughter Leah with her cleaning. . . .

7:55 A.M. Girls off to work, and I'm about ready to hang the clothes on the clothesline. Looks rainy, but I'll take my try to get it hung out. . . .

8:50 A.M. The laundry hangs on the clothesline now. The sun is peeping through the clouds. Hopefully the wash will dry.

I don't know about you, but just reading what the Amish get done before 9:00 a.m. makes me tired. It also makes me think about how I use my own time.

Psalm 90:12 says, "Teach us to realize the brevity of life, so that we may grow in wisdom." I wonder, if we truly understood the brevity of life, would we spend hours on the Internet, watching television, or shopping for items that'll be outdated and out of style in a matter of months?

The best way to honor God with our time is to make a list of our priorities. Ask yourself, *Five years from now what will I be thankful that I completed?* Reading to your child? Taking a Bible class? Exercising with your spouse?

We protect our homes; we protect our families; we protect our finances. May we all become more diligent about protecting our time.

■ ■ ■

Dear heavenly Father, I place my time in Your hands. Show me how to protect it, use it, and glorify You with it!

Truth Talks

Take control of what I say, O LORD, and guard my lips.

PSALM 141:3

When I first became a Christian, I discovered that one of the hardest habits to break was allowing unkind words to spout from my lips. For many years I'd filled my mind with wicked, idle, and unclean thoughts, and they usually pushed through my lips when I felt anger or frustration. In time, with many prayers and much confession, I began to gain control of my words, but it wasn't easy.

The Amish teach their children that their thoughts will direct their speech, their conduct, and their entire way of life. This is discussed in the devotional book *Rules of a Godly Life*, which is commonly used in conjunction with the Bible in Amish homes:

> If you desire in honorable company to be joyful take care that your merriment prove worthy of Christian love, purity, and respectability. Avoid, therefore, rude insults, mocking speech, indecent words, and filthy jokes of which respectable people would be ashamed. First, because lewd conversation of this sort is outward proof of an unregenerate heart; "For out of the abundance of the heart the mouth speaketh" (Matthew 12:34). Second, because smutty humor and immodest words smooth the road to dishonorable deeds.

Mincing your words makes it easier if you have to eat them later.

PROVERB

One of the best ways to develop strength of character is to learn how to control your tongue. This starts by guarding what enters your mind. As one of my schoolteachers used to say, "Garbage in, garbage out." If you don't fill your mind with garbage, then you won't have to worry about it slipping out in your words or actions.

Second, when the abundance of our hearts grows from the truth that is centered on Jesus, who is the Truth, lies will have no place on our tongues because we will be busy "rejoicing in the truth" (see 1 Corinthians 13:6). Living in the light of the truth will give us minds of gratitude. It will promote righteous thinking and holy living. And that will help us to guard our words.

■ ■ ■

Dear heavenly Father, give me a passion for the truth. Fill me so full of it that it's what spills out first in every situation.

Face-to-Face Friendship

A friend is always loyal, and a brother is born to help in time of need.
PROVERBS 17:17

I love sitting around with older people as they share stories. I imagine if I were to sit down with Amish siblings, I'd hear stories like this one, shared in Andy Yoder's book *Amish Boyhood Echoes.*

At times, if we knew we weren't going anywhere on Sunday, we would skip the Saturday night bath and do it the next day. One such Sunday was exceptionally cold so we closed the door between the kitchen and living room and bathed in the kitchen. The kitchen stove was kept going and in between bathers, we'd get someone to help put the tub back up on the stove. The next guy in line would wait until the water was good and warm, then get someone to help lift it off again. When it got to be Felty's turn, he went out to check the water, but didn't ask for help with the tub. After awhile he was sitting in the living room eating peanuts so Mom asked him why he didn't bathe. Felty said he'd done so already, so Mom asked who had helped him with the tub. Felty said he didn't need help, he just saw the tub was on the stove and figured that was where everybody had bathed, so he just climbed up there and bathed too.

There is nothing better than face-to-face time for reminiscing about life! In our society, through the use of social media, we have many "friends," but no technology can substitute for time spent together. Amish carve out time to spend with friends. Women gather for sewing and baking circles. They invite friends into their homes and travel to go visiting. It reminds me of this biblical example of friendship: "Two people are better off than one, for they can help each other succeed. . . . Three are even better, for a triple-braided cord is not easily broken" (Ecclesiastes 4:9, 12).

Do you have a friend you haven't seen in a while? Take time to get together and enjoy the stories you share and the new memories that you'll make.

■ ■ ■

Dear heavenly Father, sometimes I feel lonely, and I know it's because I don't take time for friends as I should. Help me, Lord, to enjoy face-to-face relationships.

Proclaiming His Works
with Our Words

I will live to tell what the LORD has done.

PSALM 118:17

I love reading the *Budget*. The articles of the scribes often contain humor, joy, a bit of snarkiness, and personal interest. I also love books written by the Amish, including *Amish Boyhood Echoes* by Andy Yoder. Why would an Amishman choose to write his story? Here are some thoughts:

> From the beautiful Iowa sunrise to its equally gorgeous set, our hands and minds were busy. After the moon had risen we would oft times still be outside working and conjuring up excitement. It seemed as if the darkness was a stimulant to an active brain. Maybe it was the slow clanking of the windmill in the soft breeze, or the flopping of hog-feeder lids. Maybe it was the lowing of cows in the pasture or the barking of neighboring dogs planning their nightly adventures. Maybe it was simply the harvest moon and wonderful youth. Whatever it may have been that inspired us, it was still God's protecting hand which kept our adventures within bounds.

If we pause to think, we have cause to thank!

PROVERB

> I got the idea of writing my story while I was still a child. Dad told us so very many stories, but he didn't want to write them. He said his Dad used to tell a lot of stories, but didn't want to write them either. They would both say, "We like to tell them, but if you want them written, you do the writing.". . . One story reminded me of another, and soon the family thought we should make a book out of them.

If you were going to write a book of stories, what would you include? Which stories of faithfulness do you need to pass on to the next generation? Isaiah 38:19 says, "The living, the living—they praise you, as I am doing today; parents tell their children about your faithfulness" (NIV).

Consider writing down, or recording, your stories for your children, family, or friends. Write from your heart. God is worthy of getting the glory for what He's done in your life, and your children or other young people need to hear stories that will inspire their own faith walks.

■ ■ ■

Dear heavenly Father, Your faithfulness overwhelms me. Help me to be faithful in sharing all You've done!

SEPTEMBER 9

Working Together for Common Good

Let us think of ways to motivate one another to acts of love and good works.
HEBREWS 10:24

We often hear of Amish women gathering for sewing circles or canning. We know Amish men gather for barn raisings, but during the harvest season men also gather for threshing time. The threshing ring, once common among the English, is just one example of how the Amish work together to harvest their crops. The rings (or circles) consist of men and boys from neighboring farms who work together to complete the harvesting of one another's crops, such as oats and corn.

During the threshing season, men run around to shock (stack) bundles as they are cut. The next step happens three weeks later when they return to thresh.

Teamwork divides the effort and multiplies the effect.

PROVERB

Even though it made you feel hotter, bundle pitchers almost always wore shoes or boots. The reason was snakes. Apparently snakes like the shocks and hide in them, probably to catch the rodents that feed on the grain. When we come along and mess up their homes, they don't like it. Most wagons have a snake or two in them when you got them empty. There were no live snakes in the grain wagon, so I shoveled grain! Occasionally, there was a dead one that went through the threshing machine. After what happened in Genesis, the Amish attitude is the only good snake is a dead snake.

Despite the heat, I loved threshing. I still do. I have been accused of being in love with a threshing machine by my Amish friends. I will always consider the men and boys of the threshing ring to be my very best friends on this earth. I hope to see all of them in the next life.

Hard work doesn't quite seem so hard when you're working side by side with neighbors. Toil bonds friends, and when you give, you receive even more in return.

Is there a task that you can share with a friend? Find a time when you can invite someone to work alongside you, or offer to share a task with someone else. Not only will you get work done, but you'll also grow your friendship!

■ ■ ■

Dear heavenly Father, I thank You for friends who come alongside me in my need. Help me to be that kind of friend to others, too.

Light of the World

You are the light of the world—like a city on a hilltop that cannot be
hidden. No one lights a lamp and then puts it under a basket. Instead,
a lamp is placed on a stand, where it gives light to everyone in the house.

MATTHEW 5:14-15

September is a time when Amish children head back to school. Many believe that Amish children only attend school in one-room schoolhouses, but many Amish scholars also go to public school. Once, I even met an Amish man who taught at a public school!

So what is it like to attend public school as an Amish person? Elizabeth Coblentz, author of *The Amish Cook,* describes it this way:

> When I was at school age, we went to a two-room public school. First to fourth grade were in one room (the little side), and fifth through eighth was called the "big side." A room for lunch buckets and coats divided the two. Then we moved to a different place, which brought us to grade nine and a high school. Was so different from a country school of eight grades. At the high school, they served a noon lunch, but who could afford it? . . . When our eight children went to public schools where lunch was prepared,

Preach faith until you have it, and then preach it because you have it.

PROVERB

I thought it was healthier to let them eat a warm meal at school. Made less work to pack the lunch and keep those buckets clean.

As you can imagine, Amish students will stand out among their peers in public school—from their faith to the way they dress to the size of their families. They aren't your typical students. Yet standing out isn't always a bad thing. God calls us to be salt and light in this world. In our daily lives, we will often interact with those who are different from us in some way. Instead of being intimidated by the situation, we have a chance to share God's love with those who may never have heard about Him. When someone takes note of you because you are different, use it as your chance to shine the light of Jesus in that person's life!

■ ■ ■

Dear heavenly Father, I often feel awkward when I am different from those around me.
Help me to use any attention I receive to glorify You.

He Overcomes

[Jesus said,] "I have told you all this so that you may have peace
in me. Here on earth you will have many trials and sorrows.
But take heart, because I have overcome the world."
JOHN 16:33

On a recent trip to Pennsylvania Amish country my friend and I wanted to stop by the Flight 93 Memorial. I plugged the location into my GPS, and when I approached the gates, I was surprised to see that I was only a mile away from Amish homes. My guess is that the Amish were some of the first people to the crash site, although, of course, there was nothing they could do for those brave victims.

The local Lancaster paper had a short article on the "Amish reaction" to the shocking events of September 11, 2001. They were as horrified as anyone else. Indeed, the plane that crashed in Pennsylvania went down in an area partly populated by Plain folk. Most of what they knew and saw came from newspapers and magazines, not TV.

**A happy home is
more than a roof
over your head;
it's a foundation
under your feet.**

PROVERB

A few flags did appear in windows, although the church did not condone such shows of "patriotism." There were auctions here organized by non-Amish, to which Amish donated many valuable items. While they do support the government, many wished there could have been a non-military solution, and surely prayers were offered for those who lost their lives on both sides of the conflict.

After the tragedy on September 11, many Americans did what the Amish have been doing for thousands of years: they turned to God. Churches were packed, and neighbors cared for and prayed for one another in ways they never had before. When our world was shaken, many turned to the unshakable foundation.

I love our country, and I'm thankful for those in the military who sacrifice so much to protect us. But each of us needs to look to God as our ultimate Source of protection and peace. Even when evil comes and fills us with fear, we must remember that in the end, God is the victor!

■ ■ ■

Dear heavenly Father, I thank You for being with us when we face troubles in this life.
You are our sure foundation. Thank You for overcoming the world in Jesus!

Truly Humble

God opposes the proud but favors the humble.

JAMES 4:6

When I look at the Amish, it makes sense to me that they are humble. Who could raise a dozen children to love and serve God without having dedicated their lives to Him? Who else could feed and clothe those children with limited resources? Who else could serve not only their families but also their communities? Who else could give generously while stocking their own cupboards from the food they've grown and canned or butchered or hunted? The Amish are able to do what they do because they realize they do not have to do it alone. Contrast that with people who willingly take personal credit for their accomplishments. People who want the spotlight. People who don't want to ask for help.

Humility is learned. We face challenges, and as we step out in faith, God shows up. He does what we cannot do, and we learn to depend on Him more.

Some people tend to think that humility is a weakness, but it's actually a strength. There will never be a time when we don't need God's grace, wisdom, and help. Humility means we realize our need, turn to Him, and walk forward with sure steps. Those who are humble know they have the God of the universe backing them up!

Humble people look to God's Word for inspiration and answers. They count on God's gracious provision. They look at impossible situations and say, "Since You, God, are with me, I'm ready to do this thing." Humble people realize that God has already given us everything we need to succeed in the tasks He has called us to.

John 1:16 says, "Out of His fullness (abundance) we have all received [all had a share and we were all supplied with] one grace after another and spiritual blessing upon spiritual blessing and even favor upon favor and gift [heaped] upon gift" (AMP).

Humility is accepting those gifts and putting them to use in daily life. You don't have to be Amish to do this. You simply have to push back pride and lean dependently on God.

> The real measure of your wealth is how much you'd be worth if you lost all your money.
>
> **PROVERB**

■ ■ ■

Dear heavenly Father, I thank You that I can turn to You. May my prideful thoughts be squeezed out day by day as I lean on You.

True Self-Esteem

You yourself must be an example to them by doing good works of every kind.
Let everything you do reflect the integrity and seriousness of your teaching.
TITUS 2:7

There is a lot of talk about self-esteem these days. We want our children to have a good view of their dignity and self-worth. We praise them and give them star charts, but true self-esteem doesn't come from puffed-up words and stickers. It comes from young people seeing a problem, tackling it, and achieving more than they ever thought possible:

A fifteen-year-old girl in Franklin County, Pennsylvania, taught twenty-five children in grades one through eight. Some of her students were scarcely a year younger than she. During her second year of teaching, her twelve-year-old sister transferred into her one-room school so that she could help by teaching the eight first-graders how to read. Parents of the school children reported that the sisters did well. If Amish youth are not supposed to take pride in their work, they are at least permitted to feel satisfaction in working hard and accomplishing tasks like these. Since hard workers are highly esteemed by adults and peers alike, they have a good foundation on which to develop a positive and robust sense of self-worth.

The more a child is valued, the better his values will be.

PROVERB

We shouldn't manufacture a sense of self-worth for our children. Instead we should teach them how to serve others. Praise for a job well done means far more than praise for praise and honor's sake. James 4:10 says, "Humble yourselves before the Lord, and he will lift you up in honor."

Peace comes from knowing God is always there to help us. And self-esteem comes from knowing who we are in Him and what we can do with His help. If you want children to have a great sense of self-worth, give them a hard task and watch them work hard to succeed!

■ ■ ■

Dear heavenly Father, too often I try to take the easy way out and use words to try to build up my kids. But I know deep down that what they need is training, coaching, and real-life experience. Use me today, Lord, to teach them how to depend on You and work hard for You.

To Help As We Are Helped

*There is no one like the God of Israel. He rides across the heavens
to help you, across the skies in majestic splendor.*

DEUTERONOMY 33:26

For Amish young people who decide to follow the ways of their ancestors and get married, work a simple job, and dedicate themselves to family and church, a "community" of resources is available. The members of their community will be there to celebrate a wedding; they will give the young couple gifts and assist in establishing a home. A new wife and, later, a new mom, can count on her sisters, her mother, and other women in the community to help and support her. But for those who want to work outside their communities or attend college, he odds are stacked against them:

> What happens when a needy student cannot get financial aid? Like other students of Amish descent, Naomi Kramer, a 2012 graduate of Goshen College, faced that dilemma because her parents did not support her decision to attend college.
>
> After five years of sacrifice and struggle, Kramer has achieved her dream. Now she is trying to help others by co-founding the Amish Descendant Scholarship Fund, which aids former Amish people who want to go to college.
>
> Kramer started the fund along with three other former Amish: her cousin, Emma Miller, who has a bachelor's degree in economics from San Diego State University; William Troyer, who is studying at the University of Akron; and Saloma Furlong, who graduated from Smith College and is the author of the memoir, *Why I Left the Amish*.
>
> In many cases the student cannot get any financial help "since the parents are not supportive of them getting their education," said Miller. . . . In addition, most students of Amish descent cannot receive federal aid because in order to qualify students must complete the Free Application for Federal Student Aid, which requires a parent's signature if the student is younger than 24.

You can tell when you're on the right track. It's usually uphill.

PROVERB

Even though their families are not often active in helping these students, God is there to help them. He is helping them with their own good futures. He's also helping others through them.

■ ■ ■

Dear heavenly Father, so many people face obstacles I can't imagine. Thank You, Lord, that Your majestic splendor reminds me of Your ability and willingness to help.

The Secret to Child Training

I have singled [Abraham] out so that he will direct his sons and their
families to keep the way of the LORD by doing what is right and just.
GENESIS 18:19

I've been asked before if the Amish have any secrets to raising children. After all, if they can have a large family that lives harmoniously—with children who can sit through a three-hour church service—there must be a magic potion or a secret. My friend Suzanne Woods Fisher says that if we could bottle up one truth about the Amish, it's this:

Instead of putting others in their place, put yourself in their place.

PROVERB

Amish children are loved but not adored. The Amish view children very differently than we do. They love and value each child—in many ways, they value marriage and family more than the non-Amish do. They consider each child to be a gift from God. The average family has six or seven children. Ten or more is not unusual! Children with physical or mental handicaps are thought of as "special children." I've heard quite a few Amish parents of handicapped children comment on how much they've learned from the gift of this "special child." . . . Amish parents believe a child belongs to God, not to them. Such a perspective allows parents to raise their children with clear boundaries and a healthy detachment. Hoped for, wanted, loved . . . but not adored. As a result, children are always involved in the life of the family—but it does not revolve around them.

Children are gifts from God, and He has good plans for their lives. Part of the plan is becoming a member of the family as a child, but much more of God's plan will unfold after a child leaves the home. If we make children the center of our world, they'll have a huge wake-up call when the world doesn't do the same. The job of parents is to direct their children and families in the way of the Lord. It's also to teach their children to do what is right and just and to realize the importance of others above themselves. That's something we all need to know.

■ ■ ■

Dear heavenly Father, it's so easy to make my children and grandchildren the center of my world. Guide me as I guide them, and may the boundaries I set mold them for a bountiful future.

A Mother's Discipline

*To discipline a child produces wisdom, but a mother
is disgraced by an undisciplined child.*

PROVERBS 29:15

One of the hardest things about raising—and disciplining—children is that our own wills get in the way. We often want our children to act right so that we ourselves can look good. This is true of the Amish society too. Imagine that everywhere you go there is a team of neighbors who are watching how your children act and react. As Proverbs 29:15 says, a mother is disgraced by an undisciplined child, yet the goal in raising children shouldn't be to make parents look good but to teach children to be obedient to them so that they will learn to be obedient to God. The best way to teach obedience is to focus on the things that matter most, knowing that other character qualities will follow. Here is one Amish mother's wise advice:

> In order to properly and loving discipline our children, we cannot afford to be stressed out and burdened with too many "extras." By teaching our children to submit and to do so cheerfully, we are doing them a great service that will last a lifetime. We may spare them countless heartaches by doing our duty now while they are young.
>
> These children are not ours, but God's. Can we fully realize the awesome responsibility of raising them to give back to the heavenly Father? Let us prayerfully strive to do our best, and may we someday hear those blessed words, "Well done, thou good and faithful servant."

If at first you succeed, try not to look astonished.

PROVERB

Mothers can best teach their children to give up *their* wills when mothers make the effort to submit their own wills to God. Are you disciplined in your daily life? Can you truly say to your children (no matter their ages), "Do what I do"? A mother's discipline can be directed toward a child. Or a mother's discipline can be something internal that guides her own steps. Both have great value to God and His Kingdom.

■ ■ ■

Dear heavenly Father, sometimes it's easier to direct others than to direct myself. Help me to do both wholeheartedly.

SEPTEMBER 17

Security in Times of Defeat

Those who trust in the LORD are as secure as Mount Zion;
they will not be defeated but will endure forever.

PSALM 125:1

For all the praise the Amish receive, some people may think that everything the Amish do succeeds. This is not the case. Jobs are lost, crops disappoint, and children choose the world's way over God's way. In some cases whole communities fail. Mary Ellis, one of my writer friends, discovered this while doing research for one of her novels.

Readers and writers of Amish fiction usually think about new settlements forming and growing larger each year. During my research of *Love Comes to Paradise*, I discovered that's not always the case. In Missouri, the oldest settlement was founded in 1953, but several communities were founded before the Civil War and went extinct. During the Civil War, the Amish were often at the mercy of both Union and Confederate troops since both sides stole their crops, cattle and pigs. The Hickory County settlement disbanded in 1882 due to crop failures, financial losses during the Civil War, and lack of congregational growth. A settlement near Centralia in Audrain County, (location of my fictional story) failed to thrive due to erratic weather, periods of drought alternating with heavy, persistent flooding. The last two Amish families moved away in 1917.

To return good for good is human, to return good for evil is divine.

PROVERB

No matter who we are, we will face times of struggle, failure, and disappointment in this life. If things were perfect here on earth, we wouldn't need God, and we wouldn't look forward to eternity! No matter how defeat comes, we are to trust in the Lord. Trust reminds us that our hearts and souls are secure even when the world around us crumbles. Trust causes us to cling to Romans 8:28: "We know that God causes everything to work together for the good of those who love God and are called according to his purpose for them."

Are you facing a disappointing struggle today? You will not be defeated when God is strong in you. Even if you have lost much in the world's eyes, you have access to even more in God's.

■ ■ ■

Dear heavenly Father, more than once I've asked why You allow such hard things into my life. Today, instead of asking why, I lift my voice in praise!

Holy Habits

*Let us not neglect our meeting together, as some
people do, but encourage one another.*

HEBREWS 10:25

The Amish have developed many habits that build their character and help them work efficiently. Here are a few:

The Amish waste no effort. They focus on the task at hand. If they are on the job site, they work hard—as a team—until the task is finished. Then they enjoy a meal together and visit. The Amish aren't focused on what they can acquire or what will make them fit in. They have no need for strolling through malls or flipping through fashion magazines. The Amish stand by their reputation. They know their good name is one of their greatest possessions.

The Amish focus on people. They seek to create a connection, and they watch out for the needs of others. The Amish also are in the habit of meeting together—especially for worship, but also in homes or at community events.

These are great habits we, too, can acquire, but it's a battle to get there, as this poem from the Amish magazine *Family Life* explains:

*Goliath's life then David took,
On the ancient hill above the brook;
A long time past and far away—
But are there giants in our day? . . .*

*Some habits bad, a selfish trait,
Or harmful thoughts of envy, hate;
And fears and worries, anger, pride,
Or something else we'd like to hide? . . .*

*If we but trust Him for His grace
'Twill be much easier to face
Those giants in our lives today,
For God will be our hope and stay!*

What solid habits would you like to establish? Doing so may seem like a giant undertaking. But habits are built one choice at a time, and God is faithful to help you grow in holiness.

■ ■ ■

Dear heavenly Father, it's so easy to focus on the giant, but help me to realize I can build a holy habit when I stay focused on You.

Giving and Caring

Listen to your father, who gave you life, and don't despise your mother when she is old.
PROVERBS 23:22

Fall is one of the most beautiful times in Amish country, with its cool, comfortable days and crisp evenings, but even more beautiful than the autumn view is the sight of a family member arriving by horse and buggy. While many parents around the States have to nag their grown children to call or visit, adult Amish children make it a goal to see that their parents' needs are taken care of:

How relaxing to see my daughter Liz and her husband Levi drive in with their horse-drawn buggy last night while in the midst of making tomato juice. Liz stepped in to help me finish processing the tomato juice. It is hard work to do, such processing. What a surprise to have them stay for the night. It's so good to have family. What would I do without family?

By perseverance the snail reached the ark.

PROVERB

Our drains, that drain away waste water, started to not be in working order, so our son Albert came yesterday. What a mess to go through, but was just glad to see those drains in good working order. Again, it is so nice to have children who come around and are helpful.

On September 4, my son-in-law Joe and my daughter Lovina were here, and with the help of my daughter Verena, the old roof from our barn, which was just replaced, was cleared away. A good meal was served to all after that hard work. . . . It looks very nice with a brand new roof sparkling in the sunshine.

I smile as I read Elizabeth's words. I can sense her relief that her house and barn are being tended to—that *she* is being tended to. God places us into families for a reason. Although it's good to have friends, family should be the first to support us, to provide for us, and to meet our physical and emotional needs. How have you been doing in the giving and caring department? It's not too late to extend a hand of love. Just imagine the smile you'll put on someone's face!

■ ■ ■

Dear heavenly Father, the busyness of life often hinders me from reaching out to my family. Soften my heart to care for those who've provided so much care for me.

When Simple Is Not Enough

*Philip said, If you believe with all your heart [if you have a conviction, full
of joyful trust, that Jesus is the Messiah and accept Him as the Author of
your salvation in the kingdom of God, giving Him your obedience, then] you
may. And he replied, I do believe that Jesus Christ is the Son of God.*

ACTS 8:37 (AMP)

I tell my missionary friend Loring that she's the most "Amish" English person I know.
Loring lives in Uganda. She washes her clothes in a tub and hangs them to dry. She
has spotty electricity and few of the conveniences that I enjoy. She lives simply among
a people who live even simpler. Loring is the first to confess that simple living doesn't
guarantee faithful living. Outside the gates of Loring's home, millions of men, women,
and children live in poverty—and all of them need Christ.

While many people look to the simple way of Amish living as a key to peace, one
Amish writer believes otherwise:

> We need to rediscover that a simple way of life, separated
> and apart from the world, is indeed God's pattern for his
> people. However scriptural simple living is, it is not an
> automatic passport to heaven. Thousands of people live
> simple lives, with just a roof above their heads and a dirt
> floor beneath their feet, and so few earthly possessions
> that they can load them all onto an oxcart. They may still
> live ungodly lives, wallowing in sin and poverty. Hand
> in hand with our simple living must be a devout faith
> in God, honesty of conviction, and an earnest desire for
> brotherhood. . . .

A good deal of
trouble in the
world has been
caused by too much
intelligence and too
little wisdom.

PROVERB

We don't need more conveniences as much as we need more convictions. In
this world of emphasis on luxury and earthly possessions, it may be difficult to be
content with little. But it is impossible to be content with much.

Maybe you've been striving to live simply, but your soul doesn't feel satisfied.
Faithful living is more important than simple living. Convictions are more important
than conveniences. Having much or little isn't nearly as important as having a devout
faith in God.

■ ■ ■

*Dear heavenly Father, sometimes I'm so focused on living more simply that I forget to live
more faithfully. Help me do so today.*

When We Give, We Receive

To those who use well what they are given, even more will be
given, and they will have an abundance. But from those who do
nothing, even what little they have will be taken away.
MATTHEW 25:29

We do much in life to care for ourselves and protect our finances. We believe that we should be good stewards of what God has entrusted to us, but sometimes we fail when we focus more on holding on to those coins than caring for others. In the Amish magazine *Family Life* a writer discusses that very thing in a piece titled "How to Win Money (and Lose Friends)." Here are a few points from that article:

Let your neighbors know they can't expect any handouts from you. If they want to give you something—well, that's up to them if they like giving things away!

People don't care about how much you know until they know how much you care.

PROVERB

Stop mailing cards and letters to people. Do you realize what postage adds up to if you keep buying stamps all the time? Just think how many stamps it takes in a year if you mail a letter or two each week. That money could well go toward something more necessary, or collect interest in the bank.

You surely get the gist of things by now. It takes a sharp eye and a shrew mind to make a go of it in today's world. But by pinching every penny, you can succeed. Oh yes, one more word of advice. It is best if you don't hold friends too high in esteem. For by following this creed you may accumulate a hoard of riches, but you will surely lack true friends.

By the world's standards it makes sense that the more we protect what we have, the more we will have in the end. But that's not how God's economy works. When we share what we have, God will bless us. What can you share with others? Your friends hold you in high esteem for doing so, and even more, God will be pleased.

■ ■ ■

Dear heavenly Father, I thank You for being gracious and giving and for not holding back
Your blessings from me.

Search My Heart

We can say with confidence and a clear conscience that we have lived with a God-given holiness and sincerity in all our dealings. We have depended on God's grace, not on our own human wisdom. That is how we have conducted ourselves before the world, and especially toward you.

2 CORINTHIANS 1:12

Many things symbolize a Christian's faith walk: attending church, acting with kindness, and maybe affixing a fish symbol on your car. The Amish have symbols too: prayer kapps, beards, and buggies are a few.

To understand the Amish, one must appreciate the central role that that horse-drawn buggy plays in their life. The horse-drawn buggy is more than a mode of transportation, it's an important symbol of separation. Embracing the automobile would be, in the minds of most Amish, surrendering the simple way of life they have embraced. . . .

In Swiss Amish communities, sheltered buggies are not permitted. These buggies expose their occupants to the elements.

The carriages can range from small two-seaters that aren't much more than a cart to sleek, plush behemoths that can comfortably carry a family of fourteen. The Eichers' buggy is very typical . . . seating all ten family members quite comfortably. Buggies are made according to the dictates of the local church rules (ordnung). Some Amish sects are vehemently opposed to the orange "slow-moving vehicle" triangle required by some states.

We like symbols of our faith because we can see those symbols. We can see a buggy, but we can't see a forgiven heart. We can mark church attendance, and we can weigh actions, but only God knows the soul.

How we conduct ourselves before the world matters to God, but how our hearts look matters even more. One simple prayer is found in Psalm 139:23-24: "Search me, O God, and know my heart; test me and know my anxious thoughts. Point out anything in me that offends you, and lead me along the path of everlasting life."

Driving a buggy or wearing a kapp is a choice, but it's grace that will usher us into eternity with Christ.

■ ■ ■

Dear heavenly Father, forgive me for the times I've judged someone by his or her outward presentation. Let me judge only my own heart. But more than that, You search me, Lord, and weigh what You see.

Joy Breaks

We were filled with laughter, and we sang for joy. And the other
nations said, "What amazing things the LORD has done for them."

PSALM 126:2

With autumn comes a list of things that need to be done before the first snow falls and the ground freezes. There is harvesting, canning, and tilling of the garden. There is also the raking of leaves. But even with all the work, the Amish make sure to take time for a little fun. Amish children rake leaves, but they also enjoy jumping into the piles. Laughter carries through the air, and more raking and jumping follow.

Even with the urgency of trying to get so many tasks done, there is always time for laughter. As Ecclesiastes 3:4 says, "A time to cry and a time to laugh. A time to grieve and a time to dance." And sometimes this dancing takes place among a pile of leaves! What good is having a dozen children if there aren't a dozen smiles once in a while?

Experience is a different teacher; giving you the test first and the lesson later.

PROVERB

Have you taken time recently to play in the leaves, to laugh, to let God's joy bubble from your lips? If not, then don't be surprised if no one wants to hear about the faith that you have to share.

I remember when I was far from God. I thought about my friends and their lack of joy. As they pursued their own self-interests, there was always drama, problems, and tears. Then I thought about my mom's Christian friends. They had kind things to say. They laughed often. As I compared the two groups, I realized that I wanted the joy my mom's friends had. When I accepted Jesus' salvation, the first glimmer of joy filled my heart, and it has continued to grow over the years!

When those around us see our laughter and our joy, they, too, will say, "What amazing things the LORD has done for them" (Psalm 126:2). Maybe they will start to seek the Lord for themselves. Too often we feel guilty for not accomplishing the daily tasks on our to-do lists, but sharing joy is something that can make a difference in eternity!

■ ■ ■

Dear heavenly Father, remind me again of all the wonderful things You have done so that my heart is filled with joy!

Loving Warnings

Which do you choose? Should I come with a rod to punish
you, or should I come with love and a gentle spirit?

1 CORINTHIANS 4:21

Sometimes we need to hear encouraging words, but sometimes we need to hear messages that cause us to pause and take a close look at our hearts. Children need praise and encouragement, but they also need loving discipline. Spouses need us to cheer them on, but we should also lovingly confront if we see our spouses straying from God's path. *Rules of a Godly Life* contains many statements that read like warnings. One part says, "Do not be proud and overbearing because you have been blessed with this world's goods . . . for God who has given can also take away, and may do so, if you through pride or contempt of others make misuse of His gifts to you."

The Bible, too, is filled with such caring warnings. Hebrews 12:13 says, "Mark out a straight path for your feet so that those who are weak and lame will not fall but become strong."

Some people find it easier to focus on the good they see in people. For others, it's easier to point out what is wrong in someone's life, but there is a middle ground: "Dear brothers and sisters, if another believer is overcome by some sin, you who are godly should gently and humbly help that person back onto the right path. And be careful not to fall into the same temptation yourself" (Galatians 6:1).

True brotherhood is talking to a brother or sister who has offended us before we talk to a lot of other people about it.

PROVERB

Through prayers and personal confrontation, the Amish follow this mandate. When someone sins, they go to that person humbly and with concern.

Is there someone in your life whom you need to lovingly confront? Perhaps you need to sit down with the Scriptures and peer into your own soul. Warnings come through words and prayers for our good. And we should offer the same to those we love.

■ ■ ■

Dear heavenly Father, one of the hardest things to do is confront someone I love. Give me peace and a gentle spirit, that I may offer Your grace with my words.

Taking Up Space

LORD, remind me how brief my time on earth will be. Remind
me that my days are numbered—how fleeting my life is.
PSALM 39:4

When I was growing up, I was taught the "right way" to do things. When hand washing dishes, I learned to wash glasses and silverware first because those things touch your lips and need to be the most sanitary. I learned to make the bed with the printed sides of sheets touching so it would look nice when I pulled back the covers. I also learned to iron dress shirts neatly. When I was married and we started adding kids to our home, I questioned how much time should be spent on doing things "right." Ironing took hours each week. So to save me time, my husband discovered permanent-press shirts! Sometimes there is an easier way that takes up less time and space. The Amish cook Lovina Eicher agrees:

Sometimes the "right" way to do something may not be the best way to do it.

PROVERB

By late September, large orange pumpkins begin to show themselves in area gardens. They are the whales of the garden! I love to grow my own pumpkins, but sometimes I can't because they take up so much room in the garden.

Mom always grew pumpkins and then canned the puree for pie filling. You can get a lot of pie filling out of a few pumpkins. Most years, Mom put a few plants out, but not every year, again because of the space. As she began to go to the grocery store more, canned pumpkin pie filling got so cheap it wasn't worth her time to can it at home.

Consider your life. Is there anything taking up space in your schedule that doesn't need to be there? Are you still doing things a certain way because "that's the way they're done"? Can you find a better way? Our time on earth is short, and there are too many important things that God desires us to do. Yes, sometimes we need to plant a pumpkin or two, but sometimes we need to tell ourselves that canned puree is okay!

■ ■ ■

Dear heavenly Father, help me to realize how short life is so that I can make space for the more important things You have for me to do.

My First Love

I have this complaint against you. You don't love
me or each other as you did at first!

REVELATION 2:4

I smiled at the elderly Amish woman riding a scooter. I chuckled at the grinning toddler peeking out of the window. Then I saw a couple who sat silently as they ate, as if they were strangers to each other. That reminded me of this letter from an Amish man to his wife:

> I think of times some twenty years ago when we were going through our courtship and first years of our marriage. We were in love then. We worked together, played together, laughed together, and mourned together.
>
> It seems in recent years, you are giving most of your love to the children. . . . My heart is not made of stone. Really, it feels like it is getting more tender as the years go by. Surely the coolness that has come between us is not the way you like it. In many ways, you do your duty well. You work hard to provide a home for me and the children, and you are very unselfish in many ways. You have many flowers and they all seem to be very well cared for, except one. It is called a bleeding heart of . . .
>
> —Your Loving Husband, John

In youth we learn; in age we understand.

PROVERB

My heart breaks when I read that letter. First, because of all the times I've focused more on my children than I have on my husband. But mostly because it makes me think of God. When I first gave my heart to Him, I couldn't believe how blessed I was. My sins were gone, and love overflowed. But over time, those emotions faded, like those described in Jeremiah 2:2: "This is what the LORD says: 'I remember how eager you were to please me as a young bride long ago, how you loved me and followed me even through the barren wilderness.'"

God has given His whole heart to us. Of course He is pleased when we serve Him, but more than anything else, He wants us to look to Him, connect with Him, open our hearts to His.

How can you do that today? Remember the One who is your First Love, and open your heart.

■ ■ ■

Dear heavenly Father, how amazing that the Creator of the universe loves me. I am overwhelmed with love for You.

Provision

> *Trust in the LORD, and do good; so shalt thou dwell*
> *in the land, and verily thou shalt be fed.*
> PSALM 37:3 (KJV)

I have a plaque in my breakfast nook that says, "Full Bellies + Full Hearts = Full Life." Isn't that the truth? My husband's face beams when he watches our little ones eat. And even during our lean years when John was in college, God always provided enough food—not necessarily extravagant food, but enough.

Have you ever wondered about the food on an Amish table? It might be a bit different from what you imagine:

Greet the dawn with enthusiasm, and you may expect satisfaction at sunset.

PROVERB

You would think, upon visiting Lancaster County, that the Plain folk top off each and every meal with a slice of their illustrious [shoofly] pie, so named because cooks would traditionally cool it on a windowsill, where its super sweet aroma would attract flies. But it's actually a once-in-a-while dessert for the People, who, with gardens and orchards and fresh milk and eggs in abundance, have a wide repertoire of desserts under their bonnets.

Following are three actual meals from an Amish family. Each meal includes homemade bread, farm-churned butter, and home-canned jelly:

-Breakfast: Eggs, cornmeal mush with ketchup, oatmeal with raisin, applesauce. "There's nothing cheaper for breakfast than cornmeal mush and eggs," Ella Yoder said.

-Dinner (lunch): Beef and carrots, scalloped potatoes, gravy, baked corn, carrot salad, graham cracker pudding, cookies, peaches.

-Supper: Vegetable soup, bologna, tomatoes and Chinese cabbage, apple sauce, chowchow, apple dumplings with milk and sugar.

Ezekiel 34:14 says, "I will give them good pastureland on the high hills of Israel. There they will lie down in pleasant places and feed in the lush pastures of the hills."

How has God been feeding you? Are you spiritually hungry? Are you hungry emotionally or physically? Ask God to feed that hunger. Imagine yourself at an Amish dinner table laden with His goodness, and see what real nourishment comes.

■ ■ ■

Dear heavenly Father, I thank You for all the ways You provide for me. Let my prayers over my meals be ones of true thanksgiving, not just rote words.

Yielded

May your Kingdom come soon. May your will be done on earth, as it is in heaven.

MATTHEW 6:10

"What is God's will for my life?" Most of us ask that question at some time. Good things happen, challenging things happen, and we wonder where God is in all of it. Sometimes we may have a clear understanding, but most of the time we muddle through, hoping that we're getting it partially right. The problem isn't that we aren't hearing the answer. The problem is that instead of trying to figure out the answer, we need to simply declare to God, "Your will be done."

That is one of the most common refrains in Amish life. Amish people submit themselves to God's will, believing that the divine will is sometimes clear and sometimes impossible to discern. For example, a minister preaching a funeral sermon for one of the victims of the Amish school shooting in Nickel Mines said that it is not God's will that people shoot one another, and in the same sermon suggested that the schoolgirls' deaths were somehow part of God's plan in a sense that humans might never fully understand. The same may be said for many of life's hardships.

Patience is trusting God's timing.

PROVERB

In some cases, people find positive ways of understanding their pain without claiming to know any ultimate purpose behind it. Ada Borkholder, an Indiana Amish woman who contracted polio as a very young child writes, "I have often said if I had to have polio, then I am glad it was when I was young so I don't remember being active." She does not romanticize her suffering or claim that her condition served some greater good. She simply concludes, "Lord, Thy will be done."

One Amish proverb says, "The yoke of God does not fit a stiff neck." Our necks are stiff if we are set in our ways and are determined to figure out for ourselves the right way. Better is realizing that Jesus *is* the right way.

So many times we try to seek the will of God when really we just need to seek God Himself. When we seek Him, we will find Him. And where He is, there is His will.

Although God sometimes chooses to withhold answers for our good, He simply knows you need Him more than you need the answers. Seek Him and declare, "Your will be done."

■ ■ ■

Yes, dear heavenly Father, Your will be done.

SEPTEMBER 29

An Open Hand

*Suppose you see a brother or sister who has no food or clothing, and you
say, "Good-bye and have a good day; stay warm and eat well"—but then you
don't give that person any food or clothing. What good does that do?*
JAMES 2:15-16

I had been telling myself for months that I needed to clean out my closet. The last straw
came when I couldn't find a hanger for my new shirt. In fifteen minutes I pulled out
a fourth of my clothes and bagged them up. That night I took them to the teen-mom
support group that I lead. I offered them to the girls, and within five minutes all the
clothes were spoken for. The saddest part is that I'd been mentally judging their too-
tight clothing choices for months. What I hadn't realized was that they would be happy
to get new ones that fit better. That night I prayed that God
would show me how to do more—sooner. That's something the
Amish do well. My friend Suzanne Woods Fisher talks about a
grocery shower at a small Amish store:

**Never lose sight of
the fact that old
age needs little, but
it needs that little
so much.**

PROVERB

Long metal shelving is filled with staples such as sugar,
salt, flour, and lots and lots of bulk candy. There's another
distinctive feature in this simple store. A cardboard box,
placed near the register, with a handwritten sign on its
front: "Grocery Shower. For Sam and Maryann Stoltzfus.
Maryann has had two surgeries for gall bladders. Expenses
are high. Let's help."

Rebecca, whose family runs this village store, explains it is an Amish custom
to have a grocery shower box. "It's a way we have of taking care of our own.
There's always someone who needs a little extra help." The box is overflowing
with goods.

"Tomorrow," Rebecca adds, "there will be another box. Just learned of a
couple whose baby was born a preemie." She said that in most communities, a
week or so after a wedding, friends have a grocery shower to help fill the couple's
pantry.

Do you know someone in need? If so, consider what you can do today to help that
person. Don't let the sun set until you reach out a hand of help.

■ ■ ■

*Dear heavenly Father, You've given me so much! Show me what I can give and to
whom today.*

Holy Women

This is how the holy women of old made themselves beautiful.
They trusted God and accepted the authority of their husbands.

1 PETER 3:5

It is a sad fact that many children in the United States grow up in single-parent homes. That is not typical in Amish communities, as *The Amish Way* describes:

> Except in cases where the husband has died or become severely disabled, the head of an Amish family is always a man. Amish men demonstrate their family leadership in a number of areas. As we have seen, family devotional practices such as prayers and scripture readings are typically led by the father, except when young children are the focus. The husband usually takes the lead in dealing with outsiders. Although most schoolteachers are women, the trustees who oversee the schools are invariably men.
>
> Most other committees in Amish communities are composed entirely of men. An Amish wife is to be "subject to her husband" and "help and support her husband in every way."

A happy marriage is a long conversation that always seems too short.

PROVERB

One might think that Amish women would despise their role, but the majority find joy in it. They receive care from their husbands and return the care. They even have fun in their roles. Here is a humorous story from the *Budget*: "This past week a young couple was on their way home from a friend's house. As they were driving the wife noticed that the curve ahead did not get the attention of her husband. He was looking the other way. She wisely checked, and seeing that there was not much of a ditch with no fence posts close, she held her tongue. A bit later Mr. Byler found himself driving in a field."

How do you see your role as a woman? If you are married, do you appreciate the role your spouse has? Do you see your own responsibilities as a gift rather than a burden?

Find a way to have fun in your role today. Doing so will lighten your load!

■ ■ ■

Dear heavenly Father, may I always see the role You've given me as a gift from You and appreciate it with a joyful heart.

FALL

Recipe for Date Pudding

Cake

2 cups chopped dates
1 teaspoon baking soda
1 cup hot water
1 cup sugar
2 tablespoons butter

1 egg
1½ cups all-purpose flour
pinch of salt
½ cup chopped pecans
whipped cream

Sauce:

3 cups water
2 cups brown sugar
1 cup sugar
5 tablespoons all-purpose flour

chunk of butter
½ teaspoon salt
1 teaspoon vanilla

Mix baking soda and hot water and pour over dates in large bowl. In a separate bowl, cream sugar, butter, egg, flour, and salt. Add pecans and stir. Combine with date mixture and bake in a greased 8- or 9-inch cake pan for 45 minutes. When cooled, cut into bite-size cubes. Cook sauce ingredients together in a saucepan until thickened. Layer cake cubes, sauce and whipped cream in a large bowl. Makes 10–12 servings.

OCTOBER 1

Looking Forward to a Good Future

History merely repeats itself. It has all been done
before. Nothing under the sun is truly new.
ECCLESIASTES 1:9

Have you ever heard the saying that everything old is new again? Old fashions are "retro." Old furniture is "repurposed." Old skills, such as knitting, crocheting, and embroidery, are embraced by a new generation. And as Amish move into new parts of the country, old manners of living are resurrected. Here is a report from visitors to a new Amish settlement in Unity, Maine.

To grow old gracefully, you must start when you are young.

PROVERB

The Community Market is still under construction and is located at the base of what looks like the central point of Community activity and endeavors and the large fields look like they grew a lot of product this past growing season.

There was a lot of activity going on outside with several Amish men using a chainsaw to cut ice from a pond and using the horses and buggies to haul it off somewhere. There was an elderly woman there who was watching this going on and said pretty loudly, " . . . I haven't seen that done in about 70 years."

God has a habit of allowing society to run in cycles. Ecclesiastes 3:15 says, "What is happening now has happened before, and what will happen in the future has happened before, because God makes the same things happen over and over again."

What can we expect to see in our spiritual lives? "'In the last days,' God says, 'I will pour out my Spirit upon all people. Your sons and daughters will prophesy. Your young men will see visions, and your old men will dream dreams'" (Acts 2:17).

We may look at the Amish lifestyle and think, *I wish we could return to a simpler life.* We may look at the ungodliness of the world and think, *I wish we had the values of the past.* But with God, the past is only a glimpse into the future. Young men and women are being raised to know God personally, and the future will be better for it. Trust God for that!

■ ■ ■

Dear heavenly Father, I'm thankful that You hold the past, present, and future in Your hands. I thank You that the "good old days" can be our future when we turn to You.

Harvest School

How joyful are those who fear the LORD—all who follow his ways! You will
enjoy the fruit of your labor. How joyful and prosperous you will be!

PSALM 128:1-2

In our home, when the children helped out with tasks, we considered those tasks their "chores." In the Amish community, harvest work is part of a child's education.

[Benny Mast's] education ended at eighth grade in a one-room schoolhouse just a few miles away. When he turns 21 he'll be free to buy land, marry and settle down. Until then he works for his father, at his brother's sawmill and for neighbors during harvest.

"This is our college," he said. "We learn by working." If the field were a classroom, the Amish men were star students.

"Hey," 15-year-old Andy Yerdon said to his horses, in a normal speaking voice. His calm draft team walked 10 feet. "Ho," he said and they stopped.

He didn't even have to touch the reins; just kept tossing bundles.

"The English ask horses to do things," he said. "We Amish, we just tell them. They know their work."

In the hours of cool morning it seemed easy. The workers were methodical. In a career of deadlines, the crisp air and steady physical labor seemed a welcome change from the usual desk shift.

Then the sun broke the tree line.

Very few burdens are heavy if everyone ifts.

PROVERB

When the sun rises and warms the sky, the work gets harder, but it's only in our "modern" society that people consider hard work a bad thing. Today, people put more stock in book knowledge than in experience, but that isn't the only knowledge there is. Knowing how to harvest corn, how to work with horses, and how to work the land is worth passing down. Sometimes we forget that the things our children learn in school are just a portion of what they need to know in life.

"Direct your children onto the right path, and when they are older, they will not leave it," we read in Proverbs 22:6. The right path encompasses more than book knowledge, and what children learn from working hard can be just as valuable.

■ ■ ■

Dear heavenly Father, strengthen my back and help me teach Your ways to the generations that come after me.

The Right Path

Trust in the LORD with all your heart; do not depend on your own understanding.
Seek his will in all you do, and he will show you which path to take.
PROVERBS 3:5-6

Have you ever had something hard in your life turn into something wonderful? Was there a time you first questioned God's plan and then later thanked Him for it?

Although the Anabaptist movement had its beginning among educated city-dwellers, it soon spread to the rural areas of Switzerland. To avoid persecution, many people also left the cities and fled to remote parts of the country to evade the authorities. Former merchants, tailors, and cobblers were suddenly farmers. At that time, it was mostly a subsistence type of farming.

In areas where persecution lessened, the Anabaptists became excellent farmers. In some instances, they led in the development of new techniques that improved productivity. Through their honest[y], integrity and good work ethics, they were recognized for their stewardship of the land and their animal husbandry. They were even invited to move to certain areas by friendly rulers who saw their farming abilities.

One of my favorite Bible stories is that of Philip and the Ethiopian: "An angel of the Lord said to [Philip], 'Go south down the desert road that runs from Jerusalem to Gaza.' So he started out, and he met the treasurer of Ethiopia, a eunuch of great authority under the Kandake, the queen of Ethiopia" (Acts 8:26-27).

Too many people want to reach the Promised Land without going through the wilderness.

PROVERB

When Philip set out, he had no idea what was in store. Still, he trusted that God knew. Following God's direction, Philip was able to meet a man and lead him to saving grace in Jesus Christ. Not only was the Ethiopian ushered into God's Kingdom, but Philip also got to be part of the process.

Perhaps you are being led to a place different from what you expected. Like Philip sent to the Ethiopian—or the Amish sent to the countryside—God has a plan for where He is taking you. Trust Him in that. Know that the paths God takes us on are not arbitrary.

■ ■ ■

Dear heavenly Father, the road is harder than I thought, and I wish I had more answers about where we're going. Still, Lord, I trust You. Help me trust You more.

From Him, through Him, in Him

Lord, through all the generations you have been our home!
Before the mountains were born, before you gave birth to the
earth and the world, from beginning to end, you are God.

PSALM 90:1-2

What did your ancestors believe about God? Do you know? The Amish do. They have a Confession of Faith that was written and adopted at a peace convention held in the Dutch city of Dordrecht on April 21, 1632:

> Whereas it is declared that "without faith it is impossible to please him [God]" (Heb 11:6), and that "he that cometh to God must believe that he is, and that he is a rewarder of them that diligently seek him," therefore we confess with the mouth, and believe with the heart, together with all the pious, according to the Holy Scriptures, that there is one eternal, almighty, and incomprehensible God, Father, Son, and Holy Ghost, and none more and none other, before whom no God existed, neither will exist after Him. For from Him, through Him, and in Him are all things. To Him be blessing, praise, and honor, for ever and ever.

When you talk you only repeat what you already know, but if you listen, you may learn something.

PROVERB

"From Him, through Him, and in Him." It's hard to wrap our minds around that, and the more we learn of God, the harder it becomes. It's like explaining the process of writing a book to my children. When they are preschoolers, they trust that when Mom types on a computer, a book comes out of it. The older they get, the more they understand the process, but they also realize the process is more complex than they thought.

Have you ever felt that way—that the more you learn about God and His Word, the more you realize how much you don't know? We don't need to understand everything about God. We simply need to put our faith in the fact that He is.

What concerns are heavy on your heart? Write those things down, and then take a closer look at them. Let peace come when you realize the answers are from Him, through Him, and in Him.

■ ■ ■

Dear heavenly Father, may my heart be open to hear and to embrace the truths shared by past generations.

Pruning

*[Jesus said,] "I am the true grapevine, and my Father is the gardener. He
cuts off every branch of mine that doesn't produce fruit, and he prunes
the branches that do bear fruit so they will produce even more."*
JOHN 15:1-2

We might tend to think that once a crop is harvested, the work is done for the year.
But when it comes to fruit, the work is never finished.

Following their harvest of apples and pears every year, Amish farmers take on the
chore of pruning all the orchards. The Amish long ago discovered that trimming
limbs, and removing the dead wood, has a powerful and regenerative effect.
Sufficient pruning stimulates new growth ensuring next season's crop is both
bountiful and flavorful.

But nature makes a grower pay a steep price when branches
are sheared too severely. Trees take longer to recover and fruit
yields are substantially reduced. Consequently, a fear of over-
cutting makes pruning ones' own groves a particularly tenuous
and even painful task.

> In this world of give
> and take, not enough
> people are willing to
> give what it takes.
>
> **PROVERB**

The Amish, however, found a brilliant solution to this
dilemma, one that reveals a keen understanding of human
nature. They discovered it was much easier for them to pare-
down someone else's trees rather than their own.

On a designated day at the onset of winter, all the farmers meet, shake hands,
and then set off to independently perform a neighbor's trimming. At dusk, the men
return to the town square to express their mutual appreciation. Each returns home
certain they were more the beneficiary than the benefactor in the exchange.

Some of us have friends we can turn to for help with our pruning. "Can you point out
my weak or dead areas?" we might ask. A good friend won't be too kind or too harsh.

If you don't have a friend like that, there is Someone else you can turn to. God the
Father cuts off every branch that does not produce fruit because He knows that proper
pruning stimulates new growth and ensures that next season's crop is both bountiful
and flavorful.

"When you follow God hard, things can get messy," says my friend Lisa Whittle.
"Don't hate the pruning. The exposure of your flaws may be hard, but it is a gift that
leaves you with no choice but to need Him."

■ ■ ■

Dear heavenly Father, I turn myself over to You in complete trust.

What Is Saved

The wise store up choice food and olive oil, but fools gulp theirs down.

PROVERBS 21:20 (NIV)

Although Benjamin Franklin's familiar adage "A penny saved, is a penny earned" has changed from his original, the concept is one the Amish believe in, as the first Amish Cook, Elizabeth Coblentz, writes:

> Thinking back then, the land wasn't selling high as it is now, and the wages were low or so it seems now. I guess it's not what you earn, it's what you save. Also, it was hard to find a job when we were first married, thirty-six years ago. Being without a job was tough, especially when those farm payments came along. But somehow, there was always a way, it seemed.
>
> No killing frost as yet. We dug out the flower bulbs that don't survive the cold winter months. Also, the sweet potatoes were dug out and the garden goodies have been taken care of except the lettuce and endive and a few other vegetables remain in the garden. We didn't buy any lettuce from the stores since last spring and it's less than two months from Christmas. Do we appreciate it enough?

Help those whom God has placed in our path.

PROVERB

What we save—money, flower bulbs, or "garden goodies"—is precious to us. Personally, I have saved boxes of wonderful treasures: baby photos, trinkets from vacations, and my grandmother's recipes.

In our culture today we often have a consumeristic mentality, but God reminds us there is a good purpose to our saving some things: so that we will have a bounty to share with others. The apostle Paul often took collections for himself and his fellow laborers. His work depended on others saving and sharing: "On the first day of each week, you should each put aside a portion of the money you have earned. Don't wait until I get there and then try to collect it all at once" (1 Corinthians 16:2).

What do you have to save? What do you have to share? Tulip bulbs grow and share beauty. A garden harvest feeds a family. Money can help the destitute. Photos share memories. And if you find it hard to share, remember how much Christ shared . . . and how you are saved because of it.

■ ■ ■

Dear heavenly Father, I would be lost now if You didn't focus on a saving work. Thank You.

Your Walk, Your Testimony

When they see their many children and all the blessings I have
given them, they will recognize the holiness of the Holy One
of Israel. They will stand in awe of the God of Jacob.
ISAIAH 29:23

My friend Kristen Jane Anderson lost both of her legs in a suicide attempt. When she was seventeen, Kristen lay in front of an approaching train, trying to end it all. But God saved her life, and He is now using her story to bring others to Him. After her attempt, Kristen dedicated her life to God, and now she glows with love for Him. People notice her physical condition, but they pay attention to her face even more. She is often asked, "What makes you so happy? Why do you have so much peace and joy?"

The Amish know that their "differences" will gain them attention, but their desire is that people will pay more attention to how they live for God than to how they live plain lives. An Amish parable discusses this very thing:

If there is a smile in your heart, your face will show it.

PROVERB

My dad orders his checks with a Bible verse printed on them. A few years ago he ordered several tons of coal and sent a check along with the neighbor man who was going to haul it home for us. The man at the coal mine looked at the check and remarked, "It should be all right. It has a Bible verse printed on it."

We do not have Bible verses printed on us, but our plain clothes should be worn as a testimony to what we believe.

Our words, actions, and dealings must correspond with our plain clothes, or it will not benefit us at all to wear them.

When people look at you, do they see a difference? Do they see something they want for themselves? Are they witnesses to your happiness, your joy, and your peace? Do they see Jesus in you?

We can have checkbooks with Bible verses, or we can wear Scripture T-shirts, but doing those things doesn't matter as much as the testimony of how we live our lives. You may be the only Bible someone reads. Let the truth of Scripture radiate through your life!

■ ■ ■

Dear heavenly Father, when people look at me, may they see You most!

Feeding a Crowd

*There's a young boy here with five barley loaves and two
fish. But what good is that with this huge crowd?*

JOHN 6:9

When my son got married a few years ago, our family and friends helped with the meal. Everyone had a great time, and the food was wonderful! The Amish often ask their friends and family members to help with the wedding cooking, too, but these days they sometimes use wedding wagons to make the preparation and service easier:

[Wedding wagons] are portable kitchens that can be hired to prepare all the wedding food. Several Amish own and rent out the kitchens as a part-time job.

The kitchens typically have five gas stoves in them, sinks, and cabinets along both sides of the wall. The cabinets contain all the dishes, stainless-steel kettles, and utensils needed to serve the hundreds of people that attend a typical wedding. The wagons are generator powered, with hot and cold running water, silverware, and over three hundred place settings, including coffee cups, glasses, and silverware. Most of them have a ramp for easy walking up and down. And a lot of times they have a cooler inside with shelves for the potato salads and things that need to be kept cool.

**Do the most
important thing first.**

PROVERB

I love the idea of wedding wagons, but I love Jesus' manner of feeding crowds even more: "'Tell everyone to sit down,' Jesus said. So they all sat down on the grassy slopes. (The men alone numbered about 5,000.) Then Jesus took the loaves, gave thanks to God, and distributed them to the people. Afterward he did the same with the fish. And they all ate as much as they wanted" (John 6:10-11).

Jesus didn't put out an invitation for a potluck. He didn't have an Amish wedding wagon. Jesus' only resource was Himself, and when we have Jesus, we don't have need of anything else either.

Whatever situation you're facing today, Jesus is enough. Just as He directed the disciples, He is able to direct a miracle in your life too. When we have the best of the world's resources, we can feed a crowd, but when we have Jesus, we can also see our faith multiply!

■ ■ ■

Dear heavenly Father, today I offer the little I have to You. Multiply it as only You can.

OCTOBER 9

Overcoming Fears

[Jesus said,] "I am leaving you with a gift—peace of mind and heart. And the peace I give is a gift the world cannot give. So don't be troubled or afraid."
JOHN 14:27

If you've ever visited the Amish community in West Kootenai, Montana, you've no doubt heard about the bachelors. Every year twenty to thirty Amish bachelors come from all over the United States to live in Montana from six months to a year to gain their resident hunting license so they can hunt in the fall. It's quite an adventure for these young men as they travel from rural farms and factories in Ohio, Pennsylvania, or Indiana to move into the wild where the deer, bear, and moose still roam. It's a good possibility they could run into a wild animal while riding their bicycles to work.

> Let us be of good cheer, remembering that the misfortunes hardest to bear are those which never come.
>
> **PROVERB**

For all those bachelors, adventure is waiting in the area. Some may also find true love while they're there. More than one Amish bachelor has written home describing not only his latest hike or hunt but also a pretty local girl who has caught his eye.

For a young Amish person in these parts, there can be many reasons to fear. Wild animals are one, but even greater can be the question *What if I don't find love?* With only a few dozen Amish families in the area, there aren't many potential spouses to choose from.

All of us experience fear. The truth is that the fear of being laughed at can be just as intense for some people as the fear of running into a large bear on a Montana dirt road.

So where do we go with our fears? Psalm 34:4 shows us: "I sought the LORD, and He answered me, and delivered me from all my fears" (NASB). God is the only One who can truly defeat fear in your heart. And He not only takes away the fear, but also replaces it with His peace. And while the perfect Amish bachelor may not show up at the right time for the right girl, God will never disappoint us!

■ ■ ■

Dear heavenly Father, I know my fear stems from a lack of trust. Help me to trust in You!

Connecting Hearts

God is working in you, giving you the desire and the power to do what pleases him.

PHILIPPIANS 2:13

I've been told that every great novel starts with a bit of fact. My first Amish novel, *Beside Still Waters*, started with more than that. A few years ago I was asked if I would ever consider writing an Amish novel. The truth is, I hadn't. But the seed of an idea was planted, and my mind started to feed and water it. That's how novels usually start.

The very day I was asked, I remembered that the parents of my daughter's friend Saretta had been raised Amish. They had moved from an Amish community in Indiana to Montana, and that is how we met. I also remembered my daughter telling me that Ora Jay and Irene had lost two daughters in a buggy accident. I remember thinking that I'd love to hear their story. Maybe someday, if I saw them again, I would ask them about it.

The next day, my daughter Leslie and I went out for some mom-and-daughter time. We went to a bookstore to browse and get coffee, and as we looked over the bargain rack, guess who walked in? Saretta. We hadn't seen her for at least six months, and there she was.

"Saretta," I told her, "I think I'm supposed to talk to your parents and hear their story."

"Sure," she said. "I think they'd love to talk to you!"

Not long after that, Ora Jay and Irene sat in my living room. They told me about being Amish, about losing their daughters, about their move from Indiana to Montana. They also talked about their faith. They shared what it meant to be Amish. They shared how their faith had grown after moving to Montana. They shared many ways God had changed their lives and their hearts. I was amazed. As I listened, their story added more water—Living Water—and sunshine to that seed of a novel planted in my heart.

> "A lot of people read bonnet fiction. Three bonnet-romance writers–Beverly Lewis, Wanda Brunstetter and Cindy Woodsmall– are New York Times best-selling authors."

God has a way of connecting our hearts to those of others. He does it so that we'll grow and change. He does it so that others will too. When we're seeking Him, God takes pleasure in working in and through us in ways we may never expect. It pleases Him, and we are blessed too.

■ ■ ■

Dear heavenly Father, I'm amazed at how Your story for me connects with Your story for others. Thank You.

Traditions

Brothers, stand firm and hold to the traditions that you were
taught by us, either by our spoken word or by our letter.
2 THESSALONIANS 2:15 (ESV)

Do you observe any traditions in your life? Most of us have some, including certain holidays. But the Amish follow some traditions that we don't have.

Every October there is an Amish religious "holiday" that often catches we non-Amish by surprise. Amish businesses are closed, and farmers are not seen working in the fields. The day is called St. Michael's Day, and is usually observed by the Amish on October 11. For the Amish, most of whom probably know very little about Michael, it is a day of rest and fasting (usually breakfast) prior to the upcoming Communion service.

So, who is St. Michael? As one of the seven archangels named in the Old Testament, he is mentioned in the book of Daniel as a "great prince" and protector of God's people. . . . But how did the Amish come to "observe" the day of a Catholic saint? In the old days in Europe, many of the Amish and Mennonites were tenant farmers. Much of the land was owned by the church or aristocrats. Farmers paid a percent of their profits to the landholder every year. The date set by the churches and monasteries in Germany for the farmers to pay their tax was St. Michael's Day, October 11th. This date fell after the harvest, when the profits and resulting tax could be most accurately assessed.

> "St. Michael's Day is celebrated in the Catholic, Lutheran, and Anglican churches on September 29th, and in the Greek church on November 8."

While the Amish no longer have to pay taxes like this, the observance of this day continues because it is a tradition. It makes me pause and think about the things I have set up in my life. Do I focus more on the traditions of my family or the doctrines shared in the Word of God?

Through holy men, God gave us His Word. How wonderful that the Bible is still around for us to read. May we be more diligent about sticking to God's holy teaching than to anything our ancestors have passed down.

■ ■ ■

Dear heavenly Father, the only way my heart will embrace Your doctrine is when
I understand it. Please give me a hunger for Your Word!

Hymns of Praise

Praise the LORD! How good to sing praises to our
God! How delightful and how fitting!

PSALM 147:1

What hymns do you like to sing? Tony Loeffler, a formerly homeless suicidal addict, is now a Christian and the founder of Solid Rock Ministries. He writes, "Hymns breathe the praise of saints, the visions of the prophets, the prayers of the penitent, and the spirit of martyrs. They bring solace to the sad, assurance to the perplexed, faith to the doubter and comfort to the oppressed. They span the centuries of history and bridge the barrier of denominations. Study hymns and spiritual songs to be pure in heart; sing them to be joyful in spirit and store them in the mind to possess a treasury of worship."

Most people assume that the only hymns that Amish sing are from the *Ausbund.* This is not the case. Singing hymns like "Amazing Grace" or "In the Sweet By and By" is popular outside of church. Here's a bit more about the Amish approach to singing:

Bend the branch while it is still young.

PROVERB

> Amish do enjoy song, and often sing informally. This may be anything from singing in the shower, the garden, or while working. Song is seen as a joyful way to pass the time and make the work go quicker. Songs are typically sung in English.
>
> Church songs are generally not sung alone or informally. Amish will gather to practice these songs. Amish married men, for instance, may gather together to practice church singing on a weekday. Christian hymns may also be sung in English at breakfast or at the end of the day.

When we sing, we have a special connection with those who've gone before us. Their praise, vision, and prayers connect with ours even though they are long gone. I look forward to the day when people from every nation and language will join together to praise God. How delightful and fitting that will be!

■ ■ ■

Dear heavenly Father, how precious You are, that Your Spirit moves on the heart of a man or woman in the words of a hymn, and then we get to participate in worship with those of other generations!

Interdependence

Submit to one another out of reverence for Christ.
EPHESIANS 5:21

Independence is self-sufficiency, self-dependency, and self-reliance. The Amish are opposed to any sort of independence. In fact, one of the first prayers they learn is this: "I must be a Christian child, gentle, patient, meek and mild. I must cheerfully obey, giving up my will and way." Yet things were very different for the first Amish settlers in the eighteenth century.

The first communities were made up of clusters of families, most of whom were related by kinship ties. There was no overall or master plan of settlement. In fact, individualism and strong family autonomy seem to have had greater reign than church control. The behavior of some Amish was inconsistent with the tradition of the Amish as we know it today. The color of their wagon tops was not yet uniform, and in Chester County the Amish had built a meeting house. The long, intense voyages across the ocean may have resulted in alliances and friendships with persons who were not Amish. For many years a single bishop, traveling by foot and horseback, performed marriages and offered communion to scattered clusters of families. The Lancaster Amish settlement was not divided until 1843, nearly a hundred years after the first Amish families arrived in America. With the growth of settlements, the Amish ordained resident bishops, and thus church control began to be exercised over family and kinship rule.

> A word to the wise is unnecessary.
>
> PROVERB

Just like the Amish, we are told to submit to one another: "You have been called to live in freedom, my brothers and sisters. But don't use your freedom to satisfy your sinful nature. Instead, use your freedom to serve one another in love" (Galatians 5:13).

Self-sufficiency, self-dependency, and self-reliance not only disconnect us from one another but also disconnect us from God. God wants us to depend on Him, and the more we submit to Him and our Christian brothers and sisters, the more we understand how God planned for us to live our lives as the body of Christ.

■ ■ ■

Dear heavenly Father, help me to depend on You more today. Help me to depend on others, too, and be dependable for them.

Memory Journals

It was there at Gilgal that Joshua piled up the twelve stones taken from the Jordan River. Then Joshua said to the Israelites, "In the future your children will ask, 'What do these stones mean?' Then you can tell them, 'This is where the Israelites crossed the Jordan on dry ground.'"

JOSHUA 4:20-22

I've been journaling for twenty years, collecting stories, prayers, and Scriptures. I have thoughts tucked inside spiral-bound notebooks and leather journals. Prayer requests—and answers—fill their pages.

I try to imagine what my children and grandchildren might think when they read through the pages. My journals contain my questions, cries of my heart, and even confessions. There are also prayers of surrender and praise. The picture my loved ones will see within my words is that I was completely human, with joys and struggles like anyone else's. Mostly, I hope they'll see that no matter what, I turned to God. That I depended on Him in all circumstances.

The Amish do not usually expose their feelings in their diaries. Instead they note down each day's rounds of boiling pear butter, collecting duck eggs, cleaning stables, taking sleigh rides or attending church. Once in a while dramatic events are recorded, but sometimes not by the diarists themselves.

"Our Dear son Dannie died this morning at 10 minutes after 8 o'clock," Samuel and Annie Esh wrote as the May 31, 1912, entry in their teenage son's worn clothbound diary. The Eshes then filled out some of the rest of the year's pages with dutiful notes on farm life in Pennsylvania.

Amish saying: Hospital . . . a place of medical care for the physically ill and hurt. Church . . . a place of spiritual care and prayer for our hearts, minds, and souls.

While I'm sure these journals are treasures, can you imagine how much more meaningful they would be if they shared real heart issues?

Have you ever set up stones of remembrance from your walk with God? Find a journal to write down your memories of God's goodness in your life. You'll be amazed by how much has already been captured in your heart!

■ ■ ■

Dear heavenly Father, thank You for all You've done in my life. May I be faithful to share that with others.

Good Intentions Made Good

Honor your father and mother, as the LORD your God commanded you. Then you will live a long, full life in the land the LORD your God is giving you.
DEUTERONOMY 5:16

My widowed grandmother has lived with our family for the last decade, and although it hasn't always been easy, I've been thankful for our time together. Some time ago I spent the afternoon with my mother-in-law. In the midst of our conversation I mentioned, "You know, if something ever happens to Dad, you are welcome to live with us. We'll make sure you're cared for."

Relief flooded her face as she said, "You don't know what it means for me to hear you say that. You just lifted a huge burden from my shoulders."

In the Amish community widows and widowers are well cared for, and some adult children find a way to organize their efforts.

Last Christmas, Julia's sister handed everyone a list of dates. "My sister Mary Sue thought it up. She assigned everyone to take a turn and help Mom for one day per week throughout the year," Julia explained. "We mow her lawns or do her laundry; whatever she needs. I thought it was a real good idea, and it's worked out well."

> Good intentions die unless they are executed.
>
> **PROVERB**

The grandchildren participate too by running errands or hoeing the garden. "Everyone plays a part," Julia said. "I like having my children see how to take good care of a grandmother. She's taken good care of all of us over the years. She's been a wonderful mother and grandmother. It's our turn, now, to take care of her."

Christmas is still a few months away—the perfect time to plan a "caring calendar" for someone in your life. Make good on your good intentions! Not only will you honor a special person, but you and your children will be blessed.

Deuteronomy 5:29 says, "Oh, that they would always have hearts like this, that they might fear me and obey all my commands! If they did, they and their descendants would prosper forever."

When we give care and honor to our parents, we will prosper in our own lives and souls. That's a promise from God.

■ ■ ■

Dear heavenly Father, I can count on Your promises. Help me to be obedient to Your Word and to give honor where it is due!

Time Wise

*Be careful how you live. Don't live like fools, but like those who are
wise. Make the most of every opportunity in these evil days.*

EPHESIANS 5:15-16

What robs you of your time? For me it's watching television, hunting for items I've
misplaced, and spending too much time on the Internet. I tell myself I'll do better
tomorrow, but "tomorrow" comes, and once again the minutes slip away. The Amish
don't have those time robbers.

> [The Amish] have a deep connection to the rhythms of nature through their
> farm, even if it's just a few acres to grow their own fruits and vegetables. They
> eschew time thieves: television, radio, newspapers. It's as if they live their life with
> an unlimited amount of time, as if they have a toe in the
> door to eternity.
>
> Common sayings promote patience as a virtue:
> "It takes a century for God to make a sturdy oak."
> "Harvest comes not every day."
> "A handful of patience is worth more than a bushel
> of brains."
> "You can't make cider without apples."
> "Don't count your eggs before they are laid."

**Children need your
presence more than
your presents.**

PROVERB

What a contrast to the English perception that there is never enough time! We tend
to view time as an enemy, or at the least, as an irritating constraint. We try to beat the
clock, and we use technology or machinery to speed up tasks. But in an ironic twist,
time seems even more elusive despite all the gadgetry that promises to save us time. We
cook with microwaves and wash with machines. We drive cars and send work through
e-mail and fax, but none of these things gains us more time.

Just how precious is your time? It's worth Christ's sacrifice. He died so that we could
live with Him for eternity, where we will no longer be bound by the limits of time.
He also wants us to follow His example on earth. Ephesians 5:2 calls us to "live a life
filled with love, following the example of Christ. He loved us and offered himself as a
sacrifice for us, a pleasing aroma to God."

The only way we can make the most of our minutes and days is through wisdom.
It's turning to God for guidance and being careful how our minutes are spent.

■ ■ ■

*Dear heavenly Father, show me how precious You consider my time, and guide me in using
it better.*

Loving Separation

*You can enter God's Kingdom only through the narrow gate. The highway
to hell is broad, and its gate is wide for the many who choose that way.*
MATTHEW 7:13

I had a best friend in the sixth grade. We did everything together, until one day she
didn't return my calls. The next day I found all the stuff I'd ever given her dumped
onto our front lawn. The hardest part was not knowing what I'd done wrong. The
Amish don't have that problem. When one of them breaks church rules, everyone
knows. And when someone refuses to return to obedience, *Meidung*, or shunning, is
often the result.

When church members break church rules, they are asked to confess their errors
before the congregation. After confession, the deed is forgotten. But if there is no
confession, the offending members are excommunicated. They
cannot return to church unless they confess. They also are
shunned by the other members:

**Trouble is easier to
get into than out of.**

PROVERB

Shunning is a form of social avoidance. It is an alteration of
behavior towards an individual who has willfully violated rules
of the church. Shunning may take the form of eating separately,
not doing business with a person, not accepting gifts or rides
from a shunned individual, and generally excluding a person from community
activities. Amish will still converse with an individual in the *Bann*, and will offer
assistance if needed. But for all intents and purposes, that individual, through his
own choice, is considered outside the flock.

While the church you attend may not have the same protocol, the Bible does tell us
to disassociate with those who claim to be believers but who are living in blatant sin: 1
Corinthians 5:11 says, "I meant that you are not to associate with anyone who claims
to be a believer yet indulges in sexual sin, or is greedy, or worships idols, or is abusive,
or is a drunkard, or cheats people. Don't even eat with such people."

When we love someone, it's easy to look past that person's sins, but God wants us
to take sin seriously. The goal is for our friend to see the sin, feel the pain of separation,
and return to God—return to the narrow gate.

■ ■ ■

*Dear heavenly Father, sometimes it's easier to ignore blatant sin than to talk to a friend
who is sinning. Give me a willing heart to start the discussion, for the sake of that person's
soul!*

The Example, the Way

Dear brothers and sisters, pattern your lives after mine,
and learn from those who follow our example.

PHILIPPIANS 3:17

Amish communities have exploded from quiet, sleepy places to tourist attractions. While the Amish are sometimes bothered by English who (disrespectfully) want to take their photographs or speed carelessly down the roads in their cars, they do benefit from the money the English bring in. This is a conflict. The goal of the Amish is to reject all that is pleasure seeking, but that is exactly what some tourists are doing. They may be visiting the area and purchasing goods not because they need them, but merely for pleasure. The Amish, who don't put much stock in entertainment, are *becoming* the entertainment. They are objects of curiosity that people travel great distances to see. They are to live separately from the world, yet they increasingly depend on the world for their income.

For the Amish, maintaining their customs in the face of tourism is not enough; they want to maintain a pure motivation for continuing those customs, a motivation aimed only at pleasing God. If they allow themselves to get too caught up in the mere practice of their religion here on earth, they will forget the Amish belief that the true purpose of this . . . life is not this life but preparation for eternal life with God. . . . And in their view, forgetting that would remove all lasting meaning from their lives.

Are there others who look up to you as an example? What is your motive in what you do? A leader, a minister, a parent, or a friend should be able to refer to his or her example and encourage others to live likewise. But the only way we can keep our motives pure is to depend on God and pray for an earnestness of our souls. And the only way we should invite others to follow our example is to make Jesus our Way.

"You shall love your neighbor as yourself in joy and affliction. Sin you shall not practice. For it is due time that we begin to do what is right, following after Christ Jesus, looking to His example."

AUSBUND,
SONG 56, VERSE 2

■ ■ ■

Dear heavenly Father, I ask You to use my body and soul as instruments of righteousness for Your service, not to benefit myself but to glorify You and bless others.

Satisfied

He fills my life with good things. My youth is renewed like the eagle's!
PSALM 103:5

Where do you find your satisfaction? What feeds your soul? I'm an introvert, so I get "recharged" when I have time for quiet, Scripture reading, and reflection. I have family members who get charged up by being with friends.

Like anyone else, the Amish have the same basic needs—for love, respect, information, community, safety, and fun—but compared with us they have very different ways of satisfying those needs. Here is how Joe Wittmer, PhD, explains it:

> Some non-Amish individuals have mistakenly assumed that the Amish are like them in need, or at least should want to be like them. For example, recently after concluding a speech I had made concerning the Amish, an individual in the audience asked, *"Are you telling us that they really don't want to drive a car, that they really don't want running water and that they really don't want to own a television set or a computer? Come on, Dr. Wittmer, this is the new millennium, the 21*st *Century! Amish people surely must secretly want those things."* The answer is an unequivocal "no!"
>
> The Old Order Amish *really* do not want to use our modern devices or appliances and they *really* do not want to be like us in most respects! Matter of fact, Amish relatives will often tell me how they truly feel sorry for certain non-Amish acquaintances of theirs because of the stressful lives they see them living.

Jesus is a friend who walks in when the world has walked out.

PROVERB

Can you relate? The world may look at us as Christians and see all that we are "missing out" on, yet we know what satisfies our souls. God is the only thing that can truly satisfy. His love never fails. His love renews, refreshes, and makes us feel as if we can soar. And the more we have of God, the less we desire anything else. We will actually end up feeling sorry for those who don't have what we have. Turn to God today and be satisfied.

■ ■ ■

Dear heavenly Father, when I attempt to find satisfaction in anything other than You, I end up feeling drained. Thank You for filling my life with good things!

Amish Dating

Can two people walk together without agreeing on the direction?

AMOS 3:3

I knew from my first date with my now-husband, John, that I was going to marry him. He was fun to be with and a great conversationalist. He had a sense of humor, and most of all he loved God.

Searching for the right person to spend your life with is always a challenge. In the Amish community, youth singings are a great place to perhaps find romance. It's also at these events that Amish dating takes place.

If an unattached young man and woman meet for the first time during one of these gatherings, or if two young people who already know each other begin to feel an attraction, the man will ask to drive her home (in his buggy). Even if a non-Amish driver brought a load of Amish from a district far away, the Amish are usually dropped off at a friend or cousin's house so that they can drive a buggy to the event. If they enjoy each other's company, he will begin picking her up and taking her home from future gatherings. If either of them has siblings who are married, they'll visit that couple while dating/courting.

Marriage may be made in Heaven, but man is responsible for the upkeep.

PROVERB

The parents of the young couple may or may not know they're seeing each other. Couples often enjoy keeping their relationship a secret.

Do you know people who are praying for and seeking spouses? That's not easy these days! Let them know that you will be their prayer support! And you might consider sharing Lamentations 3:25-29 with him or her: "GOD proves to be good to the man who passionately waits, to the woman who diligently seeks. It's a good thing to quietly hope, quietly hope for help from GOD. It's a good thing when you're young to stick it out through the hard times. When life is heavy and hard to take, go off by yourself. Enter the silence. Bow in prayer. Don't ask questions: Wait for hope to appear" (*The Message*).

■ ■ ■

Dear heavenly Father, I thank You that You see the great desire of our hearts—to love and be loved. Help me to love better. Today, I also lift up those who are looking for spouses.

Got Wisdom?

Cry out for insight, and ask for understanding. Search for them as you would for silver; seek them like hidden treasures. Then you will understand what it means to fear the LORD, and you will gain knowledge of God. For the LORD grants wisdom! From his mouth come knowledge and understanding.
PROVERBS 2:3-6

It's amazing what people will do to ensure a quality education for their children. Some parents move to a different neighborhood. Others take on a second job to pay for private school. Then they spend hours helping with homework. If these types of sacrifices produce quality education, then where does that leave the Amish?

Some people are wise, and some are otherwise.

PROVERB

To mainstream Americans who place a premium on higher education, an Amish education might raise an eyebrow. To our way of thinking, it might seem limited and restrictive. Unmarried young Amish women—without college training—teach in small, parochial schools. Amish schools use a limited amount of material in the classroom—they have created their own readers, workbooks, and texts. They stress accuracy rather than speed, drill rather than variety, proper sequence rather than critical thinking skills.

Yet illiteracy is virtually nonexistent in Amish settlements. Without television and computers, they read more than most Americans. They have a remarkable ability to learn new skills—even complicated ones—and value lifelong learning. Amish parents are heavily involved in their children's education: they donate the land and building supplies for the school, visit regularly, attend school events, and take turns caring for the facilities. . . .

And here's a note to end on that will inspire you to turn off the TV and read to your kids: Amish children in the eighth grade gave a more positive rating to their families than did non-Amish children.

Any teacher will tell you that a parent's commitment to lifelong learning makes the biggest difference. And any wise man or woman will tell you that even more important than seeking a good education is seeking God's wisdom. You don't need to pay to get it. You don't need to wear a uniform or work long hours on homework. Turn to His Word, and you will discover knowledge and understanding.

■ ■ ■

Dear heavenly Father, I desire knowledge and understanding. Thank You for offering it so freely!

Raised in a New Life

Have you forgotten that when we were joined with Christ Jesus in baptism, we joined him in his death? For we died and were buried with Christ by baptism. And just as Christ was raised from the dead by the glorious power of the Father, now we also may live new lives.

ROMANS 6:3-4

When Amish young people are ready to join the church, they must be baptized first. They are considered to be adults and able to make lifelong commitments to God and their communities.

The baptism takes place at the end of the service. After the two sermons the bishop offers a personal admonition to those being baptized. A deacon leaves the service and returns with a small pail of water and a tin cup. The applicants are reminded of the lifetime vow they have made to God. Then they kneel and are asked three questions:

1. Can you *renounce* the devil, the world, and your own flesh and blood?
2. Can you commit yourself to Christ and His church, and to abide by it and therein to live and to die?
3. And in all the order (Ordnung) of the church, according to the word of the Lord, to be *obedient* and *submissive* to it and to help therein?

"Persons are baptized when they are admitted to formal membership in the church, about the age of 17 to 20 years."

With the applicants still kneeling, the congregation then rises for prayer, and the bishop "reads one of the simple prayers from *Die Ernsthafte Christenpflicht*, a prayer book of the Swiss Anabaptists." This is a meaningful time for the Amish young people because they are now considered fully committed to God and to their community.

Have you been baptized? The baptism services you might have seen—or participated in—may look different, but the core is the same. It's a solemn profession that we have died to our lives—our wills—and have accepted Christ's in return. We live with a new reality. And the same glory that raised Christ from the dead now lives within us.

Have you taken time recently to appreciate the significance of baptism? If not, now is a perfect time to do that.

■ ■ ■

Dear heavenly Father, thank You for new life in Christ. My life is not mine. Use me, Lord, no matter what is at stake.

A Heart of Trust

Pray for us, for our conscience is clear and we want
to live honorably in everything we do.
HEBREWS 13:18

In this life it's easy to not be trustworthy. There have been a few times I've tried to help people by welcoming them into my home, only to find out they were stealing from me. I've confided in trusted friends and then discovered they were spreading rumors.

Sometimes, though, we're surprised to find that people can be trusted. That's a welcome feeling, a fresh breeze. Here's a story my friend Suzanne Woods Fisher shares about such trust:

Right is still right if nobody does it. Wrong is still wrong if everybody does it.

PROVERB

A few years ago, I called an Old Order Amish farm in Pennsylvania to make a reservation to stay for a trip I had planned. I left a message on an answering machine and received a return call just a few hours later from a woman named Viola Stoltzfus. Viola called from the phone shack down the lane from her farm. Every few minutes, her gentle voice—with just a trace of an accent—was drowned out by the clip-clop sounds of a horse and buggy passing by. After Viola wrote down the dates of my visit, I asked her how much money I should send to reserve the room.

"Well," she said, "we're too busy to make a breakfast for you. So, just send me a donation."

Nonplussed, I had absolutely no idea how much to send, so I wrote out a check for the amount I was spending at an airport hotel the night before. As I sealed that envelope to Viola and stuck a stamp on it, I couldn't remember ever feeling so good about writing someone a check. Why? Viola offered me two things that are in short supply in a secular world: She wasn't trying to unduly profit off of my visit but to receive a fair exchange for goods and services. And she trusted me to decide what that would be worth.

Do you need to open your heart to someone? God knows that honest relationships are built when the walls of self-protection are torn down.

■ ■ ■

Dear heavenly Father, I pray that I will not punish those who are trustworthy because of those who have taken advantage of my trust. Heal me so I can reach out to others.

Settle Up

Throw off your old sinful nature and your former way of life, which is corrupted
by lust and deception. Instead, let the Spirit renew your thoughts and attitudes.

EPHESIANS 4:22-23

For many years I thought my role as a mom was to make my children conform—to
see to it that they loved others, gave, served, and were sacrificial. But it's hard to make
our kids exhibit Christlike qualities if Christ isn't living in them. It was very clear when
each of my children accepted Christ and began to heed the Holy Spirit. He did a much
better job of guiding!

In Amish communities some may see a night-and-day difference in young adults
between the Rumspringa years and the time when they choose to accept Christ and
settle down. As one Amish person, who wrote in to *Family Life*, acknowledges, young
people need to be encouraged to change from the inside out.

It's a dangerous thing to pressure someone into "settling
down" without insisting that he also "settle up." For it
is quite possible for a young person to decide, when he
gets tired of being nagged by the church and parents,
that okay, he'll conform. He may be ready to get married
anyhow, and stay at home. So he agrees to drop his
"wild life," whatever that may include in his particular
community. And relatives and parents, looking only on
the outside, draw a sigh of relief—too soon. For too often
such a person has not really experienced an inner change. He has not really given
himself up, surrendered and dedicated his life to God. What he does is not out of
conviction. There is no depth to his spiritual life. He does not think to go aside
for personal prayer. He does not cherish a tender conscience and a daily walk
with God. The Bible doesn't interest him.

Each new day can
be a door to joys
we've never known
before.

PROVERB

Do you know someone who needs a life transformation? It can be easy to give
advice, to complain about that person, or to feel frustrated. Better is to pray and have
hope. Pray not that the person settles down but rather that he or she settles up with
God. God's Spirit changes people from the inside out.

■ ■ ■

Dear heavenly Father, thank You for Your Spirit who renews thoughts and attitudes.
Please, Lord, start with mine.

A Glimpse of Heavenly Faith

All the believers devoted themselves to the apostles' teaching, and to fellowship, and to sharing in meals (including the Lord's Supper), and to prayer.
ACTS 2:42

Because the Amish hold church services in homes, there is no upkeep on a building, no church parking lot or playground. There is also no bell welcoming parishioners, and no church foyer for mingling. But the joy of meeting together is not lost.

Father always drives the horse and buggy, with mother and baby beside him and the young children in the back seat. In winter, mother and baby may be tucked in the back seat of the carriage, where the air is not so sharp and raw. The sight of a dozen carriages turning single-file into the long farm lane, and the sound of still other horses trotting on the hard-surface road over the hill, evokes deep sentiments among the gathering community. Neighbors and those nearby usually walk to the service. No driver would think of passing another "rig" on the way to the service.

If you sow kindness, you will reap a crop of friends.

PROVERB

On arriving at the place of worship, the carriage halts in the barnyard, where the mother and girls dismount. Father and sons drive to a convenient stopping place, where they are met by hostlers, often sons of the host household, who help unhitch the horse and find a place for it in the stable. The horse is given hay from the supply in the barn. Meanwhile the men cluster in little groups in the stable and under the forebay of the barn, greeting one another with handshakes and in subdued voices.

The commitment the Amish have to one another is evident. Mothers and babies are cared for. No one buggy attempts to beat the others to the meeting place. "Hosts" welcome those who arrive, and the stable becomes the foyer. In these behaviors we can see that the best type of faith is steadfast, tender, patient, and welcoming. Paul wrote, "Above all, you must live as citizens of heaven, conducting yourselves in a manner worthy of the Good News about Christ. Then, whether I come and see you again or only hear about you, I will know that you are standing together with one spirit and one purpose, fighting together for the faith, which is the Good News" (Philippians 1:27).

That kind of faith gives us a glimpse of heaven to come.

■ ■ ■

Dear heavenly Father, I thank You that even on earth we can get a glimpse of heaven through the loving faith of Your servants.

A Different Kingdom

By the sweat of your brow will you have food to eat until you return to the ground
from which you were made. For you were made from dust, and to dust you will return.

GENESIS 3:19

Twyla, one of my friends, always jokes, "I don't understand it. You spend your whole life cleaning and fighting dust, and then they bury you in it." Isn't that the truth?

Our society seems to be comfortable talking about almost anything—any subject—except death. We don't like to think of not being on this earth. Yet when we realize that we are only human—only dust—we have a better grasp of time. Only when we fully acknowledge that we can't hold on to anything on this earth do we start looking ahead to eternity to come.

My friend Suzanne Woods Fisher says,

> The Amish can teach us to slow down. Time is not something to be mastered, but a boundary to be respected. They remind us that Christians should look at life from a different perspective because we are part of a different kingdom—one that stretches into infinity.
>
> "Run the race with eternity in view" and "What we do in this life echoes in eternity" are frequently quoted in sermons. And one thing the Amish know to be true: unlike humans, God is not in short supply of time. There is no limit to his days or his patience or his joy.

Either you are leaving a mark on the world, or it is leaving a mark on you.

PROVERB

Spend a few minutes thinking about your last day—your last breath. What things are you focusing on now that won't matter one bit then? Now consider what will matter most.

You will have to work by the sweat of your brow for only so many years. Then will come one moment when the sweat will be wiped away and a crown will be placed upon your head: the apostle Paul says, "The prize awaits me—the crown of righteousness, which the Lord, the righteous Judge, will give me on the day of his return. And the prize is not just for me but for all who eagerly look forward to his appearing" (2 Timothy 4:8).

■ ■ ■

Dear heavenly Father, I thank You that our time on earth is limited, because there is something so much better in store for me!

Without Ceasing

Never stop praying.

1 THESSALONIANS 5:17

The Amish believe they must cover their heads to pray and that they must be ready to pray at all times. Amish women even wear a sleeping handkerchief at night, in case they wake up and want to pray:

> One of the most symbolic of all garments among the women is the *Kapp*, or "head cap," worn by every woman and even by infants. Girls from about the age of twelve until marriage wear a black cap for Sunday dress and a white cap at home. After marriage a white cap is always worn. . . . Though this headpiece has undergone some changes in detail, the present Amish cap is essentially the same as that worn by . . . women of earlier centuries. Among partially assimilated Amish or Mennonites of Swiss-German origin the cap has become a "covering," "prayer cap," or "veiling" required of women "when praying or prophesying" (1 Cor. 11:5).

We don't have to consider all the details surrounding a kapp, but we do need to take seriously God's command to pray without ceasing. Ephesians 6:18 says, "Pray in the Spirit at all times and on every occasion. Stay alert and be persistent in your prayers for all believers everywhere."

The Amish believe that buying commercial insurance would not be trusting in God.

When I first became a follower of Christ, I didn't know what that meant, but as the years go by, I'm learning that it means to have a running conversation with God. When a child is misbehaving, my thoughts turn to God in prayer and I ask Him for wisdom. When I'm tired, I pray for strength. When I need help with a work project, I ask. I can't tell you the number of times an answer has risen up in my mind after I've prayed, when there was no answer before.

Talking with God throughout the day can be as real and symbolic as wearing a kapp. God is always there. All you have to do is start the communication.

■ ■ ■

Dear heavenly Father, I thank You that whenever I open my heart to talk to You, You are always listening.

God's Provision

Take your bow and a quiver full of arrows, and go out into
the open country to hunt some wild game for me.

GENESIS 27:3

When the gardening is finished for the year, the Amish turn their attention to other activities. They help their children with increasing schoolwork; they make sure they have enough wood or coal for the winter. They butcher chickens, and the men set their sights on hunting season. Even though the Amish do not believe in using force against others, they do use guns and bows for hunting.

Not all Amish hunt, but many do. Some Amish will visit local hunting lands when deer season comes around. Others hunt birds and larger game. Amish use both firearms and bows when hunting.

Some Amish own their own piece of hunting ground, located within or outside of the community. Still other Amish may make hunting trips to more distant areas, hiring a driver to do so. Amish may even go on trips to hunt big game in Western states.

> Those who let God provide will always be satisfied.
>
> **PROVERB**

. . . Not all Amish agree with the practice of hunting. Some Amish may consider hunting for sport and fun as frivolous and wasteful. Hunting in order to acquire a trophy may be considered prideful by some Amish. Others find fault with Amish hunters who purchase expensive hunting equipment.

Hunting reminds us that God is our provider. He provides game, and He provides hunting skill. Being on a hunt is also a great way to commune with God. In the woods, our senses are on alert, and the stillness seems almost to stop time. There is no technology to distract us. There are no busy highways to threaten our slow pace. All hunters are equal, something unusual in the divided worlds of Amish and English.

When have you last spent time in nature and gotten away with God? Even if hunting does not appeal to you, walking on a nature trail can pull you away from this busy world and take you to a place of peace where it's easier to hear God's Spirit speak to your heart.

■ ■ ■

Dear heavenly Father, thank You for those moments when the outward trappings of life are stripped away. Help me to discover Your provision in a new way today.

God Is There

*It was by faith that Abraham obeyed when God called him to
leave home and go to another land that God would give him as his
inheritance. He went without knowing where he was going.*
HEBREWS 11:8

Like anyone else, I have experienced hard times in my life—the death of a grandparent, personal struggles, and times of meager living when my husband was in college. But one of the hardest unexpected challenges came after we moved two thousand miles for my husband's job. We formerly lived in a community we loved, and we had a wonderful church and great friends. Even though I had a few friends waiting in our new location, starting over was harder than I had thought it would be. I missed familiar places, familiar people.

While some Amish live in the same community their whole lives, others move to new communities. Sometimes they do so to be closer to other family members or to find land. Lovina Eicher describes her family's preparation for a big move:

To succeed in life, use experience as a guidepost, not a hitching post.

PROVERB

It's going to take a lot of packing up with six children. Sisters Verena and Susan bought a house just around the corner from ours in Michigan, so they'll be going with us. We are excited that they found something that close to us.

We will regret pulling the children out of this school they attend now, but after visiting their new school, we were very pleased and the girls are less nervous now about moving. Everyone was very nice and helpful. There will be many memories to leave behind here in Indiana, but it's a new beginning for us.

Unlike Abraham—whom God directed to leave his country—we usually have a good idea of where we're going. But *like* Abraham, we also find differences in new places, sometimes even a different culture. We need to learn the lay of the land and make new friends.

When we feel displaced amid all the newness, we can remember the words of Malachi 3:6: "I am the LORD, and I do not change." When you're uncertain about where your journey is leading, know that God is already there. He's waiting in the good land He's already prepared.

■ ■ ■

*Dear heavenly Father, I thank You that nowhere I can go on earth is without Your
presence. I'm so grateful for Your constant care for me.*

Seeds of Faith

Don't be misled—you cannot mock the justice of God. You will always
harvest what you plant. Those who live only to satisfy their own sinful
nature will harvest decay and death from that sinful nature. But those who
live to please the Spirit will harvest everlasting life from the Spirit.

GALATIANS 6:7-8

When it comes to Amish gardens, harvesttime doesn't always mean the end of the work. Many Amish save and store seeds or buy them from others. The seeds collected are called heirloom seeds because they've been preserved for generations and will continue to be passed on.

Heirloom seeds allow a lone gardener to provide a bounty of food. The manner in which gardeners use them is scientific. Gardeners must time the plants' blossoms so the plants won't cross-pollinate. Just like the seeds, the gardeners' practices and knowledge have been passed down for generations.

"Most of the European immigrants brought some kind of seed with them," said George DeVault, a farmer and heirloom seed expert in Emmaus, Pa. "They didn't know what they would find in the New World, and they wanted a taste of home. It was the original comfort food."

"When I see an older person gardening, I'll screech the brakes, go over and offer to trade seeds," Von Saunder said. "Sometimes it works, sometimes it doesn't."

What do we allow to take root in the soil of our hearts? What we plant inside us is the only thing we have to share. We can't share what we don't have!

A man who sows wheat will reap wheat. He who sows barley will reap barley. Every kind of seed will reproduce itself. The person who sows seeds of righteousness will be rewarded, and the one who sows sinful deeds will reap destruction.

One of the best things you can do to lead your family to a growing, thriving relationship with God is to tend your own soul. Plant God's Word in your heart. Water it with the presence of Jesus, who is the Living Water. Prune back what doesn't belong, and allow the roots of faith to go deep.

"Skiretts, a root vegetable that was popular in the eighteenth-century are amongst the rare vegetables that are sold by Amishland Heirloom Seeds."

■ ■ ■

Dear heavenly Father, I pray that my faith will grow—and go deep—so I'll have plenty to share!

A Good Steward

Owe nothing to anyone—except for your obligation to love one another. If you love your neighbor, you will fulfill the requirements of God's law.
ROMANS 13:8

Nothing robs someone's peace more quickly than a pile of bills and not enough money to pay them. It's easy to spend money and get overextended. What is harder is to make the sacrifices required to do something about it. The Amish are examples of what is possible when we control what we have instead of allowing it to control us.

If the Amish don't have credit cards, how do they pay their bills when there's too much month at the end of the money? As Bishop Eli King said, "You gotta make up what you don't have; don't borrow it." It goes completely against the grain for the Amish to go into hock to pay their expenses. Instead, they will find extra jobs or things to sell to come up with the extra cash. . . .

Where there's money you'll find the devil.

PROVERB

Friends of mine were scraping for the last few hundred bucks they needed to pay moving expenses and closing costs as they moved from a rented home to their own place. "Nothing is nailed down," Rudy told me, smiling sheepishly. "We sold everything we could think of at a garage sale and then on Craigslist."

"Just as the rich rule the poor, so the borrower is servant to the lender," says Proverbs 22:7. When we owe people money, our actions must be focused on meeting our financial obligation to repay the debt. When we are free of our debts to men, then we can look to the Lord for direction in our finances. We are also free to serve and to give as He desires.

Turn to God, and ask Him to help you arrive at a place of financial freedom. It's only then that you'll be able to freely distribute what God entrusts into your care.

■ ■ ■

Dear heavenly Father, help me to do the hard things that will get me to a place of financial freedom so that I owe no one anything but love.

Finding True Love

You are altogether beautiful, my darling, beautiful in every way.

SONG OF SONGS 4:7

Before any couple is joined together in marriage, there is a time of wooing. Throughout both the Old and New Testaments there are parables, allegories, and figures of speech that describe God drawing His people—His church—to Him. Both Jews and the first Christians saw the Song of Songs as an allegory of the love between God and His people. A simple maiden is drawn by her Shepherd and escorted into comforts beyond what she can imagine, but what she wants most of all is Him.

In some Amish communities there are strict rules concerning the dating age—but age sixteen is common.

[The Amish] may use the word "dating" or "date" to mock, or make fun of, a custom held by the outsiders. However, within my community it is customary to use the word "have" rather than "date." That is to say, the young person will be asked, "Whom did you *have* last Sunday?" However, "having" as used in this context does not have any sexual connotations.

Once a young man and woman are going steady, he not only will date her on Sunday evenings but may also appear at her house during the week. On this week night the young man will not make his appearance known until the rest of the family is in bed. That is to say, even if he has to wait at the end of the lane in the cold, he does not appear until all the lights have gone out. However, she will know that he is coming and will be awaiting his arrival. . . . If they are serious about one another, they will discuss the upcoming wedding.

Through courtship and marriage we get a beautiful glimpse of the relationship between Jesus and the church. Ephesians 5:25-26 reads: "Husbands, this means love your wives, just as Christ loved the church. He gave up his life for her to make her holy and clean, washed by the cleansing of God's word."

Have you taken your love relationship with Jesus for granted? Remember how you felt when you first came to know Him, and fall in love with Him again today.

■ ■ ■

Dear heavenly Father, thank You for wooing me and drawing me to You. I am overwhelmed by Your love!

Knowing God's Word

Work hard so you can present yourself to God and receive
his approval. Be a good worker, one who does not need to be
ashamed and who correctly explains the word of truth.
2 TIMOTHY 2:15

Many people have a tendency to over-romanticize the Amish. We appreciate their resiliency and their faith, and some people believe the Amish are better—more righteous—than the rest of us. But the truth is, the Amish have the same struggles and failings that the rest of us have. Amish preachers turn to God's Word to bring help and guidance to church members:

When faith is most difficult, that is when it is most necessary.

PROVERB

Preachers draw on everyday experiences as well as stories from the Bible to convey their messages. The New Testament is emphasized. In *Amish Grace*, authors Kraybill, Nolt and Weaver-Zercher point out that "although Amish preachers recite Old Testament stories in their sermons, all the biblical texts read in Amish church services come from the New Testament," particularly Matthew, Mark, Luke, and John, as "out of the sixty chapters in the Lancaster Amish lectionary, forty come from the four Gospels."

After preaching concludes (there is typically a shorter sermon, and then a longer one, which runs around an hour), other ministers often add their own commentary or correction. In this way the Amish service is a collective effort, an idea also supported by the fact that preaching duties rotate among ministers.

To correctly explain the Word of Truth to others, you need to know the Word of Truth. How much time do you spend reading the Bible? Do you read a Scripture verse here and there, believing it is enough? Consider trying to read a novel and picking up a paragraph here and there. You might get to know a bit of the story, but the more you read, the more the story will make sense.

Years ago I felt I needed to read through the entire Bible. Since then I've done that several times, and each time I gain new understanding. It's important to spend time in God's Word and understand God's story. Make a commitment to do so.

■ ■ ■

Dear heavenly Father, thank You for giving us Your Word. The more I read it, the more I want to read it.

Ministers of the Gospel

Paul lived and worked with them, for they were tentmakers just as he was. Each Sabbath found Paul at the synagogue, trying to convince the Jews and Greeks alike.

ACTS 18:3-4

Many people do not realize that even when Amish men are chosen by lot to serve in the ministry, the work involved is something above and beyond their ordinary jobs and family life. Like the apostle Paul, they do not quit their regular jobs to become ministers. Instead, ministering becomes an extension of their jobs and lives.

A weakness of the Amish system is the fact that it provides no opportunity for its leadership to assume responsibilities wider than those of the local district. But, from the Amish point of view, this limitation is a source of strength. Leadership is not drained off. The congregation remains one united body. During the course of the week the leaders, no matter how gifted, cannot be distinguished from other Amishmen. They wear no special garb or insignia; they are not addressed with special titles. They receive no material rewards for their spiritual labors. They tend their fields and barns and make their livings as farmers. On Sunday, however, these men stand before their fellows to expound the Scriptures and their religion as the guidance of the holy Spirit and the experience gained in the daily chores move them to do.

"Ministers are responsible for preaching on Sundays. Saturday afternoon is often a time of preparation and study for the next day."

"Talent develops in silence, but character only in the stream of life," wrote Goethe in the eighteenth century. The more we work at a skill, the better we become at it. Yet character in the stream of life means that an Amish minister is fully involved in all that his congregation is involved in. When an Amish minister shares from God's Word, his words are backed up with the experience of the day-to-day concerns in his own life. His preaching isn't merely of concepts but also the fruit of experience.

It is not wrong to receive one's living from the gospel, as proclaimed in 1 Corinthians 9:14, yet we also must never become so book smart that we forget the everyday needs and questions of the people we serve.

■ ■ ■

Dear heavenly Father, today I pray for the ministers of your gospel, those who give their lives and hearts to bring Your Word to the people.

God, Our Security Guard

This I declare about the LORD: He alone is my refuge, my place of safety; he is my God, and I trust him.

PSALM 91:2

When I lived in rural Montana, it wasn't necessary to lock the doors of our house or cars. During the cold winter days, it's common to see cars parked in front of the grocery stores with their engines running so they'll stay heated up. I even have friends who don't have the keys to their front doors. This can be handy when someone needs to stop by on a bathroom break!

Now I live in Little Rock, Arkansas, a city well-known for its crime. Not only do the cars have security systems, but the houses do too. Signs in the yards warn would-be intruders of the presence of alarms and guard dogs on the properties.

The leader of one Amish group, found guilty for a series of hair- and beard-cutting attacks on other Amish, received a long prison sentence. Other members of his group, both men and women, were sentenced to serve time as well.

Robberies of Amish homes or of people driving buggies aren't common, but they do happen. Some time ago members of an Amish religious sect broke into occupied Amish homes to cut women's hair and men's beards in response to a disagreement. There are also rare incidents like the Nickel Mines school shooting, yet the Amish do not live in fear. Although they do take some measures of protection to keep their loved ones safe, they know that their real shelter is God, as we read in Psalm 40:17: "As for me, since I am poor and needy, let the Lord keep me in his thoughts. You are my helper and my savior. O my God, do not delay."

To be the object of God's thoughts means you are always on His mind, and He will show up when you are in need. When you are in God's thoughts, you can be confident that although the "thief" comes to destroy, God is with you.

To whom do you turn when you need a place of protection? Those who lack many of the usual means of protecting themselves depend on God more. When you don't have a security system, it's most important that you see God as your security guard.

■ ■ ■

Dear heavenly Father, thank You for always providing, always protecting, and always having me in Your thoughts. I long to always keep You in my thoughts as well.

God-Breathed

All Scripture is inspired by God and is useful to teach us what is
true and to make us realize what is wrong in our lives. It corrects
us when we are wrong and teaches us to do what is right.

2 TIMOTHY 3:16

Many people are at least somewhat familiar with the Amish and Mennonites, but another Anabaptist group, established in Europe some two centuries ago, is River Brethren:

> Jacob Engel separated from his Mennonite congregation, wishing only to be baptized in a scripturally correct mode. . . .
>
> Given Engel's understanding of Christ's scriptural baptism as face-forward, [triple] immersion, he and the other dissatisfied Mennonites in his society were left with no other alternative than to begin a quest to secure baptism either by a minister of an existing religious group or by mutual baptism.

River Brethren are more conservative in some ways than Old Order Amish.

The River Brethren are a small group (2010 figures indicated fewer than one thousand), and they baptize by total immersion. They live plain lives and believe in foot washing. They oppose involvement in the military, the use of alcohol and tobacco, and worldly pleasures. They also carry out missionary work in Asia and Africa.

How do people reading the same Bible have such varied means of living it out? I strive to follow God's Word, but I don't live like the Amish. The Amish, the Mennonites, and the River Brethren strive to live it out, too, and yet they do so in different ways.

God's Word is inspired. His Spirit breathed the Scriptures into His scribes. It's profitable, which means we benefit when we follow it. It convinces us of the truth and corrects us. And above all, it reveals God to us and points us to Christ.

Men and women may focus on various Scriptural teachings, but we can be all united in God's body when we choose to "major on the majors." What are those? God's creation of this world and men and women; human sin, which leads to death; and Christ's death, which leads to life.

The body of Christ may look different, and even live and worship differently, but those who focus on the big issues of God's Word can find common ground with those who look and live differently.

■ ■ ■

Dear heavenly Father, I thank You that even though I live and serve differently from other Christians, You are the breath of inspiration who changes everything.

God Sees through the Fog

My future is in your hands.
PSALM 31:15

Every year dozens of Amish lose their lives in automobile-and-buggy accidents. Sometimes the accidents are due to errors on the car driver's part. Other times weather conditions cause the trouble. The Amish Cook, Lovina Eicher, writes about her concerns with going to a family member's wedding in the typically dreary month of November.

> It turned out to be a warm and beautiful day for a wedding, the wedding of Joe's nephew Emanul. It was very foggy on our way there. It always makes me nervous to drive the buggy through fog. We had our blinking lights on, but I'm always afraid someone won't see us in time. I appreciate the covered buggy even more now with cold weather coning on. The wedding services were held at the bride's neighbors in a big buggy shed.

I get nervous driving in the fog in my car. I can't imagine the faith it takes to get into a buggy on a foggy day or evening, knowing how difficult it is for a fast-moving car to see a slow-moving buggy and knowing the damage a collision can cause. Yet if we allow it to, fear will hold us back. Fear will focus our eyes on the danger around us and remove our eyes from God.

Life is a one-way street. Live in the consciousness that you shall not pass this way again.

PROVERB

"You have decided the length of our lives," we read in Job 14:5. "You know how many months we will live, and we are not given a minute longer." Are you able to trust God with all you have, even when fog surrounds you and you can't see into the future? Even when you aren't sure whether danger is just around the corner?

True faith believes in all times. It does not give up. It ventures out and chooses to connect with others and to celebrate, even when there is potential danger in doing so. Even when you can't see through the fog, God can. He's able to protect you from danger and keep you safe. He holds your life in His hands.

■ ■ ■

Dear heavenly Father, thank You for all the times You protect me when I don't even know about it. You are my shield. You are a wall around me.

He Makes Our Hearts Home

Jesus replied, "All who love me will do what I say. My Father will love them, and we will come and make our home with each of them."

JOHN 14:23

What are some of your favorite words? Here are a few of mine: *children, laughter, togetherness,* and *home.* In Pennsylvania Dutch, the word *home* is *haymet.* And when visiting an Amish home, people shouldn't be surprised that what they'll find is humble simplicity. There is nothing in an Amish home that will be displayed in the pages of *Good Housekeeping* magazine. Instead, what is there reflects the values of the home—family, daily work, and humility.

One might assume that all Amish live in old farm houses, but some live in newer homes, and the size varies. One Amish family I visited built homes that they later sold to English. Their house was wired for electricity, but while the Amish lived there, the outlets were covered up. The home was beautiful, with fine wood floors, large windows, and custom cabinetry, yet even then it was built this way for the purpose of providing for the family who would live there. And when the current house sold, the family moved into a small cabin and started the process over again.

The exterior of most Amish homes is white or natural. Porches are common, but not for curb appeal. They are a wonderful gathering place for families when the weather is nice. Amish homes also have several rooms that are connected—or that can be opened into one large room—when families host church services. Most window coverings are white, and the floors are bare. Most Amish homes do not include closet space because they don't have much to store.

In the Bible, Jesus says that He and His Father will come to make Their home with us. He is speaking about our hearts, but what about your actual home? Would Jesus be comfortable if He visited? Is there anything in your home that you'd be embarrassed about?

Our outward homes are extensions of what's inside us. The things we maintain and collect are indications of what we feel is most important. What does your home say about your heart?

■ ■ ■

Dear heavenly Father, like my home, there are places in my heart that need decluttering. Help me, Lord, to focus on humble simplicity.

Just Enough

First, help me never to tell a lie. Second, give me neither poverty nor riches! Give me just enough to satisfy my needs. For if I grow rich, I may deny you and say, "Who is the LORD?" And if I am too poor, I may steal and thus insult God's holy name.
PROVERBS 30:8-9

My eighty-three-year-old grandmother lives with us, and she likes to live simply. She'd rather use the stove top than the microwave. She has no interest in learning how to use a computer or in having an e-mail account. She has cable television in her room, but she flips between just two channels—religious programming and the old-movie channel. She's happy and content no matter who tells her she's missing out. She doesn't have too much or too little. She is satisfied, and there's something to be said for that!

"A man is rich in proportion to the number of things which he can afford to let alone."

ATTRIBUTED TO
HENRY DAVID
THOREAU

In 1955, Jay Lehman was concerned that some day the Amish would not be able to maintain their simple ways because their non-electric products would no longer be available. He founded a store in Kidron, Ohio; today, that store is the world's largest provider of historical technology. His goal was, and still is, to provide authentic, historical products to those seeking a simpler life: Homesteaders, environmentalists, missionaries, doctors in developing nations, and others living in areas where there is no power or unreliable power rely on Lehman's. Hollywood set designers too. Lehman has supplied historically accurate period pieces for many movies.

Where do you find satisfaction? Are you always looking for the newest and greatest thing? Do you try to keep up with others, or are you content with what you have?

First Timothy 6:8 says, "If we have enough food and clothing, let us be content." Contentment is a matter of the heart; it's not a consequence of the accumulation of goods.

Consider praying Proverbs 30:8-9 today. Ask God to give you enough to satisfy your needs. You might begin to look at all you have differently when you do.

■ ■ ■

Dear heavenly Father, too often I get my needs and my wants mixed up. Help me to pray for the former and to release the desire for the latter into Your hands!

Happy Hymns

Enter with the password: "Thank you!" Make yourselves at home, talking praise. Thank him. Worship him. For GOD is sheer beauty, all-generous in love, loyal always and ever.

PSALM 100:4-5 (THE MESSAGE)

There is nothing more wonderful than joining with friends to lift up songs of praise to God. Some time ago I was on a mission trip to Europe, and one of my favorite things from the trip was singing hymns in a Czech church. While the members sang the words in Czech, our group sang in English. It was beautiful to know that we sang the same words and that God was praised by all our voices lifted together.

The Amish often praise God together with hymns. Joni Eareckson Tada shares this story of one of her visits to Amish country:

I love the Amish farms that dot the countryside along the southern edge of Pennsylvania. My friend Rebecca Stoltzfus lives in a beautiful part of this country. . . . We were right on time for a country dinner—fried chicken and mashed potatoes!

When we finished shoo-fly pie, we carried our mugs of apple cider to the backyard and sat under a colorful elm tree to enjoy the crisp afternoon air. The aroma of harvesttime, cow pastures, and cherry wood fires wafted our way. "Let's sing some hymns! Do you know any German hymns?" I asked. The Stoltzfus family and their friends made a group, all with straw hats and white head coverings. My friends and I sat opposite them and made an English-singing choir. Back and forth we sang, one hymn after the next—we in English, they in German. It was the most unusual and happy time of singing I can remember!

> When you sing your own praises, you always get the tune too high; when you sing God's praises, you can never go high enough.
>
> PROVERB

Do you want to create a special memory? Consider gathering together with friends or family to sing hymns. It doesn't matter if you know all the words (you can look them up) or have great voices. The most important part is that you join together with thanksgiving and lift your voices in praise!

■ ■ ■

Dear heavenly Father, I'm thankful that no matter what language is used to express thankfulness, the joy on someone's face makes it obvious!

Open Home, Open Heart

Don't forget to show hospitality to strangers, for some who have
done this have entertained angels without realizing it!
HEBREWS 13:2

My friend Joanna called and asked if I wanted to meet her for lunch. I thought about all I'd planned for that day. I had work projects to finish and other things I wanted to check off my to-do list. "Can I catch you next time?" I asked. She was gracious about my request and told me she'd try again.

Unfortunately there wouldn't be a "next time." Just a few months later Joanna ended up moving two hours away, and as I drove by her empty house, I wondered what had been so important that I couldn't take a few hours to catch up with a friend.

Friendship is a lamp that shines most brightly when all else is dark.

PROVERB

In the Amish community it's not uncommon for a friend to stop by unexpectedly to visit. Amish men and women always have work to do. There is never a moment when everything is checked off their lists, yet they are eager to visit with friends— or even strangers—who stop by. I was amazed when I was visiting Amish country that many people welcomed me into their homes when they didn't know me. I was thankful they offered me insight into their lives, along with a cup of tea!

When it comes to hospitality, too often I focus on myself, my schedule, and my boundaries rather than on what I can offer to another person. I often forget that sometimes what someone else needs most is my time and a simple cup of coffee or tea.

Mark 9:41 says, "If anyone gives you even a cup of water because you belong to the Messiah, I tell you the truth, that person will surely be rewarded." The reward we receive is good favor with God, but there are other rewards, too. I always feel refreshed after a long conversation with a friend, and my heart is full with joy.

Life isn't always about tasks or our own gratification. Yet sometimes when we give to others, we are gratified in ways we don't expect!

■ ■ ■

Dear heavenly Father, I'm thankful that You do not put up boundaries when I try to
approach You. Help me to open my heart more.

Something to Share

Encourage one another and build one another up, just as you are doing.

1 THESSALONIANS 5:11 (ESV)

You might be surprised, but the Amish and English communities have been working together, helping each other, supporting each other, and encouraging each other for many years. Below is a short note that was printed in the publication *Gleanings in Bee Culture*:

I received my second lot of goods all right. I think those ½-lb tumblers are "boss." Every article was found just as ordered. I am well pleased with every thing. I made quite a lot of hives and sections this spring for myself and neighbors. Bees are doing very well at present. They commenced on fruit-blossom this morning. Friend R., will you send me a lot of sample copies of *GLEANINGS*, especially Mar. 15? You ask why that date. This is a Christianlike neighborhood, and a great many of them are keeping bees. . . . The one particular feature about that issue is in Our Homes. I have lost considerable stock this winter, and from causes for which I can not account, nor can any one else whom I have seen. I have worried over it considerably: but when I read Our Homes, I took to quite a different notion, and have quit worrying and troubling myself about things which I can not help. I hear some of my neighbors are losing in the same way, and perhaps those numbers will help them. It has helped me wonderfully.

> Good friends are like good quilts; they never lose their warmth.
>
> PROVERB

That note was written by S. B. Miller, Amish, Iowa, April 23, 1886! I love the fact that this person was encouraged and wanted his neighbors to find the same encouragement.

Do you know someone who has faced a great loss? Maybe it is a loss that you have faced. If you have words that encouraged you or a Scripture verse that lifted you up, don't keep it to yourself. Ask God to show you how to reach out to others. As we have faced loss and were comforted, so we can comfort others.

■ ■ ■

Dear heavenly Father, so many times another's words have lifted my soul. Help me to be the giver and provider of such words today.

The Beauty of Silence

For God alone, O my soul, wait in silence, for my hope is from him.
PSALM 62:5 (ESV)

Autumn has a way of quieting the land. Creatures work diligently to prepare for winter. The Amish, who were previously active outside, find themselves sitting before a fire or around the table. Yet even inside large homes filled with children there isn't the noise you expect. There's no television or music playing or senseless chatter.

The Amish use their words sparingly. When people are deeply involved with each other, there is a pervasive communication with a minimum use of words. Collective awareness develops to such an extent that it becomes a religious experience—an involvement that cannot be uttered in words. Silence functions as an effective conveyor of information.

Patience is a word that carries a lot of wait.

PROVERB

Deep commitments to the faith tend to be silent rather than vocal. Prayers before and after meals are periods of uninterrupted silence. Sundays at home are spent in silence—hammering, building, and loud noises are not permitted. Silence is a defense against fright or the unknown. Silence is a way of living and forgiving, a way of embracing the community with charity. The member who confesses all before the church is forgiven, and the sin is never spoken of again.

How well do you incorporate silence into your day? Your week? I have a habit of turning on music in the car or listening to an audiobook when I'm folding laundry. But sometimes I feel a gentle stirring deep inside that says, *Just be quiet before Me.*

Silence gives your mind time to seek clarity. Silence gives your body a chance to release all the tension that has built up. And remaining silent about another's minor faults encourages that person to do the same with yours.

Can you find time for silence in your home, with your family, and even with offhand comments? Are there things you want to speak of but about which you know you should hold your tongue instead? Silence not only protects others but also guards your own heart and allows God's whispers to penetrate deep. Try it.

■ ■ ■

Dear heavenly Father, sometimes I speak before I think . . . and sometimes I just need to stop speaking so I can meditate on You. Please give me Your strength to seal my lips.

Appreciation in the Season

This is the day the LORD *has made. We will rejoice and be glad in it.*

PSALM 118:24

What do you appreciate most about this season you're in?

My friend Suzanne Woods Fisher met Simon Yoders while doing research for a book, and she shares some of his family's yearly routine in her book *Amish Values for Your Family*:

> October brings corn harvest, cider making, apple butter—and colors and serenity that only this month can offer. Apple fritters, too! "Along about the middle of the month," Simon says, "we hear a sound that we've been waiting for—the quacking and gabbling of migrating ducks and geese." As the month draws to a close, so does Simon's field work.
>
> November and December are the time to tackle the messier job of butchering meat. The Yoders keep some livestock to provide fresh meat for their family. It's also wedding season, when fields rest and there is time to devote to weddings. . . . Winter is a time of cozy fires; eating popcorn and peeled apples; quilting, reading, and playing games in the evenings; snowball fights and sleigh rides. The Yoders are stocking their icehouse.

If you can't have the best of everything, make the best of everything you have.

PROVERB

What do you appreciate most about today, the day God has given you? Appreciation means approval of something or someone. It's a way of placing value on the moments you have—and of valuing the One who gave you those moments. When you appreciate the day, the season, and the situation you're in, you're extending thankfulness for what God's done. You look around with respect and see the good in all that's happening.

Appreciation in honoring all that's around you. Those with hearts of appreciation are fun to be around. And appreciative parents train up kids who follow suit.

Will you take time to look around today and to appreciate all that this season offers? Not only will the Lord appreciate your attitude, but those around you just might pick up your attitude too!

■ ■ ■

Dear heavenly Father, I appreciate all You've given me today. Open my eyes even more to the beauty of the season so my appreciation will grow.

Good Grace

Let us come boldly to the throne of our gracious God. There we will receive
his mercy, and we will find grace to help us when we need it most.
HEBREWS 4:16

One of the best-loved writers of Amish fiction is Beverly Lewis. Her father was a pastor in Lancaster, Pennsylvania, where she was born and grew up, and it's there she became interested in her family's Plain heritage. On a recent trip back to Pennsylvania, Beverly had a chance to revisit the place where her writing began.

I also was given permission by the present owner of my childhood home to walk along the perimeter of the grove of tall Norway spruce my father planted when I was a mere fifth grader and just beginning to write my stories (and too shy to show anyone but my mother). A flood of emotions poured over me as I walked that ground, and I lingered longingly near the places where, all those years ago, I sat to write in my secret writing notebook.

> **Don't be like the wheelbarrow, which goes no farther than it is pushed.**
>
> PROVERB

And I wondered: Had I fulfilled the things I'd set out to do for God so energetically, so joyously? Even as a child, I was incredibly driven, motivated by an internal to-do list. Oh, the sometimes nearly never-ending lists of deeds I planned to accomplish! Goals centered in the heart of my newfound faith in Christ.

If I could talk to that young schoolgirl now—my preteen self—and tell her what I've learned about faith in God, I believe it would go something like this: Salvation is absolutely a gift from God. No amount of works or deeds can alter that fact.

God places gifts and talents, dreams and goals in our lives for our sake and for the sake of others, but He never wants us to be so focused on what we hope to accomplish that we forget Him and what He has already accomplished. God may call us to write books that make the *New York Times* Best Sellers list, or He may call us to offer a piece of pie and a smile to our neighbor across the next field, but everything we accomplish—big or small—is because of Him, through Him, and should be for Him.

■ ■ ■

Dear heavenly Father, I'd be nowhere without grace. Thank You for the gift of salvation.

A Pretty Necklace

*My child, don't lose sight of common sense and discernment. Hang on
to them, for they will refresh your soul. They are like jewels on a necklace.*

PROVERBS 3:21-22

What would you say are the top qualities of a good teacher? For the Amish the list
is simple: the ability to teach, commitment to the Amish faith, and common sense.
Teaching an Amish student means focusing on the basics, and the Amish schools are
efficient in doing just that.

The curriculum includes reading, arithmetic, spelling, grammar, penmanship,
history, and some geography. Classes are conducted in English, and both English
and German are taught. Parents want children to learn
to read German so that they can understand religious
writings, many of which are recorded in formal German.
Science and sex education are missing in the curriculum
as are other typical trappings of public schools—sports,
dances, cafeterias, clubs, bands, choruses, computers,
television, guidance counselors, principals, and college
recruiters.

Amish teachers, themselves trained in Amish schools,
are not required to be certified in most states. The
brightest and best of Amish scholars, they return to the
classroom to teach, often in their late teens and early
twenties. Amish school directors select them for their
ability to teach and for their commitment to Amish values. . . . Periodic meetings
with other teachers, a monthly teachers magazine, *Blackboard Bulletin*, and ample
common sense prepare them for the task.

> You may glean
> knowledge by
> reading, but you
> must separate the
> chaff from the wheat
> by thinking.
>
> **PROVERB**

We try to give our attention to so much in our lives that sometimes we forget that
only a few things are really needed. We want to prepare ourselves and any children we
may have for everything they may face in the world, but when it comes down to it,
common sense and discernment go a long way.

The Amish don't wear jewelry, but their common sense is like a pretty necklace.
Jewels are beautiful and special, and those who have common sense are mature, calm,
and attractive in a way that no real diamonds can show off.

■ ■ ■

*Dear heavenly Father, I know that common sense comes from Your Word. As I seek You,
may my life be attractive to those in a watching world.*

Creative Potential

There are many virtuous and capable women in the world,
but you surpass them all!
PROVERBS 31:29

As a mom who has raised three young people out of the teenage years, I've learned that the best way to keep children out of trouble is to keep them busy in creative ways. Two of our teens played basketball, and we also encouraged part-time jobs and personal hobbies, such as learning to play the guitar, studying sign language, and writing stories. It seems that the Amish understand the same principle:

The concept of *Gelassenheit*, submission to the authority of the church and scripture, becomes ever more clear as young people grow up. Submission to what is not available—and that will include a great many freedoms that they see around them among their English peers—can also be thoughtfully counterbalanced.

A smile is a curve that can straighten out a lot of things.

PROVERB

Cooperation paired with creative outlets for young energy and artistic gifts can become essential as the child reaches adolescence. Craftwork is always encouraged, and so beautiful baskets, quilts and runners, rocking chairs and bookcases fill the shop shelves, made by hand by young people who are working side-by-side with their parents, older siblings, aunts and uncles, cousins and friends.

It's easy to put limits on young people in our lives. It's easy to set requirements for them too. What is harder is investing the time required to lead them, guide them, and train them, yet we can share in their joy when we help them discover their creative bents. That's exactly what God asks us to do. Ephesians 6:4 says, "Fathers, do not provoke your children to anger by the way you treat them. Rather, bring them up with the discipline and instruction that comes from the Lord."

The time and influence we put into young people's lives will be multiplied as they embrace their capabilities and make God's virtues their own. And as we guide them, we need to look at ourselves. Do we continue to allow God to make us into the people He's designed us to be? We won't truly know our potential until we place ourselves in God's hands.

■ ■ ■

Dear heavenly Father, thank You for designing each of us with undiscovered potential. Help me to realize it in myself and to help others do the same.

Adornment

*Don't be concerned about the outward beauty of fancy
hairstyles, expensive jewelry, or beautiful clothes.*

1 PETER 3:3

What do you think of when you hear the word *fancy*? I think of the lobby of the Omni Parker House Hotel in Boston, with its lush carpet, gilded mirrors, and the largest bouquet of orchids I've ever seen. But fancy means different things to different people. Some might think of jewelry or fine clothes. Others might point to designer shoes or high-end cars. Some Amish use this term in reference to adornments on buggies:

In Lancaster County, buggies with gray tops belong to the Amish and all black buggies signify Old Order Mennonites. Other differences can be found in buggies based on the degrees of conservatism of the individual church district leaders. Such differences can include windows, window wipers, battery powered head-, tail- and directional lights, rubber or steel-rims, etc.

> "Of all the things you wear, your expression is the most important."
>
> ATTRIBUTED TO JANET LANE

One concession to modern civilization has been forced upon the Amish buggy. After numerous accidents at night involving fast moving cars and slow moving black buggies, the Amish have added reflective tape to the back of their buggies. Less conservative groups have added battery-powered lights and installed slow-moving vehicle triangles.

Even so, some groups have refused to "adorn" their vehicle with these "loud" or "fancy" implements. In Harmony, Minnesota, the issue divided the Amish community and resulted in a State Supreme Court ruling in favor of those who had resisted their use.

In all our hearts a battle rages. We adorn ourselves because we seek esteem. We want to receive the approval of others. We wish to be commended.

Consider how God has decorated the earth with flowers, filled the oceans with colorful fish, and graced the creatures of this world with unique beauty. Adornment isn't wrong, but focusing on others' approval rather than on God's is wrong. It's fine to look nice, but it's possible to have too much of a good thing when we're more concerned about our outward appearance than the condition of our hearts.

■ ■ ■

Dear heavenly Father, thank You for gracing this world with beauty. Help me to focus first and foremost on my inward beauty.

Words Open a World

Such things were written in the Scriptures long ago to teach us.

ROMANS 15:4

Books amaze me, especially the way writers are able to share their thoughts and ideas with those they may never meet. Words and thoughts can be passed down through generations. Good writing can take you into a new community and can open your heart and mind to another's point of view.

For many years outsiders didn't understand the Amish. It wasn't until the 1920s that Pennsylvania German writers began describing their heritage in English writings that outsiders could begin to understand.

"Faith is not belief without proof, but trust without reservation."

ATTRIBUTED TO D. ELTON TRUEBLOOD

Cornelius Weygandt, a Dutchman and a professor of English literature at the University of Pennsylvania, wrote two popular books on traditional Pennsylvania Dutch culture in this period. *The Red Hills: A Record of Good Days Outdoors and In, with Things Pennsylvania Dutch*, published in 1929, focused primarily on folk art, crafts, and antiques. . . . But most potent of all were his descriptions of the serenity and security of farm life:

What a place was the barn, say, of a November night and the cold falling. The stock, fed and bedded, voice their content with gratulatory noises, as they stir placidly at the pleasant task of eating in warm quarters. It is snug here in the stables. . . . You have a sense of all that mass of hay above you in the great lofts. It is between you and the menace of winter; it will spend but slowly, and keep all the creatures in fine fettle until there is pasture again. It is, directly or indirectly, food and shelter and money in the bank.

We have a window into ancient times and foreign people when we read the Bible. More than that, we are given the inside scoop on God's plan for humankind, His eternal perspective, and His Fatherly heart. Do you want to be able to share your inner view with another person? Write it down and pass it on. Do you want to know God's most intimate and loving thoughts? Open the Bible and allow yourself to be ushered into His heart.

■ ■ ■

Dear heavenly Father, thank You for ushering me into Your eternal world through the use of written words.

Hope in Heaven

Dear brothers and sisters, we want you to know what will happen to the believers who have died so you will not grieve like people who have no hope.

1 THESSALONIANS 4:13

At least once a day my grandma talks about heaven. She doesn't talk about it with regret at the thought of dying. Instead, her words remind me of a five-year-old waiting for a trip to Disneyland! Grandma gets frustrated with her failing body, and she's saddened by the loss of all the friends who have gone, including her husband of fifty years. Like my grandma, those in the Amish community aren't fearful of death. Here is an example of how they live out their view of death, in an excerpt about an Amish man's last days:

> John Stolzfus bore one of the most common names in the Old Order Amish community in eastern Pennsylvania where he had lived all of his life. He had an ordinary Amish life, but for many people who fear death his last days can be considered nothing less than extraordinary.
>
> In time, after what he thought of as a good life, John began to decline in vigor and in his ability to get around. In accordance with Amish customs, a small house (called a "grandfather house") was built next to the main farmhouse, and John retired there. After his retirement, John concentrated on reading his beloved Bible, whittling simple wooden toys, and spending time with his second wife, their children, and their grandchildren. When he could no longer get out of bed, both John and other members of his community realized that his death was not far off. Gradually, Amish neighbors of all ages began to come by to pray together and say good-bye one last time. John spoke openly of his coming death and used these visits to encourage others to prepare for and calmly accept their own deaths. At the age of 82, John Stolzfus died peacefully one night in his own bed, as one of his daughters sat quietly in a nearby rocking chair and two of his grandchildren slept in their own beds in the same room.

Experience, tradition, and shared attitudes help individuals and the community deal with death in Amish communities.

Do you look forward to heaven—to eternity—with expectancy? What Jesus offers in life is greater than anything this world has to offer.

■ ■ ■

Dear heavenly Father, the hope of heaven is a beautiful gift. Please take away all my fears.

Future Thinking

The Kingdom of Heaven can be illustrated by the story of a
king who prepared a great wedding feast for his son.
MATTHEW 22:2

I've been to numerous weddings, and I enjoy taking note of the traditions of the wedding feast. Some couples focus on the food, others on the entertainment, and other wedding feasts are all about the dancing—parents with children, friends with friends. One fun tradition at Amish weddings is the "pairing up" of young people. Steady couples are confirmed—and other young people wonder who will pick whom.

"[Ice cream] is a Southern staple in Amish settlements, assuming an ice house is on the premises. Otherwise homemade ice cream has to wait until winter, when Mother Nature supplies the ice."

It is the custom at the wedding supper for the young people to sit in couples; thus each boy was forced to bring a girl to the supper table whether he wanted to or not. The older boys who had "steady" girls had no difficulty in pairing off, but young boys with little or no experience in courtship showed great timidity in finding a partner.

Those who refused to find partners were seized and dragged to the door, where they were placed beside a girl. Once in line, all resistance ceased and each couple went to the table holding hands, following the example of the bridal party. The supper included roast beef, roast chicken, noodles, beef gravy, chicken gravy, mashed potatoes, cole slaw, prunes, fruit salad, potato chips, cookies, pies, cakes, and for the bridal group and cooks there were, in addition, baked oysters and ice cream.

I smile when I think about all the speculation over future marriages. We tend to speculate about many other things, too—future relationships, future occupations, future vacations—even what's for dinner! The only thing we can be certain of is that God, our Father, takes care of all the details. David wrote, "My future is in your hands" (Psalm 31:15).

Do you have hopes, dreams, and eager speculation about your future? We all do. How wonderful that God, who loves us unconditionally, is in charge of how everything will turn out!

■ ■ ■

Dear heavenly Father, I can't wait to see what good plans You have in store for me. Thank
You for holding my future in Your hands.

Finding Common Ground

Among us you are all equal. That is, we are all in a common relationship with Jesus Christ. Also, since you are Christ's family, then you are Abraham's famous "descendant," heirs according to the covenant promises.

GALATIANS 3:28 (THE MESSAGE)

It seems to be a common trait among humans to rank and classify ourselves with one another. High schools have cliques. Workplaces create teams. Churches belong to denominations. We like to have a specific place in this world. We like to surround ourselves with others with the same interests, beliefs, and lifestyles. This is true in the Amish community too. Among the Plain people there are those who are the Plainest of all.

The Swartzentrubers are generally considered to be among the most conservative sects of the Old Order Amish. The Swartzentrubers, who are named after an early bishop of the church, split from the mainline Amish church in 1917. The Swartzentrubers wanted to return to the church's less worldly ways. . . . The Swartzentrubers differentiate themselves from their other Amish brethren by wearing muted, dark clothing. Women's dresses are longer than those in other Amish churches.

The apostle Paul traveled to numerous cultures and shared the gospel message with a variety of people. What he discovered is that in sharing God's Word, we need to find common ground with those different from us: " I try to find common ground with everyone, doing everything I can to save some," we read in 1 Corinthians 9:22.

In this life there will always be those who are different from us. And while each of us can be comfortable by surrounding ourselves with like-minded friends and coworkers, we also need to reach out and appreciate others' differences. In Christ's family there will be are no divisions. All who believe in God will partake of His goodness together.

"The Swartzentruber Amish generally don't associate with more liberal Amish churches. They've also resisted perceived government intrusion on their lives more forcefully than other Amish, protesting against the orange safety triangle that many states require on the back of their buggies."

■ ■ ■

Dear heavenly Father, today help me to find common ground with someone I've previously considered "different," and may that person see Your love through my actions.

A Friend Forever

There are "friends" who destroy each other, but
a real friend sticks closer than a brother.
PROVERBS 18:24

Have you ever heard the song "Friends" by Michael W. Smith: "And friends are friends forever if the Lord's the Lord of them"? The Amish have a similar song of friendship, and it is sung at a key point in an Amish wedding reception.

Hymns were sung during the supper hour, which continued until ten o'clock. The bride and bridegroom during this time sent plates of extra delicacies—cakes, pie, and candies—from the *Eck* to their special friends seated in various parts of the house. The final selection sung after the evening meal was *Guter Geselle* ("good friend"), a religious folk song. This selection cannot be found in any of the Amish song books. It is largely sung from memory, although it has been printed in leaflet form. The first verse reads:

Guter Geselle, was sagest du mir?	*Good friend, what do you say?*
O guter Geselle ich sage dir,	*O good friend I tell you—*
Sage dir was eins ist,	*I tell you what one thing is;*
Eins ist der Gott allein,	*One is God alone,*
Der da lebet und der da schwebet,	*He who lives and He who soars,*
Und der den wahren Glauben führet	*And He who leads the true Faith*
Im Himmel und auf Erden.	*In Heaven and on Earth.*

We have friends who are there to celebrate our most important moments. There are friends for different seasons of our lives. The thing about friendship is that it must be mutual and reciprocal. There is no such thing as a one-sided friendship. Jesus wishes to be your friend today. He is the only friend who is closer than a brother—One who will never leave you. He will never forsake those who trust in and love Him. If Jesus is your truest friend for life, He will remain the same for eternity.

Today, pray and ask how you can grow in your relationship with Jesus. Strive to be a friend to others for your Savior's sake. Friendship is a gift you both give and receive.

■ ■ ■

Dear heavenly Father, thank You for choosing to be my friend before I even knew You.
Thank You for being my friend forever.

A Masterpiece

You made me; you created me. Now give me the sense to follow your commands.

PSALM 119:73

As the winter winds begin to blow, it's the perfect time to curl up under a cozy quilt. Amish quilts have a timeless quality and are highly valued for their workmanship.

> We know the Amish by their quilts. The women inside an Amish community often shared piecing and quilting patterns with each other. Sometimes patterns would be shared between women from different communities. In this way designs spread through Amish communities, across the United States.
>
> Amish quilts are most often pieced and the designs are usually simple. Their beauty comes from the way each individual quilter used color in her quilts. The solid fabrics in these quilts are plain—free from pattern. But solid fabrics don't have to be dull or quiet. Many Amish quilts are made from rich, bright, wonderful colors. . . . In many cases, if you take these quilts out of context, they look very modern. The piecing designs in Amish quilts do not have a dated look; we still use them today. Solid fabrics don't look dated the way a very old print does.

Patience is a quality most needed when it is exhausted.

PROVERB

The Amish never intended for their quilts to be timeless. For decades they've made quilts to keep their families warm, and now they are collected and appreciated far beyond Amish communities.

Like an Amish quilt, we are each uniquely created and designed. But the One who designed us is infinitely wise. He knows His intentions for us, and they are often not what we might expect. We are fashioned, fitted, shaped, and formed. We are pieced together: "You made all the delicate, inner parts of my body and knit me together in my mother's womb. Thank you for making me so wonderfully complex! Your workmanship is marvelous—how well I know it" (Psalm 139:13-14).

It feels good when others value and appreciate you, but the One who created you values and appreciates you so much more. God created you to be timeless. How amazing is that!

■ ■ ■

Dear heavenly Father, I thank You that in Your sight, I'm a masterpiece. Help me to understand my unique design more than I ever have before.

Gifts of Love

Love each other with genuine affection, and take delight in honoring each other.
ROMANS 12:10

November is wedding season for the Amish. This means that sometimes Thanksgiving celebrations are combined with wedding celebrations. Amish weddings are traditionally held on Tuesdays or Thursdays from late October through December. They are joyful community events.

My friend, Amish author Beth Wiseman, shares more about Amish weddings:

Don't expect to see a three- or four-tiered, decorated wedding cake at an Old Order Amish wedding—or a groom's cake, for that matter. However, there is an abundant offering of eatable goodies for the bride and groom in lieu of our English tradition.

Most Amish weddings are held at the bride's parents' home.

Following the wedding ceremony in the bride's home, the new couple will take their place at the *eck* (tables that form an 'L' in the corner of the room), along with their family and attendants. After the meal, guests will present the bride and groom with various gifts, mostly food. This might be a single cake, perhaps a favorite of the groom's. Or it could be a lovely decorative container filled with cookies, maybe the bride's favorite. . . . Whatever the gifts might be, they are given to the bride and groom as a token of love and remembrance of some special event or knowledge that they share.

Have you taken time lately to get together with friends? You could share a special memory with someone you care about. Show your affection by making a special dessert. Write a note of care, or spend time with someone you love over a cup of tea.

"I am giving you a new commandment: Love each other. Just as I have loved you, you should love each other," we read in John 13:34. When we love others, we bring delight to them and to God. We also reflect to the world what God followers look like. As family and friends spend time together, we can get and give a glimpse of what heaven will be like.

■ ■ ■

Dear heavenly Father, I'm thankful that You give us a glimpse of what an eternity filled with love looks like. Help me to love others more deeply.

Help in the Hard Parts

The LORD gives his people strength. The LORD blesses them with peace.

PSALM 29:11

Some may think that if you were the lone teacher of twenty-five children, the hardest part would be maintaining control of the class. But in the winter, the hardest part of a teacher's day may just be getting to and from school.

In the Allen County, Adams County, and Nappanee settlements, most Amish teachers are able to drive a buggy to school, since they live no more than several miles from the school. The greatest problem with buggy travel in all three of these settlements is that a major highway, a heavily traveled two-lane road, bisects each of these Amish communities. Many drivers drive at or above the speed limit of fifty-five miles per hour, and there is only a blinking caution light at one major intersection of an artery used by the Amish. I know teachers who must cross such busy highways every day on their way to school. I have seen driving horses get unruly having to wait to cross; I have seen one horse bolt at an inappropriate moment. Several times in winter, when the roads were very treacherous, I have seen large trucks bear down unmercifully on Amish buggies, frightening both horses and their drivers. I often thought on my way to school that I would arrive exhausted and shaking if I had to cross such roads early on a winter morning.

"The best thing you can spend on your children is your time."

ATTRIBUTED TO LOUISE HART

Is there a part of your day that frazzles your nerves? Maybe you feel troubles or challenges running at you like fast-moving vehicles on slick roads, and your whole body is tensed, just waiting to be hit. If so, cling to Psalm 5:12: "You bless the godly, O LORD; you surround them with your shield of love."

God is the One who strengthens His people. God is the One who grants them peace. God surrounds them—us—with His shield of love.

We will never have a day without frustrations. We will never have a week without worries. We will never have a month without tears. When the hard parts of our days come, God is with us. And with Him comes peace.

∎ ∎ ∎

Dear heavenly Father, I know today will have its difficulties. I also know that with You I can face them.

No Comparison

Make a careful exploration of who you are and the work you have been given, and then sink yourself into that. Don't be impressed with yourself. Don't compare yourself with others. Each of you must take responsibility for doing the creative best you can with your own life.
GALATIANS 6:4 *(THE MESSAGE)*

One thing that gets us into a lot of trouble is comparing ourselves with others. When we do this, we either come up short, or we end up thinking we are better than others and become prideful. Comparison brings on unnecessary worries and fear. It can also cause us to disassociate ourselves from others. It builds stumbling blocks within our hearts and within our communities.

True Thanksgiving is thanks-living.

PROVERB

One stumbling block had been that many Old Order communities viewed Pinecraft [Florida] as part of the technologically progressive New Order Amish. Members ride two- or three-wheel bicycles instead of horses and carriages, and they worship in a meetinghouse instead of members' homes. More significantly, these "liberal" Amish have electricity and telephones in their Florida homes, and most have air conditioning and microwaves. And if that isn't enough, many men, single and married, routinely stroll or bicycle around Pinecraft without a hat, an omission that in most communities would at least raise eyebrows, if not prompt severe criticism.

Bishops fear that exposure to such luxuries, conveniences, and examples may cause not only young people but baptized members to return home dissatisfied with kerosene lanterns and antiquated ways. Finally, the bishops ask, how will young people ever learn to develop a respect for hard work, simplicity, and self-denial when they daily observe Amish elders wasting time at shuffleboard, checkers, and even golf? What kind of example is that, they wonder.

One thing that can combat comparisons is being thankful for what you have and choosing to be content in all things.

Do comparisons fill you with worry and uncertainty? Take them to God, and focus on Him. He will help you do the creative best with your life. And it's then you'll find peace.

■ ■ ■

Dear heavenly Father, help me to keep my eyes focused on You. May the only comparison in my heart be between where I was before I followed You and where I am now. May this comparison always fill me with thankfulness!

Thanksgiving

Come, let us sing to the LORD! Let us shout joyfully to the Rock of our salvation.
Let us come to him with thanksgiving. Let us sing psalms of praise to him.

PSALM 95:1-2

What are you thankful for? How do you express it to God? Is Thanksgiving a time of thankfulness for you? Or is it just another holiday to plan for—another gathering that brings more stress than joy? Do you spend more time focusing on the menu than you do on all the things God has done for you?

When it comes to Thanksgiving, the Amish take a cue from the Pilgrims and fast. The fasting begins after dinner the night before, and lasts until the big meal, usually served around noon. The women prepare the meal during that time—no tasting allowed! The fasting applies mainly to the baptized church members. For children, the fasting is optional. . . . Before eating, the Amish family gathers together in the morning for devotions and talks about what they're thankful for.

> "Thanksgiving was never meant to be shut up in a single day."
>
> ATTRIBUTED TO ROBERT CASPAR LINTNER

A roasted turkey is often the centerpiece of the meal; rather than purchase frozen birds, many Amish raise their own or purchase them from neighbors. They may also serve mashed potatoes, cooked vegetables, salads, breads, noodles, and pie.

After dinner, it's not uncommon for the Amish to sing German hymns, taking time to give thanks to God through music. Remember that sung music is the one kind of music allowed by the Ordnung—there are no instruments in Amish homes or churches.

Think about how you can bring more thankfulness into your Thanksgiving celebration. True Thanksgiving is a matter of the heart, not a date on the calendar. It finds a moment of stillness to praise God in the midst of busyness. Thanksgiving makes God the centerpiece of the celebration. When you are truly thankful, you aren't afraid to lift your voice in song: "Enter his gates with thanksgiving; go into his courts with praise. Give thanks to him and praise his name" (Psalm 100:4).

How can you express your thankfulness to God today?

■ ■ ■

Dear heavenly Father, thank You! You are the Rock of my Salvation. You are my everything!

Adorned

I saw the holy city, the new Jerusalem, coming down from God out
of heaven like a bride beautifully dressed for her husband.
REVELATION 21:2

When my daughter was in her late teens, she and I loved to watch the TV show *Say Yes to the Dress*. It features a wide variety of potential wedding gowns, from simple to extravagant. All of them are costly, and the idea is that viewers can watch each bride choose a dress that best reflects her style. Wedding dresses in an Amish community are very different:

> Blue is the typical color chosen for Amish brides—a variety of shades of blue . . . or sometimes purple. An Amish bride usually makes her own dress, and it's similar to the dresses she wears every other day of the year. The dresses of her two attendants, known as *newehockers* (Pennsylvania Dutch for "sidesitters"), are often made from the same cloth. . . .
>
> All three dresses are plain and mid-calf length. There is no beading, no sweetheart neckline, and no train. We all know that for us Englishers the thought of wearing our wedding dress more than once would be crazy . . . yet an Amish bride wears her "wedding dress" as a nice church dress after she is married. Many times she is also buried in that dress when she dies. Or buried in the cape and apron she wore on her wedding day. There is no veil either. Often the young woman wears a black kapp to differentiate from the white one she wears daily. There is also no bouquet—the beauty reflecting from her smile is her only adornment. And her groom sees her as a beautiful bride indeed.

In some communities unmarried women wear either a white kapp or a black kapp. After they are married, they wear only white kapps.

A beautiful site to God is the new Jerusalem. It's a symbol of the heavenly world He has prepared for us, his bride. The city is splendid and glorious and more wonderful than we can imagine. It's a symbol of His eternal commitment to us.

What does it mean to you that God compares your heavenly home to a bride? Does it make you feel cherished and honored? It should.

■ ■ ■

Dear heavenly Father, thank You for all You've done to prepare a heavenly home for me. I adore You.

Too Much of a Good Thing

People ruin their lives by their own foolishness and then are angry at the LORD.

PROVERBS 19:3

If you've ever been with a child who is trying to pick out toys to buy with birthday money, then you've seen a picture of the phrase *too much of a good thing*. Instead of bringing about thankfulness, sometimes an abundance of things only makes us want more. And then—when we don't feel satisfied or fulfilled with what we have—we may blame God for not doing enough for us. This is a great concern in the Amish community.

Parents worry that instead of their children learning the value of money and hard work, they will become slothful and self-indulgent. "In my generation," recalled one great-grandfather, "nobody had enough money to buy a car, or even go to town and buy drinks. What little we did earn went to our parents until we came of age at twenty-one. Now young people are making big money and many of them are keeping all of it for themselves." A father made a similar point: "When I was a boy, our parents kept what we earned until we were twenty-one and responsible enough to spend it wisely. They would save as much as they could on our behalf until we came of age. It was also a good way to be sure we didn't spend it on cars and such foolishness. My own son has worked in construction for the past three years, and he has nothing to show for it. I'm sure that he has wasted $45,000 on vehicles and other foolishness." An Indiana father lamented the fact that "our boys working in factories can earn $1000 or $1200 a week. It's not good for them."

Those who have money are troubled about it; those who have none are troubled without it.

PROVERB

Have you ever been angry at God because you've made a foolish mistake? Have you gotten yourself into a pickle and then turned to God and pleaded for rescue? Just like any young person we sometimes make foolish choices, but like loving parents, the best thing God can do is allow us to learn from the consequences.

■ ■ ■

Dear heavenly Father, please forgive me for the times I've made foolish choices and then blamed You for not helping out or answering my prayers.

Standing By His Promise

They are like trees planted along the riverbank, bearing fruit each season. Their leaves never wither, and they prosper in all they do.
PSALM 1:3

How would your life change if you lived with the knowledge that everything comes through the hand of God and that you can trust His plan? Many of us have this knowledge in our heads, but do we believe it in our hearts? Do we dig our roots deep into that fact?

It takes a century for God to make a sturdy oak.

PROVERB

In the book *Success Made Simple: An Inside Look at Why Amish Businesses Thrive*, Erik Wesner claims that 95 percent of all Amish businesses succeed, and one of the main reasons is customer service.

Underlying the idea of customer service is the concept of brotherly good. Considering how the average Amish businessperson's life meshes with business, it's no surprise to see the Golden Rule at play both in the day-to-day and in the shop.

Bishop Menno Graber offers his two cents on doing the right thing. "The more you put in, the more you get out," he explains.

"It's like anything else. You can't get interest at the bank if you don't put no money in! It's just like charity. But you don't have to go and tell a fellow that I donated so much money for this.

"If anything happens, we repair free," says Menno, noting that he honors this guarantee on issues that appear even ten years after purchase. . . . Menno's promise reflects confidence in his chairs' craftsmanship.

There are people we trust in our lives, those we know will not fail us. More than any human person, God's "business" focuses on our good. The more we send our roots deep into Him, the more sure of Him we become. If problems arise in your life, know that God will always stand beside His work: "We know that God causes everything to work together for the good of those who love God and are called according to his purpose for them" (Romans 8:28).

Can you plant your faith deep into His promises? If so, you can be at peace, knowing that God stands by His word.

■ ■ ■

Dear heavenly Father, winter awaits just outside my window, but help me to bear good fruit in every season.

Our Word

Most of all, my brothers and sisters, never take an oath, by heaven or earth or anything else. Just say a simple yes or no, so that you will not sin and be condemned.

JAMES 5:12

"You're only as good as your word." You may have heard your parents or grandparents say this, but is this virtue still valued today? I'm guilty of tossing around words with my children: "Maybe later we're going to the park." "Maybe after dinner we'll make cookies." Keeping my word—not just big ones but small ones too—is something I'm working on.

Words carry great weight to the Amish. The most significant words an Amish person will utter are when he or she "bends at the knee" and chooses to become baptized as a church member. That one decision weighs heavily on an Amish youth, and from it springs forth all other decisions. Adult baptism is sacred to the Amish, linked to the sacrifices of their ancestors. It can be a very emotional experience, even for a people who keep their feelings under a tight rein.

There are no degrees of honesty.

PROVERB

If an Amish person chooses to leave the church before becoming baptized as a member, they are not under the ban—known as excommunication. Nor will they be shunned. But if they leave after they have become baptized, the ban will be enforced and the consequences of leaving are harsh. . . .

"Oaths are to be made only to God, binding for life," says Norman. All the brightness leaves him, like a cloud swallowing up the sun. "But some do leave. Some leave under the ban." He releases a deep sigh. "They broke a promise, you see."

How diligent are you at sticking to your word? Can others trust you to do what you say? Can God trust you to follow through with your promises to Him? Your friends and family can trust your big promises only if they already trust your small promises.

God's Word is clear that oaths are a serious matter. How would your life change if you took your words more seriously?

■ ■ ■

Dear heavenly Father, You say our words can bring blessing and cursing. Help me to better understand the power of my words.

A Perfect Gift

Don't make idols for yourselves; don't set up an image or a sacred
pillar for yourselves, and don't place a carved stone in your land
that you can bow down to in worship. I am GOD, your God.
LEVITICUS 26:1 *(THE MESSAGE)*

Cabbage Patch Kids dolls became one of the biggest fads of the 1980s, and I received one during the peak of their popularity because my mother worked at a retail outlet.

It seems that most little girls have a special doll in their childhoods. This is true of Amish girls, too.

To mistreat God's creation is to offend the Creator.

PROVERB

Authentic Amish dolls are always fitted and dressed in traditional Amish garb and do not have any facial features. The dolls are faceless because the Old Order Amish do not believe in the use of mirrors or the taking of photographs of men, women or children. This is in keeping with the very important Biblical dictate that states: "Thou shall not make unto thee any graven image, or any likeness of any thing that is in heaven above, or that is in the earth beneath, or that is in the water under the earth (Exodus 20:4)."

Although most of us do not consider dolls to be graven images, we do need to consider the things that might become idols in our lives. From the beginning, God made sure His people never tried to create an image to represent Him, yet we often find ourselves looking to things that we appreciate and applaud—million-dollar homes, luxury cars, and even people we praise simply because of their looks or talents—and placing more value on them than we should. Childhood fads can grow into adult fads, and if we're not careful, they will distract our attention from the One who is worthy of all our praise.

James 1:17 says, "Every good and perfect gift is from above, coming down from the Father of the heavenly lights, who does not change like shifting shadows" (NIV). Nothing our eye is drawn to compares to the gifts that God offers. More than that, God offers Himself, which is the greatest—most perfect—gift of all.

■ ■ ■

Dear heavenly Father, I'm thankful for the gift of You. Forgive me for the times I've turned my mind, heart, and attention to lesser things.

Soul Satisfaction

*Anyone who believes in me may come and drink! For the Scriptures
declare, "Rivers of living water will flow from his heart."*

JOHN 7:38

I remember when I first became a Christian. When I read God's Word and prayed,
I felt full to the brim. I didn't understand why I felt so refreshed, but I knew I didn't
want to stop feeling that way. More than twenty years later I still know where I need
to go to find soul satisfaction and refreshment. For some people, getting there is a
journey all its own.

Quilts are the reason that Sue Bender, a middle-aged
artist and therapist with two graduate degrees, ended up
doing dishes with the Amish. Having stumbled upon
some Amish quilts in a Long Island clothing store,
Bender was so taken by their colors and design that she
resolved to meet the people who made them, hoping to
find something to fill the "starved place" in her soul. In
Plain and Simple: A Woman's Journey to the Amish, Bender
recounts her life-changing experiences in Iowa and Ohio,
where she lived first with the Yoders and then with the
Beilers. Although never tempted to become Amish herself,
Bender insists at the end of her journey that her time with
the Amish had transformed her in profound ways. "Through them I am learning
not to rush through life in order to get the goodies," she writes. "Their way of
life delivers the goods, and that is quite different."

> "God's grace is
> immeasurable,
> His mercy is
> inexhaustible,
> and His peace is
> inexpressible."
>
> ATTRIBUTED TO
> ENOCH O. AKANJI

Do you have a starved place in your soul? Like Sue Bender, I am refreshed when
I'm around loving, godly people and when I take time to enjoy my day rather than
rush through it. Yet even that will bring only limited satisfaction for a limited amount
of time. Only Jesus can truly, deeply satisfy: "The LORD will guide you continually,
giving you water when you are dry and restoring your strength," reads Isaiah 58:11.
"You will be like a well-watered garden, like an ever-flowing spring."

Is your soul feeling thirsty? Open God's Word. Ask God to fill you as you read. And
be prepared to be filled up and soul satisfied!

■ ■ ■

*Dear heavenly Father, You are amazing. Thank You for Your Living Water that will never
leave me dry.*

A Good Name

A good name is more desirable than great riches; to be esteemed is better than silver or gold.

PROVERBS 22:1 (NIV)

When I received my first Bible, it came with a bookmark that read "Tricia, Noblewoman" and included the words of Proverbs 22:1. At the time I didn't understand that verse. If someone gave me great riches, silver or gold, I'd have been happy to change my name to Heather or Dawn. I didn't realize until later that our name is a reflection of who we are. Our "name" is our reputation or character, and having a good reputation is worth a lot. In the book *Our Amish Neighbors*, the author describes common Amish names:

A bird is known by its feathers.

PROVERB

One learns here that the good old biblical names are still common with the Amish but are in competition with modern or more euphonious ones. The names of the children of large families are often a study in contrasts. In one family there are, for example, Benjamin, Samuel, Isaac, Stephen, John, Israel, Christ, Barbara, Mary, Hannah, Annie, Mattie, and Lizzie. Another family has chosen these names for its children: Sarah, Lizzie, Samuel, Benjamin, John, Annie, Marie, Daniel, David, Enos, Sylvia, and Malinda. Then there are three Amish brothers named Isaac, Levi, and Elmer. One wonders how Vesta, Delila, Dena, Saloma, Drusilla, or Verba, or boys' names like Junie, Venus, or Aquilla came into strict Christian families?

This book quoted above was written in 1962, but not much has changed. Amish families still use biblical or traditional names. I've never heard of an Amish child named Brittney or Cayden, and I'd be surprised if I ever did.

Have you ever taken time to consider how your name represents you? How do people respond when they hear your name—that says a lot about who you are and how you display yourself to the world.

God proved that a good name matters by honoring His Son in that way. "God elevated him to the place of highest honor and gave him the name above all other names, that at the name of Jesus every knee should bow" Philippians 2:9-10.

Take a moment and lift up Jesus' name today. Not because you have to but simply because you can.

■ ■ ■

Dear Jesus, I thank You that someday Your name will be exalted high above the earth!

Busy Hands, Clothed Family

She finds wool and flax and busily spins it. . . . Her hands are busy spinning thread, her fingers twisting fiber. . . . She has no fear of winter for her household, for everyone has warm clothes.

PROVERBS 31:13, 19, 21

An Amish mother sits by the fire, warming herself as her fingers work with the wool in her hands. Not many Amish women spin wool or flax, but more Amish women can be found knitting.

In the early days, Amish women knit shawls and capes, mittens and gloves, typically in solid dark colors consistent with the plain dark clothing worn by men and women. Between 1860 and 1920, Old Order Amish women in Lancaster County, Pennsylvania, knit colorful knee-length stockings, many with scalloped tops in vivid contrasting hues from purple, rose, and pink to brown, green, and blue. These stockings were part of private dress, as the long dresses and laced black boots hid their stockings. . . .

The Amish began to buy their stockings and mittens during the first half of the twentieth century, though some knitters continued to make mittens and stockings for their families. Women also knit and crocheted rugs, placemats, and lamp mats to place beneath kerosene lamps.

> Keeping a neat house is like threading beads on a string with no knot on it.
>
> **PROVERB**

It's amazing really how women have the honor of clothing and caring for their families. Our children don't have to worry about clothes to wear or food to eat because of us!

Proverbs 31:21 puts it this way: "When it snows, she has no fear for her household; for all of them are clothed in scarlet" (NIV). The term *scarlet* has spiritual meanings, too. The scarlet color can be applied to the robe of righteousness. As one commentary puts it "the righteousness of Christ . . . is a hiding place from the wind, and a covert from the storm; a sufficient shelter from the cold of snow, and all inclemencies of the weather; by which the vindictive wrath and justice of God may be signified."

Godly mothers do more than just clothe their children with physical garments. We wrap them with the Word of God and cover them with our prayers. And the garment of salvation is one our children can wear for life!

■ ■ ■

Dear heavenly Father, thank You for the strength to care for my family. Thank You that Your righteousness can clothe them for eternity!

Loving Your Enemies

Bless those who curse you. Pray for those who hurt you. . . . Give, and you will receive. Your gift will return to you in full—pressed down, shaken together to make room for more, running over, and poured into your lap. The amount you give will determine the amount you get back.
LUKE 6:28, 38

There was a time when someone spread an untrue rumor about me, and my e-mail box was filled with horrible notes from the very young people that I was trying to serve. The matter got cleared up eventually, but I still remember the horrible feeling of wanting to defend myself, even though I knew I was in the right.

"From the winds and rains of adversity comes abundant growth and a beautiful life."

ATTRIBUTED TO
LAURA LEWIS
LANIER

Thirty years ago the Amish were viewed as a backward sect living by oppressive customs and exploiting the labor of their children. Amish parents were sent to prison for not allowing their children to go to school beyond the elementary grades. They were viewed as a group that renounced both modern conveniences and the American dreams of progress. Thirty years ago national magazines described the Amish as a "dying breed." Today they are featured in national magazines as hearty Americans. . . .

The Amish provide models of how modern people may choose to survive—physically, culturally, and spiritually. The fear on the part of modern parents that their children may join cult movements does not exist among the Amish. My personal files are bulging with inquiries from children, adults, and old people asking how to become Amish.

The hardest thing to do is to love those who curse you and to pray for those who hurt you, yet that's what the Amish did. And the result? They are not only accepted by mainstream society but are also honored and valued. People vacation to see them, read books about them, and want to join them.

It's a struggle to love those who we feel have disrespected us, but we'll never know what good can come about until we do. God determines how we'll be rewarded, and He always goes above and beyond what we expect.

■ ■ ■

Dear heavenly Father, I can't love and forgive those who hurt me without Your help. I want to obey Your command. Please help me to do so.

Peace

That Sunday evening the disciples were meeting behind locked doors because they were afraid of the Jewish leaders. Suddenly, Jesus was standing there among them! "Peace be with you," he said.

JOHN 20:19

[On] December 7, 1941, the U.S. enters World War II after the Japanese attack Pearl Harbor and begins military conscription. About 772 Old Order Amish men are drafted, and all of them declare themselves CO's [conscientious objectors].

But that wasn't the only time the Amish were asked to serve in our country's military. It happened first during World War I:

Late Spring, 1917

> **A peaceful heart leads to a healthy body.**
>
> **PROVERBS 14:30**

The U.S. begins a national conscription service; some Amish boys receive exemptions for farm deferments as conscientious objectors, but others are required to report to Army camps. Drafted Amish who refuse to enter armed service are sent to the Army camps for non-combatant service and are often subjected to abuse.

Some members of the Amish community express concern over Amish boys being pulled away from the church and not returning to their home communities following their service.

One headline from a 1918 newspaper read, "Amish People Getting Themselves Disliked: Refused to Take Any Part in Patriotic Movements Creates Enmity to Sect."

It is hard enough living in a country that is facing war. Even harder is knowing that those around you see *you* as an enemy. In life, there will always be times of trouble. There will always be conflicts. Because of this there is conflict within our souls. There is only one answer to this: peace. And there is only one place where true peace comes from: Jesus. "Peace be with you," He said.

When the angels announced Christ's birth, they declared, "Glory to God in highest heaven, and peace on earth to those with whom God is pleased" (Luke 2:14). Not peace from war. Not peace from community conflict. But peace deep in our hearts that no one can steal from us.

■ ■ ■

Dear heavenly Father, I thank You for the peace that Christ gives. I thank You that it is greater than any conflict this world has.

Books Change Things

Think about what I am saying. The Lord will help you understand all these things.
2 TIMOTHY 2:7

My life changed forever when our family moved near a library when I was in elementary school. I lived close enough to ride my bike there after school and on weekends. I hadn't read much before that time, but I fell in love with books. Through the years I continued to read, and I eventually became a writer myself. The Amish spend many winter nights reading, and sometimes books change them more than they think.

Occasionally young people's love for reading or simple curiosity about ideas or the outside world entices them to delve into reading materials that the community finds objectionable. Non-Amish co-workers or local librarians sometimes recommend and even provide books that promote critical thinking or encourage additional formal education. For some readers, these ideas provoke a discontent with their limited education and stimulate a desire for more learning. Some of these Amish young people eventually leave.

> You can't stumble when you are on your knees.
>
> PROVERB

. . . For every reader who leaves the Amish, many more Old Order youth remain to become self-educated. They now function as successful draftsmen, veterinary technicians, midwives, unofficial chiropractors, mechanics, hydraulic and pneumatic technicians, inventors, tax accountants, writers, historians, and even occasionally computer programmers for outside businesses—all without the benefit of high school or college. Most of them demonstrate the ability to analyze both mainstream and Amish society.

Has reading changed your life? Reading books may change your choice of career or even your choice of community, but only God's Word can change you from the inside out. Psalm 12:6 says, "The LORD's promises are pure, like silver refined in a furnace, purified seven times over." Books give knowledge, but God's Word provides pure wisdom. Books can inspire, but only God's Word can transform.

Schedule a time soon to dig deep into God's Word, and ask God to give you His wisdom to understand and change from the inside out.

■ ■ ■

Dear heavenly Father, thank You for the written word . . . and for Your Word that changes everything.

Sing!

Let the message about Christ, in all its richness, fill your lives. Teach
and counsel each other with all the wisdom he gives. Sing psalms
and hymns and spiritual songs to God with thankful hearts.

COLOSSIANS 3:16

I remember as a child standing in church next to my grandmother, listening to her sing, and thinking she had the most beautiful voice. Just last week I had the same thought. Even though she doesn't always sing on key—and sometimes messes up the words—still, Grandma sings with all her heart.

Singing hymns at home is common for Amish families. It's part of their lives, and sometimes part of their daily ritual.

Mose and Eva sing their hymn as a morning and evening ritual, a pattern to start and end each day. Mose may not have many more days. His lips are blue, his skin color is gray. He has already had one heart attack and two serious operations. He finally decided to toss out the medications—which were only making him sicker, he realized—and trust his remaining time on earth to the Lord. "I've already lived two years past the doctor's prediction," he said, looking a little pleased. "But I get winded easily now. I'm just happy to be alive.

"I'm ready to go," he added. "But only the Lord knows the day." Mose shrugged. "Whatever," he added, sounding a lot like an English teen. He smiled slightly, at peace with his future.

Mose and Eva lift their faces slightly, eyes closed in reverence as they sing. Their tinny voices aren't exactly easy on the ears. But they just keep singing, unconcerned by the fact that their voices are neither beautiful nor professional.

After all, they're not singing for themselves.

Awake, you Christians all. And grasp it courageously With a sound rich in joy, Reach for this crown Which God has promised to us. Through His Holy Spirit He wants to show us His help, That we may praise Him In affliction most of all.

AUSBUND,
SONG 100, VERSE 8

Consider making singing part of your morning ritual. Sing your prayers, sing in the shower, just sing!

■ ■ ■

Dear heavenly Father, help me to remember that the quality of my voice is not as important as the quality of my heart. I praise You today!

DECEMBER 10

Be Brave, and Wait

Wait patiently for the LORD. Be brave and courageous.
Yes, wait patiently for the LORD.
PSALM 27:14

"Mom, can you believe it? All my friends are getting married this year. All of them."
Even though my daughter didn't say it, I could read her thoughts from her sorrowful
gaze. *What about me?*

It was true. Most (four, to be exact) of my daughter's closest friends were getting
married. And as I gave my daughter a hug, I told her that it would be okay. After all,
she was only twenty.

Apple butter, just like relationships, takes time to boil, time to cool, and time to turn out wonderfully.

PROVERB

Many young Amish people turn earnestly to the question
of family and marriage in the year after receiving the
sacrament of baptism. The years in between baptism and
marriage can be filled with a variety of experiences available
to young Amish adults within the boundaries of social
expectations and the *Ordnung*. Both young women and men
can become school teachers, though most teachers today are
young women, as in the past. Young people may become
full partners in a family business or look for a farm of their
own. Some young people hire out as maids in other large
households, or go to work in area restaurants and shops that
cater to English tourists. Young men may sign on with building crews or become
apprentices for a trade with specialists in the Amish community such as the
blacksmith or harness-maker.

Running as a theme throughout these days is the search for the marriage
partner, the husband or wife who will be a match in purpose for the plain life in
the Amish world. All paths have been leading to this end.

God knows that waiting is hard, and that's why He tells us to be brave and courageous. Being brave isn't just about stepping out into danger; it's also stepping back
when you're tempted to make something happen on your own instead of waiting for
God. Being courageous isn't just standing up to an enemy; it's sitting down and allowing God to do His good work inside you, preparing you for what's ahead.

■ ■ ■

*Dear heavenly Father, so often I want to run ahead, but Your love holds me back. Today
I give You my anxious worries, and thank You for settling my heart.*

Daily Bread

Give us today our daily bread.
MATTHEW 6:11 (NIV)

For me the Christmas season starts with the arrival of a care package from my step-mother. Every year Susan packages up peanut brittle, chocolate-dipped Oreos, exquisite sugar cookies, and other homemade creations.

"I don't know what it is about food your mother makes for you, especially when it's something that anyone can make—pancakes, meat loaf, tuna salad—but it carries a certain taste of memory," writes Mitch Albom. The same is true in an Amish home.

A few of one Amish family's favorite foods include pumpkin pie, chicken noodle soup, apple butter, chow-chow, soft pretzels, homemade doughnuts, and half-moon pies. Cooking is often a family event. Here is an example from the book *Visits with the Amish*:

> Since it's 11:00 in the morning, the girls begin to prepare dinner, their main meal of the day.
>
> Grace washes and tears apart some fresh leaf lettuce. "It's from our sister Mary Edna's garden," says Annie. "This year we couldn't plant lettuce because it rained so much. But my sister's garden is on a slope, so she could get hers in."
>
> Annie mixes a meatloaf using beef they butchered last fall. Regina peels potatoes and shows me how to poke the potatoes into a crank-style stainless steel shredder without getting my fingers nicked. . . .
>
> In the large Yoder kitchen, long and wide counters provide spacious work areas for all the daughters.

For the Amish, food brings not only the "taste of memory," but its preparation makes memories too.

The daily bread that God's Word speaks of refers to everything necessary to sustain life. Just as our bodies are dependent on food, our lives are daily dependent on God. We need Him, and that's exactly the way it should be.

"In winter, families will cut blocks of ice and store them, covered with sawdust, in well-insulated ice houses. They place the ice in the top compartments of their refrigerators; as the ice slowly melts, the cold water streams down the back into a catch basin and the air inside is kept cool."

■ ■ ■

Dear heavenly Father, thank You for our daily bread and for memories that come from enjoying food with family.

Called Out

The LORD had said to Abram, "Leave your native country, your relatives, and your father's family, and go to the land that I will show you."
GENESIS 12:1

Every time I merge onto the freeway by my home, I remember the first time I drove on it. I was trying to follow the GPS through a detoured construction zone. I'd moved from rural Montana to the "big city" of Little Rock, and I felt frazzled and zapped on most days as I tried to adjust.

For the Amish, moving isn't as big a deal, and many of them become experts at it! Here is writer David Schafer's observation about when he moved to Amish country.

> We popped in at Henry's shop from time to time. . . . On one visit Henry gave us some shocking news.
>
> "We'll be moving down to Windsor, Missouri, this fall." . . .
>
> They left behind lovingly worked gardens, bird houses and fences and yard plantings. They left neighbors, relatives, and friends.
>
> To most people, there is a loss of security in moving homes. It's traumatic for children who have to make new friends, go to new schools, and learn new areas. . . . But none of that applies to the Amish.
>
> They move to a place that has a school exactly like the last one. Same dress code, same curriculum, same holidays, same school bus (their own two feet or a pony and small buggy if they live farther away). Friends and relatives are probably already there and the new neighbors will soon be good friends that share chores and home church meetings and become part of their daily lives.

Love always finds a home in the heart of a friend.

PROVERB

Sometimes God asks us to step out of our comfort zones, and most of the time we don't find the new place the same as the old one. I'm so thankful that in the midst of life's changes, God never changes. He led Abram to a new place, not only to discover a Promised Land, but also so Abram would know God's promises better.

Are you feeling called out of your comfort zone? God will be with you wherever you go!

■ ■ ■

Dear heavenly Father, when I step out into the unknown, I'm thankful it gives me a chance to know You better.

Judge Not Yourselves

I, Paul, appeal to you with the gentleness and kindness of Christ—though I realize
you think I am timid in person and bold only when I write from far away.

2 CORINTHIANS 10:1

One of my favorite books about the Amish is *Plain Wisdom: An Invitation into an Amish
Home and the Hearts of Two Women*. It's written by two women, Cindy Woodsmall and
Miriam Flaud—one English and one Amish. They write about their unlikely friendship and how, over the years, the walls between them have broken down. Here's a bit
of Miriam's description of Cindy's first visit:

> The sound of a push reel mower could be heard from my
> kitchen window as my son Mark made the last few rounds
> in the front yard. We had been looking forward to this day
> for months. . . .
>
> Suddenly I went from being a little nervous to a
> lot nervous. What if she came all this way and was
> disappointed not only in my ability to hold a reasonable
> conversation but also in me as a person? We'd shared
> letters and long phone conversations, but what if I fell way
> short of her expectations once we were together?

"Experience is a
hard teacher. She
gives the test first,
then the lesson
afterward."

ATTRIBUTED TO
ALBERT EINSTEIN

It's only natural to worry about what other people think of us. We want approval.
We want to fit in. Sometimes we start fretting when we compare ourselves with
others—but sometimes we make the comparison with the "real" us and the person we
like to portray ourselves to be.

God judges people by what's in their hearts, not by the coolness of their personalities. Acts 10:34-36 puts it this way: "Peter fairly exploded with his good news: 'It's
God's own truth, nothing could be plainer: God plays no favorites! It makes no difference who you are or where you're from—if you want God and are ready to do as
he says, the door is open. The Message he sent to the children of Israel—that through
Jesus Christ everything is being put together again—well, he's doing it everywhere,
among everyone'" (*The Message*).

God is no respecter of persons, and He wants you to be the same, even with yourself.

■ ■ ■

*Dear heavenly Father, sometimes the person I'm the hardest on is me. Please help me to
offer myself the same grace that You give to me.*

Welcome Friends

Be inventive in hospitality.

ROMANS 12:13 (*THE MESSAGE*)

For years we had a small-group Bible study. In addition to the six couples, there were triple that many kids. We'd snack on food, study God's Word, and hope the kids weren't tearing up the upstairs too badly.

The Amish also find gathering with friends important. It's common to "go visiting" on the Sundays when there are no church services.

Families that go visiting on Sunday enjoy a diversity of age groups similar to their own. It is customary to arrive at the friend's house in the forenoon, often

It is better to be short on cash than short on character.

PROVERB

an hour before lunch. Three or four families may be present for the occasion. The men unhitch their horses and talk as they find their way to the house, where the women have been setting a long table with delicious foods. The sitting room fills with people who seat themselves in a circle and wait until the women call the men to dinner. Men gather around the table first, and the women stand back and take the unoccupied seats. A second seating is often necessary. The noon meal is the highlight of the day. An outdoor picnic or eating in cafeteria style, practiced by some Midwestern Amish families, is not considered good hospitality by the most formal Amish groups, to whom sitting at the table is important.

Do you have a group of friends that you can gather? Open your doors for a simple potluck, or be inventive—meet at a park or at a kid-friendly restaurant. Plan a regular time to read and study God's Word together.

Colossians 1:9-10 says, "We ask God to give you complete knowledge of his will and to give you spiritual wisdom and understanding. Then the way you live will always honor and please the Lord, and your lives will produce every kind of good fruit. All the while, you will grow as you learn to know God better and better." What a wonderful way to grow your friendships deeper!

Connecting your heart with others' is more important than what you do together, and I bet your friends will agree! You'll produce every kind of good fruit while laying out a good spread.

■ ■ ■

Dear heavenly Father, investments always take sacrifice, but I know that when I open my home to others, I'll realize that my sacrifice is a blessing instead!

Prince of Peace

A child is born to us, a son is given to us. . . . And he will be called:
Wonderful Counselor, Mighty God, Everlasting Father, Prince of Peace.

ISAIAH 9:6

These days there is more than enough Christmas cheer to go around. There are holiday parties, cookie exchanges, and children's programs. There are gifts to buy, and maybe cards to mail and homes to decorate as bright and beautiful as the magazine covers on the rack at the grocery store. Yet there is little peace. And on some busy, frantic holiday days I'm certain that I've forgotten that the whole thing is supposed to be about the Prince of Peace.

That title holds a lot of meaning.

Prince: "Jesus came and told his disciples, 'I have been given all authority in heaven and on earth'" (Matthew 28:18). We've given Jesus authority over our souls and our homes, but have we given Him authority over our Christmas celebrations?

Peace: "You will keep in perfect peace all who trust in you, all whose thoughts are fixed on you!" (Isaiah 26:3). When our minds are filled with all the tasks of Christmas, peace comes when we focus on the Prince of Christmas.

In the Amish home, preparations for Christmas start a few days (not a few months) before the holiday. If gifts are given, they are simple gifts for the children. There is often an Amish school Christmas program that focuses on Christ. In fact, in a book for Amish schoolteachers a new verse to the familiar carol "O Little Town of Bethlehem" was added:

O little Inn of Bethlehem
How like we are to you;
Our lives are crowded to the brim
With this and that to do.

We're not unfriendly to the King,
We mean well without doubt;
We have no hostile feelings,
We merely crowd Him out.

It seems even the youngest children know what Prince needs to reign in their Christmas! Can you make an effort to remember the same?

■ ■ ■

Dear heavenly Father, forgive me for my busy plans that tend to push You out. Help me to focus my thoughts on You today. It is there that I will find peace.

DECEMBER 16

Freedom!

If the Son sets you free, you are truly free.
JOHN 8:36

Sometimes I'm amazed at the freedoms we now take for granted that older generations couldn't appreciate. My grandma still seems horrified when I dress my little girls in cute blouses and jeans for church instead of putting them in dresses! Things change, and we embrace new kinds of freedom. This is even true of Christmas decorations in Amish homes. Author Cindy Woodsmall writes,

> I'm sure it won't surprise you when I say that the Amish use almost no decorations. Most Amish consider such "trappings" a distraction from the story of Christ's birth.

Freedom is not the right to do as you please but the liberty to do as you ought.

PROVERB

> But for many decades they've enjoyed making or buying Christmas cards, and they enjoy sending and receiving them. They often hang up the cards throughout their homes as a form of simple holiday trimming. Also, many Amish have traditionally put candles in the window and light them after dark, giving the house a warm, homey feel during Christmastime.
>
> Even the Amish, however, are not immune to change. As the years have progressed, they are enjoying a few more freedoms . . . and decorations. It is now common for some Amish to place battery-operated candles in their windows, although this wouldn't take place in several of my Amish friends' homes.
>
> Most Amish are comfortable putting candles surrounded by wreaths on surfaces throughout the house. But you won't find a Christmas tree or stockings hanging inside an Amish home. Based on the second commandment, which says not to make any graven image, you won't find a nativity scene or angel figurines, and definitely no traces of Santa.

Are there freedoms you are appreciating that earlier generations didn't get to experience? What about the freedoms that the next generation will embrace? Are you willing to have an open mind and heart about those things? The more we grow in our relationship in Christ, the more we understand that we have more freedoms than we first believed. Take time to consider whether the "shall nots" that you cling to are truly from God or from generations that came before you. When you grow in Christ's freedom, you are free indeed!

■ ■ ■

Dear heavenly Father, thank You for the freedom You give. Help me to embrace it more.

Thriving Vines

Your mother was like a vine planted by the water's edge. It had lush, green foliage because of the abundant water. Its branches became strong— strong enough to be a ruler's scepter. It grew very tall, towering above all others. It stood out because of its height and its many lush branches.

EZEKIEL 19:10-11

One of the hardest jobs in the world is being a parent. Children come with numerous needs, and when you add more than one child to the family, those needs seem to multiply. There are often more parenting requirements than minutes in the day, and as every parent knows, time is limited:

> Children are considered a gift from God and family size attests to that: the average Amish family has seven children. . . . With such a high birthrate, the Amish have become the fastest growing population in the United States. As of 2009, the Young Center for Anabaptist and Pietist Studies at Elizabethtown College in Pennsylvania calculated there are over 233,000 Amish. Over half the population is under eighteen years of age.
>
> "Children are the poor man's wealth," says one proverb. . . . One father wrote in *Family Life* magazine, "Children have only one childhood. We can fail in business and often times start over and make good. But if we fail in the teaching and training of our children, we never get another chance."

Children are living messages we send to a world we will not see.

PROVERB

Comments like these could make the role of parenting seem overwhelming, yet we are not left on our own in our efforts. John 15:4-5 says, "Remain in me, and I will remain in you. For a branch cannot produce fruit if it is severed from the vine, and you cannot be fruitful unless you remain in me. Yes, I am the vine; you are the branches. Those who remain in me, and I in them, will produce much fruit. For apart from me you can do nothing."

Yes, God's Word calls mothers a plant by the water's edge, but God does not make us struggle for all that we need. Jesus gives us more than tools to help us be good parents; He gives us Himself. Walk with Him today, and those in your family will be blessed!

■ ■ ■

Dear heavenly Father, how amazing it is that I can depend on You so that I might flourish!

Look at the Heart

*The LORD said to Samuel, "Don't judge by his appearance or height, for
I have rejected him. The LORD doesn't see things the way you see them.
People judge by outward appearance, but the LORD looks at the heart."*
1 SAMUEL 16:7

We shouldn't have judged the couple in our small Bible study, but when we looked at
their stylish clothes and model looks, my husband and I couldn't help it. They were
nice enough, but they just seemed too perfect. As the years passed, we got to know
their hearts, and they became our closest friends.

For many years Amish people's outward appearance was the last thing people
noticed. Back then the biggest difference was within their hearts.

**Not every cloud
brings rain.**

PROVERB

From the time the Amish came to the New World as part of
Penn's experiment, they worked hard, bonding together and
helping one another. Each patterned his life and person after
the humility and servant-likeness of Christ, drawing inner
strength from serving his fellow man.

The bonding reached beyond all boundaries. Everyone
stuck together, eyes open to love of God and neighbor, and free
from the religious persecution they had endured in 17th-century Europe (the Old
Country).

At first there was little distinction between the outward appearance of the Amish
and English (anyone not Amish). A spirit of brotherhood prevailed as both groups
embraced an agrarian style of life and spoke an unwritten dialect they brought from
the Old Country. Both the way of life and dialect originated with German Lowland
peasants in medieval times, known today as Pennsylvania Deitsch.

. . . Over time, the non-Amish changed in outward appearance and spoke
mainly English. But to this day, the Old Order clings to customs and dialect they
carried over from the Old Country.

Do you ever judge others by their outward appearance? If so, make an effort to find
out more about people than just what they wear. Some of the deepest—most bonded—
relationships can grow with those who appear different. Ask the Lord to show you
someone whose faith can be an example to you or whose fear you can calm today.

■ ■ ■

*Dear heavenly Father, forgive me when I focus only on what I can see in others. Show me
the hearts of those in my life—and guide me to unexpected friendships as only you can.*

The Shepherds' Story

After seeing [the baby], the shepherds told everyone what had
happened and what the angel had said to them about this child.
All who heard the shepherds' story were astonished.

LUKE 2:17-18

Have you shared any good news lately? I'm thankful that I'm able to share the Good News of Jesus through the written word and in that way touch the lives of people I'll never be able to meet. What an honor to tell others what Jesus has done in my life!

The Amish community does this, too, through their own publishing company. A distributor of their books states "Many Amish and Mennonite church schools, as well as homeschool families, use Pathway's popular Pathway Readers series. . . . Pathway also publishes numerous juvenile and adult fiction titles, as well as books on marriage, family life, and Amish beliefs and way of life." And it all started on an ordinary day in 1964:

The planning for this enterprise began in a wheatfield, as sheaves were being loaded for threshing, when two Amish farmers, David Wagler and Joseph Stoll, discussed the possibility of starting an Amish publishing company. Both men knew of old books that they believed should be reprinted. At the same time, an Amish minister had written a manuscript, "Worth Dying For," and was seeking a publisher. Wagler decided to open a bookstore and mail-order service in his farm home. The following year a third Amish farmer, Jacob Eicher, an experienced operator of threshing machines and sawmills, volunteered to operate a printing press. . . .

A child can read a parent's character before he can read the alphabet.

PROVERB

The offices of Pathway Publishers are housed in a single building on Rural Route 4, Aylmer, Ontario. There are no electric wires running from the community's power line to the building, for the presses and "electric" typewriters are operated with hydraulic fluid from a diesel motor.

All of us have been asked to proclaim the work of Jesus. Some do it with their voices, others through the written word. Sometimes God calls people who are well-schooled and well-funded to spread His Good News, but all He really needs—as Pathway Publishers proves—is a few humble servants with willing hearts.

■ ■ ■

Dear heavenly Father, I am astonished by how amazing You are. Use me in whatever manner You wish, for I know You'll go with me.

Remember Him

[Jesus] took some bread and gave thanks to God for it. Then he
broke it in pieces and gave it to the disciples, saying, "This is my
body, which is given for you. Do this to remember me."
LUKE 22:19

What are your family traditions? As Christmas nears, most of us have them. Do you attend a candlelight service on Christmas Eve? Go caroling or sing hymns around the piano? Do you open presents with other family members? To members of younger generations traditions may seem outdated or boring, but the Amish demonstrate that traditions will be valued later only if they are kept now:

The light that shines farthest, shines brightest at home.

PROVERB

We consider tradition as being spiritually helpful. Tradition can blind you if you adhere only to tradition and not the meanings of the tradition, but we really maintain a tradition. . . . We have some traditions, that some people question and I sometimes myself question, that are being maintained just because they are a tradition. This can be adverse, but it can also be a benefit. Tradition always looks bad if you're comparing one month to the next or one year to the next, but when you're talking fifty or more, tradition looks more favorable.

We may follow many spiritual traditions. But do we keep those traditions because they are truly helpful to us or only because we've always done certain things that way?

When Jesus instituted what we call the Lord's Supper, He was following the spiritual tradition of Passover, which was an important reminder of God's mercy to His people in Egypt. He didn't just want to add another tradition but was instituting a commemoration and an observation of His life and death for us. He wanted us to remember the manner of our salvation through all generations.

This Christmas, instead of observing traditions only for tradition's sake, take time to remember the meaning behind them. Consider the Presence behind the presents. Focus on the "Him" behind the hymns. Give your heart in service, both during a candlelight service and after the Christmas season. Finally, focus on the Christ in Christmas Day.

You might also think about new traditions you would like to start, traditions that will turn your heart to Jesus now and the hearts of coming generations in the future.

■ ■ ■

Dear heavenly Father, You are the reason for the season. May this be more than just
a catchy phrase to me in the days to come.

Wise Men and Women

About that time some wise men from eastern lands arrived in Jerusalem, asking, "Where is the newborn king of the Jews? We saw his star as it rose, and we have come to worship him."

MATTHEW 2:1-2

Some of the most memorable gifts we receive don't have great monetary value. Their value comes from the memories attached to them. My friend Elizabeth Byler Younts shares her mother's favorite Christmas memory from her Amish childhood.

> The melody of "Silent Night" weaved its way through the crevices of our old house. The wind echoed in tempo. I closed my eyes and sang in my heart the words. *Silent Night, Holy Night, All is calm, All is bright.*
>
> Every Christmas Eve *Deddy* would play a new harmonica, every Christmas song we knew, one after another, until the house was asleep. The next morning it would be gifted to one of us, one of the nine. In the moments I listened to this little concert, I pictured the special place I picked for *Mem* to place my three gifts. We didn't have a tree like my public schoolmates. I was sure it would be a dress and a piece of fruit. Would the third gift be a harmonica this year? Was it my turn?
>
> I fell asleep hoping I would be the lucky one to get the harmonica this year. I promised myself that if I did, I would learn to play better than anyone else. I promised that I would love to play as much as my *Deddy*.

To him hath God prepared, impearled
A crown eternity shall hold;
It shall not pass away, O world,
Away then, with your gain and gold.

FROM THE *AUSBUND*

You'll be happy to hear that Esther did receive the harmonica that year and still plays all the time.

Long ago, wise men saw a star rise, and they followed it to worship the King of the Jews. Today wise men—and wise women—worship Him in other ways. They worship Him by sharing hymns. They worship Him by creating special memories with their children. They worship Him by giving gifts. Wise people today may not give gold, frankincense, and myrrh, but their gifts are still meaningful.

■ ■ ■

Dear heavenly Father, sometimes the simplest things make the most impact. Show me what to focus on this Christmas season so that I will touch a loved one's heart.

No Ordinary Men

The members of the council were amazed when they saw the boldness of Peter and John, for they could see that they were ordinary men with no special training in the Scriptures. They also recognized them as men who had been with Jesus.
ACTS 4:13

One thing about being Amish is that you're recognized wherever you go. A woman wearing a kapp is setting a standard not only for herself but for her entire community. Amish men also have their own "dress code."

An Amish man begins growing a chin beard the preceding week of his marriage, but the upper lip and neck are kept clean shaven. This is in keeping with their non-conformity to "worldly" values and ways as an "outsider" where a mustache is often in evidence. A straight line is shaved across the back of his neck and his hair is bobbed in a "crock-like" appearance. An Amishman does not part his hair and it is not "tapered" on the sides. The men wear large, broad-brimmed black hats, suspenders, shirts without buttons or pockets, pants without hip pockets or zippers and underwear without stripes. All shirts are sewn in such a manner so as to necessitate being put on and removed by slipping them over the head. These are considered "orders" of the local church. Such "orders" may vary from one Amish community to another.

"Most of the Amish wear only plain, muted colors like blue, green, gray and black. No prints of any kind are allowed."

While most of us don't wear clothing that can distinguish us from others, no greater compliment can be given than the one Peter and John received from the council: "They also recognized them as men who had been with Jesus."

These men were open, confident, and concerned about others. They weren't educated in religious pursuits and weren't in public office, yet the words that came out of their mouths made the members of the council marvel.

Who comes to mind when you read the verse above? Can others say that it's obvious you've been with Jesus? When you walk with Him, it will be evident to others!

■ ■ ■

Dear heavenly Father, fill me today so my life can reflect Your light to a watching world.

Strong in His Hands

Mary responded, "Oh, how my soul praises the Lord. How my spirit rejoices in God my Savior! For he took notice of his lowly servant girl, and from now on all generations will call me blessed."

LUKE 1:46-48

One of my favorite Scripture verses is 1 Corinthians 1:27: "God chose the foolish things of the world to shame the wise; God chose the weak things of the world to shame the strong" (NIV). In an interesting way, God used simple Amish families to play a part in the larger story of land ownership in the United States in the eighteenth century. They proved to be shining examples for those around them and for generations to come.

In large part the Amish could acquire land as readily as they did because they were not like many of their colonial neighbors in an important respect. The Amish had immigrated as free people with the ability to control the terms and conditions of their work. During the eighteenth century, however, only about a quarter of all those who came to British North America did so as free labor. The Amish may not have realized how relatively unusual their status was, but that status was crucial to their communities' growth and economic success.

You can tell how big a person is by what it takes to discourage him.

PROVERB

If the Amish position as free laborers was notable, so too was their refusal to own slaves. . . . No records exist of any Amish family ever owning slaves.

Sometimes we feel as if we can't do much for God. We look to others with money or influence to make a difference, but in a way only God can, He chose to use simple things in life—simple people—to have the most impact. Mary was a "lowly servant girl," yet God asked her to be the mother of His Son. Her example of willing obedience to whatever God asked of her is remembered generations later.

Do you believe that God can use you in the same way? He can. Like Mary, listen when He calls you and rejoice at the task, even when you wonder how you'll ever accomplish it. You can never achieve what God desires, but *He can* through you. Trust Him in that.

■ ■ ■

Dear heavenly Father, I thank You for using the weak things of the world to shame the strong. I glorify You today and place myself in Your hands!

Christmas Laundry

Though your sins are like scarlet, I will make them as white as snow.
Though they are red like crimson, I will make them as white as wool.
ISAIAH 1:18

Do you like doing laundry, or do you consider it more a "necessary evil" in your life? Here's an example of an Amish wash day from years ago, and for Amish women, it hasn't changed much.

Wash day was the favorite day of the week for twins Lena and Wilma, now maiden ladies in their late fifties. On Monday mornings, after the breakfast dishes had been cleaned, the girls and their mother would collect dirty laundry from the last week and take it down to the wash house, separate from the house. . . . Each pile would be put into five-gallon pails, old paint pails given to them from the hardware store, then they would fill the pails with water and let the clothes soak for a few hours.

> Our duty is not to see through one another but to see one another through.
>
> PROVERB

Before lunch, the girls' mother would start boiling large kettles of water over a fire. . . . The girls' father helped to fill the wash tub with hot water before he went back to the fields for the afternoon. Their mother would first put the church clothes in the tub and add some soap. She took a plunger and agitated the soap, working the suds deep into the clothes for a few minutes. Then she got a long wooden stick—like a shepherd's crook—to lift the clothes out and into the rinse tub, filled with clean water.

Have you ever thought of the meaning behind Christmas laundry? Those swaddling clothes didn't wash themselves. It was the first time in eternity that God—the Everlasting One—needed someone to clean His clothes. In Jesus, God became fully human. A baby, a boy, a young man, and an adult who needed someone to scrub at His grass stains.

Jesus, God-come-to-earth, had a mind, a will, emotions, a body, and laundry. How amazing is it that the divine Son of God would not only take on our humanity but that He'd need fellow humans to help care for His humanity too!

■ ■ ■

Dear heavenly Father, thank You for humbling Yourself and allowing human beings to do Jesus' laundry so that He could wash our sins as white as snow.

Peace to Us

Christ himself has brought peace to us. He united Jews and
Gentiles into one people when, in his own body on the cross,
he broke down the wall of hostility that separated us.

EPHESIANS 2:14

When the Amish celebrate Christmas, there is no Santa Claus, no twinkling lights or decorated trees. They enjoy a feast, play games, throw snowballs if there's snow, and sing Christmas carols. They may decorate simply with candles and holly, but the focus is on the Christ child.

The Amish Cook, Lovina Eicher, describes a few things the Amish have in common with many of us: her love of a white Christmas and a growing family.

> We had a cold weekend, with the temperature going down to 2° F, and it was very windy. It's harder to keep the house cozy when that wind blows. Most of the snow is gone now. I keep hoping we might get just enough snow to cover the ground before Christmas.
>
> I always like to see a white Christmas. I guess we are never satisfied, are we? We should accept the weather however God sends it. Saturday is Christmas Day already.
>
> We will be home and take time to spend the day with the children. Let us take time to thank God for his many, many blessings on this day our dear Savior, Jesus Christ, was born. . . .
>
> Five of us daughters have moved to different places this year. Six of the oldest grandchildren have a "special" friend now. So along with the two new babies in the family this year, the family is growing in another way.

The best gift to the world was wrapped in a manger.

PROVERB

Isn't that a wonderful thing about Christmas—to see a bit of snow and new family members?

When Jesus came into the family of Mary and Joseph, everything changed. The Prince of Peace made the lives we live possible. Whether Amish or English, we can find true peace, for Christ Himself brought peace to us.

Whatever you do, no matter how you celebrate Christmas, may Jesus be at the center of your celebration, just as He was the center of God's gift of love to us.

■ ■ ■

Dear heavenly Father, thank You for the greatest gift of all, Your Son, and for the peace He brought to us.

The Most Important Role

*Children born to a young man are like arrows in a warrior's
hands. How joyful is the man whose quiver is full of them!*
PSALM 127:4-5

Some time ago my husband and I welcomed two foster children into our home. These children came with worries and fears and bad habits we needed to cope with. Some days I felt as if I were just spinning my wheels. What helped the most was thinking of my three grown children. They each love God and share the light of Jesus in numerous ways. When I saw that, I realized the daily work was worth it. Today, tomorrow, I'm gently molding my children into the adults they will someday be.

Author Louise Stoltzfus shares how one minister shared this truth in a unique way during an Amish church service:

The foundation of understanding is the willingness to listen.

PROVERB

On this particular Sunday morning, a minister from another Amish district was present and was asked to give the main morning sermon.

In the warm, lilting, singsong cadence of Amish preachers, he spoke about personal responsibility in the church. At one point, Esther says, he paused to ask the question, "Who has the most important role in the church? The deacon? The minister? The bishop?"

Turning to face the side of the room where most of the women were seated, he proclaimed, "No, it is not the deacon, the minister, or the bishop; it is the mothers with babies on their laps who have the most important task in our church." A hush fell over the already quiet room.

Mothers with babies on their laps snuggled them a bit closer.

Fathers nodded their heads ever so slightly.

The day after Jesus' birth, no one knew the impact He would have on the world, on our souls. It's amazing that God chose to free the world by offering a babe in a manger.

Only God can see the potential of the children in our lives, and while it might take dozens of years for us to see it, know that when you give the gift of yourself to a child, you are having an impact on posterity in immeasurable ways.

■ ■ ■

*Dear heavenly Father, I thank You for all those who poured themselves into me. I pray that
You will use me to do the same for others.*

A Grandparent's Love

Naomi took the baby and cuddled him to her breast.
And she cared for him as if he were her own.

RUTH 4:16

Do you remember who loved you first? Did your grandparents pop into your head? I remember curling up next to my grandfather and watching old John Wayne movies while my grandmother cooked up a special lunch. I remember sitting between them in the front seat of their Buick and listening to hymns on their 8-track tape player. I remember them taking me shopping to get a sweatshirt jacket just like Olivia Newton-John's.

Amish novelist Jerry S. Eicher shares some special memories of his Amish grandparents.

> [Grandfather Eicher's] preaching is still a distinct memory. When I remember him speaking, I see his face lifted toward the ceiling, his hands clasped in front of him, his white beard flowing over his arms. He could chant a thousand miles an hour, or so it seemed to me. A person could lose himself in that voice. It was as if I were enveloped in love and acceptance. In his preaching, he was never going anywhere particular. He had no agenda. He simply exalted in the holy words, as if he were glad to be part of such a great thing.
>
> Grandmother Eicher could chatter during the week about as fast as Grandfather Eicher did on Sundays. She'd say hi, give out a long stream of words, and then bustle on. There was always something going on at her house. She came from Arthur, Illinois. Grandfather made contact with her from his world in Davies County, Indiana. My guess is they met when he visited Arthur on weekends for weddings or funerals, typical Amish reasons to travel to another town.

First love does not rust.

PROVERB

It's said that grandchildren are a special gift to grandparents, but the opposite is true too. Do you have special memories of a grandparent? Take time to write them down for your children or grandchildren. If you still have a grandparent living, make a point to give him or her a call. A grandparent's love is to be cherished and enjoyed!

■ ■ ■

Dear heavenly Father, I thank You for the grandparents who first loved me and opened my heart to the love of others.

Ask. Seek. Knock. Share!

*I tell you, even though he will not get up and give you the bread
because of friendship, yet because of your shameless audacity
he will surely get up and give you as much as you need.*

LUKE 11:8 (NIV)

Whenever a new Amish community starts, someone always has to go first. Here's a portion of a story from Ezra E. Miller, who moved from Michigan to Sikeston, Missouri, with his wife and four small children in 1927.

"Not a day passes over the earth, but men and women of no note do great deeds, speak great words, and suffer noble sorrows."

CHARLES READE,
*THE CLOISTER AND
THE HEARTH*

I went to the bank for money but the banker said he couldn't give me any and that I should ask Manassas Bontrager for some. I went to Manasses. He gave me a check of fifteen dollars. I took this to the Tanner store. I bought $5.00 worth of groceries for the family. The rest of the money he gave me in change: 5¢, 10¢, and 25¢. I had a pocketful of money. This paid my trip to Arthur, Illinois.

I arrived at Ed Yoder's at one o'clock at night, the evening before Thanksgiving. Friday and Saturday I husked corn. Then it snowed and I could not husk any more. I then went to Dan Otto's shop. His wife was my wife's cousin. From Thanksgiving until Christmas there were only four days I could husk. But I worked at Dan Otto's. The money I got I sent to my wife and children. I left for home the day after Christmas.

We like to provide for ourselves, but sometimes, like the neighbor in Luke 11, we must plead our case to others. A woman needed bread for a visitor, and she knocked at her neighbor's door until she received some. Did she get chided for this wake-up call? No.

Sometimes God provides through extraordinary means, but sometimes God brings others to help us. It's also a reminder of how we must look to God: "I tell you, keep on asking, and you will receive what you ask for. Keep on seeking, and you will find. Keep on knocking, and the door will be opened to you" (Luke 11:9).

Ask. Knock. Receive. Share!

■ ■ ■

Dear heavenly Father, thank You for those who help and give, and thank You for always answering my prayers.

A Watchful Eye

Look at the birds. They don't plant or harvest or store food in barns, for your heavenly Father feeds them. And aren't you far more valuable to him than they are?

MATTHEW 6:26

In the spring, baby robins stretch their necks for food. Ducks and ducklings cross the road. The spring air around an Amish home echoes with birdsong, but spring isn't the only time the Amish enjoy the birds. Many Amish in eastern Ohio take part in the Christmas Bird Count. This count is organized and run by the National Audubon Society, and it has become a fun Christmas tradition for many families. From December 14 through January 5, Amish birders and others observe, count, and record their findings.

The Christmas Bird Count (CBC) began in 1900 when ornithologist Frank Chapman became concerned about the slaughter of birds and mammals around Christmas. People would celebrate the holiday by going out and shooting anything that moved. Chapman, a prominent ornithologist, organized instead a day for bird-counting rather than bird-shooting. He got local groups to count and record the numbers of birds and numbers of species they had seen during a pre-chosen, 24-hour period within a pre-determined count circle. During the first count, around Christmas 1900, 25 groups—which included 27 participants—recorded 90 species and more than 18,000 individual birds.

"Use what talent you possess: the woods would be very silent if no birds sang except those that sang the best."

ATTRIBUTED TO HENRY DAVID THOREAU

The Amish community in Holmes County, Ohio, has become one of the more popular places to find rare birds. Local birding enthusiasts—mainly Amish birders—even started a birding journal, the *Bobolink*.

Watching birds reminds us of our Savior's care. It also reminds us of the wonder of being unique and individual, just like the different species of birds. If God has a plan for each small bird, doesn't He also have a plan for each of us? If God cares for the small creatures who live in the harsh elements, won't He provide for us, too? The next time you see a bird, remember this: God's care for us is even greater than His care for the birds. He watches us, counts us, and records the joy we bring to Him.

■ ■ ■

Dear heavenly Father, I thank You for Your faithful care for me, so much greater than for the sparrows. Thank You, Lord, that Your watchful eye is always on me!

Wholehearted Devotion

Commit yourselves wholeheartedly to these words of mine. Tie them to your hands and wear them on your forehead as reminders. Teach them to your children.
DEUTERONOMY 11:18-19

In the Amish community, work connects families and the communities. The Amish believe that work is God given, and there is joy to be had in work together. That's a good thing because there's a lot of it!

The floors must be scrubbed, the beds made, and the living areas tidied and dusted. Windows and walls need to be washed and the porches swept. Sewing and mending for all the family members seem to be never-ending tasks. Outside, there's lawn mowing and planting and weeding to be done. Chickens must be watered and fed and fresh eggs gathered. In season, the family garden must be harvested, and hundreds of jars of food need to be preserved for the coming winter. Making quilts to sell or working in a cottage industry on the property can also take up hours in her day.

A family that works together grows together.

PROVERB

The list of tasks is long, but the Amish know how to work. In fact, their industriousness is one of the stumbling blocks for people seeking to join their communities. If people haven't been taught to work hard when they're young, it's difficult to catch that work ethic later in life. For the Amish, working hard is embraced as part of what it means to be an adult. And because their work serves the purpose of caring for those they love, it's considered a joy by most of them.

As I read this, I couldn't help but think how our children's lives would be different if we taught them such a work ethic. Even more, if we taught them to be as diligent in learning about God and turning to Him in prayer.

First John 5:14-15 says, "We are confident that he hears us whenever we ask for anything that pleases him. And since we know he hears us when we make our requests, we also know that he will give us what we ask for."

It's up to us to train our children in what they need to know for this life and for eternity.

■ ■ ■

Dear heavenly Father, please give me wholehearted devotion in training children to have wholehearted devotion.

God's Help from Old Year to New

GOD is good, a hiding place in tough times. He recognizes and
welcomes anyone looking for help, no matter how desperate the
trouble. But cozy islands of escape He wipes right off the map.

NAHUM 1:7-8 (*THE MESSAGE*)

If you could create a perfect end to your year, what would that be? Sitting by a cozy fire, playing puzzles and games, or maybe spending time outside having snowball fights and sleigh rides? The perfect end to the year is also a great time to seek God for the year to come. Has reading about the Amish had an impact on you? Is your relationship with God closer? Have you made an attempt to put aside some of the world's ways to follow God's ways more faithfully?

Take a few moments and write down any changes you may already have made. Are there goals you would still like to work toward in the coming year?

> May our lives be like arithmetic: friends added, enemies subtracted, sorrows divided, joys multiplied.
>
> PROVERB

[The Amish] dress differently and travel differently, but their goals are essentially the same as the goals of most other people: to live happily in this life and to do the same in the next life. They just happen to have chosen a road less traveled to reach their goals.

Their beliefs tell them that cars and other modern gadgets won't help them find happiness or salvation, but Amish life isn't about what they don't have. Instead, it's about what they do have. They have strong Christian faiths, strong families and communities, and their lives aren't really as simple as they may appear. . . . Amish lives still focus on God, family, and hard work, but their lives are definitely not the same as they were in the 1700s, as some writers like to romanticize.

You may have discovered that you're more like an Amish person than you thought, and when you seek God, He will help with faith, family, and community. He is the One who brings peace. He can keep us from the distractions of the world and guide us in focusing on simplicity of the heart. Seek Him faithfully in the year to come, and in Him you will find help.

■ ■ ■

Dear heavenly Father, thank You for the year that has finished, and for the year to come.
I can face the future knowing You are already there.

Endnotes

January 4: "to the next": www.funtrivia.com/en/subtopics/Those-Amazing-Amish-346109.html.

January 10: "done by hand": www.articles3k.com/article/460/160039/Amish_Quilting
_Was_Once_Thought_Revolutionary/.

January 17: "among others": http://amishamerica.com/amish_folks_lik/.

January 21: "men do not": http://christianity.about.com/od/Amish-Religion/a/Amish-Life
-And-Culture.htm.

January 27: "she left behind": *Ausbund*, 113:18.

January 28: "My friend Kendra": Kendra's name, along with others in the book have been
changed to protect the individuals' privacy.

February 3: "heartfelt mystery": *The Brethren Hymnal: A Collection of Psalms, Hymns, and
Spiritual Songs* (Elgin, IL: Brethren Publishing House, 1901), no. 344.

February 6: "together on this day": The typical district has about eighty adults and about ninety
children under age nineteen. Based on data collected from Lancaster county. Kraybill (2001),
p. 91.

February 6: "in financial need": www.jamesfreespiritual.org/2012/09/the-amish-just-what-you
-really-need-to.html.

February 7: "of preserving foods": www.rachaelray.com/recipe.php?recipe_id=1339.

February 11: "the years 1535–1540": http://amishamerica.com/ausbund/.

February 12: "in High German": www.padutchcountry.com/towns-and-heritage/amish
-country/amish-religious-traditions.asp.

February 17: "bonnet at all": http://amishwoodworks.com/history_of_the_amish.htm.

February 17: "near Andover, Ohio": http://amishamerica.com/what-colors-are-amish-buggies/.

February 19: "King James translation": http://amishamerica.com/which-bible-do-the-amish-use/.

February 21: "settlement remains today": www.religionfacts.com/christianity/denominations
/amish.htm.

February 22: "a chain letter": www.friendshipbreadkitchen.com/amish-friendship-bread.

February 23: "or write it": www.apostolicfriendsforum.com/archive/index.php/t-23900.html.

February 27: "eighteen to twenty years": "Amish Population Trends 2012, One-Year Highlights,"
The Young Center for Anabaptist and Pietist Studies, Elizabethtown College. Available at
www2.etown.edu/amishstudies/Population_Trends_2012.asp.

March 2: "traditional prayer": Donald B. Kraybill, *The Riddle of Amish Culture* (Baltimore:
Johns Hopkins University Press, 1989), 123.

March 5: "practice stands out": http://amishamerica.com/the-holy-kiss.

March 8: "Suzanne Woods Fisher": Suzanne Woods Fisher, *Amish Values for Your Family*
(Grand Rapids, MI: Revell, 2011), 19.

March 10: "hands of God": Donald B. Kraybill, "Why the Amish Forgive so Quickly," *Christian
Science Monitor,* October 2, 2007. Available at www.csmonitor.com/2007/1002/p09s02-coop.
html

March 11: "or to ponder": *Merriam-Webster's Collegiate Dictionary*, 11th edition, see
"contemplate." Regarding the start of new Amish communities, see www.thecontemplation
.com/index.php/2012/07/28/religion-news-the-amish-are-coming.

March 11: "three and a half weeks": Nap Nazworth, "Study: New Amish Community Founded Every 3½ Weeks," *The Christian Post*, August 5, 2012. Available at www.christianpost.com /news/study=new=amish=community=founded=every=3=1=2=weeks=79491/.

March 17: "fifty United States": www.washingtontimes.com/news/2012/aug/9/amish-enjoy -unexpected-boom-in-numbers/?page=all.

March 18: "perfect example": Mary Miller, *Our Heritage, Hope and Faith* (Mary Miller, 2000), 321.

March 18: "into the ground": http://dying.about.com/b/2006/10/07/amish-death-dying-and -funeral-traditions.htm.

March 20: "gifts to you": *Rules of a Godly Life*, part 3, section 7, www.pbs.org/wgbh /americanexperience/features/primary-resources/amish-rules/.

March 21: "drained, empty": www.terilynneu.com/2012/11/when-god-draws-near-our-need -for-redemption/?utm_source=feedburner&utm_medium=email&utm_campaign=Feed%3A +PleasingToYou+%28Teri+Lynne+Underwood%29.

March 21: "hope": http://dictionary.reference.com/browse/trust?s=t.

March 22: "greater punishment": *Rules of a Godly Life*, part 1, section 7, www.pbs.org/wgbh /americanexperience/features/primary-resources/amish-rules.

March 23: "take for granted": Donald B. Kraybill, Steven M. Nolt, and David L. Weaver-Zercher, *The Amish Way: Patient Faith in a Perilous World* (San Francisco: Jossey-Bass, 2010), 94.

March 24: "my fellow-men": Arthur Bennett, ed., *The Valley of Vision* (Edinburgh, Scotland: Banner of Truth, 1975), 327.

March 26: "repent and believe": www.800padutch.com/amishfaith.shtml.

March 29: "to listen to": http://toginet.com/shows/amishwisdom.

March 29: "adjacent house": www2.etown.edu/amishstudies/Family.asp.

March 30: "lives managing them": Mark Batterson, *The Circle Maker: Praying Circles around Your Biggest Dreams and Greatest Fears* (Grand Rapids, MI: Zondervan, 2011), 168.

March 31: "on the ground": http://dictionary.reference.com/browse/humble.

Spring: "Fastnachts": Recipe from www.amyclipston.com/recipe-fastnachts.html.

April 2: "Pennsylvania in 1681": www.cosimobooks.com/classics_author.php?author=4619.

April 2: "[William's father]": www.cosimobooks.com/classics_author.php?author=4619.

April 2: "Lancaster County, Pennsylvania": www.ushistory.org/penn/bio.htm.

April 6: "helping a neighbor": Melea Burke, "Simply Serving: Amish Community Lends a Hand to Valley View Family," *Valley Journal*, December 14, 2011. See also www.valleyjournal .net/Article/770/Simply-serving-Amish-community-lends-a-hand-to-Valley-View-family.

April 9: "labor-intensive hours": www.purecanadamaple.com/pure-maple-syrup/how-maple -syrup-is-made.

April 10: "more acceptable": Lorilee Craker, *Money Secrets of the Amish: Finding True Abundance in Simplicity, Sharing, and Saving* (Nashville: Nelson, 2011), 10.

April 14: "seem like work": http://blog.thebarninn.com/2012/04/amish-community-work -ethic-and.html.

April 17: "forth to sow": http://accad.osu.edu/~midori/Game/intro_religion.html.

April 17: "voice and melody": http://accad.osu.edu/~midori/Game/intro_religion.html.

April 18: "atonement": Mary Miller, *Our Heritage, Hope and Faith* (Mary Miller, 2000), 82.

April 18: "coming year": www.amishnews.com/featurearticles/easter.htm.

April 19: "dandelions": Lovina Eicher and Kevin Williams, *The Amish Cook at Home* (Riverside, NJ: Andrews McMeel, 2008), 2.

April 19: "winter is through": Lovina Eicher and Kevin Williams, *The Amish Cook at Home* (Riverside, NJ: Andrews McMeel, 2008), 14.

April 20: "end of harvest": http://accad.osu.edu/~midori/Game/intro_religion.html.

April 23: "laundry": Elizabeth Byler Younts, "Hanging Laundry" (November 26, 2012), http://notquiteamishliving.com/2012/11/hanging-laundry.

April 25: "shed for us": Mary Miller, *Our Heritage, Hope and Faith* (Mary Miller, 2000), 77.

April 27: "break from them": www.pbs.org/wgbh/americanexperience/features/primary-resources/amish-rules.

April 27: "Communion Service": http://aboutamish.blogspot.com/2011/04/amish-communion-service.html.

April 29: "Matthew 6:9-13": Donald B. Kraybill, Steven M. Nolt, and David L. Weaver-Zercher, *The Amish Way: Patient Faith in a Perilous World* (San Francisco: Jossey-Bass, 2010), 26.

April 30: "all the world": Brad Igou, *The Amish in Their Own Words* (Scottdale, PA: Herald Press, 1999), 248.

May 1: "while plowing": www.ehow.com/facts_7376208_amish-plows-cultivators.html.

May 1: "soil deficiencies": http://accad.osu.edu/~midori/Game/intro_farm.html.

May 2: "truly tested": David Luthy, *The Amish in America: Settlements That Failed, 1840–1960* (LaGrange, IN: Pathway, 1986).

May 2: "from working": Doyle Yoder and Leslie A. Kelly, *America's Amish Country* (Millersburg, OH: America's Amish Country Publications, 1992), 48.

May 7: "glorify Thee": Mary Miller, *Our Heritage, Hope and Faith* (Mary Miller, 2000), 68.

May 8: "our hearts": Mary Miller, *Our Heritage, Hope and Faith* (Mary Miller, 2000), 55.

May 9: "in 1693": www.welcome-to-lancaster-county.com/amish-community.html.

May 11: "again by age": http://aboutamish.blogspot.com/2011/04/amish-communion-service.html.

May 13: "twenty minutes": http://aboutamish.blogspot.com/search?q=foresinger.

May 13: "grow cold": www.homecomers.org/mirror/ausbund.htm.

May 15: "put them in": Joe Eicher, quoted in Lovina Eicher and Kevin Williams, *The Amish Cook at Home* (Riverside, NJ: Andrews McMeel, 2008), 11.

May 16: "imprints": www.padutchcountry.com/members/mud_sales.asp.

May 16: "their area": www.libbymt.com/news/2010/06/AmishAuctioninRexfor.htm.

May 17: "generation to generation": Suzanne Woods Fisher, *Amish Proverbs: Words of Wisdom from the Simple Life* (Grand Rapids, MI: Revell, 2010), 12.

May 18: "medical technicians": Jon Rutter, "Amish, Other Plain, Fill Ranks of Fire and Ambulance Companies," *Lancaster Sunday News*, July 8, 2012. See also www.whitehorsefire.org/apps/public/news/newsView.cfm?News_ID=462.

May 18: "before they're married": www.pennlive.com/midstate/index.ssf/2012/07/amish_firefighters.html.

May 20: "was avoided": John A. Hostetler, *Amish Society* (Baltimore: Johns Hopkins, 1993), 373.

May 22: "talkative children": http://amishamerica.com/at-the-amish-table.

May 23: "better use": Brad Igou, *The Amish in Their Own Words* (Harrisonburg, VA: Herald Press, 1999), 187.

May 24: "between hymns": http://amishamerica.com/at-an-amish-youth-singing.

May 28: "renewed": Lovina Eicher and Kevin Williams, *The Amish Cook at Home* (Riverside, NJ: Andrews McMeel, 2008), 1.

May 29: "(exalt) this?": Mary Miller, *Our Heritage, Hope and Faith* (Mary Miller, 2000), 87.

May 29: "needs arise": Donald B. Kraybill, Karen M. Johnson-Weiner, and Steven M. Nolt, *The Amish* (Baltimore: Johns Hopkins University Press, 2013), 85.

May 30: "than the rest": http://amishamerica.com/ausbund/?cid=25594.

June 1: "Amish community": www.amishmennonitequilts.com/child2.html.

June 3: "minute of it": Jennifer Hatmaker, *A Modern Girl's Guide to Bible Study* (Colorado Springs: NavPress, 2006), 16.

June 4: "adult life": Lovina Eicher and Kevin Williams, *The Amish Cook at Home* (Riverside, NJ: Andrews McMeel, 2008), 51.

June 5: "bare feet": http://derdutchman.wordpress.com/2010/07/22/how-do-amish-beat -the-heat.

June 6: "no pressures": http://notquiteamishliving.com/2012/12/family-memories.

June 14: "they repent": www.welcome-to-lancaster-county.com/amish-community.html.

June 15: "teaching the child": http://amishamerica.com/how-do-amish-discipline-children.

June 16: "He makes": www.mamalisa.com/?t=es&p=1247&c=169.

June 16: "from others": www.reviveourhearts.com/articles/growing-in-gratitude-a-30-day -challenge.

June 17: "group witness": Steven M. Nolt, *A History of the Amish* (Intercourse, PA: Good Books, 2003), 5.

June 17: "outside the faith": http://pittsburgh.about.com/cs/pennsylvania/a/amish_3.htm.

June 18: "government control": Steven M. Nolt, *A History of the Amish* (Intercourse, PA: Good Books, 2003), 10.

June 18: "punishable by death": www.welcome-to-lancaster-county.com/amish-belief.html.

June 19: "city walls": Steven M. Nolt, *A History of the Amish* (Intercourse, PA: Good Books, 2003), 12.

June 19: "and Moravia": Steven M. Nolt, *A History of the Amish* (Intercourse, PA: Good Books, 2003), 12.

June 20: "the Anabaptists": Steven M. Nolt, *A History of the Amish* (Intercourse, PA: Good Books, 2003), 14.

June 21: "church discipline": Steven M. Nolt, *A History of the Amish* (Intercourse, PA: Good Books, 2003), 14.

June 22: "our lives": http://notquiteamishliving.com/2012/11/almost-amish-five-more-principles -for-a-slower-simpler-more-sustainable-life.

June 22: "good home": http://notquiteamishliving.com/2012/11/almost-amish-five-more -principles-for-a-slower-simpler-more-sustainable-life.

June 24: "school year": Lovina Eicher and Kevin Williams, *The Amish Cook at Home* (Riverside, NJ: Andrews McMeel, 2008), 52.

June 24: "Ohio and Indiana": http://pittsburgh.about.com/cs/pennsylvania/a/amish.htm.

June 25: "in 1693": http://pittsburgh.about.com/cs/pennsylvania/a/amish_3.htm.

June 26: "some worth!": Mary Miller, *Our Heritage, Hope and Faith* (Mary Miller, 2000), 242.

June 27: "in God's glory": http://notquiteamishliving.com/2012/12/a-childs-funeral-song.

June 28: "he said": *The Budget*, PO Box 249, Sugarcreek, Ohio 44681. See also http:// notquiteamishliving.com/2012/09/the-amish-in-their-own-words.

June 29: "piercing wisdom": Suzanne Woods Fisher, *Amish Peace: Simple Wisdom for a Complicated World* (Grand Rapids, MI: Revell, 2009), 45.

June 30: "bigger wrongs": Nancy Sleeth, *Almost Amish: One Woman's Quest for a Slower, Simpler, More Sustainable Life* (Carol Stream, IL: Tyndale, 2012), 209.

Summer: "Happiness": Author unknown.

July 1: "bounty of grain": http://accad.osu.edu/~midori/Game/intro_religion.html.

July 2: "their disobedience": http://christianity.about.com/od/Amish-Religion/a/Amish-Beliefs .htm.

July 4: "displays of patriotism": http://amishamerica.com/a-note-on-the-amish-patriotism-and-july-4th.

July 4: "granting time off": http://amishamerica.com/the-amish-and-easter-monday.

July 5: "spiritual kingdom": http://amishamerica.com/why-dont-amish-serve-in-the-military.

July 6: "settled in 1808": Doyle Yoder and Leslie A. Kelley, *America's Amish Country II* (Millersburg, OH: America's Amish Country Publications), 6.

July 7: "values and visibility": Richard A. Stevick, *Growing Up Amish: The Teenage Years* (Baltimore: Johns Hopkins University Press, 2007), 232–33.

July 8: "school system": www.amishnews.com/amisharticles/amishchildren.htm.

July 9: "head scarves": www.irawagler.com/?p=673.

July 10: "property in common": Hans Betz, *Ausbund*, 108:5–6. See also bm-www.homecomers.org/mirror/ausbund.htm.

July 10: "torture in 1537": http://thecommonlife.com.au/SoS/10.pdf.

July 12: "seemed hopeless": Malinda Detweiler, *I Was Amish: A Personal Story of an Amish Girl and Her Life* (Bloomington, IN: Exlibris, 2011), 90.

July 13: "from others": www.amishnews.com/amisharticles/amishchildren.htm.

July 13: "non-Amish women": Donald B. Kraybill, Steven M. Nolt, and David L. Weaver-Zercher, *The Amish Way: Patient Faith in a Perilous World* (San Francisco: Jossey-Bass, 2010), 184.

July 14: "wedding feast": www.padutchcountry.com/towns-and-heritage/amish-country/amish-religious-traditions.asp.

July 15: "family liabilities": Richard A. Stevick, *Growing Up Amish: The Teenage Years* (Baltimore: Johns Hopkins University Press, 2007), 44.

July 16: "skates, and more": Mindy Starns Clark, *A Pocket Guide to Amish Life* (Eugene, OR: Harvest House, 2010), 80.

July 17: "as they term it": Richard A. Stevick, *Growing Up Amish: The Teenage Years* (Baltimore: Johns Hopkins University Press, 2007), 43.

July 18: "on a scooter": Mindy Starns Clark, *A Pocket Guide to Amish Life* (Eugene, OR: Harvest House, 2010), 87.

July 19: "church districts": www2.etown.edu/amishstudies/Diversity.asp.

July 20: "faith foundation": Richard A. Stevick, *Growing Up Amish: The Teenage Years* (Baltimore: Johns Hopkins University Press, 2007), 38.

July 20: "evening singings": Richard A. Stevick, *Growing Up Amish: The Teenage Years* (Baltimore: Johns Hopkins University Press, 2007), 40.

July 21: "with requests": Louise Stoltzfus, *Amish Women: Lives and Stories* (Intercourse, PA: Good Books, 1994), 57–58.

July 21: "for the father": http://amishbuggy.tripod.com/amishtidbits.htm.

July 22: "Amish circles": Steven M. Nolt, *A History of the Amish* (Intercourse, PA: Good Books, 2003), 20–21.

July 23: "is permitted": Charles Scott Rice and John B. Shenk Rice, *Meet the Amish: A Pictorial Study of the Amish People* (New Brunswick, NJ: Rutgers University Press, 1947), 7.

July 24: "over the matter": Charles Scott Rice and John B. Shenk Rice, *Meet the Amish: A Pictorial Study of the Amish People* (New Brunswick, NJ: Rutgers University Press, 1947), 16.

July 24: "barns he builds": Charles Scott Rice and John B. Shenk Rice, *Meet the Amish: A Pictorial Study of the Amish People* (New Brunswick, NJ: Rutgers University Press, 1947), 7.

July 25: "way of life": http://suzannewoodsfisher.com/blog/2012/12/thursday-on-amish-wisdom-2.

July 26: "core values": Richard A. Stevick, *Growing Up Amish: The Teenage Years* (Baltimore: Johns Hopkins University Press, 2007), 5.

July 26: "get a GED": Mindy Starns Clark, *A Pocket Guide to Amish Life* (Eugene, OR: Harvest House, 2010), 103.

July 27: "recipe for success": *Merriam-Webster's Collegiate Dictionary*, 11th edition, see "recipe."

July 29: "united as a people": Mindy Starns Clark, *A Pocket Guide to Amish Life* (Eugene, OR: Harvest House, 2010), 47–48.

July 31: "something right": Suzanne Woods Fisher, "Plain Talk about the Amish: Why Do They Fascinate Us?" (August 31, 2011). See http://blogs.christianpost.com/amish-principles -for-families/plain-talk-about-the-amish-why-do-they-fascinate-us-6842.

August 2: "forget that": Joe Wittmer, PhD, *The Gentle People: Personal Reflections of Amish Life* (Minneapolis: Educational Media Corporation, 1990), 35.

August 2: "by a tornado": Doyle Yoder and Leslie A. Kelley, *America's Amish Country* (Millersburg, OH: America's Amish Country Publications), 18.

August 3: "bestowed upon me": Joe Wittmer, PhD, *The Gentle People: Personal Reflections of Amish Life* (Minneapolis: Educational Media Corporation, 1990), 77.

August 5: "14,000 steps": http://well.blogs.nytimes.com/2010/10/19/the-pedometer-test -americans-take-fewer-steps.

August 6: "relish": www.amishnews.com/featurearticles/pennsylvania_dutch_food_favorite.htm.

August 7: "fall myself in luff": *Ferhoodled English, a Collection of Quaintly Amusing Expressions Heard Among the Pennsylvania Dutch Folks* (Gettysburg, PA: Conestoga Crafts, 1964).

August 10: "all eternity": Amy Schlabach, *Times of Trial: Poem Stories of Anabaptist Martyrs for Children* (Sugar Creek, OH: Carlisle Press, 2011), 14–15.

August 12: "moved again": Suzanne Woods Fisher, "Plain Talk about the Amish: Seventy Times Seven" (Sepember 11, 2012), http://blogs.christianpost.com/amish-principles-for-families /plain-talk-about-the-amish-seventy-times-seven-11874/.

August 13: "come on home": Brad Igou, *The Amish in Their Own Words* (Scottdale, PA: Herald Press, 1999), 161–62.

August 14: "coming generations": *Family Life*, June 2010, 2–3.

August 15: "your visitors": *Family Life,* June 2010, 3.

August 16: "own them": Brad Igou, *The Amish in Their Own Words* (Scottdale, PA: Herald Press, 1999), 159.

August 17: "freshly baked pies": Lovina Eicher and Kevin Williams, *The Amish Cook's Anniversary Book* (Riverside, NJ: Andrews McMeel, 2010), 1.

August 17: "was created": http://suzannewoodsfisher.com/blog/2011/07/thursday-on-amish -wisdom-the-amish-cooks-kevin-williams-with-guest-host-judy-christie.

August 18: "blessings from above": Lovina Eicher and Kevin Williams, *The Amish Cook's Anniversary Book* (Riverside, NJ: Andrews McMeel, 2010), 1.

August 18: "wear a veil": www.cindywoodsmall.com/2012/09/18/amish-wedding-day/.

August 20: "to show love": http://notquiteamishliving.com/2013/02/dating-daughters-and -sons.

August 21: "something new": David Weaver-Zercher, *Writing the Amish: The Worlds of John A. Hostetler* (University Park, PA: Pennsylvania State University Press, 2005), 183.

August 21: "believe in": http://christianity.about.com/od/Amish-Religion/a/Amish -Beliefs.htm.

August 22: "even unspoken": Laura Katz Olson, ed., *Age through Ethnic Lenses: Caring for the Elderly in a Multicultural Society* (Lanham, MD: Rowman and Littlefield, 2001), 144.

August 22: "cooperative": www.mesacc.edu/~chr2137038/PracticeTest2fall.html.

August 22: "not a nationality": http://wiki.answers.com/Q/What_are_Amish_people
_called_other_then_Amish

August 23: "former member": http://aboutamish.blogspot.com/2009/12/shunning.html.

August 24: "Janet's feet": http://notquiteamishliving.com/2013/02/attending-an-amish-service.

August 25: "all of them": http://amishamerica.com/at-an-amish-youth-singing.

August 25: "Amish youth": http://amishamerica.com/at-an-amish-youth-singing.

August 26: "Tim Gingerich": Sherry Gore, *Simply Delicious Amish Cooking: Recipes and Stories
from the Amish of Sarasota, Florida* (Grand Rapids, MI: Zondervan, 2013), 56.

August 27: "other way around": Henry L. Tischler, *Introduction to Sociology* (Belmont, CA:
Wadsworth, Cengage Learning, 2011), 130.

August 29: "we move on": Martha Zimmerman, from *The Budget* (December 2, 2009).

August 30: "only an hour": http://blogs.christianpost.com/amish-principles-for-families/plain
-talk-about-the-amish-expecting-to-wait-14163/#more.

August 31: "he said": www.christianitytoday.com/ct/2007/septemberweb-only
/136-54.0.html.

September 1: "too much": *John Newton's Olney Hymns* (Minneapolis: Curiosmith, 2011), 34.

September 2: "learning and doing": Brad Igou, *The Amish in Their Own Words* (Scottdale, PA:
Herald Press, 1999), 172.

September 3: "the 'right' one": Brad Igou, *The Amish in Their Own Words* (Scottdale, PA:
Herald Press, 1999), 152.

September 4: "blessings of God": *Family Life,* June 2010, 5.

September 5: "wash will dry": Lovina Eicher and Kevin Williams, *The Amish Cook's Anniversary
Book* (Riverside, NJ: Andrews McMeel, 2010), 92.

September 6: "dishonorable deeds": www.pbs.org/wgbh/americanexperience/features
/primary-resources/amish-rules.

September 7: "bathed too": Andy Yoder, *Amish Boyhood Echoes* (Oconto, WI: Bay Impressions,
1997).

September 8: "book out of them": Andy Yoder, *Amish Boyhood Echoes* (Oconto, WI: Bay
Impressions, 1997), i.

September 9: "the next life": http://amishamerica.com/amish-threshing-or-thrashing-oats
/?cid=32203.

September 10: "buckets clean": Lovina Eicher and Kevin Williams, *The Amish Cook's
Anniversary Book* (Riverside, NJ: Andrews McMeel, 2010), 103.

September 11: "the conflict": www.amishnews.com/amisharticles/peopleofpeace.htm.

September 13: "self-worth": Richard A. Stevick, *Growing Up Amish: The Teenage Years*
(Baltimore: Johns Hopkins University Press, 2007), 45.

September 14: "younger than 24": www.mennoworld.org/2013/2/4/goshen-grad-helps-former
-amish-realize-college-dre/?page=1.

September 15: "around them": Suzanne Woods Fisher, "Children Are Loved but Not Adored,"
http://notquiteamishliving.com/2013/02/children-are-loved-but-not-adored-plus-a-giveaway.

September 16: "faithful servant": *Family Life,* June 2010, 9.

September 17: "in 1917": www.amishreader.com/2013/02/05/extinct-amish-communties.

September 18: "hope and stay": *Family Life,* June 2010.

September 19: "sunshine": Lovina Eicher and Kevin Williams, *The Amish Cook's Anniversary
Book* (Riverside, NJ: Andrews McMeel, 2010), 137.

September 20: "with much": Brad Igou, *The Amish in Their Own Words* (Scottdale, PA: Herald
Press, 1999), 90–91.

September 21: "lack true friends": *Family Life,* June 2010, 6.

September 22: "some states": Lovina Eicher and Kevin Williams, *The Amish Cook at Home* (Riverside, NJ: Andrews McMeel, 2008), 72.

September 24: "gifts to you": Lovina Eicher and Kevin Williams, *The Amish Cook at Home* (Riverside, NJ: Andrews McMeel, 2008), 111.

September 25: "at home": Lovina Eicher and Kevin Williams, *The Amish Cook at Home* (Riverside, NJ: Andrews McMeel, 2008), 126.

September 26: "Husband, John": Brad Igou, *The Amish in Their Own Words* (Scottdale, PA: Herald Press, 1999), 101–02.

September 27: "milk and sugar": Lorilee Craker, *Money Secrets of the Amish: Finding True Abundance in Simplicity, Sharing, and Saving* (Nashville: Nelson, 2011), 180.

September 28: "will be done": Donald B. Kraybill, Steven M. Nolt, and David L. Weaver-Zercher, *The Amish Way: Patient Faith in a Perilous World* (San Francisco: Jossey-Bass, 2010), 155–56.

September 29: "couple's pantry": http://notquiteamishliving.com/2013/01/the-grocery-shower.

September 30: "single-parent homes": http://datacenter.kidscount.org/data/acrossstates/Rankings.aspx?ind=107.

September 30: "every way": Donald B. Kraybill, Steven M. Nolt, and David L. Weaver-Zercher, *The Amish Way: Patient Faith in a Perilous World* (San Francisco: Jossey-Bass, 2010), 117–18.

September 30: "in a field": http://notquiteamishliving.com/2012/11/more-amish-in-their-own-words.

Fall: "Date Pudding": Courtesy of Sherry Gore, author and radio host, www.sherrygore.com.

October 1: "70 years": http://amishamerica.com/unity-maine-amish-settlement.

October 2: "tree line": www.dailygazette.net/standard/ShowStoryTemplate.asp?Path=SCH/2012/09/23&ID=Ar00100&Section=National.

October 3: "farming abilities": *Family Life*, June 2010, 30.

October 4: "ever and ever": Mary Miller, *Our Heritage, Hope and Faith* (Mary Miller, 2000), 114.

October 5: "the exchange": http://markccrowley.com/21st-century-leadership-advice-from-the-amish/.

October 6: "appreciate it enough": Lovina Eicher and Kevin Williams, *The Amish Cook's Anniversary Book* (Riverside, NJ: Andrews McMeel, 2010), 36.

October 7: "wear them": Brad Igou, *The Amish in Their Own Words* (Scottdale, PA: Herald Press, 1999), 376.

October 8: "kept cool": Lovina Eicher and Kevin Williams, *The Amish Cook at Home* (Riverside, NJ: Andrews McMeel, 2008), 138.

October 10: "best-selling authors": www.canadianmennonite.org/articles/peeking-under-bonnet.

October 11: "accurately assessed": www.amishnews.com/amisharticles/michael.htm.

October 11: "November 8": www.amishnews.com/amisharticles/michael.htm.

October 12: "treasury of worship": http://starministry.org/cristian.htm.

October 12: "end of the day" http://amishamerica.com/do-amish-enjoy-music-and-singing.

October 13: "kinship rule": John A. Hostetler, *Amish Society* (Baltimore: Johns Hopkins, 1993), 64.

October 14: "life in Pennsylvania": http://evekahn.com/index.php?/newyorktimes/dear-amish-diary/.

October 14: "and souls": Mary Miller, *Our Heritage, Hope and Faith* (Mary Miller, 2000), 112.

October 15: "care of her": Suzanne Woods Fisher, *Amish Peace: Simple Wisdom for a Complicated World* (Grand Rapids, MI: Revell, 2009), 88–89.

October 16: "they are laid": Suzanne Woods Fisher, *Amish Proverbs: Words of Wisdom from the Simple Life* (Grand Rapids, MI: Revell, 2010), 17–18.

October 17: "outside the flock": http://amishamerica.com/why-do-the-amish-practice -shunning.

October 18: "their lives": http://web.missouri.edu/~hartmanj/rs150/papers/t1harrisonfs02.html.

October 19: "see them living": Joe Wittmer, PhD, *The Gentle People: Personal Reflections of Amish Life* (Minneapolis: Educational Media Corporation, 1990), 5.

October 20: "relationship a secret": www.cindywoodsmall.com/2013/02/07/amish-dating.

October 21: "non-Amish children": www.publishersweekly.com/pw/by-topic/columns-and -blogs/soapbox/article/54670-amish-reading-list.html.

October 22: "to help therein": Donald B. Kraybill, *The Riddle of Amish Culture* (Baltimore: Johns Hopkins University Press, 2001), 119.

October 22: "Swiss Anabaptists": John A. Hostetler, *Amish Society* (Baltimore: Johns Hopkins, 1993), 80.

October 22: "20 years": www.religionfacts.com/christianity/denominations/amish.htm.

October 23: "would be worth": Suzanne Woods Fisher, *Amish Proverbs: Words of Wisdom from the Simple Life* (Grand Rapids, MI: Revell, 2010), 29–30.

October 24: "doesn't interest him": Joe Wittmer, PhD, *The Gentle People: Personal Reflections of Amish Life* (Minneapolis: Educational Media Corporation, 1990), 121–22.

October 25: "subdued voices": John A. Hostetler, *Amish Society* (Baltimore: Johns Hopkins, 1993), 210–11.

October 26: "his joy": Suzanne Woods Fisher, *Amish Proverbs: Words of Wisdom from the Simple Life* (Grand Rapids, MI: Revell, 2010), 18.

October 27: "prophesying": John A. Hostetler, *Amish Society* (Baltimore: Johns Hopkins, 1993), 240.

October 28: "hunting equipment": http://amishamerica.com/do-amish-hunt.

October 29: "beginning for us": Lovina Eicher and Kevin Williams, *The Amish Cook's Anniversary Book* (Riverside, NJ: Andrews McMeel, 2010), 172.

October 30: "sometimes it doesn't": www.washingtonpost.com/wp-dyn/content/article/2010 /11/15/AR2010111506504.html.

October 30: "Heirloom Seeds": www.williamrubel.com/online-vegetable-seed-catalogs.

October 31: "Craigslist": Lorilee Craker, *Money Secrets of the Amish: Finding True Abundance in Simplicity, Sharing, and Saving* (Nashville: Thomas Nelson, 2011), 128–29.

November 1: "upcoming wedding": Joe Wittmer, PhD, *The Gentle People: Personal Reflections of Amish Life* (Minneapolis: Educational Media Corporation, 1990), 128.

November 2: "among ministers": http://amishamerica.com/the-amish-ministry.

November 3: "them to do": William I. Schreiber, *Our Amish Neighbors* (Wooster, OH: College of Wooster, 1990), 133–34.

November 3: "next day": http://amishamerica.com/the-amish-ministry.

November 4: "as well": www.nytimes.com/2013/02/09/us/amish-sect-leader-gets-15-years-in -beard-cutting-attacks.html?_r=0.

November 5: "mutual baptism": Margaret C. Reynolds, *Plain Women: Gender and Ritual in the Old Order River Brethren* (University Park, PA: Pennsylvania State University Press, 2001), 21, 23.

November 6: "buggy shed": Lovina Eicher and Kevin Williams, *The Amish Cook's Anniversary Book* (Riverside, NJ: Andrews McMeel, 2010), 186.

November 8: "many movies": Suzanne Woods Fisher, *Amish Peace: Simple Wisdom for a Complicated World* (Grand Rapids, MI: Revell, 2009), 53.

November 9: "I can remember": Bobbie Wolgemuth and Joni Eareckson Tada, *Hymns for a Kid's Heart, vol. 2* (Wheaton, IL: Crossway, 2004), 83.

November 11: "helped me wonderfully": S. B. Miller, "Trouble Teaching Us How to Sympathize with Each Other," in *Gleanings in Bee Culture*, vol. 14, (Medina, OH: A. I. Root, 1886), 426.

November 12: "spoken of again": John A. Hostetler, *Amish Roots: A Treasury of History, Wisdom, and Lore* (Baltimore: Johns Hopkins University Press, 1989), 7–8.

November 13: "icehouse": Suzanne Woods Fisher, *Amish Values for Your Family* (Grand Rapids, MI: Revell, 2011), 102.

November 14: "alter that fact": www.beverlylewis.com/blog/262-scripture-of-the-month-nov.

November 15: "for the task": Donald B. Kraybill, Carl Desportes Bowman, and Carl F. Bowman, *On the Backroad to Heaven: Old Order Hutterites, Mennonites, Amish, and Brethren* (Baltimore: Johns Hopkins University Press, 2001), 114.

November 16: "cousins and friends": Ruth Irene Garrett and Deborah Morse-Kahn, *Born Amish* (Paducah, KY: Turner Publishing, 2004), 120–21.

November 17: "resisted their use": Doyle Yoder and Leslie A. Kelley, *America's Amish Country* (Millersburg, OH: America's Amish Country Publications), 9.

November 18: "money in the bank": David Walbert, *Garden Spot: Lancaster County, the Old Order Amish, and the Selling of Rural America* (New York: Oxford University Press, 2002), 70–71.

November 19: "same room": Charles A Corr and Donna M. Corr, *Death and Dying: Life and Living* (Belmont, CA: Wadsworth, 2009, 2013), 46.

November 20: "ice cream": John A. Hostetler, *Amish Society* (Baltimore: Johns Hopkins, 1993), 198.

November 20: "supplies the ice": Kevin Williams and Lovina Eicher, *Amish Cooks Across America: Recipes and Traditions from Maine to Montana* (Riverside, NJ: Andrews McMeel, 2013), 112.

November 21: "Amish churches": Kevin Williams and Lovina Eicher, *Amish Cooks Across America: Recipes and Traditions from Maine to Montana* (Riverside, NJ: Andrews McMeel, 2013), 112.

November 21: "back of their buggies": Kevin Williams and Lovina Eicher, *Amish Cooks Across America: Recipes and Traditions from Maine to Montana* (Riverside, NJ: Andrews McMeel, 2013), 112.

November 22: "and on Earth": John A. Hostetler, *Amish Society* (Baltimore: Johns Hopkins, 1993), 198.

November 23: "old print does": Becky Goldsmith and Linda Jenkins, *Amish-Inspired Quilts: Tradition with a Piece O'Cake Twist* (Lafayette, CA: C&T Publishing: 2006), 5.

November 24: "they share": Beth Wiseman, "Do Amish Weddings Include a Cake?" www.rtbookreviews.com/rt-daily-blog/spotlight-traditional-amish-wedding.

November 25: "winter morning": Stephen Bowers Harroff, *The Amish Schools of Indiana: Faith in Education* (West Lafayette, IN: Purdue University Press, 2004), 62–63.

November 26: "they wonder": Richard A. Stevick, *Growing Up Amish: The Teenage Years* (Baltimore: Johns Hopkins University Press, 2007), 122–123.

November 27: "homes or churches": www.amishreader.com/2009/10/26/holidays-amish-style.

November 28: "bride indeed": Tricia Goyer, "An Amish Wedding Dress," RT Book Reviews,

June 21, 2012. Available at www.rtbookreviews.com/rt-daily-blog/spotlight-traditional-amish-wedding.

November 29: "good for them": Richard A. Stevick, *Growing Up Amish: The Teenage Years* (Baltimore: Johns Hopkins University Press, 2007), 97.

November 30: "chairs' craftsmanship": Erik Wesner, *Success Made Simple: An Inside Look at Why Amish Businesses Thrive* (San Francisco: Jossey-Bass, 2010), 82.

December 1: "you see": Suzanne Woods Fisher, *Amish Peace: Simple Wisdom for a Complicated World* (Grand Rapids, MI: Revell, 2009), 174–75.

December 2: "under the earth": Joe Wittmer, PhD, *The Gentle People: Personal Reflections of Amish Life* (Minneapolis: Educational Media Corporation, 1990).

December 3: "quite different": Donald B. Kraybill, Steven M. Nolt, and David L. Weaver-Zercher, *The Amish Way: Patient Faith in a Perilous World* (San Francisco: Jossey-Bass, 2010), 181.

December 4: "Christian families": William I. Schreiber, *Our Amish Neighbors* (Wooster, OH: College of Wooster, 1990), 147.

December 5: "kerosene lamps": Susan M. Strawn, *Knitting America: A Glorious Heritage from Warm Socks to High Art* (Minneapolis: Voyageur Press, 2011), 65.

December 5: "may be signified": John Gill, *Exposition of the Entire Bible,* http://gill.bible commenter.com/proverbs/31.htm.

December 6: "become Amish": John A. Hostetler, *Amish Society* (Baltimore: Johns Hopkins, 1993), 397.

December 7: "[conscientious objectors]": www.pbs.org/wgbh/americanexperience/features /timeline/amish.

December 7: "following their service": www.pbs.org/wgbh/americanexperience/features /timeline/amish.

December 7: "Enmity to Sect": www.pbs.org/wgbh/americanexperience/features/timeline/amish.

December 8: "Amish society": Richard A. Stevick, *Growing Up Amish: The Teenage Years* (Baltimore: Johns Hopkins University Press, 2007), 74–75.

December 9: "singing for themselves": Suzanne Woods Fisher, *Amish Peace: Simple Wisdom for a Complicated World* (Grand Rapids, MI: Revell, 2009), 204–205.

December 10: "to this end": Ruth Irene Garrett and Deborah Morse-Kahn, *Born Amish* (Paducah, KY: Turner Publishing, 2004), 150–51.

December 11: "taste of memory": Mitch Albom, *For One More Day* (New York: Hyperion, 2006).

December 11: "all the daughters": Linda Egenes, *Visits with the Amish: Impressions of the Plain Life* (Iowa City, IA: University of Iowa Press, 2000), 25.

December 11: "kept cool": www.amishreader.com/2010/10/22/fun-amish-fact-ice-houses.

December 12: "daily lives": David Schafer, *Simply the Greatest Life: Finding Myself in the Country* (Bloomington, IN: Balboa Press, 2012), 61–62.

December 13: "were together": Cindy Woodsmall and Miriam Flaud, *Plain Wisdom: An Invitation into an Amish Home and the Hearts of Two Women* (Colorado Springs: WaterBrook Press, 2011), 6–7.

December 14: "table is important": John A. Hostetler, *Amish Society* (Baltimore: Johns Hopkins, 1993), 221.

December 15: "crowd Him out": www.amishnews.com/christmas.html.

December 16: "no traces of Santa": www.sherrygore.com/blog/blog/how-the-amish-decorate -for-christmas.

December 17: "another chance": Suzanne Woods Fisher, *Amish Proverbs: Words of Wisdom from the Simple Life* (Grand Rapids, MI: Revell, 2010), 68.

December 18: "Old Country": J. B. Fisher, *Outside of Paradise: Growing Up Amish* (Houston, TX: Strategic Book Publishing, 2011), 3–4.

December 19: "way of life": http://pathway-publishers.com/.

December 19: "diesel motor": John A. Hostetler, *Amish Society* (Baltimore: Johns Hopkins, 1993), 378.

December 20: "more favorable": Donald B. Kraybill, *The Riddle of Amish Culture* (Baltimore: Johns Hopkins University Press, 2001), 49–50.

December 21: "my Deddy": http://notquiteamishliving.com/2012/12/an-amish-christmas-serenade.

December 22: "or another": Joe Wittmer, PhD, *The Gentle People: Personal Reflections of Amish Life* (Minneapolis: Educational Media Corporation, 1990), 35–36.

December 22: "are allowed": www.ehow.com/facts_5965953_amish-dress-code_.html.

December 23: "owning slaves": Steven M. Nolt, *A History of the Amish* (Intercourse, PA: Good Books, 2003), 82.

December 24: "clean water": Suzanne Woods Fisher, *Amish Values for Your Family* (Grand Rapids, MI: Revell, 2011), 61–62.

December 25: "another way": Lovina Eicher and Kevin Williams, *The Amish Cook's Anniversary Book* (Riverside, NJ: Andrews McMeel, 2010), 187–88.

December 26: "ever so slightly": Louise Stoltzfus, *Amish Women: Lives and Stories* (Intercourse, PA: Good Books, 1994), 64–65.

December 27: "another town": Jerry Eicher, *My Amish Childhood: A True Story of Faith, Family, and the Simpler Life* (Eugene, OR: Harvest House, 2013), 17.

December 28: "after Christmas": John A. Hostetler, *Amish Roots: A Treasury of History, Wisdom, and Lore* (Baltimore: Johns Hopkins University Press, 1989), 50.

December 29: "individual birds": www.peacefulsocieties.org/NAR07/071220amis.html.

December 30: "most of them": Georgia Varozza, *What the Amish Can Teach Us about the Simple Life: Homespun Hints for Family Gatherings, Spending Less, and Sharing Your Bounty* (Eugene, OR: Harvest House, 2013), 40.

December 31: "to romanticize": Bill Simpson, *Guide to the Amish Country* (Gretna, LA: Pelican Publishing, 2003), 8.

Do-able. Daily. Devotions.

START ANY DAY THE ONE YEAR WAY.

For Women

The One Year® Devotions for Women on the Go

The One Year® Devotions for Women

The One Year® Devotions for Moms

The One Year® Women of the Bible

The One Year® Coffee with God

For Men

The One Year® Devotional of Joy and Laughter

The One Year® Women's Friendship Devotional

The One Year® Devotions for Men on the Go

The One Year® Devotions for Men

The One Year® Father-Daughter Devotions

For Families

The One Year®
Family
Devotions, Vol. 1

For Couples

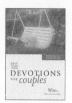

The One Year®
Devotions for
Couples

The One Year®
Love Language
Minute Devotional

The One Year®
Love Talk
Devotional for
Couples

For Teens

The One Year®
Devos for Teens

For Teens
(continued)

The One Year®
Devos for Sports
Fans

The One Year®
Be-Tween You
and God

For Personal Growth

The One Year®
at His Feet
Devotional

The One Year®
Uncommon Life
Daily Challenge

The One Year®
Recovery Prayer
Devotional

For Bible Study

The One Year®
Praying through
the Bible

The One Year®
Praying the
Promises of God

The One Year®
Through the
Bible Devotional

The One Year®
Experiencing
God's Presence
Devotional

The One Year®
Unlocking the
Bible Devotional

It's convenient and easy to grow
with God the One Year way.
TheOneYear.com

CP0145